T0400035

Contemporary Muslim Travel Cultures

This timely volume brings together various issues in Muslim consumer cultures and provides a comprehensive account of Muslim tourism and tourist behaviour.

Islam is a major international religion, and Muslims are a majority of the population in many countries in Asia, the Middle East and North Africa. The growth of a substantial middle class, the development of Islamic consumer cultures, rising Muslim market consumption in non-Muslim majority destinations and the growing significance of intra-Muslim traffic and rising outbound tourism expenditure in emerging Muslim markets have all contributed to substantial interest in Muslim tourism. However, travel by Muslims is about far more than the Hajj and Umrah, as important as they are as acts of devotion. Instead, although often portrayed in the West as a monolithic religion, Muslim travel and leisure behaviour is very diverse, with different traditions and cultures leading to a range of expressions of tourism-related consumption culture and practices. Drawing on a range of empirical studies undertaken in different social and economic contexts and countries, this book provides a well-balanced portrayal of the Muslim tourism experience and practices.

This book makes a substantial contribution to an improved understanding of Muslim travel culture and will be required reading for anyone interested in this fast-growing market.

C. Michael Hall is Professor Ahurei in the Department of Management, Marketing and Entrepreneurship, University of Canterbury, New Zealand; Visiting Professor and Docent in Geography, University of Oulu, Finland; Visiting Professor in Tourism at Linnaeus University, Kalmar, Sweden; Guest Professor in the Department of Service Management and Service Studies, Lund University, Helsingborg, Sweden and Visiting Professor, Centre for Research and Innovation in Tourism, Taylor's University, Malaysia. He has written widely on tourism, regional development, heritage, food and global environmental change.

Siamak Seyfi is Assistant Professor in the Geography Research Unit, University of Oulu, Finland. Using a multi-disciplinary approach and informed by diverse disciplinary perspectives, his research interests focus on tourism politics and geopolitics with a primary focus on the MENA region, cultural heritage, Gen Z, resilience, sustainability and qualitative sociological/ethnographic research methods in tourism.

S. Mostafa Rasoolimanesh is Associate Professor and Director of the Centre for Research and Innovation in Tourism (CRiT), Taylor's University, Malaysia. His research interest areas contain sustainable tourism, community participation, residents' perceptions toward tourism development, and advanced quantitative analysis approaches. He serves as an editorial team and board member of more than 20 reputed tourism and hospitality journals.

Contemporary Geographies of Leisure, Tourism and Mobility
Series Editor: C. Michael Hall, *Professor at the Department of Management, College of Business and Economics, University of Canterbury, Christchurch, New Zealand*

The aim of this series is to explore and communicate the intersections and relationships between leisure, tourism and human mobility within the social sciences.

It will incorporate both traditional and new perspectives on leisure and tourism from contemporary geography, e.g. notions of identity, representation and culture, while also providing for perspectives from cognate areas such as anthropology, cultural studies, gastronomy and food studies, marketing, policy studies and political economy, regional and urban planning, and sociology, within the development of an integrated field of leisure and tourism studies.

Also, increasingly, tourism and leisure are regarded as steps in a continuum of human mobility. Inclusion of mobility in the series offers the prospect to examine the relationship between tourism and migration, the sojourner, educational travel, and second home and retirement travel phenomena.

Routledge Studies in Contemporary Geographies of Leisure, Tourism and Mobility is a forum for innovative new research intended for research students and academics, and the titles will initially be available in hardback only. Titles include:

Socialising Tourism
Rethinking Tourism for Social and Ecological Justice
Edited by Freya Higgins-Desbiolles, Adam Doering and Bobbie Chew Bigby

Tourism Dynamics in Everyday Places
Before and After Tourism
Edited by Aurélie Condevaux, Maria Gravari-Barbas and Sandra Guinand

Contemporary Muslim Travel Cultures
Practices, Complexities and Emerging Issues
C. Michael Hall, Siamak Seyfi and S. Mostafa Rasoolimanesh

For more information about this series, please visit: www.routledge.com/ Contemporary-Geographies-of-Leisure-Tourism-and-Mobility/book-series/ SE0522

Contemporary Muslim Travel Cultures

Practices, Complexities and Emerging Issues

Edited by C. Michael Hall, Siamak Seyfi and S. Mostafa Rasoolimanesh

Routledge
Taylor & Francis Group

LONDON AND NEW YORK

First published 2023
by Routledge
4 Park Square, Milton Park, Abingdon, Oxon OX14 4RN

and by Routledge
605 Third Avenue, New York, NY 10158

Routledge is an imprint of the Taylor & Francis Group, an informa business

British Library Cataloguing-in-Publication Data
A catalogue record for this book is available from the British Library

Library of Congress Cataloging-in-Publication Data
A catalog record for this book has been requested

ISBN: 978-0-367-47740-0 (hbk)
ISBN: 978-1-032-30803-6 (pbk)
ISBN: 978-1-003-03629-6 (ebk)

DOI: 10.4324/9781003036296

Typeset in Bembo
by Apex CoVantage, LLC

This book is dedicated to those travellers that 'long for that place to which one belongs' (Ibn al-'Arabi).

Contents

Figures

Tables

Contributors

Rasool Akbari, Department of Religion and Comparative Mysticism, Ferdowsi University of Mashhad, Iran; ORCID: 0000-0002-0193-4302

Hazel Andrews, Liverpool John Moores University, Liverpool, UK; ORCID: 0000-0002-6160-8568

Qurat-ul-Ann Ayesha, Hazara University, Mansehra, Pakistan; ORCID: 0000-0002-1594-2549

Morteza Bazrafshan, Tourism and Hospitality Department, Higher Education Complex of Bam, Bam, Iran; ORCID: 0000-0001-6134-856X

Neil Carr, Department of Tourism, University of Otago, Dunedin, New Zealand; ORCID: 0000-0002-9410-4710

Ayla Deniz, Department of Geography, Faculty of Languages, History and Geography, Ankara University, Ankara, Turkey; ORCID: 0000-0001-5964-0131

Gözde Emekli, Department of Geography, Ege University, Izmir, Turkey; ORCID: 0000-0001-8528-5209

Fernando Almeida Garcia, Department of Geography, Faculty of Tourism, Universidad of Malaga, Spain; ORCID: 0000-0001-6560-8752

Abolfazl Siyamiyan Gorji, PhD student in Tourism, Faculty of Tourism, Universidad of Malaga, Spain; ORCID: 0000-0002-2632-0366

Zohair Siyamiyan Gorji, Shahid Beheshti University, Iran; ORCID: 0000-0001-5694-8229

C. Michael Hall, Department of Management, Marketing and Entrepreneurship, University of Canterbury, Christchurch, New Zealand; Linnaeus University School of Business and Economics, Kalmar, Sweden; Geography, Oulu University, Finland; Taylor's University, Malaysia, ORCID: 0000-0002-7734-4587

Mohd Hafiz Hanafiah, Faculty of Hotel and Tourism Management, Universiti Teknologi MARA Malaysia; ORCID ID: 0000-0002-3378-7300

Seyedasaad Hosseini; PhD student in Tourism, Faculty of Tourism, Universidad of Malaga, Spain; ORCID: 0000-0001-7066-3035

Kübra İlban; Department of Geography, Faculty of Art & Science, Süleyman Demirel University, Isparta, Turkey; ORCID: 0000-0002-9649-2673

Bahar Kaba; ORCID: 0000-0001-9729-8605

İsmail Kervankiran; Department of Geography, Faculty of Art & Science, Süleyman Demirel University, Isparta, Turkey; ORCID: 0000-0001-9202-7320

Salar Kuhzady, Department of Tourism Management, University of Kurdistan, Sanandaj, Iran; ORCID: 0000-0001-7601-4159

Rafael Cortes Macias; Department of Geography, Faculty of Tourism, Universidad of Malaga, Spain; ORCID: 0000-0002-2120-3515

Mahshid Ahdiyeh Mahdavi, Department of Management, Marketing and Entrepreneurship, University of Canterbury, Christchurch, New Zealand; https://orcid.org/0000-0001-8736-9414

Amie Matthews, School of Social Sciences and Psychology, Western Sydney University, Australia

Boshra Mohajer, PhD Candidate in Tourism Management, University of Allameh Tabatabai, Tehran, Iran; ORCID: 0000-0003-1615-7291

Farisha Nazmeen Nisha, The University of the South Pacific, Fiji; ORCID: 0000-0002-1083-6747

Youri Oh, Department of Management, Marketing and Entrepreneurship, University of Canterbury, Christchurch, New Zealand; ORCID: 0000-0002-9753-7247

Hera Oktadiana, College of Business, Law and Governance, James Cook University, James Cook Drive, Townsville, Queensland 4811, Australia; Trisakti School of Tourism, Jakarta, Indonesia; ORCID: 0000-0002-7897-2534

Philip L. Pearce, College of Business, Law and Governance, James Cook University, Townsville, Queensland, Australia; ORCID: 0000-0003-3829-4449

Felicity Picken, School of Social Sciences and Psychology, Western Sydney University, Australia; ORCID: 0000-0001-6717-5145

Intan Purwandani, Faculty of Cultural Sciences, University of Gadjah Mada, Indonesia; ORCID: 0000-0001-9592-1520

S. Mostafa Rasoolimanesh, School of Hospitality, Tourism and Events, Taylor's University, No. 1, Jalan Taylor's, Subang Jaya, 47500, Malaysia; ORCID: 0000-0001-7138-0280

Tazayian Sayira, Independent scholar, Liverpool, UK; ORCID: 0000-0002-3005-4742

Maryam Sedaghat, Tourism Department, Kharazmi University, Tehran, Iran; ORCID: 0000-0001-7298-0907

Siamak Seyfi, Geography Research Unit, University of Oulu, Oulu, Finland; ORCID: 0000-0002-2427-7958

Ismail Shaheer, Department of Tourism, University of Otago, Dunedin, New Zealand; ORCID: 0000-0002-9202-3335

İlkay Südaş; ORCID: 0000-0003-2778-7942

Songsin Teerakunpisut; Faculty of Management Sciences, Prince of Songkla University, Songkhla, Thailand; ORCID: 0000-0002-1726-6361

Julie Jie Wen, School of Social Sciences and Psychology, Western Sydney University, Australia; ORCID: 0000-0003-2869-8407

Omneya Mokhtar Yacout, Faculty of Commerce, Alexandria University, ElShatby, Egypt; ORCID: 0000-0001-9316-8563

Preface and acknowledgments

Michael would like to thank colleagues and friends with whom he has had relevant conversations or conducted research with over the years in relation to this work. In particular, thanks go to Bailey Adie, Alberto Amore, Inoor Azman, Dorothee Bohn, Chris Chen, Tim Coles, Hervé Corvellec, David Duval, Martin Gren, Dikte Grønvold; Fahimeh Hatefhabar, Johan Hultman, Tyron Love, Mahshid Mahdavi, Dieter Müller, Yuri Oh, Girish Prayag, Yael Ram, Anna Laura Raschke, Jarkko Saarinen, Anna Dóra Sæþórsdóttir, Daniel Scott, Samaneh Soleimani, Kimberley Wood, and Maria José Zapata-Campos for their thoughts on tourism and cultural practices, as well as for the stimulation of Agnes Obel, Ann Brun, Beirut, Paul Buchanan, Nick Cave, Bruce Cockburn, Elvis Costello, Stephen Cummings, David Bowie, Ebba Fosberg, Mark Hollis, Margaret Glaspy, Aimee Mann, Larkin Poe, Vinnie Reilly, Henry Rollins, Matthew Sweet, Emma Swift, TISM, Henry Wagon, *The Guardian*, BBC6, JJ, and KCRW – for making the world much less confining. Special mention must also be given to the Malmö Saluhall; Balck, Packhuset and Postgarten in Kalmar; and Nicole Aignier and the Hotel Grüner Baum in Merzhausen. Finally and most importantly, Michael would like to thank the Js and the Cs who stay at home and mind the farm.

Nobody has been more important to me in the pursuit of this project than the members of my family. I would like to thank my parents, especially my late father whose love and guidance are with me in whatever I pursue. And, most importantly, I wish to thank my loving and supportive wife, Mina, for her enduring love and patience. My thanks are extended to various friends and colleagues for their advice and warm encouragement at times of despair. I won't mention their names; I am just thinking about them. – Siamak

We also wish to gratefully acknowledge the help and support of Jody Cowper-James for proofreading and editing. Finally, we would both like to thank Emma Travis, Lydia Kessell, Harriet Cunningham and all at Routledge for their continuing support.

Abbreviations

AQR	*Āstān Qods Razavī* (the Sacred Threshold of Imam Reza).
COMCEC	Standing Committee for Economic and Commercial Cooperation of the Organization of Islamic Cooperation
IRNA	Islamic Republic News Agency
MFT	Muslim-friendly tourism
OIC	Organisation of Islamic Cooperation
TCEB	Thailand Convention & Exhibition Bureau
TPB	Theory of Planned Behaviour

Part I

Introduction and context

1 Muslim travel cultures

Introduction and context

C. Michael Hall, Siamak Seyfi and
S. Mostafa Rasoolimanesh

Introduction

Travel is central to the Muslim experience of the world. From its origins with the Prophet Muhammad (PBUH) and his family and companions and also in its Abrahamic roots, travel has been seen to be integral to Islamic life. The Qur'an includes numerous passages that encourage both men and women to travel to gain knowledge and to learn about the world into which we have been born (Al-Qur'an: Al-An'aam 6:11; Al-Qur'an: Al-Naml 27:69). Importantly, such travel is in addition to such pillars of Islam as pilgrimage and travelling to Makkah for either Hajj in the twelfth Hijri month of Dhūl-Ḥijjah, or Umrah, which involves visiting the city at any time of the year. In the Qur'an Allah says: "Travel in the land and see how He originated creation, then Allah bringeth forth the later growth. Lo! Allah is Able to do all things" (Al-Qur'an: al-'Ankaboot 29:20).

Hashim et al. (2007) indicate that many verses on travelling in the Quran encourage Muslims to see the creations of Allah and feel for his greatness. These verses include Al-Imran (The Amramites) 3:137; Al-An'am (Livestock) 6:11; Yunus (Jonah) 10:22; Yusuf (Joseph) 12:109; Al-Nahl (The Bee) 16:36; Al-Hajj (The Pilgrimage) 22:46; Al-'Ankaboot (The Spider) 29:20; Al-Rum (The Romans) 30:42/9; Saba' (Sheba) 34:18; Faater (Initiator) 35:44; Ghafer (Forgiver) 40:82/21; Muhammad 47:10; and Al-Mulk (Kingship) 67:15. Travel in Islam can be divided into several forms, musafir, rehlah, siyahah, Umrah, and Hajj (Eickelman & Piscatori, 1990; Hasan et al., 2010; Taheri, 2016; Razak et al., 2020a) (Table 1.1).

Travel is therefore an essential element of Islamic spirituality. However, Muslim interest in travel is increasingly directed towards holiday, leisure, and recreational tourism, not just pilgrimages associated with faith-based journeys, such as Hajj and Umrah. In modernity, notions of Islamic travel and recreation have therefore expanded to incorporate more contemporary notions of leisure (Saad Aly, 2010). As such, ideas of what constitutes Muslim tourism culture have arguably gone through the same challenges as broader Islam with respect to notions of sacred and the profane and the relationship to modern consumerism (Gökarıksel & McLarney, 2010). This last point is extremely important

DOI: 10.4324/9781003036296-2

Table 1.1 Traditional understandings of travel in Islam

Term	Use	Origin
Musafir	Means a traveller but is also used for guest	Originated from the Arabic word *Safara,* meaning going, walking, and wandering Al-Maidah: verse 6
Rihlah	Also *rehlah* or *rihla.* Refers to both a journey and the oral, written, and more recently visual, i.e. documentary, account of that journey. In the Middle Ages *rihla* consisted of three types: *Rihla* – a journey within a region, particularly Morocco, usually to meet other pilgrims before travelling beyond the local area. *Rihla hijaziyya* – a journey to the Hejaz (the western coastal region of the Arabian Peninsula, which includes the holy cities of Mecca and Medina). *Rihla sifariyya* – a journey to Muslim and non-Muslim lands. The most famous *rihla* based on such a journey is *The Travels of Ibn Battuta* (*Riḥlat Ibn Baṭūṭah*).	Originated from the Arabic word *Rahala,* meaning travelling/trading Quraish: verse 6
Ziyarah	A visit to the tomb of a saint or a holy person, including a visit to the tomb of the Prophet Muḥammad in the mosque at Medina. This may occur for reasons of gaining a blessing or cure although the legitimacy of such a visit is debated depending on the perspective of different schools of Islamic thought.	Originated from the Arabic word *Zara,* meaning visiting or paying a visit Al Takathur: verse 2; Al Kahfi: verse 17
Siyahah	Often used as synonymous with travel and tourism. However, it is also connected to gaining knowledge and learning, including travelling to see the wonders of creation.	Originated from the Arabic word *Saha,* meaning wander the earth Al Taubah: verse 112
Umrah and hajj	Umrah is an Islamic pilgrimage to Mecca that can be made at any time of year. It is also known as the minor pilgrimage. In contrast, the *Hajj* (also *Hadj, Hadji* or *Haj)* is the major pilgrimage that is a required religious duty for Muslims that must be undertaken at least once in the lifetime of all adult Muslims who are financially and physically able to make the journey. The *hajj* is one of the pillars of Islam that according to Islamic teaching go back to the time of Prophet Abraham. *Hajj* is performed over five or six days, beginning on the eighth and ending on the thirteenth day of *Dhu al-Hijjah,* the last month of the Islamic lunar calendar.	Originated from the Arabic word *Saha,* meaning a worshiping obligation for capable Muslims Ayat surah Al Baqarah: 196

Source: Eickelman & Piscatori, 1990; Hasan et al., 2010; Taheri, 2016; Razak et al., 2020

with respect to the increased importance attached to halal certification and Islamic tourism because of the issues that are raised about the commodification of the religious experience and the sacred (Reader, 2013; Redden, 2016). For example, Sandıkcı (2018) notes how the development of the concept of the Muslim consumer is linked to the growing influence of neoliberalism and the expansion of market logic into the religious sphere and the sacred, with the development of halal certification and halal standards as clear examples of such processes.

Islamic knowledge, performances and identities are increasingly being contrasted through material commodities and consumption practices (Fischer, 2011, 2015, 2016; Bergeaud-Blackler et al., 2015). As Gökarıksel and McLarney (2010, p. 2) observe, "Muslims identify as such and connect with one another through Islamic products and spaces, forming new, transnational and transregional 'Muslim networks'. . . . At the same time, networks forged through capitalist consumption practices create new marginalizations, leaving some unconnected". Tourism is a very good example of such networks and transnational flows of people, as well as the marginalizations that can occur in terms of constraints on travel and the impacts that can result from tourism. Therefore, Islamic tourism is an excellent space in which to examine some of the new transnational flows of tourism and tourist practices, as well as the emergence of new travel cultures, and it is these issues that the various chapters in the book address.

This first chapter aims to provide a brief introduction to the book. It first discusses some of the definitional issues involved in Muslim travel and the implications that this has for research. It then touches on some of the issues involved in undertaking research on tourism and Islam before providing an outline of the book.

Definitional issues

Although, at first glance, Muslim tourism can be simply stated as the travel, activities and experiences of Muslim tourists, substantial definitional difficulties exist (Hall & Prayag, 2020a). There is a lack of agreement over what constitutes halal, Muslim-friendly, Muslim, Islamic, and sharia tourism and hospitality, with terms often being used interchangeably (Henderson, 2009; Razzaq et al., 2016; Khan & Callanan, 2017; Boğan & Sarıışık, 2018; Vargas-Sánchez & Moral-Moral, 2018; Hall & Prayag, 2020a, 2020b). Definitions are important as they help assist with answering significant questions, for example, as to whether halal tourism is "really halal" (El-Gohary, 2016) and consequent issues of consumer and business trust (Khan & Callanan, 2017). Indeed, much of the concern regarding halal tourism matches similar questions in hospitality and food services, where there is no fully agreed upon set of regulations on halal. Razak et al. (2020a) suggest that much of the halal tourism and hospitality literature tends to focus on the more conservative interpretations of idealized

Muslim behaviour, and it is significant that the OIC explicitly describe Islamic tourism as a "religious conservative" concept

> The religious conservative concept for Islamic tourism is based on the conservative interpretation and understanding of Islam. Merging elements of the extremely conservative Islamic lifestyle with the modern tourism industry could indeed present new tourism options, spaces, and spheres. For a growing conservative intra Arab and intra Muslim tourism market, the implementation of a religious conservative concept in tourism planning as an extra option and as an insertion into the existing mainstream tourism could indeed have a positive economic and social effect.
>
> (OIC, 2017, p. 28)

This conservative framing of Islam and tourism is also often reflected in government policies as well as in some of the statements of the OIC regarding tourism. For example, the OIC suggest that as a cultural concept

> Islamic tourism includes visions and ideas that outline the inclusion of Islamic religious cultural sites in tourism programs with "pedagogical" and self-confidence building elements. It tries to encourage a reorientation inside the tourist destinations towards less consumption and "western culture" loaded sites towards more Islamic historical, religious and cultural sites.
>
> (OIC, 2017, p. 28)

Although visits to Islamic attractions and destinations are undoubtedly important, the OIC (2017) arguably ignore the interests and needs of the many Muslim travellers to non-Islamic countries and regions as part of their broader interest in the world around them. Such an insular approach is seemingly at odds with the extollation in the Qur'an to travel to experience and witness all of God's creation (Al-Qur'an: al-'Ankaboot 29:20). Furthermore, research on halal tourism suggests that there are significant gaps between government statements on the positioning of destinations for conservatively oriented halal tourism and the on-the-ground realities of what is offered. For example, no significant difference was identified in the communication of halal attributes on the websites of accommodation providers in Malaysia – a Muslim-majority country (Razak et al., 2020b) – and New Zealand, a country with only a very small Muslim population (Razzaq et al., 2016). Such a situation clearly raises substantive, unresolved questions over what various descriptors really mean and the extent to tourism is drawn into the commoditization of religious values. As Khan and Callanan (2017) noted in their study of definitional issues in the "Halalification" of tourism, they could find no substantive difference between the various terms (e.g., halal, Muslim friendly, Islamic, Sharia) that were used in their content analysis of popular UK media, UK-based tour operators' websites and tourism strategies of destinations popular with Muslim tourists.

However, the implications of definition move beyond product categories. Definition of a subject also influences how a field of study is analysed and progresses. It determines what is included and what is left out. Just as importantly it determined policy fields, as it is difficult to generate and implement policy unless the policy field is defined. Hence why there is a danger in researchers applying the OIC approach to Muslim travel behaviour, as noted earlier, because it is a self-avowed conservative interpretation that marginalizes or, potentially even worse, demeans or deprecates behaviours by Muslims outside of that particular approach. As Hall and Prayag (2020a) concluded, there is often a lack of critique by researchers in the presentation of notions of halal, Muslim and Islamic tourism, and the governments that promote it:

> At times, some of the contextualisation of halal, especially in conference papers and open access journals, almost takes the form of attempts to prove the piety of the author rather than critically assess halal matters. There is also often insufficient criticism of poor halal certification procedures, the (lack of or partial) enforcement of halal by responsible government agencies, and the large gap that may exist between what business and enterprises say they do and what actually happens. Such lack of criticism or a willingness to discuss negative aspects of halal or Islamic tourism may be because of not wanting to appear to be critical of either Islam or one's country. However, it may also be that a somewhat unbalanced portrayal of research topics and subjects is presented.
>
> (Hall & Prayag, 2020a, p. 342)

One example of this is the lack of more detailed assessment of what constitutes a Muslim tourist. Realistically, this may require a research intervention that provides for understanding the relative religiosity of the subject within Islam. But this is rarely undertaken and, in some research contexts, may even be hard to do because of the institutional pressures and social norms on individuals to meet the religious requirements of authorities in that context. Similarly, in statistical terms the figures for Muslim travel are dubious. It would be much more accurate to discuss the growth in international travel from and to *Muslim-majority countries*, but that is usually not the terminology used, with governmental positions about Islamic religious identity often being used unquestionably by many researchers in their studies. Arguably, another major gap is a failure by researchers to better identify which of the sharia traditions adherents follow and the particular *madhhab* (school of jurisprudence), especially as this has implications for considerations of halal and therefore consequent tourist behaviours (Hall & Prayag, 2020b).

Research practices and reflexivity

Issues of definition also affect research interpretation and, potentially, practice (Hall, 2011). However, significant issues associated with good research practice in an Islamic context and their implications are relatively little discussed and reflected upon or made overt. Of particular importance is the implications of gender for research access and information provision, especially when a researcher is wanting to interview someone from the opposite sex (Wan Hassan, 2011). This, combined with cultural and institutional norms, can make accurate information gathering extremely difficult with, in some situations, responses having to be mediated by third parties such as a *mahram* (a male relative of a woman). Nevertheless, as several chapters in this volume indicate, gender related and gendered spaces are an extremely significant factor to consider in research on travel culture and practices, and there is clearly a need for a greater understanding of gendered travel practices, e.g. that of single women, being undertaken in different contexts, e.g. within non-Muslim majority countries. In addition, in several Muslim-majority countries or regions opinions on subjects may need to go through the male head of household as a courtesy or standard cultural practice.

Research practices may also affected by the influence of religious and political authorities on the interpretation and publication of material. Clearly particular interpretations of policy may be affected by the role of authorities and the desire for attractions, activities, communities and destination to be framed and presented in specific ways. In some locations this may affect discussion of leisure travel behaviours that may otherwise be negatively portrayed. Clearly, such issues are not unique to Islamic tourism research (Hall, 2011), but they remain nevertheless significant and require further examination in the literature in order to gain a fuller and more transparent understanding of the research process and its outcomes.

While there is a oneness in Islam there is also great diversity. Muslims are not all the same, but there is often insufficient framing of difference in the way the results of Muslim travellers are presented. This may potentially be because of a desire to portray the work, the research subjects, and/or the authors in particular ways or of not recognizing that such differences are legitimate. However, as the following collection of chapters indicate, there is considerable diversity in Muslim travel culture and practice.

Outline of the book

The various chapters of the book are organised around several main themes. Chapters 1 to 3 provide an introduction to the literature on Muslim travel and tourism. Chapter 2 provides an introductory review of various dimensions of Muslim travel culture, highlighting the range of Muslim tourism experiences depending on context, degrees of religiosity, and gender. Chapter 3 by Mohajer et al. provides a narrower and more conservative focus on Muslim tourism in journal-based literature that highlights the substantial growth in this topic since 2010 (see also Rasul, 2019).

The second part, Chapters 4 to 6, examined issues of Muslim tourism behaviour and motivation. Chapter 4, by Pearce and Oktadiana, raises an important fundamental question about Muslim travel behaviour, namely how different the behaviour of Muslim tourists is from others. They argue that, although novelty, escape, and relaxation are viewed as important core travel motives for all groups of travellers, Muslims especially emphasise the value of (strengthening) relationships while adding the value of seeing nature as a core travel driver. Muslim travellers, compared to other groups, also highlight stimulation and nostalgia as travel motives. They conclude that their results confirm the understanding Muslim tourists is about far more than specifying needs for halal food and prayer rooms but instead, like any other travel market segment, can be built on recognizing strong and distinctive emphases in their motivational profile. Chapter 5, by Hanafiah, explores Turkish tourists' motivation and perception towards Muslim-friendly tourist (MFT) destinations and also highlights significant market differences. The Turkish MFT visiting tourists prefer the islands, nature and beauty, modest Islamic culture, and Halal branded restaurants when travelling to MFT destinations. However, Turkish non-MFT tourists perceived MFT destinations as having limited brand value and brand image. Significantly they value MFT less and do not favour MFT attributes as their primary motivation to travel. Yacout's examination of the travel motivations of Egyptian tourists (Chapter 6) identified three motivation-based segments of Egyptian tourists that vary with tourism experience value and core identity attributes. Interestingly, she also found that the clusters also showed clear differences in terms of age, gender and family life cycle, also suggesting at the possibility of important generational and gender differences in tourism motivations and experiences.

Chapters 7 to 9 examine issues related to pilgrimage. Chapter 7 by Nisha reports on the results of a qualitative study on the pre-trip experiences of Fijian Hajj pilgrims. The chapter highlights the significance of family and communities sharing in the pre-trip preparation. Chapter 8, by Akbari, uses a material religion approach to investigate Twelver Shiite pilgrimage in Mashhad. The relationship between pilgrims and their material surroundings are understood as a multidimensional "assemblage" with hybrid formations of tangible and intangible resources and multi-fold values in the setting of relations among human and non-human agents. Different actors are seen to use cultural resources to enact and materialize various dimensions of pilgrimage religiosities as well as non-religious elements. As such, the chapter has strong resonance with wider research on material religion (Insoll, 2009; Meyer et al., 2010) but potentially also with marketing research on servicescapes (Bideci & Bideci, 2021; Alhothali et al., 2021). Chapter 9, by Gorji et al., provides an ethnographic account of the lived experiences of Iranian Arbaeen foot-pilgrims in Iraq. As the authors note, present-day Western literature on pilgrimages undertaken on foot tend to focus on pilgrimages such as that of the Santiago de Camino. The chapter discusses the largest annual pilgrimage by the Shiite communities in Karbala-Iraq, known as the *Arbaeen*, which attracts more than 20 million travellers. The travellers who go on this journey are known as *Zawars* in Arabic. Against this backdrop, this chapter aims to analyze the lived experiences and motivations of Iranian foot-pilgrim's Zawars in their journey to Karbala.

Chapters 10 to 13 focus on gender as a significant aspect of Islamic tourism, a major issue that is also discussed in more detail in Chapter 2 (this volume). Gorji et al. (Chapter 10) provides an alternative perspective on issues of culture and discrimination in their study of Uzbek women's perspective of female solo travelling in a conservative post-Soviet Muslim society. They note that, even though regulatory and legal efforts have been made to expand women's rights, these have no effect on patriarchal gender norms and attitudes regarding solo women's travel, especially that of younger, unmarried women. The findings of this study showed that women encounter constrains in three main themes: (i) individually perceived constraints; (ii) family-related constraints; and (iii) gendered-imposed constraints. Such an analysis raises substantial questions for researchers of being able to disaggregate conservative interpretations of Islam from other conservative cultural perspectives and the interplay between them. Similar issues of institutionalized male power emerge in Chapter 11, by Sayira et al., which examines the restrictions on women's travel in Pakistan. The authors argue that, although women in Pakistan do travel, it is not a practice enjoyed by many of the women in the study areas of Chilas and Abbottabad who work in hospitality and tourism. As the study recognizes, for many women in Chilas and Abbottabad, movements in daily life are restricted and their roles in tourism and hospitality largely hidden. The chapter concludes that the study's findings not only highlight gender inequality in Pakistan but also the inequalities between the toured and the tourees.

Chapters 12 and 13 both report on studies of Turkish female travellers. Chapter 12 by Kervankiran et al. compares the travel patterns and experiences of secular and conservative Turkish female outbound tourists. Their study found that the travel patterns between the two groups if tourists grew more similar over time. All women interviewed also experienced an increase in their cultural capital through their travel. In Chapter 13 Emekli et al. examine the travel motivations and experiences of Turkish solo women travellers. Their results indicate that Turkish solo women travellers are single, well-educated and economically independent, travelling mostly to European countries. Desire for freedom and independence, meeting new people, learning, self-discovery and risk-taking are the main motivations. However, they encountered socio-spatial constraints including limited destination choice and moving only at certain times of the day because of security concerns and fear of harassment. In addition, a number of cultural and economic constraints were also experienced.

The final series of chapters deal with issues relating to the interaction between consumers and the tourism industry. Shaheer and Carr (Chapter 14) explore the intentions of Muslims boycotting tourism products and destinations. Chapter 15 by Purwandani examines Spanish Muslim tourist operators' motivations for providing Halal services and amenities. However, while the subjects were operators, there were significant inter-relationships between their personal travel histories and experiences and the importance they place on *da'wa* in their business lives, with the intersection between the two clearly being an important point of future research especially because, as the authors conclude, *da'wa* may potentially be seen in every single thing a Muslim does. In Chapter 16, Teerakunpisut et al. discuss the interactions between Muslims and non-Muslims in the Thai MICE market. The findings suggest that, while understanding varied between Muslim clientele, the significance of Islam to Muslim clients' lives was generally well recognized and respected.

The concluding chapter by Seyfi et al. (Chapter 17) provides a brief account of some of the more significant trends and issues to be addressed in the Muslim Travel Market. The chapter notes the importance of developing a far more sophisticated and empirically grounded critical assessment of Muslim tourism than what has previously usually been the case, especially with emerging themes such as gender, the environment, and inter-generational differences and the millennial market. The chapter concludes with thoughts on the future of research on Muslim practices of tourism consumption and production in the context of businesses, communities, destinations, and the wider socio-political context.

Conclusion

This chapter has provided a brief introduction to some of the themes and issues in this book. As noted, there is a lack of clear terminology with respect to Muslim travel and tourism, which affects statistical and empirical data (Khan & Callanan, 2017). Arguably, there is also at times insufficient reflexivity with respect to the positionality of researchers and the capacity to critically assess some of the significant issues that emerge in Muslim travel cultures, particularly with respect to women and gender in tourism (Yosry, 2021) as well as contestation within Muslim culture (Seyfi & Hall, 2019; Vliek, 2020). Indeed, such critical assessment is vital because, as the various chapters in this volume attest, there is no one Muslim travel culture. Instead, there is a rich diversity that shares various religious and ethical features that wait to be explored.

The following chapters therefore serve to remind the reader of the central role that travel plays in Islam but also of the different perspectives and constraints that exist. Travel often brings personal change and may generate reflection on personal and home environments. These are not necessarily harmful to faith. If anything, the opportunity to experience and enjoy the world can serve to reinforce personal belief systems. However, it is something that all should be able to enjoy. As such, tourism policymakers and researchers around the world need assist a more inclusive tourism both within Muslim-majority countries and international travel. We hope that this edited book is one small step towards generating awareness of some of the constraints that Muslims face in travelling both internationally and within their own country and potentially leads to positive change.

References

Alhothali, G. T., Elgammal, I., & Mavondo, F. T. (2021). Religious servicescape and intention to revisit: Potential mediators and moderators. *Asia Pacific Journal of Tourism Research*, *26*(3), 308–328. https://doi.org/10.1080/10941665.2020.1862885

Bergeaud-Blackler, F., Fischer, J., & Lever, J. (Eds.). (2015). *Halal matters: Islam, politics and markets in global perspective*. Routledge.

Bideci, M., & Bideci, C. (2021). Framing the visitor experience in sacred places. *The TQM Journal*, ahead-of-print. https://doi.org/10.1108/TQM-02-2021-0044

Boğan, E., & Sarıışık, M. (2018). Halal tourism: Conceptual and practical challenges. *Journal of Islamic Marketing*, *10*(1), 87–96. https://doi.org/10.1108/JIMA-06-2017-0066

Eickelman, D. F., & Piscatori, J. P. (Eds.). (1990). *Muslim travellers: Pilgrimage, migration and the religious imagination*. University of California Press.

El-Gohary, H. (2016). Halal tourism, is it really Halal? *Tourism Management Perspectives*, *19*, 124–130. https://doi.org/10.1016/j.tmp.2015.12.013

Fischer, J. (2011). *The Halal frontier: Muslim consumers in a globalized market*. Palgrave Macmillan.

Fischer, J. (2015). *Islam, standards, and technoscience: In global halal zones*. Routledge.

Fischer, J. (2016). Manufacturing halal in Malaysia. *Contemporary Islam*, *10*(1), 35–52. https://doi.org/10.1007/s11562-015-0323-5

Gökarıksel, B., & McLarney, E. (2010). Introduction: Muslim women, consumer capitalism, and the Islamic culture industry. *Journal of Middle East Women's Studies*, *6*(3), 1–18. https://muse.jhu.edu/article/394242

Hall, C. M. (Ed.). (2011). *Fieldwork in tourism*. Routledge.

Hall, C. M., & Prayag, G. (2020a). Emerging and future issues in halal hospitality and Islamic tourism. In C. M. Hall & G. Prayag (Eds.), *The Routledge handbook of halal hospitality and Islamic tourism* (pp. 339–346). Routledge.

Hall, C. M., & Prayag, G. (Eds.). (2020b). *The Routledge handbook of halal hospitality and Islamic tourism*. Routledge.

Hasan, B., Mohammad Mahyuddin, K., & Mohd Ahsrof Zaki, Y. (2010). Pelancongan dari perspektif Islam: Analisis pendekatan fiqh. In Y. Mohd Asmadi, I. Huzaimah, & I. Taki-yuddin (Eds.), *Prosiding seminar pengurusan perhotelan & pelancongan Islam 2010* (pp. 1–17). Universiti Teknologi Mara.

Hashim, N. H., Murphy, J., & Hashim, N. M. (2007). Islam and on-line imagery on Malaysian tourist destination websites. *Journal of Computer-Mediated Communication*, *12*(3), 1082–1102.

Hassan, M. W. (2011). Studying halal restaurants in New Zealand: Experiences and perspectives of a Muslim female researcher. In C. M. Hall (Ed.), *Fieldwork in tourism* (pp. 126–140). Routledge.

Henderson, J. C. (2009). Islamic tourism reviewed. *Tourism Recreation Research*, *34*(2), 207–211. https://doi.org/10.1080/02508281.2009.11081594

Insoll, T. (2009). Materiality, belief, ritual-archaeology and material religion: An introduction. *Material Religion*, *5*(3), 260–264. https://doi.org/10.2752/175183409X12550007729824

Khan, F., & Callanan, M. (2017). The "Halalification" of tourism. *Journal of Islamic Marketing*, *8*(4), 558–577. https://doi.org/10.1108/JIMA-01-2016-0001

Meyer, B., Morgan, D., Paine, C., & Plate, S. B. (2010). The origin and mission of material religion. *Religion*, *40*(3), 207–211. https://doi.org/10.1016/j.religion.2010.01.010

OIC. (2017). *International tourism in the OIC countries: Prospects and challenges 2017*. The Statistical, Economic and Social Research and Training Centre for Islamic Countries (SESRIC).

Rasul, T. (2019). The trends, opportunities and challenges of halal tourism: A systematic literature review. *Tourism Recreation Research, 44*(4), 434–450. https://doi.org/10.1080/0 2508281.2019.1599532

Razak, N. H. A., Hall, C. M., & Prayag, G. (2020a). Understanding halal hospitality. In C. M. Hall & G. Prayag (Eds.), *The Routledge handbook of halal hospitality and Islamic tourism* (pp. 21–52). Routledge.

Razak, N. H. A., Hall, C. M., & Prayag, G. (2020b). Malaysian accommodation providers' understanding of halal hospitality. In C. M. Hall & G. Prayag (Eds.), *The Routledge handbook of Halal hospitality and Islamic tourism* (pp. 70–82). Routledge.

Razzaq, S., Hall, C. M., & Prayag, G. (2016). The capacity of New Zealand to accommodate the halal tourism market – Or not. *Tourism Management Perspectives, 18*, 92–97.

Reader, I. (2013). *Pilgrimage in the marketplace*. Routledge.

Redden, G. (2016). 'Revisiting the spiritual supermarket: Does the commodification of spirituality necessarily devalue it? *Culture and Religion, 17*(2), 231–249.

Saaf Aly, N. M. E. (2010). *Ramadan culture in modern Cairo: Young females' leisure patterns and the politics of piety, unity and authenticity* [Doctoral dissertation, University of Groningen]. https://core.ac.uk/download/pdf/148293247.pdf

Sandıkcı, Ö. (2018). Religion and the marketplace: Constructing the "new" Muslim consumer. *Religion, 48*(3), 1–21. https://doi.org/10.1080/0048721X.2018.1482612

Seyfi, S., & Hall, C. M. (2019). Deciphering Islamic theocracy and tourism: Conceptualization, context, and complexities. *International Journal of Tourism Research, 21*(6), 735–746. https://doi.org/10.1002/jtr.2300

Taheri, B. (2016). Emotional connection, materialism, and religiosity: An Islamic tourism experience. *Journal of Travel & Tourism Marketing, 33*(7), 1011–1127.

Vargas-Sánchez, A., & Moral-Moral, M. (2018). Halal tourism: State of the art. *Tourism Review, 74*(3), 385–399. https://doi.org/10.1108/TR-01-2018-0015

Vliek, M. (2020). (Re) Negotiating embodiment when moving out of Islam: An empirical inquiry into 'a secular body'. In M. den Berg, L. L. Schrijvers, J. O. Wiering, & A.-M. Korte (Eds.), *Transforming bodies and religions* (pp. 159–177). Routledge.

Yosry, H. (2021). From sexual union to the divine – the teachings of Ibn al-'Arabi. *Psyche*. https://psyche.co/ideas/from-sexual-union-to-the-divine-the-teachings-of-ibn-al-arabi

2 Contemporary Muslim travel and tourism

Cultures and consumption

*C. Michael Hall, Mahshid Ahdiyeh Mahdavi,
Youri Oh and Siamak Seyfi*

Introduction

As of 2020, there are over 1.9 billion Muslims in the world, comprising nearly one-fourth of the world's population, making Islam the world's second largest religion after Christianity (World Population Review, 2021). However, the Muslim population is a diverse community of peoples from diverse ethnic backgrounds and languages and different sharia traditions (Seyfi & Hall, 2019), spanning the globe. Muslims make up a majority of the population in 49 countries around the world, and, by far, the Asia-Pacific region contains the highest number of Muslims in the world, followed by the Middle East and North Africa. Russia, China, India and the USA also have sizable Muslim populations with growing populations in Australasia and Europe. These staggering numbers together with the emergence of large middle-classes in many Muslim majority countries help illustrate why Muslim travel is a fast-growing market attracting the interest of the tourism and hospitality industry worldwide (Henderson, 2016; Scott & Jafari, 2010). Variously also sometimes described as halal tourism, sharia tourism or Islamic tourism (Jafari & Scott, 2014; Mohsin et al., 2016; Hall & Prayag, 2020b), according to the World Travel Market (2019), the outbound tourism expenditure by Muslims is predicted to reach US$274 billion by 2023, up from US$177 billion in 2017 (excluding Hajj and Umrah).

The Muslim population is generally young (Pew Research Center, 2015) and Muslim women have a high fertility rate (an average of 2.9 children in 2017) (Lipka & Hackett, 2017). On current trends the Muslim population is expected to increase 70% by 2060 (Pew Research Center, 2015). However, such global generalisations mask the substantial variation that exists between different countries. Muslims share the common tenets of Islam, but the community displays enormous ethnic and cultural diversity. Although Muslims are largely populated in southern and south-eastern Asia and in the Middle East-North Africa region (Pew Research Center, 2015), members of the Islamic faith are to be found throughout the world, particularly as the result of migration. Consequently, there is a growing number of Muslims in North America, Europe (Desilver & Masci, 2017; Pew Research Center, 2017), and Oceania (Kettani, 2010). On sheer numbers alone, Muslims now constitute a significant

DOI: 10.4324/9781003036296-3

consumer market. However, such generalised descriptions of the Muslim market, which are unfortunately quite common among many non-Muslims, do not give justice to the difficulties in developing accurate statistical assessments if Islamic tourism (see Chapter 1, this volume), the complexity of Muslim consumer culture or its significance for travel and tourism.

Globalisation, marked by advances in transport and information technology, ease in moving capital and reductions in travel restrictions for the more well off, has served to ease the geographical mobility of tourists and increase demand for travel (Hall, 2005; Mihajlović & Krželj, 2014; UN World Tourism Organization (UNWTO), 2017). The diversification and expansion of tourism industry has led tourism to tourism often being described as one of the world's fast-growing (UNWTO, 2017) and largest industries (e.g., Conrady & Buck, 2008), even though in strict terms it is not an industry but an amalgamation of different sectors that benefit from the consumption of people outside of their normal home environment. Nevertheless, as the economic effects of the COVID-19 pandemic has shown, the provision of services to tourists is significant, and its temporary decline has greatly affected many sectors, especially aviation, accommodation and hospitality (Seyfi et al., 2020). Similarly, tourism is a complex multidisciplinary phenomenon with numerous dimensions, e.g., economic, social, cultural, environmental (Darbellay & Stock, 2012), and perhaps Franklin's (2004) notion of a 'heterogeneous assemblage' would be an useful description of tourism. Nevertheless, an improved understanding of the cultural dimensions, particularly when outside of the dominant Western construction of tourism, would have substantial benefits for generating insights into consumer markets that are often more constructed in terms of being 'other' than for their inherent characteristics.

Increasing affluence and greater ease of travel has fuelled the growing demand for tourism by Muslims (Eddahar, 2016), often referred to as Islamic or halal tourism (Hall et al., 2020; Hanafiah & Hamdan, 2020; Henderson, 2016; Scott & Jafari, 2010). Pre-COVID more than 230 million Muslim tourists were expected to travel by 2026 with their travel expenditure projected to reach US$300 billion (Mastercard-CrescentRating, 2019a). With the substantial growth of a middle-class and young Muslim population, the potential level of tourism expenditure means that Muslim travellers are increasingly portrayed as a significant segment in global tourism (Henderson, 2016; The Standing Committee for Economic and Commercial Cooperation of the Organization of the Islamic Cooperation, 2016), while Islamic majority countries also become interested in the economic benefits of tourism (FaladeObalade & Dubey, 2014). The growing significance of intra-Muslim traffic as well as domestic tourism has led to both Islamic majority countries such as Malaysia, the United Arab Emirates, Indonesia and Turkey and non-Islamic majority countries, e.g. Japan and Korea, to develop campaigns to attract the Muslim market (Al-Hamarneh & Steiner, 2004). However as noted earlier, the Islamic market is much more diverse than what is often portrayed in both national marketing campaigns and in academic literatures (Seyfi & Hall, 2019). Although there is growing demand for new travel products and services, these cover a wide range of offerings. For example, many international hotels in some Muslim majority countries often provide products that would normally not be regarded as halal, such as alcohol and often do not explicitly promote themselves as halal (Razak et al., 2020). There are emerging demands for domestic and international tourism opportunities from emerging Islamic middle classes, Muslim millennial travellers and second and third generation Muslim communities in Europe and North America, each with their own characteristics (Wong, 2007). To these consumer demands can be added the implications of the development of Islamic consumer cultures, the role of gender in Islamic travel cultures and the growth of Islamic cosmopolitanism as a result of greater mobility, including study abroad.

Muslim travel not only comprises religious elements, such as pilgrimage – *Hajj* and *Umrah* – but also involves hospitality and consumption. However, religion should not be disregarded in this context as Muslims are bound by Islamic principles and religious requirements, e.g. shariah and halal, which frame Muslim consumption practices (Seyfi & Hall, 2019). The growing number and influence of Muslim travellers in the global tourism market pose a challenge to the tourism industry to learn and understand Islam and the needs of Muslim travellers. The tourism industry has for long been set in Western perspectives, while at times there has also been a hardening of views towards non-Western people and cultures among some politicians and members of the public, often exacerbated by the global refugee crisis, terrorist events, and Islamophobia (Michel, 2004; Mooij, 2019; Soldatenko & Backer, 2019). Nevertheless, with a burgeoning number of tourists from different cultures (Tsang & Ap, 2016), gaining a better understanding of different cultures becomes essential in order to meet the needs of tourists from around the world (Jung et al., 2018).

As Chapter 1 noted, this situation is not helped by much of the writing on Muslim travel, both from official and academic sources, which has tended to favour quite conservative interpretations of Islamic travel behaviour. Therefore, this chapter seeks to provide a broad overview of contemporary Muslim travel and tourism consumption. It first provides a discussion of the diverse nature of the Muslim market and the different hospitality and tourism cultures that exist, before discussing the relationship between religion and consumption, including with respect to Islam. These include not only traditional notions of pilgrimage but also different interpretations of leisure tourism. The chapter then discusses the one of the more contested areas of Muslim travel culture, which is women's mobility, which is a subject that illustrates the way in which religious interpretations and sharia are intersected by gender, regulation and patriarchal societies. The chapter concludes by reinforcing the diverse nature of Muslim travel cultures and the context that this provides for the various chapters in the book.

Muslim travel: Diverse market

While Islam is the predominant religion in many Arab and non-Arab societies, these societies are not identical, and they do not they share many cultural norms (Hourani, 1992; Almuhrzi et al., 2017). This differentiation between Arab world, the Islamic world, the Middle East and Asia has been highlighted by several scholars (Feghali, 1997; Jafari & Scott, 2014). Despite the fact that Islam's origins may be traced back to the Middle East, notably the Arabian Peninsula's western coast, Arabs presently constitute a minority within the Islamic world (Seyfi & Hall, 2019). Interestingly, the top five countries with the largest number of Muslims are non-Arabic speaking states: Indonesia, Pakistan, India, Bangladesh and Nigeria. Thus, as Seyfi and Hall (2019) note, when a tourism phenomenon is under investigation, this distinction between the Islamic and Arab worlds should be taken into consideration. In terms of inbound and outbound travel, the Muslim travel market is a stunning phenomenon that has grown into a powerful economic force and one of the most lucrative and quickly rising market sectors in the business, offering great potential for the tourist industry globally (Scott & Jafari, 2010). Thus, recently, there has been an expanding literature dealing with this market (Hall & Prayag, 2020b). Muslim demand for leisure travel is growing in tandem with the global Muslim population, highlighting the need for destinations and businesses to cater to this market.

Hospitality, tourism and travel cultures

Culture is an influential factor in consumer research in hospitality and tourism (Li, 2012; Watkins, 2006), especially with respect to consumers' decision making, behaviour and perceptions (Mooij, 2019; Overby et al., 2005). From a services perspective, the customer experience lies at the core of tourism and hospitality (Otto & Ritchie, 1996). As a result, culturally aware customer-oriented strategies have gained attention in marketing, management (Panni, 2012) and tourism (Gallarza et al., 2012). Hosts and guests – and their relationships, e.g., economic exchanges, interactions and communication (Smith, 1989) – have also become a widely studied and important topic in tourism because of the different cultural dimensions (Půtová, 2018; Lehto et al., 2020; Liu-Lastres & Cahyanto, 2021). There is no host without a guest; in other words, the role of host is to be hospitable – friendly, courteous and knowledgeable to the guests (Willits, 1987). Significantly, hospitality is a central element of Islam and is therefore an important element of Muslim understanding of the visitor and guest experience (Hall & Prayag, 2020a). Akpinar (2007, pp. 26–27) claims that hospitality "is a virtue that lies at the very basis of the Islamic ethical system." Nevertheless, while the benefits of tourism for host communities are often widely emphasised at the macro level, especially by the industry and policymakers, for example, with respect to social benefits (Liu et al., 2012), economic advantages and employment (Zaei & Zaei, 2013) and infrastructure development (Mathieson & Wall, 1982), the micro realities of host–guest inter-action are often not always positive. For example, while providing hospitality is often positioned as a means of empowering gender equality by enhancing women's participation in the labour force and providing an income source (Cole, 2018; Fillmore, 1994; Suarez, 2018), it is simultaneously reinforcing the notion of hospitality as "women's work" and stereotypical gender roles (Adib & Guerrier, 2003; Dyer et al., 2010). Hospitality is often typically portrayed as a kind of sanctuary, a meeting of needs and entertaining generously with the pleasure of the guests in mind (Lashley & Morrison, 2013; Telfer, 2013). These views mainly highlight hospitality as the role of the hosts rather than of the guests.

Brotherton and Wood (2000, p. 142) define hospitality as 'A contempo-raneous human exchange, which is voluntarily entered into, and designed to enhance the mutual wellbeing of the parties concerned through the provision of accommodation, and/or food, and/or drink'. Although such a definition does capture the notion of commercial hospitality, by highlighting specific ele-ments such as accommodation, food and drink it also stresses that hospitality is a reciprocal process, an interaction between the host and the guest based on respect and intimacy for mutual benefits (Siddiqui, 2015; Hall & Prayag, 2020a). As Reynolds (2010, p. 175) expressed it in terms of hospitality from the perspective of 'people of the book' (e.g., Qur'an 2.62),

> Hospitality is a bestowal of welcome that opens toward another as loved by God. But in the transaction a strange reversal occurs. The host who initially offers a gift to the guest ends up becoming blessed by the guest, receiving the presence of God. As boundaries are crossed, blessing leads to blessing in mutually enriching ways.

Indeed, being a guest involves a kind of hospitality as it entails a readiness to enter the world of the other and risking being welcomed into a strange place or setting (Reynolds, 2010; Siddiqui, 2015). As de Béthune (2007, p. 12) stated, 'to enter into the mystery of hospitality, one must know the experience of receiving hospitality'. Therefore, in considering hospitality in an Islamic context it is important to recognise that there are significant responsibilities for both the host and the guest. 'Serve Allah, and join not any partners with Him, and do good – to parents, kinsfolk, orphans, those in need, neighbors who are near, neighbors who are strangers, the Companion by your side, the way-farer (you meet)' (Qur'an 4.36).

Religion and consumption

One of the key aspects of experiencing tourism, regardless of whether being the host or the guest, is consumption (Saarinen & Manwa, 2008). Tourism provides spaces of consumption (Leslie & Reimer, 1999) by providing com-modities, knowledge, experiences and services to be produced and consumed.

Therefore, considerable emphasis is given in tourism to the importance of understanding consumer motivation and satisfaction of consumers (Gazley & Watling, 2015; Otto & Ritchie, 1996), in which the tourist's cultural background is given substantial significance (Landauer et al., 2014).

Religion is a distinctive component of culture (Shreim, 2009; Usunier & Lee, 2005). Geertz (1966, p. 16) defines religion as a cultural system that 'formulate[s] conceptions of a general order of existence' and that establishes purpose, motivation, and process that affect individual believers' behaviour. Hunt and Vitell (2006) recognise religion as a personal characteristic that influences personality structure and that principally influences religiously affiliated consumer behaviour. In consumer behaviour religion is widely recognised as an important and influential factor in consumption (Coşgel & Minkler, 2004; Delener, 1990; Mathras et al., 2016; Mokhlis, 2008, 2009; Orellano et al., 2020; Raggiotto et al., 2018; Sheth & Mittal, 2004), e.g. ethics (Arli, 2017; Pace, 2013; Vitell et al., 2005), quality evaluation (Mokhlis, 2009), materialism (Choudhury, 2019; Pace, 2013; Qin, 2016; Stillman et al., 2012), perspectives (Kurenlahti & Salonen, 2018; Sheth & Mittal, 2004) and attitudes (Cleveland & Chang, 2009; Minton et al., 2016).

The majority of the world's religions tend to condemn (self-centred) materialism (Baker et al., 2013) as it is often viewed as opposite of religious values, e.g. collectiveness and moderation (Burroughs & Rindfleisch, 2002). Miles (1998, p. 2) viewed consumption as 'we are indeed what we consume', which reflects consumption as an expression of one's identity, including religious traits (Porter, 2013). However, consumption can be carried out deliberately or unintentionally, with some consumers having limited awareness of the role of religion and belief systems in their consumption, although researchers have found religiosity to be a stronger predictor of consumer behaviour than religious affiliation (Choi et al., 2010; Essoo & Dibb, 2010; McDaniel & Burnett, 1990; Mokhlis, 2008).

Physical circumstances, e.g. surroundings, environment and objects and availability of products also affect consumer behaviours, particularly in changing consumption patterns (Umpfenbach, 2014). The significance of the environment in consumption is often found in diet and health related literatures. Gerbens-Leenes and Nonhebel (2002) found difference in food consumption practice worldwide, by different geographical areas, religion, culture, personal preference and availability of resources. They also note that consumption patterns are not fixed but can be altered by numerous factors. Significantly, Pink (2009) suggests that Muslims' consumption behaviour is not only influenced by religion but also other social, cultural and economic factors. Tourism may therefore encourage different consumption behaviours as a result of a temporary change in tourists' consumption environment, while in some cases tourists may deliberately seek exotic and unusual experiences or destinations (Center for the Promotion of Imports (CBI), 2020; Mergen, 1978; Mitchell, 1998; Vester, 1987) or may travel to destinations with a similar environment to their home country (Chen et al., 2021). Regardless of the places people travel to, culture influences one's behaviour either as a traveller or as a consumer (Pizam et al., 1999). Then, how does Islam view consumption? How does Islam influence Muslims' travel culture and their consumption practice in tourism? What are the contemporary Muslim travel culture and consumption practices while travelling?

Islam, religiosity and consumption

Islam means peace and submission to God, *Allah*, and those who practice Islam and believe in the teachings and message of Muhammad, the Prophet and last messenger of God, are called Muslims. As any religion, Islam has a moral and ethical theological requirement for Muslims to follow – for example, consuming halal food, praying five times a day and showing modesty. Religions in general have prescriptions on certain types of consumption, and dietary restrictions are extremely common. Tourism – and globalisation in general – also brings different belief systems regarding consumption into close contact with one another. Western consumption is primarily based on individualism and market-driven modes of consumption. As such Islam was viewed by some as a rejection of Western modernisation process with "incompatible" values and practices from Western consumer culture perspectives (Sandıkcı, 2018; Turner, 1994). Islam prohibits Muslims from asceticism and encourages a modest lifestyle (Khan, 1992; Sandıkcı, 2018). However, as Stearns (2001) explains, Islam is by no means averse to wealth as long as wealthy Muslims perform *zakat* (almsgiving, one of the duties as Muslim), and there are many examples of Muslim wealth accumulation and conspicuous consumption (Sandıkcı & Ger, 2007; Zakaria et al., 2021).

One under-researched aspect of Islamic consumption in a tourism context is that of Muslim ethical and green consumption. Islamic teaching emphasises the importance of living in harmony with Allah's creation (Hope & Jones, 2014), including the environment. Human beings are regarded as custodians of Allah's creation, with the Quran and the Sunnah imposing a moral responsibility of Muslims to the environment (Khalid, 2010), while other aspects of the importance of doing good (Reynolds, 2010) emphasise Muslim consumers' potential interest and practice with respect to ethical consumption (Abutaleb et al., 2020; Sharif, 2016).

Muslims are encouraged to consume only that which is *halal*, that which is permissible and allowed for Muslims to consume or undertake. Gambling, alcoholic drink consumption and adultery are strictly prohibited in Islam. When it comes to clothing, Islam emphasises modesty (Khan, 2003). Muslim men and women should cover their torso, Muslim men are mandated to cover their navel to the upper knees and Muslim women are additionally required to be modest, which may be interpreted to cover their hair to only expose their face (Deng et al., 1994; Khan, 2003). Muslim women have a stricter dress code than men in many Muslim-majority countries. However, this may reflect particular interpretations of Islam and/or cultural strictures rather than Islam per se.

Nevertheless, gender differentiates and restricts women's role in many Islamic countries. For example, Iraqi females have limited access to education, employment, and healthcare and suffer from high levels of violence and are constrained to traditional reproductive roles (Vilardo & Bittar, 2018). Until 2018 women in Saudi Arabia were not allowed to drive or go out in public without a male guardian's (father or husband) permission unless they were accompanied by a male relative. In terms of promotion and advertising, Muslims have also been identified as a more sensitive consumer group than other religious groups. In Fam et al.'s (2004) study of religiously-affiliated consumers' views on advertisement of controversial products, e.g. alcohol, cigarettes, contraceptives, underwear, gambling, weight loss programs and political parties, Muslim consumers were found to have more offensive or sensitive views in general than other religious groups. The study also found religiosity as a significant influence in Muslim respondents, as the more devout respondents find the controversial product advertisement more offensive compared to less devout Muslims.

Religiosity has been conceptualised as the degree of being religious (Run et al., 2010), compliance to theological rules (McDaniel & Burnett, 1990) and the significance of religion in one's life (Macionis & Plummer, 2008). Religiosity is important in influencing the degree of compliance to theological requirements in determining consumption (Azam et al., 2011; Beit-Hallahmi & Argyle, 1997; Budiman, 2012; Fontaine et al., 2005). For example, Hosseini et al. (2019) found religiosity as a moderator in Muslim consumers' willingness in purchasing halal certified food. Vitell et al. (2005) also addressed religiosity as one of the antecedents on consumer ethics. Studies have found an association between religiosity and green consumption (Chai & Tan, 2009; Granzin & Olsen, 1991; Hassan, 2014; Mohamad et al., 2012; Rice, 2006). Religiosity was also found to be an influential factor in Pakistani Muslim consumers' organic food purchase (Bukhari et al., 2020). Yet the influence of religiosity may be less significant in some circumstances. Choi et al. (2010) found religiosity was a less influential factor than traditional customs and collectivism in religiously affiliated Koreans' consumption behaviour. There was no significance linkage found between religiosity and green consumption in Canadian consumers (Kalamas et al., 2014) or among Muslim students in India (Khan & Kirmani, 2018) and Muslim students in Malaysia (Wan et al., 2014). Ahmad et al. (2013) found price and taste as more influential factors in Muslim consumers' food purchase over halal. Therefore, Muslim individuals' religiosity, willingness to overlook religious guidance and the effectiveness of religious teachings and ideas on individual Muslim in consumption vary across different countries, cultures, generations and consumption contexts (Mukhtar & Butt, 2012; Yousaf & Malik, 2013).

Muslim travellers' consumption

By its definition of consumption away from the normal home environment, tourism creates novel consumption spaces for the tourist. As a result, religious practices such as prayer or halal food consumption may be difficult to maintain in new environments. However, devout Muslim tourists tend to maintain strict religious practice while travelling as they demand prayer rooms, services and the Quran in their accommodation and lodging (Ozdemir & Met, 2012), which implies the important influence of religiosity in Muslim travellers' consumption. In general, studies find that Muslims are very conscious in their food consumption and mostly consume food in accordance with theological guidance (Han et al., 2019; Mastercard-CrescentRating, 2015). Nevertheless, this does now equate to neophobia as Muslim tourists prefer to try local cuisines when travelling (Korea Tourism Organization, 2018).

In consideration of food consumption, Muslims in Islamic majority countries tend to address concerns and issues of halal food consumption within their local community context. Personal trust and awareness in different halal certifications is a concern in halal consumption in Islamic countries (Ambali & Bakar, 2013; Omar et al., 2018; Rezai et al., 2012; Salman & Siddiqui, 2011). Muslims have also pointed out the importance of food being halal for them to consume in non-Islamic majority countries such as the UK (Ahmed, 2008; Jamal & Sharifuddin, 2015), Australia (Ali, 2014; Hegarty, 2020), France (Bonne et al., 2007) and New Zealand (Alhazmi, 2013). Despite their desire for halal food in non-Islamic countries, consuming halal food is not necessarily easy because of differences in the food environment and low availability of and accessibility to halal food (Afreen, 2018; Bonne & Verbeke, 2006; Fuseini, 2017; Hegarty, 2020). Poor legislation and/or consumer protection can also mean inappropriate attribution of food as halal, e.g. use of unapproved halal labels (Pointing et al., 2008), improper animal slaughtering practices (Jalil et al., 2018; Nakyinsige et al., 2012) and cross-contamination with non-halal or haram elements (Riaz & Chaudry, 2004). Although halal food is a significant concern in Muslims' consumption activities, Muslims nevertheless generally consume and have a positive attitude and intention in purchasing non-food halal certified products (Demirel & Yasarsoy, 2017; Mukhtar & Butt, 2012; Rahman et al., 2015).

As noted earlier, the purpose of travel of Muslim individuals varies substantially, and not all Muslim travellers perceive religious practice as compulsory. While many tourists spend on religious experience, some will spend more on leisure activities not related to religious principles. Muslim tourists do spend hours in shopping at luxury malls and fashion boutiques like other tourists (Bevins, 2017). As such, shopping is as an important travel activity segment for the Muslim market as it is for other tourists (The Standing Committee for Economic and Commercial Cooperation of the Organization of the Islamic Cooperation (COMCEC), 2016). Mastercard-CrescentRating's (2015) report on Muslim travellers estimated the total expenditure of Muslim travellers as $145 billion in 2015, with a total of $62 billion spent on shopping and dining. The survey was mostly conducted on Southeast Asian Muslim travellers who identified shopping as an important consideration for choice of destination. Souvenirs were the top component of their shopping purchase, followed by local and Islamic clothing (Mastercard-CrescentRating, 2015). Halal and Muslim-friendliness of facilities were also highlighted as concerns for Muslim travellers in the report. Nevertheless, shopping was reported as the key experience Muslim travellers expected and prefer to do while travelling in a non-Islamic majority country. However, the findings in Kim et al.'s (2015) study of Malaysian Muslim tourists in Asia showed significant gender differences in product preferences in tourism shopping between males and females with females indicating greater preference for fashion items while males are more disposed to electronics. However, this is consistent with other studies where gender reflects different preferences in tourism shopping (Li & Bihu, 2013).

Muslim travellers' consumption is a complex issue in which religious and secular lifestyles are entwined and different consumption cultures and behaviours exist within the basic framework of the teachings of Islam (Scott & Jafari, 2010). Such differences in consumption may only be amplified when Muslims are travelling to non-Islamic majority countries (Fauzihana & Ayob, 2020). However, Islamic consumption principles do travel with Muslim tourists and, as a result of the social and economic exchange that occurs between local and tourist cultures, there has been increased demand for halal products in destination countries (Fan et al., 2017). Islamic tourism is therefore a product of the interaction between the various elements of the tourism system – such as destinations – and Muslim travellers, who can take a variety of different expressions depending on where Muslim tourists are in the different stages of the tourist trip and of their tourism lifecourse (Hall, 2005).

Islamic/halal/sharia tourism, and Muslim travel culture

Religious tourism, also referred to as sacred or faith tourism, remains a popular form of tourism (Wiśniewski, 2018). Religious tourism is one of the oldest form of tourism (e.g. pilgrimage) and includes the participation in worship and ceremonies, visiting a shrine and meditation and prayer (Center for the Promotion of Imports (CBI), 2020; Wiltshier, 2019). However, it does not necessarily solely rely on the fulfilment of religious obligations or motivations (Buzinde et al., 2014; Wang et al., 2016). Pilgrimage, for example, is commonly recognised as a journey for the attainment of enlightenment. This will mean *hajj* or *umrah* for Muslims, but such feelings can be derived from cultural and intellectual curiosity (Wang et al., 2016; Wiśniewski, 2018). Religious fulfilment is only one intention of Muslims' travel, but like many other tourists it can also be based on motives such as leisure, education, VFR, health or other purposes.

Muslim travellers' perceptions of a destination are often categorised as religious or non-religious. The former consider more religious elements such as availability of halal food and prayer rooms, while the latter is concerned more with socio-cultural attraction and safety (Abdul Rashid et al., 2019). However, regardless of the purpose of travel, Muslims are mandated to consume halal and comply with Shariah law. Therefore, the provision of halal food, halal eateries, prayer rooms and other services that satisfy the requirements of Islamic teachings is significant for Muslim travellers' destination selection and subsequent consumption (Han et al., 2019; Jafari & Scott, 2014; Liu et al., 2018; Ryan, 2016).

Islamic tourism, particularly that which is targeted at Muslims (Organisation of Islamic Cooperation (OIC) & The Statistical, Economic and Social Research and Training Centre for Islamic Countries (SESRIC), 2017), is also often described as halal tourism, shariah tourism, or Muslim-friendly tourism (Akyol & Kilinç, 2014; OIC & SESRIC, 2017). The major components of Islamic tourism are similar to those of conventional tourism although, according to OIC and SESRIC (2017), it must entail Islamic and Shariah principles. Thus Islamic tourism is a form of tourism that includes all tourism goods and services designed, produced and provided to cater to Muslims in accordance with Islamic requirements (Bangsawan et al., 2019; Chookaew et al., 2015; Hamza et al., 2012; Shafaei & Mohamed, 2015), including halal food, mosques or prayer rooms, halal eateries and accommodation. Table 2.1 briefly illustrates some of the applicable principles for tourism product providers for tourism in compliance with Islam.

Table 2.1 Applicable principles for Islamic tourism

	Islamic principles for tourism product providers	*Implications*
Salat	• Prayer rooms	• Provide prayer rooms with prayer carpet, washing facility (*ghusl*), prayer direction • Provide the Quran at the facility • Islamic call to prayer
Zakat	• Compliance of tourism product providers with *zakat* values	• Perform *zakat* (almsgiving)
Halal food	• Serves halal (certified) food • Prohibition of non-halal and haram food, e.g., pork, alcohol	• Obtain halal certification • Serves halal (certified) food • Owned and served by Muslims
Gender	• Gender segregation requirements in facilities	• Staff serve same gender customers only • Gender-segregated restaurant (seating), swimming pool, spa, sauna and gym
Activities	• Prohibition of activities against Islamic principles • Involves in sustainable activities	• No gambling • No pornography • Provide recycling bin • Perform green consumption
Identity	• Halal certification (or at least Muslim-friendly) • Islamic dress code • Muslim staff	• Obtain halal certification/Muslim-friendly • Implement dress code in accordance with Islamic requirements

Source: The authors

An increasing number of countries, regardless of whether Islam is the main religion or not, have tourism industries that have introduced halal-friendly tourism services to attract more Muslim travellers (Hassan & Hall, 2003; Razzaq et al., 2016; Han et al., 2019). Muslim-friendly tourism can be differentiated as being neither completely halal nor strictly complying with Islamic teachings but nevertheless providing options for Muslims to consume, e.g. available or willing to serve halal food (using halal ingredients or segregation of cooking) while providing non-halal goods or services at the premises. Although the concept does not denote 'everything is halal', it has become a significant element in promotions to Muslim tourists (Bangsawan et al., 2019). For example, the Korea Tourism Organization (KTO, 2017) introduced Muslim-friendly business classifications with labels and pictograms and also initiated an annual Halal restaurant week promotion in order to improve halal awareness (Choi, 2017) and encourage government and industry to provide prayer rooms to cater to Muslims during their travel in Korea (KTO, 2016, 2018).

Destination image influences tourist perception and behaviour as well as the selection of travel destination (Bigné et al., 2001; Carballo et al., 2015; Liu et al., 2018; Chen et al., 2021). Much of the literature suggests that Muslim travellers prefer to visit destinations that provide services and facilitates safeguard of their religious interest and needs (Han et al., 2019; Hassani & Moghavvemi, 2019; Liu et al., 2018; Mohamed, 2018), which are thus characterised as 'Islamic destinations' (Shafaei & Mohamed, 2015). The importance of Islamic attributes for Muslim travellers in choosing destinations is therefore often highlighted in the research literature (Fauzihana & Ayob, 2020; Han et al., 2019; Henderson, 2016; Mastercard-CrescentRating, 2019a; Mohsin et al., 2016; Stephenson, 2014). For example, Timothy and Iverson (2006) found that Muslim travellers felt more comfortable and welcomed in Islamic destinations as it made the practice of their religious obligations more flexible. Religiosity has also been found to influence Muslim travellers' selection of destination with it being suggested that Muslim travellers whose intention of travel are motivated by Islamic factors prefer to visit Islamic countries, while those influenced by non-Islamic motivations tend to avoid Islamic destinations (Hassani & Moghavvemi, 2019). Such findings are important, but they also need to be treated with some caution, as Hall and Prayag (2020c, p. 342) commented in reflecting on halal hospitality and tourism research

> At times, some of the contextualisation of halal, especially in conference papers and open access journals, almost takes the form of attempts to prove the piety of the author rather than critically assess halal matters. There is also often insufficient criticism of poor halal certification procedures, the (lack of or partial) enforcement of halal by responsible government agencies, and the large gap that may exist between what business and enterprises say they do and what actually happens. Such lack of criticism or a

willingness to discuss negative aspects of halal or Islamic tourism may be because of not wanting to appear to be critical of either Islam or one's country. However, it may also be that a somewhat unbalanced portrayal of research topics and subjects is presented.

Such criticisms apply both to the production of Islamic tourism products as well as their consumption. People do not always meet the aspirations of the religious beliefs of either others or themselves. However, even though that is what makes the personal spiritual journey so interesting, respondents may find it difficult to admit that they have taken a different path or had a particular experience if they then feel they will be seen or portrayed as 'bad' Muslims. While honesty is a value to be praised, it is not always forthcoming when researching religious matters,

> Food consumption is an everyday practice and dining options are an important concern for tourists. Muslim travellers' food consumption has attracted significant research interest (e.g. Abodeeb et al., 2015; Hariani, 2016; Hassan & Hall, 2003; Mannaa, 2019; Mohsin et al., 2016; Nawawi et al., 2017; Stephenson, 2014). Halal food is as an important issue or at least concern for many Muslim travellers, particularly when they are travelling to non-Islamic destinations (Abodeeb et al., 2015; Han et al., 2019; Hariani, 2016; Hassan & Hall, 2003; Syed, 2001). The need for halal restaurants and hotels in non-Muslim country has been addressed by Muslim respondents in a number of studies (Chookaew et al., 2015; Kim et al., 2015). In Kim et al.'s study (2015) Malaysian Muslim travellers found the availability and accessibility of prayer facilities, amenity, public awareness of Islam as important segments in their travel to non-Muslim countries. In addition, Muslim travellers may also be concerned with Islamophobia as a potential risk to their travel to non-Islamic destinations.
>
> (Aji et al., 2020)

Nevertheless, even as domestic travellers in Muslim majority countries, tourists can encounter difficulties in finding products that cater to their religious needs. Ozdemir and Met's (2012) study of Turkish Muslim domestic tourists found that devout Muslims considered maintaining religious practices more important than less religious tourists. The devout groups considered the prohibition of non-halal and haram elements e.g. alcohol, the segregation of gender in facilities e.g. swimming pools and prayer as their most important needs during their travel. However, they did not find that local Islamic accommodations do not satisfy their religious expectations. Interestingly, assumptions with respect to the promotion and availability of halal services in Muslim majority countries may not always hold. For example, when Razak et al. (2020) examined the online promotion of halal services by accommodation providers in Malaysia, there was no significant difference between halal services in Malaysia and those in New Zealand (Razzaq et al., 2016).

Whether domestic or international travellers, a significant emerging research theme is that of tourism by young Muslims, between 18 and 36, who have been recognised as key agents for contemporary Muslim travel (Cuesta-Valiño et al., 2020; Mastercard-CrescentRating, 2020; Wong, 2017; Zaini, 2016). The Muslim population is the youngest among all religious groups, with a median age of 24 in 2015, which is 7 years younger than the non-Muslim median age of 32 (Lipka & Hackett, 2017). Considering Muslims' high fertility rate, greater disposable income and demand for travel and travel expenditure, young Muslims have become a lucrative segment (Zaini, 2016). Their exposure to advanced technology and ease of access to information via applications and websites, e.g. indication of prayer time and direction of Mecca (Fakhruroji, 2019), make their religious practice easier no matter where they are travelling. In order to cater to their religious needs, there are number of online-based information website e.g. halalzilla.com, primarily established for young Muslim travellers, that provide suggestions and information about halal food, prayer and lifestyle for different countries. However, as suggested earlier, religious observance is perhaps best understood contextually in both space and time in relation to the different stages of travel and the tourism lifecourse. For example, Bahardeen (2018) and Eum (2009) found that young Muslim travellers tended to balance faith-based values with other values and interests while travelling.

Another important set of consumers is Muslim women travellers, who comprise 45 percent of global Muslim travel market (Mastercard-CrescentRating, 2020). According to Mastercard-CrescentRating (2019b), Muslim female travellers have some of the same interests as other female travellers around the world, with their major travel purpose being leisure and shopping being the most popular activity that Muslim female travellers seek when travelling, followed by religion. Muslim women mostly travel with their family (71 percent), while an estimated 28 percent travel alone (Mastercard-CrescentRating, 2019b), reflecting highly gendered tourism practices (Ibrahim et al., 2009). Yet the report also notes that 29 percent travel in an all-female group, and 22 percent travel in a mixed gender group. Significantly, the number of Muslim women tourists seeking independent travel is increasing (Mastercard-CrescentRating, 2019b). As the next section discusses in more depth, like Muslim tourist consumers as a whole, significant differences and issues emerge in Muslim women's travel practices.

Muslim women's travel

Out of a total of 6,660 verses in the Quran, only 6 establish some kind of male authority over women. In Islam, women were never forbidden going out for work, sports or travel (Thimm, 2017). However, there are numerous misconceptions about gendered Islamic practices with respect to women's travel. Nevertheless, religious dogmas and their political, patriarchal and regulatory interpretations do have effects on travel choices and behaviour in general, including that of many Muslim women. Table 2.2 illustrates this with respect

Table 2.2 Constraints on women's agency and freedom of movement in OIC member states

Country	Can a woman choose where to live in the same way as a man?	Can a woman travel outside her home in the same way as a man?	Can a woman apply for a passport in the same way as a man?	Can a woman travel outside the country in the s ame way as a man?
Africa				
Algeria	Yes	Yes	No	Yes
Benin	No	Yes	Yes	Yes
Burkina Faso	No	Yes	Yes	Yes
Cameroon	No	Yes	No	Yes
Chad	No	Yes	Yes	Yes
Comoros	No	Yes	Yes	Yes
Djibouti	Yes	Yes	Yes	Yes
Egypt	Yes	No	No	Yes
Gabon	No	Yes	No	Yes
Gambia	Yes	Yes	Yes	Yes
Guinea	Yes	Yes	Yes	Yes
Guinea–Bissau	No	Yes	Yes	Yes
Ivory Coast	Yes	Yes	Yes	Yes
Libya	Yes	Yes	No	Yes
Mali	No	Yes	No	Yes
Mauritania	Yes	Yes	Yes	Yes
Morocco	Yes	Yes	Yes	Yes
Mozambique	Yes	Yes	Yes	Yes
Niger	No	Yes	Yes	Yes
Nigeria	No	Yes	No	Yes
Senegal	No	Yes	Yes	Yes
Sierra Leone	Yes	Yes	Yes	Yes
Somalia	No	Yes	Yes	Yes
Sudan	No	No	No	No
Togo	Yes	Yes	Yes	Yes
Tunisia	Yes	Yes	Yes	Yes
Uganda	No	Yes	Yes	Yes
By region	48.1%	92.6%	70.4%	96.3%
Asia				
Afghanistan	No	No	Yes	Yes
Azerbaijan	Yes	Yes	Yes	Yes
Bahrain	No	No	Yes	Yes
Bangladesh	Yes	Yes	Yes	Yes
Brunei	No	No	Yes	Yes
Indonesia	Yes	Yes	Yes	Yes
Iran	No	No	No	No
Iraq	No	No	No	No
Jordan	No	No	Yes	No
Kazakhstan	Yes	Yes	Yes	Yes
Kuwait	No	No	Yes	Yes
Kyrgyzstan	Yes	Yes	Yes	Yes
Lebanon	Yes	Yes	Yes	Yes
Malaysia	No	No	Yes	Yes

Country	Can a woman choose where to live in the same way as a man?	Can a woman travel outside her home in the same way as a man?	Can a woman apply for a passport in the same way as a man?	Can a woman travel outside the country in the same way as a man?
Maldives	Yes	Yes	Yes	Yes
Oman	No	No	No	No
Pakistan	Yes	Yes	No	Yes
Palestine★	No	No	Yes	No
Qatar	No	No	Yes	No
Saudi Arabia	Yes	Yes	Yes	Yes
Syria@	No	No	Yes	No
Tajikistan	Yes	Yes	Yes	Yes
Turkey	Yes	Yes	Yes	Yes
Turkmenistan#	n/a	n/a	n/a	n/a
United Arab Emirates	Yes	Yes	Yes	Yes
Uzbekistan	Yes	Yes	Yes	Yes
Yemen	No	No	No	Yes
By region	50%	50%	80.8%	73.1%
Europe				
Albania	Yes	Yes	Yes	Yes
By region	100%	100%	100%	100%
South America				
Guyana	Yes	Yes	No	Yes
Suriname	Yes	Yes	Yes	Yes
By region	100%	100%	50%	100%
OIC total average	51.8%	73.2%	75%	85.8%
World total average	81.1%	92.1%	82.6%	95.8%

★ The World Bank refers to the West Bank and Gaza; @ suspended from OIC as of January, 2022; # No World Bank data available

Source: Derived from World Bank. (2021). Women, Business and the Law: Mobility, https://wbl.worldbank.org/en/data/exploretopics/wbl_gp

to the regulatory constraints on women's agency and freedom of movement that exist in OIC member states. Significantly, the table illustrates differences between Islamic majority states. For example, Asian Muslim majority countries tend to be restrictive with respect to women's mobility. Although it is notable that OIC countries are more restrictive overall compared to other countries.

One of Islam's central obligations to perform hajj and umrah, pilgrimage to Mecca, provides an opportunity for women to travel. However, as noted earlier, more generally women travel to seek knowledge, for employment and for leisure (Muhamad, 2008). For Mohee (2012) gendered identities remain grounded in religious or cultural beliefs that draw on different understandings of culture, religion, race and ethnicity. Travel can therefore reflect the choices women make independently by questioning interpretations of religious dogmas while negotiating and navigating their roles and identity as a Muslim and as a woman.

According to Scott and Jafari (2010) travelling supports the unity of Muslims and strengthens the brother- and sisterhood of Muslims all over the world. Islam positions men and women as equals albeit with different role priorities, which reflects that Islam and the Quran do not establish any inherent spiritual, intellectual or physical inferiority of women (Shah, 2018). For example, since the early 2000s, the emergence of young, educated, financially stable Muslim women in the tourism market illustrates their capability to travel across borders and challenge bigotry and gender bias. The growth of Muslim women travellers contests the view that gendered interpretations of religious texts promote patriarchal orientation in a Muslim community that suppresses women leisure. Some Asian Muslim families, for example, are becoming more liberal with men supporting the travel endeavours of women (Ratthinan & Selamat, 2018). The changing social roles represent a significant driver of the emerging patterns in this market.

Prejudicial and cultural pressures

Both religiosity and norm-based attitudes are considered part of personal identity. People are socialised over their lifecourse (Glenn, 2003; Spierings, 2015). However, both religiosity and (gender-equality) attitudes can change over time. The two concepts are generally treated as part and parcel of a larger cultural cluster. Because most dominant interpretations of religions contain strong patriarchal norms, people for whom religion plays an important role in their life are likely to be socialised in the norms and values set by this religious institution (Burdette et al., 2005).

Gender inequity has been described as a 'freedom deficit' (Haass, 2003). Religion and cultural norms demarcate, shape and affirm the role and rights of women in public spaces. Women within patriarchal systems do advance challenges to male dominance but not necessarily for purposes to do with 'emancipation' or 'equality' (Ridzuan, 2011). Nevertheless, in a tourism context, it is crucial to consider the extent of religious jurisdictions coupled with traditional beliefs that impact women's empowerment. Islam sets the relationship between men and women in a form of fraternity and not in a form of a contention (Al-Khayat, 2003). Muslim women are often represented as trapped in an Islamic religious paradox and denied of their liberation to engage in leisure activities, as well as religious and formal gatherings. However, most feminist arguments of empowerment are grounded in 'Western' interpretations in which religious obligations are often framed as foundations of patriarchal structures (Sehlikoglu, 2018).

According to Pyke and Johnson (2003), by constructing ethnic culture as impervious to social change and as a site where resistance to gender oppression is impossible, women can accommodate and reinforce rather than resist the gender hierarchal arrangements of such locales. For example, from a tourism perspective, this could contribute to a self-fulfilling prophecy as female tourists who hold gender egalitarian views may feel compelled to retreat from interactions in particular cultural and ethnic settings, thus (re)creating particular ethnic cultures as strongholds of patriarchy.

Past theorising emphasises gender as a socially constructed phenomenon rather than an innate and stable attribute (Lucal, 1999). Gender is something people 'do' in social interaction. As such, gender is manufactured out of the fabric of culture and social structure and has little, if any, causal relationship to biology (Lorber, 2008). Gender displays are 'culturally established sets of behaviors, appearances, mannerisms, and other cues that we have learned to associate with members of a particular gender' (Lucal, 1999, 91–97). These displays can frame particular travel pursuits as expressions of masculine and feminine 'natures', while the 'doing' of gender involves its display as a seemingly innate component of an individual (West & Zimmerman, 1987).

In terms of Islam, Alexander and Welzel (2011) found that 'Muslim support for patriarchal values is robust against various controls'. Similarly, in a more refined analysis of this relationship, Glas et al. (2018) show that several dimensions of Islamic religiosity (e.g. attending religious service and devotion) fuel opposition towards gender equality in the Middle East. Hence, socialisation in dominant Islamic interpretations appears to weaken support for gender equality. The connection between religiosity and gender equality attitudes is therefore highly gendered itself and not straightforward (Röder & Mühlau, 2014). While women's rights movements have highlighted the historical and cultural specificities of gendered inequalities for some decades (Cutrufelli, 1983), issues relating to religious differences have remained largely unexplored (Bracke, 2008), particularly with regard to the differences within and across Muslim communities. This is in part due to the historically contentious relationship between Islam and the 'West' (Mahmood, 2001) as well as differences within Islam.

One of the most important approaches to these hidden religious differences is Islamic culture and prejudice, and the most obvious sign for Muslim women is the issue of hijab. Just as images of the veil can be reifying and etherising, Muslim women are often perceived as a homogeneous entity with similar cognitions, affects and behaviours (Hoodfar, 1992; Minces, 1980). Such an approach tends to suppress the heterogeneity of the subjects it sets out to analyze (Howarth, 2002). This leads to the construction of a 'third-world difference', a stable, a-historical force that supposedly oppresses most women in these regions (Mohanty, 1988).

Generally, the teaching of Islam in countries such as the United States has been characterised by numerous stereotypes, distortions, omissions, textbook inaccuracies and within the boundaries of politically motivated narrative (Douglass & Dunn, 2003). This has only worsened in the post 9/11 environment. The Sunni and Shiite sects of Islam encompass a wide spectrum of doctrine, opinion and schools of thought. The branches are in agreement on many aspects of Islam, but there are considerable disagreements within each, with considerable implications for consumer culture and tourism practices (Hall & Prayag, 2020b). Both branches include worshipers who run the gamut from secular to fundamentalist. Because of the different paths the two sects took, Sunnis emphasize God's power in the material world, sometimes including the public and political realm, while Shiites value martyrdom and sacrifice (Harney, 2016).

More conservative women support arguments espoused by religious thinking, which compels women to create their identity around specific interpretations of religious tenets (e.g., wearing the veil), including with respect to travel. They thereby perpetuate stereotypes but gain the support of their group. There is no denying that some women follow this course of cultural conservative pressures as the easiest way of securing acknowledgement by 'their people' and thereby become socially included (Wagner et al., 2012). This is a political decision for those concerned. This is particularly true for societies that are still deeply gendered in everyday divisions of labour, activities and spaces (Illich, 1990).

Women in Islamic society are also subject to sexual segregation for religious and cultural reasons (Kazemi, 2000), which can have significant implications for tourism. Her mobility outside home is restricted because of the rationale of modesty (*Haya*), family honour (*Ghairat*), and tribal tradition (*Rivaj*). Modesty is related to the concepts of shame (*Sharm*) and humility (*Ijz*). It imposes physical and psychological boundaries on Muslim women. Modesty is embodied by the veil in many Muslim countries and serves as an institution of sexual segregation (Syed et al., 2005). A woman in the male space is 'considered provocative and offensive'. By entering male space, she 'upset[s] the male's order and his peace of mind . . . actually committing an act of aggression against him merely by being present where she should not be. If the woman is unveiled, the situation is aggravated' (Storti, 1990, pp. 66–67). According to Maudoodi (1991), in addition to the generalisation of the meaning of the aforementioned verses for all women, orthodox Ulema (Islamic scholars) cite a large number of traditions of the Prophet in support of their position on Muslim woman's veiled and other forms of seclusion as well as modesty.

Yet comparatively liberal voices are not heard in many parts, notably the Arab states and the Indian subcontinent. Despite official ratification of several international instruments on gender equity and human rights, major barriers continue to restrict women's opportunities in Islamic society (UNDP, 2004). Female modesty is hegemonic – with some variations – throughout Islamic society. Some opinion is moderate but more restrictive. Detailed Islamic codes govern dress, ornamentation, conversation, voice-pitch and segregation (Syed et al., 2005). However, cultural and prejudicial stereotyping and projecting an unjustified uniformity are a potent and dangerous mix, which can lead to violence against women and sustain a bigoted form of religion (Halim & Meyers, 2010; Wagner et al., 2012), with significant implications not only for women but also specially for consumer culture and Muslim women's travel practices.

Conclusion

Muslim travellers are diverse by culture, gender, age, ethnicity and nationality. Their travel habits, patterns, purposes and needs do vary and should not be cast as being uniform. However, Islam shapes their consumption and tourism lifestyle by virtue of theological requirements (Arham, 2010) but with adherence best understood on a continuum rather than in absolute terms. Although, as discussed in this chapter, some Muslims may be less forthcoming about their engagement in some tourism consumption practices because they may not be acceptable to some interpretations of sharia or religious community norms.

The Muslim population is fast expanding along with the increasing middle class in countries with large Muslim populations. Thus, many businesses and destinations started to adapt their products and services to cater to Muslim travellers resulting in rise in the availability of Muslim-friendly services. Despite such growth and significance of Muslim travellers in global tourism, there is relative paucity of studies on Muslim travellers' leisure activities (Jafari & Scott, 2014), understanding the needs of Muslim travellers (Eid & El-Gohary, 2015), and more broadly Muslim travellers' behaviour in a cultural context (Reisinger & Moufakkir, 2015), especially from more critical perspectives (Hall & Prayag, 2020b). Nevertheless, the emergence of a substantial young Muslim tourist market, together with the rise of Muslim women travellers and a desire among Muslim travellers to visit less popular sites, highlight the importance of research in Muslim tourism consumer culture in tourism and hospitality studies. With the growth of the Muslim traveller as a niche market and the diverse nature of this market and their influence in the global tourism industry, there is a need to acknowledge the needs and values of this increasingly large travel market and to develop more sophisticated and critical assessments of Muslim travel culture. These issues will be discussed in the next chapters of the book.

References

Abdul Rashid, N. R. N., Ali Akbar, Y. A., Laidin, J., & Wan Muhamad, W. S. A. (2019). Factors influencing Muslim tourists satisfaction travelling to non-Muslim countries. In F. Hassan, I. Osman, E. S. Kassim, B. Haris, & R. Hassan (Eds.), *Contemporary management and science issues in the Halal Industry: Proceedings of the International Malaysia Halal Conference (IMHALAL)* (pp. 139–150). Springer.

Abodeeb, J., Wilson, E., & Moyle, B. (2015). Shaping destination image and identity: Insights for Arab tourism at the Gold Coast, Australia. *International Journal of Culture, Tourism and Hospitality Research, 9*(1), 6–21. https://doi.org/10.1108/IJCTHR-06-2014-0051

Abutaleb, S., El-Bassiouny, N. M., & Hamed, S. (2020). A conceptualization of the role of religiosity in online collaborative consumption behavior. *Journal of Islamic Marketing, 12*(1), 180–198. https://doi.org/10.1108/JIMA-09-2019-0186

Adib, A., & Guerrier, Y. (2003). The interlocking of gender with nationality, race, ethnicity and class: The narratives of women in hotel work. *Gender, Work & Organization, 10*(4), 413–432. https://doi.org/10.1111/1468-0432.00204

Afreen, T. (2018). *Experiences and adaptations of Muslim students on the campus of California State University, Long Beach* [Master's thesis, California State University, Long Beach]. http://search.proquest.com/docview/2154863536/abstract/5481D5018C3A4CFEPQ/1

Ahmad, N. A., Tunku Abaidah, T. N., & Abu Yahya, M. H. (2013). A study on halal food awareness among Muslim customers in Klang Valley. *4th International Conference on Business and Economic Research (4th ICBER 2013) Proceedings, March 4, 1074*, 1–15.

Ahmed, A. (2008). Marketing of halal meat in the United Kingdom: Supermarkets versus local shops. *British Food Journal, 110*(7), 655–670. https://doi.org/10.1108/00070700810887149

Aji, H. M., Muslichah, I., & Seftyono, C. (2020). The determinants of Muslim travellers' intention to visit non-Islamic countries: A halal tourism implication. *Journal of Islamic Marketing, 12*(8), 1553–1576. https://doi.org/10.1108/JIMA-03-2020-0075

Akpinar, S. (2007). Hospitality in Islam. *Religion East and West, 7*(1), 23–27.

Akyol, M., & Kilinç, Ö. (2014, Summer). Internet and halal tourism marketing. *International Periodical for the Languages, Literature and History of Turkish or Turkic, 9/8*, 171–186. http://dx.doi.org/10.7827/TurkishStudies.7278

Alexander, A. C., & Welzel, C. (2011). Islam and patriarchy: How robust is Muslim support for patriarchal values? *International Review of Sociology, 21*(2), 249–276. https://doi.org/10.1080/03906701.2011.581801

Al-Hamarneh, A., & Steiner, C. (2004). Islamic tourism: Rethinking the strategies of tourism development in the Arab world after September 11, 2001. *Comparative Studies of South Asia, Africa and the Middle East, 24*(1), 173–182.

Alhazmi, H. K. H. (2013). *New Zealand Muslim consumer attitudes towards purchasing Halal foods* [Master's thesis, Auckland University of Technology].

Ali, M. Y. (2014, December 1). Australian multicultural consumer diversity: A study on Muslim consumers' perception towards Halal labeling. *Proceedings of the Australia New Zealand Marketing Academy Conference 2014*. ANZMAC 2014, Brisbane. https://doi.org/10.13140/2.1.3098.7208

Al-Khayat, M. H. (2003). *Woman in Islam and her role in human development*. World Health Organization.

Almuhrzi, H., Alriyami, H., & Scott, N. (Eds.). (2017). *Tourism in the Arab world: An industry perspective*. Channel View Publications.

Ambali, A. R., & Bakar, A. N. (2013). Ḥalāl food and products in Malaysia: People's awareness and policy implications. *Intellectual Discourse, 21*(1), 7–32.

Arham, M. (2010). Islamic perspectives on marketing. *Journal of Islamic Marketing, 1*(2), 149–164. https://doi.org/10.1108/17590831011055888

Arli, D. (2017). Does ethics need religion? Evaluating the importance of religiosity in consumer ethics. *Marketing Intelligence & Planning, 35*(2), 205–221. https://doi.org/10.1108/MIP-06-2016-0096

Azam, A., Qiang, F., Abdullah, M. I., & Abbas, S. A. (2011). Impact of 5D of religiosity on diffusion rate of innovation. *International Journal of Business and Social Science, 2*(17), 177–185.

Bahardeen, R. (2018). Halal travel. *Global Citizenship Review*. https://globecit.com/halal-travel/

Baker, A. M., Moschis, G. P., Ong, F. S., & Pattanapanyasat, R.-P. (2013). Materialism and life satisfaction: The role of stress and religiosity. *Journal of Consumer Affairs, 47*(3), 548–564.

Bangsawan, S., Ms, M., Rahman, M. M., & Razimi, M. S. A. (2019). Muslim friendly tourism and accommodation of Malaysian hotel industries. *Utopía y Praxis Latinoamericana, 24*(5), 9.

Beit-Hallahmi, B., & Argyle, M. (1997). *The psychology of religious behaviour, belief and experience.* Taylor & Francis.

Bevins, V. (2017, June 6). Halal tourism: Kuala Lumpur welcomes the Muslim travellers others didn't want. *The Guardian.* www.theguardian.com/cities/2017/jun/06/halal-tourism-kuala-lumpur-muslim-travellers-malaysia

Bigné, J. E., Sánchez, M. I., & Sánchez, J. (2001). Tourism image, evaluation variables and after purchase behaviour: Inter-relationship. *Tourism Management, 22*(6), 607–616. https://doi.org/10.1016/S0261-5177(01)00035-8

Bonne, K., & Verbeke, W. (2006, May). Muslim consumer's motivations towards meat consumption in Belgium: Qualitative exploratory insights from means-end chain analysis. *Anthropology of Food, 5.* http://journals.openedition.org/aof/90

Bonne, K., Vermeir, I., Bergeaud-Blackler, F., & Verbeke, W. (2007). Determinants of halal meat consumption in France. *British Food Journal, 109*(4–5), 367–386. https://doi.org/10.1108/00070700710746786

Bracke, S. (2008). Conjugating the modern/religious, conceptualizing female religious agency: Contours of a 'post-secular' conjuncture. *Theory, Culture & Society, 25*(6), 51–67. https://doi.org/10.1177/0263276408095544

Brotherton, B., & Wood, R. (2000). Hospitality and hospitality management. In C. Lashley & A. Morrison (Eds.), *In search of hospitality* (pp. 134–156). Routledge.

Budiman, S. (2012). Analysis of consumer attitudes to purchase intentions of counterfeiting bag product in Indonesia. *International Journal of Management, Economics and Social Sciences, 1*(1), 1–12.

Bukhari, F., Hussain, S., Ahmed, R. R., Streimikiene, D., Soomro, R. H., & Channar, Z. A. (2020). Motives and role of religiosity towards consumer purchase behavior in Western imported food products. *Sustainability, 12*(1), 356. https://doi.org/10.3390/su12010356

Burdette, A. M., Ellison, C. G., & Hill, T. D. (2005). Conservative Protestantism and tolerance toward homosexuals: An examination of potential mechanisms. *Sociological Inquiry, 75*(2), 177–196. https://doi.org/10.1111/j.1475-682X.2005.00118.x

Burroughs, J. E., & Rindfleisch, A. (2002). Materialism and well-being: A conflicting values perspective. *Journal of Consumer Research, 29*(3), 348–370. https://doi.org/10.1086/344429

Buzinde, C. N., Kalavar, J. M., Kohli, N., & Manuel-Navarrete, D. (2014). Emic understandings of Kumbh Mela pilgrimage experiences. *Annals of Tourism Research, 49*, 1–18. https://doi.org/10.1016/j.annals.2014.08.001

Carballo, M. M., Araña, J. E., León, C. J., & Moreno-Gil, S. (2015). Economic valuation of tourism destination image. *Tourism Economics, 21*(4), 741–759. https://doi.org/10.5367/te.2014.0381

Center for the Promotion of Imports (CBI). (2020). *The European market potential for religious tourism.* Center for the Promotion of Imports (CBI). www.cbi.eu/node/1057/pdf

Chai, L. T., & Tan, B. C. (2009). Religiosity as an antecedent of attitude towards green products: An exploratory research on young Malaysian consumers. *ASEAN Marketing Journal, 1*(1), 29–36. https://doi.org/10.21002/amj.v1i1.1979

Chen, N. C., Hall, C. M., & Prayag, G. (2021). *Sense of place and place attachment in tourism.* Routledge.

Choi, K. (2017, September 8). S. Korea pins hopes on halal foods to woo Muslim tourists. *Yonhap News Agency.* https://en.yna.co.kr/view/AEN20170907010900320

Choi, Y., Kale, R., & Shin, J. (2010). Religiosity and consumers' use of product information source among Korean consumers: An exploratory research. *International Journal of Consumer Studies, 34*(1), 61–68. https://doi.org/10.1111/j.1470-6431.2009.00850.x

Chookaew, S., Chanin, O., Charatarawat, J., Sriprasert, P., & Nimpaya, S. (2015). Increasing halal tourism potential at Andaman Gulf in Thailand for Muslim country. *Journal of Economics, Business and Management, 3*(7), 739–741. https://doi.org/10.7763/JOEBM.2015. V3.277

Choudhury, K. (2019). Materialism, consumerism, and religion: A Buddhist vision for non-profit marketing. *International Journal of Nonprofit and Voluntary Sector Marketing, 24*(3), e1634. https://doi.org/10.1002/nvsm.1634

Cleveland, M., & Chang, W. (2009). Migration and materialism: The roles of ethnic identity, religiosity, and generation. *Journal of Business Research, 62*(10), 963–971. https://doi. org/10.1016/j.jbusres.2008.05.022

Cole, S. (2018). Gender equality and tourism: Beyond empowerment. In S. Cole (Ed.), *Gender equality and tourism: Beyond empowerment* (pp. 1–13). CABI.

Conrady, R., & Buck, M. (2008). *Trends and issues in global tourism 2008.* Springer Science & Business Media.

Coşgel, M. M., & Minkler, L. (2004). Religious identity and consumption. *Review of Social Economy, 62*(3), 339–350. https://doi.org/10.1080/0034676042000253945

Cuesta-Valiño, P., Bolifa, F., & Núñez-Barriopedro, E. (2020). Sustainable, smart and Muslim-friendly tourist destinations. *Sustainability, 12*(5), 1778. https://doi.org/10.3390/ su12051778

Cutrufelli, M. R. (1983). *Women of Africa: Roots of oppression.* Zed Press.

Darbellay, F., & Stock, M. (2012). Tourism as complex interdisciplinary research object. *Annals of Tourism Research, 39*(1), 441–458. https://doi.org/10.1016/j.annals. 2011.07.002

de Béthune, P. (2007). Interreligious dialogue and sacred hospitality. *Religion East and West, 7*(1), 1–22.

Delener, N. (1990). The effects of religious factors on perceived risk in durable goods purchase decisions. *Journal of Consumer Marketing, 7*(3), 27–38. https://doi.org/10.1108/ EUM0000000002580

Demirel, Y., & Yasarsoy, E. (2017). Exploring consumer attitudes towards halal products. *Journal of Tourismology, 3*(1), 34–43.

Deng, S., Jivan, S., & Hassan, M.-L. (1994). Advertising in Malaysia – A cultural perspective. *International Journal of Advertising, 13*(2), 153–166. https://doi.org/10.1080/026504 87.1994.11104569

Desilver, D., & Masci, D. (2017, January 31). *World Muslim population more widespread than you might think.* Pew Research Center. www.pewresearch.org/fact-tank/2017/01/31/ worlds-muslim-population-more-widespread-than-you-might-think/

Douglass, S. L., & Dunn, R. E. (2003). Interpreting Islam in American schools. *The Annals of the American Academy of Political and Social Science, 588*(1), 52–72. https://doi.org/10.1 177/0002716203588001005

Dyer, S., McDowell, L., & Batnitzky, A. (2010). The impact of migration on the gendering of service work: The case of a West London hotel. *Gender, Work & Organization, 17*(6), 635–657. https://doi.org/10.1111/j.1468-0432.2009.00480.x

Eddahar, N. (2016). *Muslim friendly tourism branding in the global market.* Islamic Centre for Development of Trade. www.oic-oci.org/docdown/?docID=1772&refID=1071

Eid, R., & El-Gohary, H. (2015). The role of Islamic religiosity on the relationship between perceived value and tourist satisfaction. *Tourism Management, 46*, 477–488. https://doi. org/10.1016/j.tourman.2014.08.003

Essoo, N., & Dibb, S. (2010). Religious influences on shopping behaviour: An exploratory study. *Journal of Marketing Management, 20*(7–8), 683–712.

Eum, I. (2009). A study on Islamic consumerism from a cultural perspective: Intensification of Muslim identity and its impact on the emerging Muslim Market★. *International Area Review, 12*(2), 3–19. https://doi.org/10.1177/223386590901200201

Fakhruroji, M. (2019). Digitalizing Islamic lectures: Islamic apps and religious engagement in contemporary Indonesia. *Contemporary Islam, 13*(2), 201–215. https://doi.org/10.1007/s11562-018-0427-9

FaladeObalade, T. A., & Dubey, S. (2014). Managing tourism as a source of revenue and foreign direct investment inflow in a developing country: The Jordanian experience. *International Journal of Academic Research in Economics and Management Sciences, 3*(3), 16–42. https://doi.org/10.6007/IJAREMS/v3-i3/901

Fam, K. S., Waller, D. S., & Erdogan, B. Z. (2004). The influence of religion on attitudes towards the advertising of controversial products. *European Journal of Marketing, 38*(5/6), 537–555. https://doi.org/10.1108/03090560410529204

Fan, D. X. F., Zhang, H. Q., Jenkins, C. L., & Lin, P. M. C. (2017). Does tourist – host social contact reduce perceived cultural distance? *Journal of Travel Research, 56*(8), 998–1010. https://doi.org/10.1177/0047287517696979

Fauzihana, S. A. N. B., & Ayob, N. (2020). Perceptions of Muslim travellers toward Halal lifestyle in South Korea. *Trends in Undergraduate Research, 3*(1), 9–16. https://doi.org/10.33736/tur.1552.2020

Feghali, E. (1997). Arab cultural communication patterns. *International Journal of Intercultural Relations, 21*(3), 345–378. https://doi.org/10.1016/S0147-1767(97)00005-9

Fillmore, M. (1994). *Women and tourism: Invisible hosts, invisible guest*. EQUATIONS.

Fontaine, J. R. J., Duriez, B., Luyten, P., Corveleyn, J., & Hutsebaut, D. (2005). Consequences of a multidimensional approach to religion for the relationship between religiosity and value priorities. *The International Journal for the Psychology of Religion, 15*(2), 123–143. https://doi.org/10.1207/s15327582ijpr1502_2

Franklin, A. (2004). Tourism as an ordering: Towards a new ontology of tourism. *Tourist Studies, 4*(3), 277–301. https://doi.org/10.1177/1468797604057328

Fuseini, A. (2017). Halal food certification in the UK and its impact on food businesses: A review in the context of the European Union. *CAB Reviews: Perspectives in Agriculture, Veterinary Science, Nutrition and Natural Resources, 12*(007), 1–21. https://doi.org/10.1079/PAVSNNR201712007

Gallarza, M. G., Gil-Saura, I., & Holbrook, M. B. (2012). Customer value in tourism services: Meaning and role for a relationship marketing approach. In R. H. Tsiotsou & R. E. Goldsmith (Eds.), *Strategic marketing in tourism services* (pp. 147–162). Emerald.

Gazley, A., & Watling, L. (2015). Me, my tourist-self, and I: The symbolic consumption of travel. *Journal of Travel & Tourism Marketing, 32*(6), 639–655. https://doi.org/10.1080/10548408.2014.954690

Geertz, C. (1966). Religion as a cultural system. In M. Banton (Ed.), *Anthropological approaches to the study of religion* (pp. 1–46). Tavistock.

Gerbens-Leenes, P. W., & Nonhebel, S. (2002). Consumption patterns and their effects on land required for food. *Ecological Economics, 42*(1), 185–199. https://doi.org/10.1016/S0921-8009(02)00049-6

Glas, S., Spierings, N., & Scheepers, P. (2018). Re-understanding religion and support for gender equality in Arab countries. *Gender & Society, 32*(5), 686–712. https://doi.org/10.1177/0891243218783670

Glenn, N. D. (2003). Distinguishing age, period, and cohort effects. In J. T. Mortimer & M. J. Shanahan (Eds.), *Handbook of the life course* (pp. 465–476). Springer. https://doi.org/10.1007/978-0-306-48247-2_21

Granzin, K. L., & Olsen, J. E. (1991). Characterizing participants in activities protecting the environment: A focus on donating, recycling, and conservation behaviors. *Journal of Public Policy & Marketing, 10*(2), 1–27. https://doi.org/10.1177/074391569101000201

Haass, R. N. (2003). Toward greater democracy in the Muslim world. *The Washington Quarterly, 26*(3), 137–148. https://doi.org/10.1162/016366003765609624

Halim, S., & Meyers, M. (2010). News coverage of violence against Muslim women: A view from the Arabian Gulf. *Communication, Culture & Critique, 3*(1), 85–104. https://doi.org/10.1111/j.1753-9137.2009.01059.x

Hall, C. M. (2005). *Tourism: Rethinking the social science of mobility.* Pearson.

Hall, C. M., & Prayag, G. (Eds.). (2020a). Preface. In C. M. Hall & G. Prayag (Eds.), *The Routledge handbook of Halal hospitality and Islamic tourism* (pp. xviii–xx). Routledge.

Hall, C. M., & Prayag, G. (2020b). *The Routledge handbook of Halal hospitality and Islamic tourism.* Routledge.

Hall, C. M., & Prayag, G. (Eds.). (2020c). Emerging and future issues in halal hospitality and Islamic tourism. In C. M. Hall & G. Prayag (Eds.), *The Routledge handbook of Halal hospitality and Islamic tourism* (pp. 339–346). Routledge.

Hall, C. M., Razak, N. H. A., & Prayag, G. (2020). Introduction to Halal hospitality and Islamic tourism. In C. M. Hall & G. Prayag (Eds.), *The Routledge handbook of Halal hospitality and Islamic tourism* (pp. 1–18). Routledge.

Hamza, I., Chouhoud, R., & Tantawi, P. (2012). Islamic tourism: Exploring perceptions & possibilities in Egypt. *African Journal of Business and Economic Research, 7*(1 & 2), 86–99.

Han, H., Al-Ansi, A., Olya, H. G. T., & Kim, W. (2019). Exploring halal-friendly destination attributes in South Korea: Perceptions and behaviors of Muslim travelers toward a non-Muslim destination. *Tourism Management, 71*, 151–164. https://doi.org/10.1016/j.tourman.2018.10.010

Hanafiah, M. H., & Hamdan, N. A. A. (2020). Determinants of Muslim travellers Halal food consumption attitude and behavioural intentions. *Journal of Islamic Marketing, 12*(6), 1197–1218. https://doi.org/10.1108/JIMA-09-2019-0195

Hariani, D. (2016). Halal Japanese culinary as attraction for Muslim travellers to visit Japan. *Advances in Economics, Business and Management Research, 28*, 174–176. https://doi.org/10.2991/ictgtd-16.2017.32

Harney, J. (2016, January 4). How do Sunni and Shia Islam differ? *The New York Times*, A6.

Hassan, M. W., & Hall, C. M. (2003). The demand for halal food among Muslim travellers in New Zealand. In C. M. Hall, L. Sharples, R. Mitchell, N. Macionis, & B. Cambourne (Eds.), *Food tourism: Around the world* (pp. 81–101). Elsevier.

Hassan, S. H. (2014). The role of Islamic values on green purchase intention. *Journal of Islamic Marketing, 5*(3), 379–395. https://doi.org/10.1108/JIMA-11-2013-0080

Hassani, A., & Moghavvemi, S. (2019). Muslims' travel motivations and travel preferences: The impact of motivational factors on Islamic service, hedonic and product preferences. *Journal of Islamic Marketing, 11*(2), 344–367. https://doi.org/10.1108/JIMA-11-2018-0215

Hegarty, K. (2020). Meanings in everyday food encounters for Muslims in Australia. In C. M. Hall & G. Prayag (Eds.), *The Routledge handbook of halal hospitality and Islamic tourism* (pp. 303–312). Routledge.

Henderson, J. C. (2016). Halal food, certification and halal tourism: Insights from Malaysia and Singapore. *Tourism Management Perspectives, 19*, 160–164. https://doi.org/10.1016/j.tmp.2015.12.006

Hoodfar, H. (1992). The veil in their minds and on our heads: The persistence of colonial images of Muslim women. *Resources for Feminist Research, 22*(3/4), 5–18.

Hope, A. L. B., & Jones, C. R. (2014). The impact of religious faith on attitudes to environmental issues and Carbon Capture and Storage (CCS) technologies: A mixed methods study. *Technology in Society, 38*, 48–59. https://doi.org/10.1016/j.techsoc.2014.02.003

Hosseini, S. M., Mirzaei, M., & Iranmanesh, M. (2019). Determinants of Muslims' willingness to pay for halal certified food: Does religious commitment act as a moderator in the relationships? *Journal of Islamic Marketing, 11*(6), 1225–1243. https://doi.org/10.1108/JIMA-02-2018-0043

Hourani, A. (1992). *Islam in European thought*. Cambridge University Press.

Howarth, C. (2002). Identity in whose eyes? The role of representations in identity construction. *Journal for the Theory of Social Behaviour, 32*(2), 145–162. https://doi.org/10.1111/1468-5914.00181

Hunt, S. D., & Vitell, S. J. (2006). The general theory of marketing ethics: A revision and three questions. *Journal of Macromarketing, 26*(2), 143–153. https://doi.org/10.1177/0276146706290923

Ibrahim, Z., Mohd Zahari, M. S., Sulaiman, M., Othman, Z., & Jusoff, K. (2009). Travelling pattern and preferences of the Arab tourists in Malaysian Hotels. *International Journal of Business and Management, 4*(7), 3–9. https://doi.org/10.5539/ijbm.v4n7p3

Illich, I. (1990). *Gender*. Heyday Books.

Jafari, J., & Scott, N. (2014). Muslim world and its tourisms. *Annals of Tourism Research, 44*, 1–19. https://doi.org/10.1016/j.annals.2013.08.011

Jalil, N. S. A., Tawde, A. V., Zito, S., Sinclair, M., Fryer, C., Idrus, Z., & Phillips, C. J. C. (2018). Attitudes of the public towards halal food and associated animal welfare issues in two countries with predominantly Muslim and non-Muslim populations. *PLoS ONE, 13*(10), 1–18. https://doi.org/10.1371/journal.pone.0204094

Jamal, A., & Sharifuddin, J. (2015). Perceived value and perceived usefulness of halal labeling: The role of religion and culture. *Journal of Business Research, 68*(5), 933–941. https://doi.org/10.1016/j.jbusres.2014.09.020

Jung, T. H., Lee, H., Chung, N., & tom Dieck, M. C. (2018). Cross-cultural differences in adopting mobile augmented reality at cultural heritage tourism sites. *International Journal of Contemporary Hospitality Management, 30*(3), 1621–1645. https://doi.org/10.1108/IJCHM-02-2017-0084

Kalamas, M., Cleveland, M., & Laroche, M. (2014). Pro-environmental behaviors for thee but not for me: Green giants, green Gods, and external environmental locus of control. *Journal of Business Research, 67*(2), 12–22. https://doi.org/10.1016/j.jbusres.2013.03.007

Kazemi, F. (2000). Gender, Islam and politics. *Social Research, 67*(2), 453–474. www.jstor.org/stable/40971480

Kettani, H. (2010). Muslim population in Oceania: 1950–2020. *International Journal of Environmental Science and Development, 1*(2), 165–170.

Khalid, F. (2010). Islam and the environment – Ethics and practice an assessment. *Religion Compass, 4*(11), 707–716. https://doi.org/10.1111/j.1749-8171.2010.00249.x

Khan, A. (2003). *Islam, Muslims, and America: Understanding the basis of their conflict*. Algora Publishing.

Khan, M. F. (1992). Theory of consumer behaviour in an Islamic perspective. In S. Tahir & A. Ghazali (Eds.), *Readings in microeconomics: An Islamic perspective* (pp. 69–80). Longman Malaysia.

Khan, M. N., & Kirmani, M. D. (2018). Role of religiosity in purchase of green products by Muslim students: Empirical evidences from India. *Journal of Islamic Marketing, 9*(3), 504–526. https://doi.org/10.1108/JIMA-04-2017-0036

Kim, S. (Sam), Im, H. H., & King, B. E. (2015). Muslim travelers in Asia: The destination preferences and brand perceptions of Malaysian tourists. *Journal of Vacation Marketing*, *21*(1), 3–21. https://doi.org/10.1177/1356766714549648

Korea Tourism Organization (KTO). (2016). *Muslim gwangwangaek yuchi anneseo [Information to accommodate Muslim tourists]*. Korea Tourism Organization.

Korea Tourism Organization. (2017). *Muslim-friendly restaurants in Korea*. Korea Tourism Organization. http://english.visitkorea.or.kr/e_book/access-e/ecatalog_pt2.jsp?callmode=&catimage=&Dir=600&um=pt2&cpage=120

Korea Tourism Organization. (2018). *2018nyon banghan Muslim gwangwang siltae josa* [Report on Muslim tourists visiting Korea in 2018]. Korea Tourism Organization.

Kurenlahti, M., & Salonen, A. (2018). Rethinking consumerism from the perspective of religion. *Sustainability*, *10*(7), 2454. https://doi.org/10.3390/su10072454

Landauer, M., Haider, W., & Pröbstl-Haider, U. (2014). The influence of culture on climate change adaptation strategies: Preferences of cross-country skiers in Austria and Finland. *Journal of Travel Research*, *53*(1), 96–110. https://doi.org/10.1177/0047287513481276

Lashley, C., & Morrison, A. (Eds.). (2013). *In search of hospitality*. Routledge.

Lehto, X., Davari, D., & Park, S. (2020). Transforming the guest – host relationship: A convivial tourism approach. *International Journal of Tourism Cities*, *6*(4), 1069–1088. https://doi.org/10.1108/IJTC-06-2020-0121

Leslie, D., & Reimer, S. (1999). Spatializing commodity chains. *Progress in Human Geography*, *23*(3), 401–420. https://doi.org/10.1177/030913259902300304

Li, M. (2012). Cross-cultural tourist research: A meta-analysis. *Journal of Hospitality & Tourism Research*, *38*(1), 40–77. https://doi.org/10.1177/1096348012442542

Li, M., & Bihu, W. (2013). *Urban tourism in China*. Routledge.

Lipka, M., & Hackett, C. (2017, April 6). *Why Muslims are the world's fastest-growing religious group*. Pew Research Center. www.pewresearch.org/fact-tank/2017/04/06/why-muslims-are-the-worlds-fastest-growing-religious-group/

Liu, W., Vogt, C. A., Luo, J., He, G., Frank, K. A., & Liu, J. (2012). Drivers and socioeconomic impacts of tourism participation in protected areas. *PloS One*, *7*(4), e35420.

Liu, Y. C., Li, I. J., Yen, S. Y., & Sher, P. J. (2018). What makes Muslim friendly tourism? An empirical study on destination image, tourist attitude and travel intention. *Advances in Management and Applied Economics*, *8*(5), 27–43.

Liu-Lastres, B., & Cahyanto, I. P. (2021). Exploring the host-guest interaction in tourism crisis communication. *Current Issues in Tourism*, *24*(15), 2097–2109. https://doi.org/10.1080/13683500.2020.1817876

Lorber, J. (2008). *Paradoxes of gender*. Yale University Press.

Lucal, B. (1999). What it means to be gendered me: Life on the boundaries of a dichotomous gender system. *Gender & Society*, *13*(6), 781–797. https://doi.org/10.1177/089124399013006006

Macionis, J. J., & Plummer, K. (2008). *Sociology: A global introduction*. Pearson Prentice Hall.

Mahmood, S. (2001). Feminist theory, embodiment, and the docile agent: Some reflections on the Egyptian Islamic revival. *Cultural Anthropology*, *16*(2), 202–236. https://doi.org/10.1525/can.2001.16.2.202

Mannaa, M. T. (2019). Halal food in the tourist destination and its importance for Muslim travellers. *Current Issues in Tourism*, 1–12. https://doi.org/10.1080/13683500.2019.1616678

Mastercard-CrescentRating. (2015). *Muslim travel shopping index 2015*. https://newsroom.mastercard.com/asia-pacific/files/2015/09/MTSI-2015-28th-September-2015.pdf

Mastercard-CrescentRating. (2019a). *Global Muslim travel index 2019*. Mastercard-CrescentRating. www.crescentrating.com/reports/mastercard-crescentrating-global-muslim-travel-index-gmti-2018.html

Mastercard-CrescentRating. (2019b). *Muslim women in travel 2019*. Mastercard-Crescent Rating. www.crescentrating.com/reports

Mastercard-CrescentRating. (2020). *Top 16 trends to watch in 2020*. Mastercard-Crescent Rating. www.crescentrating.com/reports

Mathieson, A., & Wall, G. (1982). *Tourism: Economic, physical, and social impacts*. Longman.

Mathras, D., Cohen, A. B., Mandel, N., & Mick, D. G. (2016). The effects of religion on consumer behavior: A conceptual framework and research agenda. *Journal of Consumer Psychology, 26*(2), 298–311. https://doi.org/10.1016/j.jcps.2015.08.001

Maudoodi, A. (1991). *Purdah and the status of women in Islam*. Islamic Publications.

McDaniel, S. W., & Burnett, J. J. (1990). Consumer religiosity and retail store evaluative criteria. *Journal of the Academy of Marketing Science, 18*(2), 101–112. https://doi.org/10.1007/BF02726426

Mergen, B. (1978). Travel as play. In V. Turner & E. T. I. by D. Ross (Eds.), *Image and pilgrimage in Christian culture* (pp. 103–111). Columbia University Press.

Michel, F. (2004). *Désirs d'ailleurs: Essai d'anthropologie des voyages*. Presses Université Laval.

Mihajlović, I., & Krželj, Z. (2014, August). The impact of globalisation on the development of tourism within social and economic changes. *European Scientific Journal*, 108–120. http://eujournal.org/index.php/esj/article/view/4014/3825

Miles, S. (1998). *Consumerism: As a way of life*. SAGE.

Minces, J. (1980). *The house of obedience: Women in Arab society*. Zed Press.

Minton, E. A., Kahle, L. R., Jiuan, T. S., & Tambyah, S. K. (2016). Addressing criticisms of global religion research: A consumption-based exploration of status and materialism, sustainability, and volunteering behavior. *Journal for the Scientific Study of Religion, 55*(2), 365–383. https://doi.org/10.1111/jssr.12260

Mitchell, R. D. (1998). Learning through play and pleasure travel: Using play literature to enhance research into touristic learning. *Current Issues in Tourism, 1*(2), 176–188. https://doi.org/10.1080/13683509808667838

Mohamad, Z. F., Idris, N., Baharuddin, A., Muhammad, A., & Nik Sulaiman, N. M. (2012). The role of religious community in recycling: Empirical insights from Malaysia. *Resources, Conservation, and Recycling, 58*, 143–151. https://doi.org/10.1016/j.resconrec.2011.09.020

Mohamed, N. (2018). *The influence of religiosity upon Muslim tourists' travel decision-making processes for an Islamic leisure destination* [PhD thesis, Heriott-Watt University].

Mohanty, C. (1988). Under Western eyes: Feminist scholarship and colonial discourses. *Feminist Review, 30*(1), 61–88. https://doi.org/10.1057/fr.1988.42

Mohee, S. (2012). *Young British South Asian Muslim women: Identities and marriage* [Doctoral dissertation, University College London].

Mohsin, A., Ramli, N., & Alkhulayfi, B. A. (2016). Halal tourism: Emerging opportunities. *Tourism Management Perspectives, 19*, 137–143. https://doi.org/10.1016/j.tmp.2015.12.010

Mokhlis, S. (2008). Consumer religiosity and the importance of store attributes. *The Journal of Human Resource and Adult Learning, 4*(2), 122–133.

Mokhlis, S. (2009). Religious differences in some selected aspects of consumer behaviour: A Malaysian study. *The Journal of International Management Studies, 4*(1), 67–76.

Mooij, M. (2019). *Consumer behavior and culture: Consequences for global marketing and advertising*. Sage.

Muhamad, N. (2008). *Muslim consumers' motivation towards Islam and their cognitive processing of performing taboo behaviors* [Doctoral dissertation, University of Western Australia].

Mukhtar, A., & Butt, M. M. (2012). Intention to choose Halal products: The role of religiosity. *Journal of Islamic Marketing, 3*(2), 108–120. https://doi.org/10.1108/17590831211232519

Nakyinsige, K., Man, Y. B. C., & Sazili, A. Q. (2012). Halal authenticity issues in meat and meat products. *Meat Science, 91*(3), 207–214. https://doi.org/10.1016/j.meatsci.2012.02.015

Nawawi, M. S. A. M., Radzi, C. W. J. W. M., Mamat, M. Z., Hasbullah, M., Mokhtar, M. I., Jenatabadi, H. S., Man, S., Othman, A. H., Azizan, S. A., & Pauzi, N. (2017). Halal food industry in Thailand: History, prospects, and challenges. In *1st International Halal management conference (IHMC 2017)* (pp. 302–307). Sejong University.

Omar, W. M. W., Muhammad, M. Z., & Omar, M. A. C. (2018). An analysis of the Muslim consumers' attitudes towards 'halal' food products in Kelantan. In *ECER regional conference 2008*. UiTM Kelantan

Orellano, A., Valor, C., & Chuvieco, E. (2020). The influence of religion on sustainable consumption: A systematic review and future research agenda. *Sustainability, 12*(19), 1–21. https://doi.org/10.3390/su12197901

Organisation of Islamic Cooperation (OIC), & The Statistical, Economic and Social Research and Training Centre for Islamic Countries (SESRIC). (2017). *Strategic roadmap for development of Islamic tourism in OIC member countries*. The Statistical, Economic and Social Research and Training Centre for Islamic Countries (SESRIC). www.oic-oci.org/docdown/?docID=1777&refID=1071

Otto, J. E., & Ritchie, J. R. B. (1996). The service experience in tourism. *Tourism Management, 17*(3), 165–174. https://doi.org/10.1016/0261-5177(96)00003-9

Overby, J. W., Woodruff, R. B., & Gardial, S. F. (2005). The influence of culture upon consumers' desired value perceptions: A research agenda. *Marketing Theory, 5*(2), 139–163. https://doi.org/10.1177/1470593105052468

Ozdemir, I. M., & Met, O. (2012). The expectations of Muslim religious customers in the lodging industry: The case of Turkey. In A. Zainal, S. M. Radzi, R. Hashim, C. T. Chik, & R. Abu (Eds.), *Current issues in hospitality and tourism: Research and innovations* (pp. 323–328). CRC Press.

Pace, S. (2013). Does religion affect the materialism of consumers? An empirical investigation of Buddhist ethics and the resistance of the self. *Journal of Business Ethics, 112*(1), 25–46. https://doi.org/10.1007/s10551-012-1228-3

Panni, M. F. A. K. (2012). CKM and its influence on organizational marketing performance: Proposing an integrated conceptual framework. In K. Hans-Ruediger (Ed.), *Customer-centric marketing strategies: Tools for building organizational performance* (pp. 103–125). IGI Global. https://doi.org/10.4018/978-1-4666-2524-2.ch006

Pew Research Center. (2015). *The future of world religions: Population growth projections, 2010–2050*. Pew Research Center. https://assets.pewresearch.org/wp-content/uploads/sites/11/2015/03/PF_15.04.02_ProjectionsFullReport.pdf

Pew Research Center. (2017). *Europe's growing Muslim population*. Pew Research Center. www.pewforum.org/2017/11/29/europes-growing-muslim-population/

Pink, J. (2009). *Muslim societies in the age of mass consumption: Politics, culture and identity between the local and the global*. Cambridge Scholars Publishing.

Pizam, A., Mansfeld, Y., & Chon, K. S. (1999). *Consumer behavior in travel and tourism*. Psychology Press.

Pointing, J., Teinaz, Y., & Shafi, S. (2008). Illegal labelling and sales of halal meat and food products. *The Journal of Criminal Law*, 72(3), 206–213. https://doi.org/10.1350/jcla.2008.72.3.496

Porter, C. (2013). *The religion of consumption and Christian neighbor love* [PhD thesis, Loyola University Chicago].

Půtová, B. (2018). Anthropology of tourism: Researching interactions between hosts and guests. *Czech Journal of Tourism*, 7(1), 71–92. https://doi.org/10.1515/cjot-2018-0004

Pyke, K. D., & Johnson, D. L. (2003). Asian American women and racialized femininities: "Doing" gender across cultural worlds. *Gender & Society*, 17(1), 33–53. https://doi.org/10.1177/0891243202238977

Qin, V. Y. (2016). *When consumption embraces faith: How religious beliefs and practices influence consumption* [PhD in Business Administration, Duke University].

Raggiotto, F., Mason, M. C., & Moretti, A. (2018). Religiosity, materialism, consumer environmental predisposition. Some insights on vegan purchasing intentions in Italy. *International Journal of Consumer Studies*, 42(6), 613–626. https://doi.org/10.1111/ijcs.12478

Rahman, A. A., Asrarhaghighi, E., & Rahman, S. A. (2015). Consumers and Halal cosmetic products: Knowledge, religiosity, attitude and intention. *Journal of Islamic Marketing*, 6(1), 148–163. https://doi.org/10.1108/JIMA-09-2013-0068

Ratthinan, S. P., & Selamat, N. H. (2018). Being Muslim: Unveiling the voices of Asian Muslim women travellers. *Gender Issues*, 35(4), 302–317. https://doi.org/10.1007/s12147-018-9215-3

Razak, N. H. A., Hall, C. M., & Prayag, G. (2020). Malaysian accommodation providers' understanding of halal hospitality. In C. M. Hall & G. Prayag (Eds.), *The Routledge handbook of Halal hospitality and Islamic tourism* (pp. 70–82). Routledge.

Razzaq, S., Hall, C. M., & Prayag, G. (2016). The capacity of New Zealand to accommodate the halal tourism market – Or not. *Tourism Management Perspectives*, 18, 92–97. https://doi.org/10.1016/j.tmp.2016.01.008

Reisinger, Y., & Moufakkir, O. (2015). Cultural issues in tourism, hospitality and leisure in the Arab/Muslim world. *International Journal of Culture, Tourism and Hospitality Research*, 9(1). https://doi.org/10.1108/IJCTHR-01-2015-0003

Reynolds, T. E. (2010). Toward a wider hospitality: Rethinking love of neighbour in religions of the book. *Irish Theological Quarterly*, 75(2), 175–187. https://doi.org/10.1177/0021140009360497

Rezai, G., Mohamed, Z., & Shamsudin, M. N. (2012). Assessment of consumers' confidence on Halal labelled manufactured food in Malaysia. *Pertanika Journal of Social Science and Humanities*, 20(1), 33–42.

Riaz, M. N., & Chaudry, M. M. (2004). *Halal food production*. CRC Press.

Rice, G. (2006). Pro-environmental behavior in Egypt: Is there a role for Islamic environmental ethics? *Journal of Business Ethics*, 65(4), 373–390. https://doi.org/10.1007/s10551-006-0010-9

Ridzuan, N. B. (2011). *Women, Islam and feminism in postcolonial Malaysia and Singapore* [Doctoral dissertation, National University of Singapore].

Röder, A., & Mühlau, P. (2014). Are they acculturating? Europe's immigrants and gender egalitarianism. *Social Forces*, 92(3), 899–928. https://doi.org/10.1093/sf/sot126

Run, E. C. de, Butt, M. M., Fam, K.-S., & Jong, H. Y. (2010). Attitudes towards offensive advertising: Malaysian Muslims' views. *Journal of Islamic Marketing*, 1(1), 25–36. https://doi.org/10.1108/17590831011026204

Ryan, C. (2016). Halal tourism. *Tourism Management Perspectives*, 19, 121–123. https://doi.org/10.1016/j.tmp.2015.12.014

Saarinen, J., & Manwa, H. (2008). Tourism as a socio-cultural encounter: Host-guest relations in tourism development in Botswana. *Botswana Notes and Records, 39*, 43–53.

Salman, F., & Siddiqui, K. (2011). An exploratory study for measuring consumers awareness and perceptions towards halal food in Pakistan. *Interdisciplinary Journal of Contemporary Research in Business, 3*(2), 639–652.

Sandıkcı, Ö. (2018). Religion and the marketplace: Constructing the 'new' Muslim consumer. *Religion, 48*(3), 453–473. https://doi.org/10.1080/0048721X.2018.1482612

Sandıkcı, Ö., & Ger, G. (2007). Constructing and representing the Islamic consumer in Turkey. *Fashion Theory, 11*(2–3), 189–210. https://doi.org/10.2752/136270407X202754

Scott, N., & Jafari, J. (Eds.). (2010). *Tourism in the Muslim world.* Emerald Group Publishing.

Sehlikoglu, S. (2018). Revisited: Muslim Women's agency and feminist anthropology of the Middle East. *Contemporary Islam, 12*(1), 73–92. https://doi.org/10.1007/s11562-017-0404-8

Seyfi, S., & Hall, C. M. (2019). Deciphering Islamic theocracy and tourism: Conceptualization, context, and complexities. *International Journal of Tourism Research, 21*(6), 735–746. https://doi.org/10.1002/jtr.2300

Seyfi, S., Hall, C. M., & Shabani, B. (2020). COVID-19 and international travel restrictions: The geopolitics of health and tourism. *Tourism Geographies,* https://doi.org/10.1080/14616688.2020.1833972.

Shafaei, F., & Mohamed, B. (2015). Involvement and brand equity: A conceptual model for Muslim tourists. *International Journal of Culture, Tourism and Hospitality Research, 9*(1), 54–67. https://doi.org/10.1108/IJCTHR-06-2014-0050

Shah, S. (2018). 'We are equals'; datum or delusion: Perceptions of Muslim women academics in three Malaysian universities. *British Journal of Sociology of Education, 39*(3), 299–315. https://doi.org/10.1080/01425692.2017.1343126

Sharif, K. (2016). Investigating the key determinants of Muslim ethical consumption behaviour amongst affluent Qataris. *Journal of Islamic Marketing, 7*(3), 303–330. https://doi.org/10.1108/JIMA-01-2015-0001

Sheth, J. N., & Mittal, B. (2004). *Customer behavior: A managerial perspective.* Thomson/South-Western.

Shreim, M. (2009). *Religion and sports apparel consumption: An exploratory study of the Muslim market* [Master's thesis, University of Windsor].

Siddiqui, M. (2015). *Hospitality and Islam: Welcoming in God's name.* Yale University Press.

Smith, V. L. (Ed.). (1989). *Hosts and guests: The anthropology of tourism.* University of Pennsylvania Press.

Soldatenko, D., & Backer, E. (2019). A content analysis of cross-cultural motivational studies in tourism relating to nationalities. *Journal of Hospitality and Tourism Management, 38*, 122–139. https://doi.org/10.1016/j.jhtm.2018.12.004

Spierings, N. (2015). Gender equality attitudes among Turks in Western Europe and Turkey: The interrelated impact of migration and parents' attitudes. *Journal of Ethnic and Migration Studies, 41*(5), 749–771. https://doi.org/10.1080/1369183X.2014.948394

Stearns, P. N. (2001). *Consumerism in world history: The global transformation of desire.* Psychology Press.

Stephenson, M. L. (2014). Deciphering 'Islamic hospitality': Developments, challenges and opportunities. *Tourism Management, 40*, 155–164. https://doi.org/10.1016/j.tourman.2013.05.002

Stillman, T. F., Fincham, F. D., Vohs, K. D., Lambert, N. M., & Phillips, C. A. (2012). The material and immaterial in conflict: Spirituality reduces conspicuous consumption. *Journal of Economic Psychology, 33*(1), 1–7. https://doi.org/10.1016/j.joep.2011.08.012

Storti, C. (1990). *The art of crossing cultures*. Intercultural Press.

Suarez, P. V. (2018). Tourism as empowerment: Women artisan's experiences in central Mexico. In S. Cole (Ed.), *Gender equality and tourism: Beyond empowerment* (pp. 46–54). CABI.

Syed, J., Ali, F., & Winstanley, D. (2005). In pursuit of modesty: Contextual emotional labour and the dilemma for working women in Islamic societies. *International Journal of Work Organisation and Emotion*, *1*(2), 150–167. https://doi.org/10.1504/IJWOE.2005.008819

Syed, O. A. (2001, October 10). Catering to the needs of Muslim travellers. In *Second conference of ministers from Muslim countries, tourism: Challenges and opportunities*. Kuala Lumpur.

Telfer, E. (2013). The philosophy of hospitableness: Otyf haodsepsi:t a noecsiasl. In C. Lashley & A. Morrison (Eds.), *In search of hospitality* (pp. 56–73). Routledge. https://doi.org/10.4324/9781315042817-5

The Standing Committee for Economic and Commercial Cooperation of the Organization of the Islamic Cooperation (COMCEC). (2016). *Muslim friendly tourism: Understanding the demand and supply sides In the OIC member countries*. www.comcec.org/wp-content/uploads/2016/05/7-TUR-AN.pdf

Thimm, V. (2017). *Commercialising Islam in Malaysia:'Ziarah'at the intersection of Muslim pilgrimage and the market-driven tourism industry*. Institut Kajian Etnik, Universiti Kebangsaan Malaysia.

Timothy, D., & Iverson, T. (2006). Tourism and Islam: Considerations of culture and duty. In D. Timothy (Ed.), *Tourism, religion and spiritual Journeys* (pp. 186–205). Routledge.

Tsang, N. K. F., & Ap, J. (2016). Tourists' perceptions of relational quality service attributes: A cross-cultural study. *Journal of Travel Research*, *45*(3), 355–363. https://doi.org/10.1177/0047287506295911

Turner, P. B. S. (1994). *Orientalism, postmodernism and globalism*. Routledge.

Umpfenbach, K. (2014). *Influences on consumer behaviour*. Ecologic Institute.

United Nations Development Program (UNDP). (2004). *Human development report: Cultural liberty in today's diverse world*. UNDP.

UN World Tourism Organization (UNWTO). (2017). *UNWTO tourism highlights: 2017 edition*. World Tourism Organization (UNWTO). https://doi.org/10.18111/9789284419029

Usunier, J. C., & Lee, J. A. (2005). *Marketing across cultures* (4th ed.). Financial Times/Prentice Hall.

Vester, H. G. (1987). Adventure as a form of leisure. *Leisure Studies*, *6*(3), 237–249. https://doi.org/10.1080/02614368700390191

Vilardo, V., & Bittar, S. (2018). *Gender profile – Iraq: A situation analysis on gender equality and women's empowerment in Iraq*. Oxfam, UN Women. https://doi.org/10.21201/2018.3460

Vitell, S. J., Paolillo, J. G. P., & Singh, J. J. (2005). Religiosity and consumer ethics. *Journal of Business Ethics*, *57*(2), 175–181. https://doi.org/10.1007/s10551-004-4603-x

Wagner, W., Sen, R., Permanadeli, R., & Howarth, C. S. (2012). The veil and Muslim women's identity: Cultural pressures and resistance to stereotyping. *Culture & Psychology*, *18*(4), 521–541. https://doi.org/10.1177/1354067X12456713

Wan, N. Z. N., Bakar, R. A., Razak, S. A., & San, S. (2014). The Importance of Halal to Muslim consumers: Are they powerful stakeholders? *Journal of Applied Environmental and Biological Sciences*, *4*(6S), 50–55.

Wang, W., Chen, J. S., & Huang, K. (2016). Religious tourist motivation in Buddhist mountain: The case from China. *Asia Pacific Journal of Tourism Research*, *21*(1), 57–72. https://doi.org/10.1080/10941665.2015.1016443

Watkins, L. (2006). *Culture, values and Japanese tourism behaviour* [Doctoral dissertation, University of Otago].

West, C., & Zimmerman, D. H. (1987). Doing gender. *Gender & Society*, *1*(2), 125–151. https://doi.org/10.1177/0891243287001002002

Willits, W. L. (1987). The hospitality host role in the travel/tourism industry. *Visions in Leisure and Business*, *5*(4), https://scholarworks.bgsu.edu/visions/vol5/iss4/5.

Wiltshier, P. (2019, February 28). Religious tourism: What is it and why is it so important? *The CABI Blog*. https://blog.cabi.org/2019/02/28/religious-tourism-what-is-it-and-why-is-it-so-important/

Wiśniewski, Ł. (2018). Religious tourism in Christian sanctuaries: The implications of mixed interests for the communication of the faith. *Church, Communication and Culture*, *3*(3), 199–220. https://doi.org/10.1080/23753234.2018.1537674

Wong, L. (2007). Market cultures, the middle classes and Islam: Consuming the market? *Consumption, Markets and Culture*, *10*(4), 451–480. https://doi.org/10.1080/10253860701566440

Wong, S. (2017, October 27). Young Muslims catch a $100 billion travel bug. *Bloomberg.Com*. www.bloomberg.com/news/articles/2017-10-27/young-muslims-have-caught-a-100-billion-travel-bug-report-says

World Bank. (2021). *Women, business and the law: Mobility*. https://wbl.worldbank.org/en/data/exploretopics/wbl_gp

World Population Review. (2021). *Muslim population by country 2021*. https://worldpopulationreview.com/country-rankings/muslim-population-by-country

World Travel Market (2019). *Top halal tourism trends for 2019*. Retrieved from https://news.wtm.com/top-halal-tourism-trends-for-2019/

Yousaf, S., & Malik, M. S. (2013). Evaluating the influences of religiosity and product involvement level on the consumers. *Journal of Islamic Marketing*, *4*(2), 163–186. https://doi.org/10.1108/17590831311329296

Zaei, M. E., & Zaei, M. E. (2013). The impacts of tourism industry on host community. *European Journal of Tourism Hospitality and Research*, *1*(2), 12–21.

Zaini, R. (2016, October). What does travel mean to Muslim millennials? *CrescentRating*. www.crescentrating.com/magazine/opinion/3930/muslim-millennials-what-does-travel-mean-to-us.html

Zakaria, N., Wan-Ismail, W.-N. A., & Abdul-Talib, A.-N. (2021). Seriously, conspicuous consumption? The impact of culture, materialism and religiosity on Malaysian Generation Y consumers' purchasing of foreign brands. *Asia Pacific Journal of Marketing and Logistics*, *33*(2), 526–560. https://doi.org/10.1108/APJML-07-2018-0283

3 Muslim tourism

A systematic literature review

Boshra Mohajer, Salar Kuhzady, Morteza Bazrafshan and Maryam Sedaghat

Introduction

Religion is a universal and authoritative socio-cultural system that has an inspiring influence on an individual's beliefs, values and behaviors for both people and society (El-Gohary, 2016; Seyfi & Hall, 2019). Tourism is always seeking a new customer segment. However, one relatively unexplored segment is the religiously concerned tourists (Battour et al., 2017). Researchers have been eager to realize the effect of religion and also Islam in tourism, and this is proven by growing academic articles published about Halal or Islamic tourism over the last few years (Jamal & El-Bassiouny, 2019; Hall & Prayag, 2020). In fact, 'Halal tourism' refers to the activities and appropriate manners for Muslims which are determined based on holy Qurān and traditions of the Prophet Muhammad (PBUH), which is named 'Shari'ah' (Jamal & El-Bassiouny, 2019). The connection between Islam and tourism seems to include religious issues such as Hajj and pilgrimage, but it is not limited to these issues and includes more cases and deeper meanings (Jafari & Scott, 2014). This increasing attentiveness in Halal tourism might be relevant to the growth of the Muslim population around the world (Battour & Ismail, 2016). Muslim customers constitute a global market of approximately 1.82 billion people (Battour et al., 2017), making up about 24% of the world population, which is expected to increase to nearly 3 billion in 2060 (Lipka & Hackett, 2017).

The Halal tourism industry was a niche market at first but now has become an established and recognized market (Hall & Prayag, 2020). The main reason for this could be their disposable income and even their younger generation in comparison with other nations. According to the report of the Mastercard-CrescentRating (2019) *Global Muslim Travel Index* (2019), it is estimated that the number of Muslim travellers would reach 230 million. Additionally, it is also estimated that the contribution of Muslims to the world economy would be raised to US$300 billion (Preko et al., 2020). Based on this situation, halal tourism, alternatively Islamic tourism or Muslim friendly tourism, as one of the influential growing trends in tourism and hospitality has captured the attention of business, destinations and scholars (Said et al., 2020). To respond to this emerging trend and get more share of this market, in the past few years many

DOI: 10.4324/9781003036296-4

Muslim countries (e.g., Turkey, Malaysia and Indonesia) and non-Muslim destinations (e.g., South Korea and Japan) have launched plans to attract Muslim travellers and become Muslim friendly destinations (Han, Al-Ansi, Olya, et al., 2019). To be successful, they need tourism service providers that offer a halal-friendly environment (Han, Al-Ansi, Olya, et al., 2019). To meet the needs of destinations and tourism and hospitality service providers on how to deal with this emerging market, Muslim tourism and its related issues have captured the attention of academic researchers. Scholars have investigated various areas. For example, identifying the requirements of being a Muslim friendly hotel (Jeaheng et al., 2019), the antecedent of Muslim tourists' satisfaction (Wardi et al., 2018) and motivation to travel (Preko et al., 2020). More recently, review studies to identify knowledge gaps have also attracted interest. For instance, Vargas-Sánchez and Moral-Moral (2019), who clarify the concept of halal tourism and identify the essential requirements for a Muslim friendly destination, have reviewed only 58 articles from both WOS and Scopus databases. Rasul (2019), by using systematic review and reviewing 27 articles, has explored characters, principles and impacts of halal tourism. In addition, they have articulated the trends, opportunities and challenges of halal tourism. Yagmur et al. (2019), have investigated the bibliometric data of 60 articles indexed in the WOS database. They have been examined in terms of number by years, journals, countries, institutes, authors etc. The conducted review studies are limited to halal tourism studies and do not cover other related fields such as Muslim tourism, Islamic tourism and sharia tourism. To cover this gap and provide an up-to-date big picture of what is known and what needs to be further explored, the present study aims to: (1) provide an overview of the published articles on Muslim travel by years and journals; (2) study the countries' contribution and collaboration in Muslim travel; (3) explore the most frequently studied variables; (4) cluster the research areas in Muslim travel and (5) define the Muslim friendly destination's requirements.

Literature review

Tourism and religion

Religion is one of the most influential elements of society and culture. It is linked to people's lives and behaviors such as dress, food and drink, social and political views and travel behaviors (Nyaupane et al., 2015). The relevance of religious beliefs and behaviors can be considered from two aspects: First, beliefs impact the behaviors according to taboos and obligations; second, religions create societies' norms, customs and culture, which influence behaviors (Heydari Chianeh et al., 2018). Travel behaviors, therefore, are related to religious motivations for undertaking pilgrimages or visiting religious places (Eslami et al., 2021); visiting religious buildings, participating in rituals, festivals and ceremonial events (Henderson, 2003); asking forgiveness of sins, performing religious duties etc. As religion has long been a strong motivating factor, it can be said that religious tourism is not a new phenomenon (Durán-Sánchez et al., 2018). In other words, any trip motivated, either exclusively or partly, by religious reasons can be called religious tourism (Durán-Sánchez et al., 2018). Religious tourism, to some researchers such as El-Gohary (2016), is referred to as faith tourism, which the author defines as 'travel with the core motive of experiencing religious forms or the products they include, like art, culture, traditions, and architecture' (El-Gohary, 2016, p. 2). El-Gohary (2016) also quotes a classification of religious tourism from the FICCI Religious Tourism Report (Strategic Initiatives & Government Advisory (SIGA) Team, 2012):

- Pilgrimages,
- Missionary travel,
- Leisure (fellowship) vacations,
- Faith-based cruising,
- Crusades, conventions, and rallies,
- Retreats,
- Monastery visits and guest-stays,
- Faith-based camps,
- Religious tourism attractions (El-Gohary, 2016, p. 2).

Pilgrimage as one of the categories of religious tourism is an outstanding feature of the world's major religions such as Buddhism, Hinduism, Islam, Judaism and Christianity. It is believed to be the root of modern tourism (Collins-Kreiner, 2010). Kim et al. (2020) argue that religious tourism has been reviewed in a variety of contexts such as responsible tourism, ashram tourism, pilgrimage tourism, festival tourism, secular pilgrimage tourism, ecotourism, route-based tourism, slow tourism, alternative tourism, cultural tourism, heritage tourism, rural tourism, new tourism and Islamic tourism. Islamic tourism seems to be a new concept to tourism researchers and practitioners. However, its concepts are old and are rooted in Islamic Shari'ah and date back to the early days of the Islamic civilization (El-Gohary, 2016). Jafari and Scott (2014, p. 9) believe it is 'a new touristic interpretation of pilgrimage that merges religious and leisure tourism'. Islamic tourism has recently been taken on different aspects such as political (Jafari & Scott, 2014), geopolitical (Eslami et al., 2021) and regional development (Kovjanić, 2014).

Islamic tourism and Halal tourism, are they synonymous?

Islamic tourism is highly linked to and dependent on Islamic Shari'ah, as every Muslim is required to visit Meccah and El-Madana to conduct Hajj and Umrah. Tourism in Islam, however, is broader than these two concepts and encompasses visiting shrines (Heydari Chianeh et al., 2018) and tombs of prophets, known as a pilgrimage, participating in religious ceremonies (Nolan & Nolan, 1992) such as Arba'een (Eslami et al., 2021) and visiting the mosques (Wahyono & Razak, 2020). Out of these origins, some seemingly synonymous terms such as pilgrimage, Muslim friendly tourism, spiritual tourism, mystical tourism and various Halal tourism concepts have developed. However, as Chapter 2 (this volume) noted, not all such concepts necessarily refer to the same experiences.

Oktadiana et al. (2016) claim that Halal tourism is a synonym of Muslim travel and refers to products, recreation and social intentions according to Islamic teaching. Rasul (2019) also argues that Halal tourism and Islamic tourism are indistinguishable and refer to a general term that is religiously acceptable. Nevertheless, a closer review of related literature shows no clear definition and conceptualization of Halal tourism, and using Halal tourism and Islamic tourism interchangeably is questionable. One of the challenges of academicians and practitioners is the exact terminology of the terms 'Halal tourism' and 'Islamic tourism' as, due to the multidisciplinary scope of tourism, many researchers use them interchangeably. Hence, 'since the Qur'an does differentiate between the terms Mu'minoon' (Islamic Person) and Muslim (person who profess to be Muslims), it is necessary to clarify the difference between the terms Islamic, Halal and Islamic related' (Battour, 2018, p. 4).

One of the common notions in various definitions of tourism is mobility, which mainly refers to the movement of people of any religion. It shapes the demand side of tourism. On the other hand, their needs should be met by different activities and facilities that represent tourism's supply side. Therefore, in the case of Muslim tourists' behaviors, the demand side, which is the need of Muslim travellers in the scope of Halal tourism, should be considered.

The core meaning of pilgrimage, Halal tourism (Rasul, 2019), Islamic tourism (Carboni et al., 2014), Islamic travel, Halal travel, Muslim friendly tourism, Shari'ah tourism (Asih & Asih, 2015) and Halal transportation is their compliance with the rules and guidance of Halal concepts and Islamic Shari'ah (Boğan & Sarıışık, 2019; Hall & Prayag, 2020). Battour et al. (2017) believe that, in defining Islamic tourism and Halal tourism, Islamic law (sharia), the target customers (i.e., Muslims or non-Muslims), the location of the activity (i.e., Muslim vs. non-Muslim country), the product and service offered (i.e., food, facilities) and the purpose of travel should be considered more. According to Battour (2018, p. 6), the activity can be referred to as 'Halal tourism if all the activities, facilities, actions, and objectives are permissible according to Islamic teachings'. Thus, Halal tourism can be by non–Muslim tourists as well. Components of Halal tourism include Halal food, Halal transportation, Halal hotel and Halal logistics, among others (El-Gohary, 2016; Hall & Prayag, 2020). On the other hand, Islamic tourism focuses on a wide variety of issues including 'participation and engagement (by Muslims), tourism palaces and destinations (Islamic destinations), product(s) (residential places, food, entertainment, beverage, etc.), dimensions (social, economic, cultural, religious, etc.), and managing the offered service processes (marketing, ethical consideration, etc.)' (El-Gohary, 2016, p. 2).

As research in Halal tourism developed, various Muslim friendly concepts such as mobile phone applications, Muslim friendly airports and Muslim friendly destinations have also emerged. To some authors such as Aziz (2018),

Muslim friendly tourism is a synonym of Islamic tourism and wider than Halal tourism and signifies providing a condition for Muslims to perform their religious duties while travelling and optimize their tourism experience.

Study method

As the focal objective of this research is to study the existing literature on Muslim travel as an emerging area (Said et al., 2020), a systematic review was adopted. A systematic review by applying strict criteria during the review process not only can help to ensure reliability and validity of the results (Russen et al., 2021) but also would be helpful to mapping and reviewing the past studies (Kim, 2020), exploring literature gaps and emerging subjects and creating a reliable direction for the future studies (Christofi et al., 2017). To achieve the aim, a review protocol was developed based on PRISMA. The drive behind using PRISMA is related to its wide acceptance, its comprehensiveness and its ability to boost consistency across reviews (Pahlevan-Sharif et al., 2019). The PRISMA protocol involves four main steps. They are identification, screening, eligibility and including (Nave et al., 2021). By developing questions, first, an exploratory search in Google Scholar was done to recognize the related search terms. The search resulted in the following terms: 'Muslim tourist', 'sharia tourism', 'Muslim Travel', 'halal tourism', 'Islamic tourism' and 'Muslim Traveler'. The search and data collection were conducted in September 2020 on the WOS database, by identification of search terms. In total, 320 items were identified. Finally, 160 peer-reviewed articles were identified by excluding book reviews ($n = 67$), book chapters ($n = 32$), proceedings ($n = 42$), editorial material ($n = 8$) and others ($n = 6$) and non-English language research. The retrieved journal articles were manually checked; 159 eligible articles were identified and their contents (e.g., authors, years, journal, affiliations) were exported.

Findings

Overview of the published articles on Muslim travel

The first attempts published in journals to investigate Muslim travel began in 2010 with a study on Islamic tourism in Iran and Saudi Arabia (Zamani-Farahani & Henderson, 2010). This article was published by the *International Journal of Tourism Research* and, with 162 citations, is the most cited. Analyzing the overall retrieved articles shows that remarkable growth has occurred since. However, of the 159 studies, more than 66% ($N = 105$) were published since 2019 (32 in 2019, 43 in 2020 and 30 by the time the study was undertaken in 2021).

Sixty-five journals have published studies on Muslim travel-related issues. Among them, the *Journal of Islamic Marketing* with 21.38 % ($n = 34$) articles has become a dominant source. This is followed by *Tourism Management Perspectives* with 15 (which had a special issue on halal tourism following a conference in New Zealand) and the *International Journal of Tourism Research* and *Tourism Management* with 7 articles each.

Countries' contribution and collaboration in Muslim travel research

Based on affiliations of authors, it was identified that a total of 49 countries contributed to publishing on Muslim tourism-related issues. Figure 2 shows the countries with more than five articles. The leading countries are Malaysia ($n = 49$), Indonesia ($n = 28$), the United Kingdom ($n = 14$) and Egypt ($n = 13$). Additionally, Malaysia is the leading country in the field of co-authorship with scholars from other countries. In this relation, Egypt with seven articles, is the main co-authored country for Malaysia (Table 3.1). As it can be concluded from Table 3.1, the most collaborations are between Muslim majority countries and Asian countries. Additionally, the most common geographical focus of studies was Asia and Africa.

THE MOST FREQUENTLY STUDIED VARIABLES

Keyword analysis was applied to identify the most studied variables. Keywords have generally been identified as necessary "indicators of the content of an article" (Weismayer & Pezenka, 2017). Accordingly, keywords could be helpful to identify the main aims, focus, applied theories, and techniques (Madani & Weber, 2016). A keyword analysis starts from information science (Chiang, 2020). Frequency analysis is the primary method for keyword analysis. However, it is not without trouble. Typically, some of the keywords with the highest occurrence are often so common and rarely can show unique features (Hu et al., 2018). Therefore, the extracted keywords were manually checked. In this step, the most common keywords like Muslim, Islam, tourism, travel, Muslim traveler, and tourist were removed, and related keywords were grouped (e.g., satisfaction and tourism satisfaction and planned behavior and planned behavior). Motivation, satisfaction, halal, and Islamic attributes were the most

Table 3.1 Contribution and collaboration by country of author

Country by contribution	Document	Citations	Country by collaboration	Collaboration	Main co-country
Malaysia	49	1015	Malaysia	23	Egypt (7)
Indonesia	28	168	Egypt	17	Malaysia (7)
United Kingdom	14	494	Indonesia	14	Malaysia (4)
Egypt	13	553	China	13	South Korea (4)
China	12	245	United Kingdom	12	Egypt (3)
Turkey	12	89	United Arab Emirates	9	United Kingdom (3)

studied variables. These results show that researchers have mostly sought to investigate travel stimuli and factors affecting Muslim satisfaction. The results also indicate that halal tourism, identifying Muslim needs and factors influencing the formation of a Muslim friendly destination have been among other topics of interest to researchers.

Title analysis was applied to identify and cluster the covered areas. In this regard, all titles were imported to Maxquda and coded one by one. The results showed that titles could be clustered into ten categories, namely: conceptual development; behavior intentions; perception toward Muslim tourism; satisfaction; the situation of Muslim tourism in a specific destination; needs; travel motivation; Muslim friendly destination/services; gender and review (Table 3.2). As Table 3.2 shows, most of the studies were related to the conceptual cluster. These studies were mainly focused on definitions, scope and boundaries of related terms such as Islamic and halal tourism. For instance, Khan and Callanan (2017) have identified the scope and boundaries between Islamic/Muslim/halal/sharia tourism. The next cluster was linked to explore the effects of considering Islamic attributes on behavior intentions to revisit (Sulaiman et al., 2021), purchase behavior (Jeaheng et al., 2019) and word of mouth (WOM)

Table 3.2 Research areas in Muslim travel

Cluster	F	Example
Conceptual development	29	'Halal tourism: conceptual and practical challenges'
Behavior intentions	23	'Muslim tourists' purchase intention of halal food in Spain'
Perception	20	'The impact of tourists' perceptions on halal tourism destination: a structural model analysis'
Satisfaction	18	'Impacts of Halal-friendly services, facilities and food and beverages on Muslim travellers' perceptions of service quality attributes, perceived price, satisfaction, trust and loyalty'
Specific destination	15	'Halal tourism potential: an investigation in Bromo Tengger Indonesia'
Needs	13	'The needs of Muslim hotel customers: evidence from Russian guests'
Motivation	13	'What travel motivational factors influence Muslim tourists toward MMITD?'
Muslim friendly	10	'Key attributes of Muslim friendly hotels' service quality: voices from booking.com'
Gender	9	'The flag-bearers of change in a patriarchal Muslim society: narratives of Iranian solo female travellers on Instagram'
Systematic review	9	'Halal tourism: literature review and experts' view'

(Wardi et al., 2018). The third category is associated with studies that have evaluated the perceptions and attitudes of the local community (Yıldırgan et al., 2020), tourists (Rahman et al., 2020) and businesses (Abbasian, 2021) toward Muslim tourism. Looking into the influential factors on satisfaction is the fourth cluster. These studies suggested factors such as perceived value (Rahman et al., 2020), service quality and perceived price (Jeaheng et al., 2020). Exploring the tourism potential of a specific destination in the field of Muslim tourism is the next group. They were followed by classifying the needs (Shnyrkova & Predvoditeleva, 2019) and drivers/motivation of Muslim travellers (Rahman et al., 2017). Exploring the antecedents of service/destination friendly for Muslims is the eighth cluster. These types of studies have suggested factors such as halal food, place of worship, alcohol-free places, and halal-friendly activities (Han, Al-Ansi, Olya, et al., 2019). Some scholars have highlighted the experiences of Muslim women (Nikjoo et al., 2021), and some, by focusing on gender, have investigated the mediating role of gender in intention to book (Tiamiyu et al., 2020) and intention to travel domestically (Krishnapillai & Kwok, 2020). More recently, review studies have attracted the attention of researchers by increasing the number of studies on Muslim tourism (Table 3.2).

Muslim friendly destinations' requirements

As a growing trend worldwide, many destinations have started to introduce themselves as Muslim friendly destinations (Katuk et al., 2020). Based on this trend, exploring the factors that make a destination friendly for Muslim travellers has captured the attention of scholars. With an emphasis on hospitality (food and hotel), various attributes have been suggested to make a destination or service Muslim friendly. Battour et al. (2011) divided attributes into two groups, namely, tangible and intangible. Tangibles are mainly related to halal food, non-alcoholic drinks and prayer facilities. Intangible attributes are associated with Islamic entertainment, segregated swimming pools, Islamic morality and Azan (Table 3.3).

Discussion and conclusions

Muslim/Islamic/halal tourism, Muslim friendly tourism, halal-friendly hotel or destination are commonly used terms for the emerging trends that aim to fulfil the demands of Muslim travellers (Hall & Prayag, 2020; see Chapter 2, this volume). While these terms are used interchangeably, nonetheless, some scholars acknowledged their differences. The motivation to travel in Islamic tourism is mainly related to religion, and the favorite destination is one of the Muslim countries. Conversely, in halal tourism travel drivers are not limited to religious motivation but also involve broader recreational activities, and the destination does not necessarily have to be an Islamic country (Yousaf & Xiucheng, 2018). The share of Muslim tourists on the international scale is outstanding in a way that, in 2019, there were 160 million international Muslim travellers.

Table 3.3 Muslim friendly destinations' requirements

Requirements	Factors	Author(s)
Tangible	Service for prayers (mosques, Qibla sticker, Islamic toilets)	Fajriyati et al., 2020
	Halal food and alcohol-free drinks	Harahsheh et al., 2019
	No decorations that illustrate nudity	Han, Al-Ansi, Olya, et al., 2019
	Ablution area	Suci et al., 2021
	Shariah-compliant hotel	Sulaiman et al., 2021
	Halal flight, Ramadhan service	Vargas-Sánchez & Moral-Moral, 2019
Intangible	Muslim friendly leisure activities and venues for entertainment, 'Islamic dress codes, Azan, and Islamic morality'	Battour et al., 2011
	Accessibility to Sharia-friendly TV channels	Eid & El-Gohary, 2015
	Sharia-based financial, carry out zakat	Suci et al., 2021
	Segregated services	Papastathopoulos et al., 2021

Concerning the COVID-19 pandemic, Muslim arrivals dropped to 42 million in 2020, of which about 90% of them performed their trips in the first quarter of the year. The Muslim travel market is forecasted to recover up to 80% of the 2019 level in 2023. Although Muslim tourists make up a great portion of international tourists, reviewing the literature shows that still more research is required to be done. As Muslim tourism-related studies are still in an early stage (Suhartanto et al., 2020), the number of retrieved articles in this study ($n = 159$) reinforce that Muslim tourism is a relatively new concept. Accordingly, conducting a systematic review of existing literature can be helpful to provide an overview of the field.

This review shows the remarkable growth of attention toward Muslim tourism, especially since 2019 with more than 69% ($N = 105$) of the total number of studied articles being published since then. Overall, 65 journals had published relevant studies with, perhaps not surprisingly, the *Journal of Islamic Marketing* being the most significant. In terms of analyzing publications by country the majority of studies have been conducted by scholars from Muslim-majority countries with Malaysia ($n = 49$) and Indonesia ($n = 28$) being most significant. It is not surprising because Malaysia is a well-known destination for the halal market and the Malaysian government is offering significant investments to turn Malaysia into a hub for halal products (Rejeb et al., 2021). In Indonesia, Muslims formed 87% of the total population. Regarding the most studied variables, analysis demonstrates that halal food and hotel, the antecedents of satisfaction, motivation to travel and identifying factors that make a destination or tourism service providers Muslim friendly are the most examined. Food and accommodation are critical tangible attributes for Muslim travellers; accordingly food and accommodation have also caught the attention of researchers (Vargas-Sánchez & Moral-Moral, 2019). Regarding satisfaction, scholars have suggested service quality, perceived value, Islamic/ halal attributes, engagement, religiosity and gender as the main antecedents of satisfaction (Abror et al., 2019). Overall, ten clusters of research were identified with the leading cluster being related to conceptual development, potentially reflecting the lack of precise definitions of related concepts such as halal/ Islamic/Muslim tourism (Vargas-Sánchez & Moral-Moral, 2019).

References

Abbasian, S. (2021). Good idea but not here! A pilot study of Swedish tourism stakeholders' perceptions of Halal tourism. *Sustainability*, *3*(5), 2646. https://doi.org/10.3390/su13052646

Abror, A., Wardi, Y., Trinanda, O., & Patrisia, D. (2019). The impact of Halal tourism, customer engagement on satisfaction: Moderating effect of religiosity. *Asia Pacific Journal of Tourism Research*, *24*(7), 633–643. https://doi.org/10.1080/10941665.2019.1611609

Asih, S. M., & Asih, S. K. (2015). Marketing strategy implementation in developing Sharia tourism in Indonesia. *International Proceedings of Economics Development and Research*, *84*, 133.

Aziz, A. H. B. A. (2018). Muslim friendly tourism: Concept, practices and challenges in Malaysia. *International Journal of Academic Research in Business and Social Sciences*, *8*(11), 355–363. http://dx.doi.org/10.6007/IJARBSS/v8-i11/4908

Battour, M. (2018). Muslim travel behavior in halal tourism. In L. Butowski (Ed.), *Mobilities, tourism and travel behavior – contexts and boundaries* (pp. 3–16). InTech.

Battour, M., & Ismail, M. N. (2016). Halal tourism: Concepts, practices, challenges and future. *Tourism Management Perspectives*, *19*, 150–154. https://doi.org/10.1016/j.tmp.2015.12.008

Battour, M., Ismail, M. N., & Battor, M. (2011). The impact of destination attributes on Muslim tourist's choice. *International Journal of Tourism Research*, *13*(6), 527–540. https://doi.org/10.1002/jtr.824

Battour, M., Ismail, M. N., Battor, M., & Awais, M. (2017). Islamic tourism: An empirical examination of travel motivation and satisfaction in Malaysia. *Current Issues in Tourism*, *20*(1), 50–67. https://doi.org/10.1080/13683500.2014.965665

Boğan, E., & Sarıışık, M. (2019). Halal tourism: Conceptual and practical challenges. *Journal of Islamic Marketing*, *10*(1), 87–96. https://doi.org/10.1108/JIMA-06-2017-0066

Carboni, M., Perelli, C., & Sistu, G. (2014). Is Islamic tourism a viable option for Tunisian tourism? Insights from Djerba. *Tourism Management Perspectives*, *11*, 1–9. https://doi.org/10.1016/j.tmp.2014.02.002

Chiang, C. T. (2020). Developing an eMarketing model for tourism and hospitality: A keyword analysis. *International Journal of Contemporary Hospitality Management*, *32*(10), 3091–3114. https://doi.org/10.1108/IJCHM-03-2020-0230

Christofi, M., Leonidou, E., & Vrontis, D. (2017). Marketing research on mergers and acquisitions: A systematic review and future directions. *International Marketing Review*, *34*(5), 629–651. https://doi.org/10.1108/IMR-03-2015-0100

Collins-Kreiner, N. (2010). The geography of pilgrimage and tourism: Transformations and implications for applied geography. *Applied Geography*, *30*(1), 153–164. https://doi.org/10.1016/j.apgeog.2009.02.001

Durán-Sánchez, A., Álvarez-García, J., Río-Rama, D., De la Cruz, M., & Oliveira, C. (2018). Religious tourism and pilgrimage: Bibliometric overview. *Religions*, *9*(9), 249. https://doi.org/10.3390/rel9090249

Eid, R., & El-Gohary, H. (2015). The role of Islamic religiosity on the relationship between perceived value and tourist satisfaction. *Tourism Management*, *46*, 477–488. https://doi.org/10.1016/j.tourman.2014.08.003

El-Gohary, H. (2016). Halal tourism, is it really Halal? *Tourism Management Perspectives*, *19*, 124–130. https://doi.org/10.1016/j.tmp.2015.12.013

Eslami, M., Bazrafshan, M., & Sedaghat, M. (2021). Shia geopolitics or religious tourism? Political convergence of Iran and Iraq in the light of Arbaeen pilgrimage. In F. J. B. S. Leandro, C. Branco, & F. Caba-Maria (Eds.), *The geopolitics of Iran* (pp. 363–385). Palgrave Macmillan.

Fajriyati, I., Afiff, A. Z., Gayatri, G., & Hati, S. R. H. (2020). Generic and Islamic attributes for non-Muslim majority destinations: Application of the three-factor theory of customer satisfaction. *Heliyon*, *6*(6), e04324. https://doi.org/10.1016/j.heliyon.2020.e04324

Hall, C. M., & Prayag, G. (Eds.). (2020). *The Routledge handbook of halal hospitality and Islamic tourism*. Routledge.

Han, H., Al-Ansi, A., Olya, H. G., & Kim, W. (2019). Exploring halal-friendly destination attributes in South Korea: Perceptions and behaviors of Muslim travelers toward a non-Muslim destination. *Tourism Management*, *71*, 151–164. https://doi.org/10.1016/j.tourman.2018.10.010

Henderson, J. C. (2003). Managing tourism and Islam in peninsular Malaysia. *Tourism Management*, *24*(4), 447–456. https://doi.org/10.1016/S0261-5177(02)00106-1

Heydari Chianeh, R., Del Chiappa, G., & Ghasemi, V. (2018). Cultural and religious tourism development in Iran: Prospects and challenges. *Anatolia*, *29*(2), 204–214. https://doi.org/10.1080/13032917.2017.1414439

Hu, K., Wu, H., Qi, K., Yu, J., Yang, S., Yu, T., Zheng, J., & Liu, B. (2018). A domain keyword analysis approach extending Term Frequency-Keyword Active Index with Google Word2Vec model. *Scientometrics*, *114*(3), 1031–1068. https://doi.org/10.1007/s11192-017-2574-9

Jafari, J., & Scott, N. (2014). Muslim world and its tourisms. *Annals of Tourism Research*, *44*, 1–19. https://doi.org/10.1016/j.annals.2013.08.011

Jamal, A., & El-Bassiouny, N. (2019). Islamic tourism: The role of culture and religiosity. In A. Jamal, R. Raj & K. Griffin (Eds.), *Islamic toursim: Management of travel destinations* (pp. 10–25). CABI.

Jeaheng, Y., Al-Ansi, A., & Han, H. (2019). Halal-friendly hotels: Impact of halal-friendly attributes on guest purchase behaviors in the Thailand hotel industry. *Journal of Travel & Tourism Marketing*, *36*(6), 729–746. https://doi.org/10.1080/10548408.2019.1631940

Jeaheng, Y., Al-Ansi, A., & Han, H. (2020). Impacts of Halal-friendly services, facilities, and food and beverages on Muslim travelers' perceptions of service quality attributes, perceived price, satisfaction, trust, and loyalty. *Journal of Hospitality Marketing & Management*, *29*(7), 787–811. https://doi.org/10.1080/19368623.2020.1715317

Katuk, N., Ku-Mahamud, K. R., Kayat, K., Hamid, M. N. A., Zakaria, N. H., & Purbasari, A. (2020). Halal certification for tourism marketing: The attributes and attitudes of food operators in Indonesia. *Journal of Islamic Marketing*, *12*(5), 1043–1062. https://doi.org/10.1108/JIMA-03-2020-0068

Khan, F., & Callanan, M. (2017). The "Halalification" of tourism. *Journal of Islamic Marketing*, *8*(4), 558–577. https://doi.org/10.1108/JIMA-01-2016-0001

Kim, B., Kim, S., & King, B. (2020). Religious tourism studies: Evolution, progress, and future prospects. *Tourism Recreation Research*, *45*(2), 185–203. https://doi.org/10.1080/0 2508281.2019.1664084

Kim, M. (2020). A systematic literature review of the personal value orientation construct in hospitality and tourism literature. *International Journal of Hospitality Management*, *89*, 102572. https://doi.org/10.1016/j.ijhm.2020.102572

Kovjanić, G. (2014). Islamic tourism as a factor of the Middle East regional development. *Turizam*, *18*(1), 33–43.

Krishnapillai, G., & Kwok, S. Y. (2020). Uncovering the Muslim leisure tourists' motivation to travel domestically – do gender and generation matters? *Tourism and Hospitality Management*, *26*(1), 213–231. https://doi.org/10.20867/thm.26.1.12

Lipka, M., & Hackett, C. (2017). Why Muslims are the world's fastest-growing religious group. *Pew Research Center*. www.pewresearch.org/fact-tank/2017/04/06/why-muslims-are-the-worlds-fastest-growing-religious-group/

Madani, F., & Weber, C. (2016). The evolution of patent mining: Applying bibliometrics analysis and keyword network analysis. *World Patent Information*, *46*, 32–48. https://doi.org/10.1016/j.wpi.2016.05.008

Mastercard-CrescentRating (2019). *Muslim women in travel 2019*. www.crescentrating.com/reports/muslim-women-in-travel-2019.html

Nave, A., do Paço, A., & Duarte, P. (2021). A systematic literature review on sustainability in the wine tourism industry: Insights and perspectives. *International Journal of Wine Business Research*, *33*(4), 457–480. https://doi.org/10.1108/IJWBR-09-2020-0046

Nikjoo, A., Markwell, K., Nikbin, M., & Hernández-Lara, A. B. (2021). The flag-bearers of change in a patriarchal Muslim society: Narratives of Iranian solo female travelers on Instagram. *Tourism Management Perspectives*, *38*, 100817. https://doi.org/10.1016/j.tmp.2021.100817

Nolan, M. L., & Nolan, S. (1992). Religious sites as tourism attractions in Europe. *Annals of Tourism Research*, *19*(1), 68–78. https://doi.org/10.1016/0160-7383(92)90107-Z

Nyaupane, G. P., Timothy, D. J., & Poudel, S. (2015). Understanding tourists in religious destinations: A social distance perspective. *Tourism Management*, *48*, 343–353. https://doi.org/10.1016/j.tourman.2014.12.009

Oktadiana, H., Pearce, P. L., & Chon, K. (2016). Muslim travellers' needs: What don't we know? *Tourism Management Perspectives*, *20*, 124–130. https://doi.org/10.1016/j.tmp.2016.08.004

Pahlevan-Sharif, S., Mura, P., & Wijesinghe, S. N. (2019). A systematic review of systematic reviews in tourism. *Journal of Hospitality and Tourism Management*, *39*, 158–165. https://doi.org/10.1016/j.jhtm.2019.04.001

Papastathopoulos, A., Koritos, C., & Mertzanis, C. (2021). Effects of faith-based attributes on hotel prices: The case of halal services. *International Journal of Contemporary Hospitality Management*, *33*(8), 2839–2861. https://doi.org/10.1108/IJCHM-01-2021-0044

Preko, A., Mohammed, I., Gyepi-Garbrah, T. F., & Allaberganov, A. (2020). Islamic tourism: Travel motivations, satisfaction and word of mouth, Ghana. *Journal of Islamic Marketing*, *12*(1), 124–144. https://doi.org/10.1108/JIMA-04-2019-0082

Rahman, M., Moghavvemi, S., Thirumoorthi, T., & Rahman, M. K. (2020). The impact of tourists' perceptions on halal tourism destination: A structural model analysis. *Tourism Review*, *75*(3), 575–594. https://doi.org/10.1108/TR-05-2019-0182

Rahman, M. K., Zailani, S., & Musa, G. (2017). What travel motivational factors influence Muslim tourists towards MMITD? *Journal of Islamic Marketing*, *8*(1), 48–73. https://doi.org/10.1108/JIMA-05-2015-0030

Rasul, T. (2019). The trends, opportunities and challenges of halal tourism: A systematic literature review. *Tourism Recreation Research*, *44*(4), 434–450. https://doi.org/10.1080/0 2508281.2019.1599532

Rejeb, A., Rejeb, K., Zailani, S., Treiblmaier, H., & Hand, K. J. (2021). Integrating the Internet of Things in the halal food supply chain: A systematic literature review and research agenda. *Internet of Things*, *13*, 100361. https://doi.org/10.1016/j.iot.2021.100361

Russen, M., Dawson, M., & Madera, J. M. (2021). Gender diversity in hospitality and tourism top management teams: A systematic review of the last 10 years. *International Journal of Hospitality Management*, *95*, 102942. https://doi.org/10.1016/j.ijhm.2021.102942

Said, M. F., Adham, K. A., Muhamad, N. S. A., & Sulaiman, S. (2020). Exploring halal tourism in Muslim-minority countries: Muslim travellers' needs and concerns. *Journal of Islamic Marketing*. https://doi.org/10.1108/JIMA-07-2020-0202

Seyfi, S., & Hall, C. M. (2019). Deciphering Islamic theocracy and tourism: Conceptualization, context, and complexities. *International Journal of Tourism Research*, *21*(6), 735–746. https://doi.org/10.1002/jtr.2300

Shnyrkova, A., & Predvoditeleva, M. (2019). The needs of Muslim hotel customers: Evidence from Russian guests. *Journal of Islamic Marketing*. https://doi.org/10.1108/ JIMA-09-2018-0172

Strategic Initiatives & Government Advisory (SIGA) Team. (2012). *Diverse beliefs: Tourism of faith, religious tourism gains ground*. SIGA. https://ficci.in/spdocument/20207/diverse-beliefs-tourism-of-faith.pdf

Suci, A., Junaidi, Nanda, S. T., Kadaryanto, B., & van FC, L. L. (2021). Muslim-friendly assessment tool for hotel: How halal will you serve? *Journal of Hospitality Marketing & Management*, *30*(2), 201–241. https://doi.org/10.1080/19368623.2020.1775746

Suhartanto, D., Dean, D., Wibisono, N., Astor, Y., Muflih, M., Kartikasari, A., Sutrisno, R., & Hardiyanto, N. (2020). Tourist experience in Halal tourism: What leads to loyalty? *Current Issues in Tourism*, *24*(14), 1976–1990. https://doi.org/10.1080/13683500.2020. 1813092

Sulaiman, Z. A., Iranmanesh, M., Foroughi, B., & Rosly, O. (2021). The impacts of Shariah-compliant hotel attributes on Muslim travellers revisit intention: Religiosity as a moderator. *Journal of Islamic Marketing*. https://doi.org/10.1108/JIMA-06-2020-0179

Tiamiyu, T., Quoquab, F., & Mohammad, J. (2020). Muslim tourists' intention to book on Airbnb: The moderating role of gender. *Journal of Islamic Marketing*. https://doi. org/10.1108/JIMA-08-2020-0253

Vargas-Sánchez, A., & Moral-Moral, M. (2019). Halal tourism: Literature review and experts' view. *Journal of Islamic Marketing*, *11*(3), 549–569. https://doi.org/10.1108/ JIMA-04-2017-0039

Wahyono, Z., & Razak, M. A. A. (2020). Islamic tourism in Southeast Asia: The concept and its implementation. *International Journal of Halal Research*, *2*(2), 90–105.

Wardi, Y., Abror, A., & Trinanda, O. (2018). Halal tourism: Antecedent of tourist's satisfaction and word of mouth (WOM). *Asia Pacific Journal of Tourism Research*, *23*(5), 463–472. https://doi.org/10.1080/10941665.2018.1466816

Weismayer, C., & Pezenka, I. (2017). Identifying emerging research fields: A longitudinal latent semantic keyword analysis. *Scientometrics*, *113*(3), 1757–1785. https://doi. org/10.1007/s11192-017-2555-z

Yagmur, Y., Ehtiyar, R., & Aksu, A. (2019). Evaluation of halal tourism in terms of bibliometric characteristics. *Journal of Islamic Marketing*, *11*(6), 1601–1617. https://doi. org/10.1108/JIMA-05-2019-0101

Yıldırgan, R., Bilgiçli, İ., Baysal, H. T., & Batman, O (2020). Local people's perception of Halal tourism and Arab tourists: The case of Sapanca. *Eskişehir Osmangazi Üniversitesi İktisadi ve İdari Bilimler Dergisi, 15*(3), 849–874. https://doi.org/10.17153/oguiibf.540961

Yousaf, S., & Xiucheng, F. (2018). Halal culinary and tourism marketing strategies on government websites: A preliminary analysis. *Tourism Management, 68*, 423–443. https://doi.org/10.1016/j.tourman.2018.04.006

Zamani-Farahani, H., & Henderson, J. C. (2010). Islamic tourism and managing tourism development in Islamic societies: The cases of Iran and Saudi Arabia. *International Journal of Tourism Research, 12*(1), 79–89. https://doi.org/10.1002/jtr.741

Part II

Non–religious travel and tourism

4 Travel Motivation of Muslim Tourists

Are They Really Different?

Philip L. Pearce and Hera Oktadiana

Introduction

Consistent problems appear when describing a tourist group. Studies of any one group in isolation can produce 'floating data'; that is a record of attributes such as motives, attitudes and evaluations that are hard to interpret. A fundamental question, which is not fully addressed by such descriptive studies with floating data, is how a target group compares to similar cohorts. The comparison can be in terms of areas of emphasis or, by way of contrast, themes and issues that appear equally or less important. In this chapter the researchers consider the motives of tourists from one religious group – Muslims from South East Asia. The problem of floating data and interpretation difficulties are relevant to this kind of interest. Research designs involving benchmarking have been used previously to address interpretation difficulties when studying tourist samples (Hermans, 2018). For example, there are benchmarking studies of diverse senior tourists (Johann & Panchapakesan, 2016), travellers with varied accommodation preferences (Doran et al., 2015), backpackers from different nationalities (Pearce, 2005a) and tourists with sustainability concerns (Bergin-Seers & Mair, 2009). Such studies address the issues of the distinctiveness of any specific group and effectively ground or contextualise the data by offering an appreciation of the results from other samples. Without such comparisons, superficial generalisations can be made; an outcome that is not only conceptually unsound but also of little use for applied purposes.

A benchmarking approach to the study of Muslim tourist motivation has not yet been carried out. By using an established scheme – the travel career pattern (TCP) approach to study motivation – and then assembling published data from multiple sources, a better contextualised analysis of what Muslims want from their travels can be developed. At the very least, this comparative approach begins to identify desired holistic differences and or similarities among markets rather than focusing heavily on specialist pragmatic needs. The researchers use data derived from studies in a number of Asian and western markets. Recent studies involving Muslims from South East Asia are the special focus, and, building on the researchers' knowledge of the Muslim world, a differentiated view of Muslim travel motivation is offered.

DOI: 10.4324/9781003036296-6

In terms of the structure of the work, the chapter outlines the advantages and reviews the key factors involved in preparing benchmarking appraisals in tourism study. This review is then married with a consideration of the TCP approach, a comprehensive perspective used to capture a diverse array of tourists' motives. The findings take the form of 'Muslim tourist are more likely to exhibit [nominated motives]'; a format that requires the comparative data being assembled in this chapter to build such statements. In brief, the study aims are to compare and benchmark the travel motivation between Muslim and other comparable tourist groups. The interest in Muslim travel is directed towards holiday and recreational tourism, not pilgrimages to Mecca associated with faith-based journeys such as Haj and Umrah.

Benchmarking in Tourism Research

Political, economic and social comparison processes among humans have operated throughout history (Blainey, 2013). The focus of the comparisons can be at a molar scale such as East versus West, the Muslim versus Christian world or between countries, cities and communities (Huntington, 1993; Ma'oz, 2009; Morris, 2011). Instead of focusing on the varied representations of other people and societies, management and tourism researchers have attempted to use the comparison process to improve their understanding of specific organisations and cases (Kozak, 2002; Wöber, 2002). Wöber's (2002) book on this theme documents ways to benefit from comparing the relative success of Austrian businesses in the small-scale accommodation and restaurant sector. Much of the other foundation benchmarking work in tourism and hospitality addresses the performance of destinations and provides assessment and ratings along specified dimensions. In formative studies, Fuchs and Weiermair (2004) used the approach to determine tourists' relative satisfaction with destinations, while Wöber and Fesenmaier (2004) were more concerned with comparing the online marketing efforts that help attract tourists to specific places. The expansion of the idea of benchmarking and comparative studies has been extended to sustainability achievements (Cernat & Gourdon, 2012), AirBnB comparisons among European cities (Zekan et al., 2019) and the characteristics of different groups of tourists as noted earlier (Kumar et al., 2019).

Two main forms of benchmarking can be considered (Hermans, 2018). Internal benchmarking applies to repeated testing of the units of interest over time. In the case of studying tourists' motives this would mean the repeated assessment of the interest among tourists in choosing a destination over a number of years. From this internal benchmarking, the rising or declining appeal of the destination or attraction could be assessed. By way of contrast, external benchmarking refers to the assessment of an entity of interest with other cases (Fuchs, 2002). As an example, Pearce and Benckendorff (2006) reviewed the different levels of tourists' satisfaction across a range of natural environment attractions. They were able to identify an overall mean score and plot the ranges for high performing and less well-received settings.

Three foundation points help direct benchmarking studies. The first issue lies in the selection of comparison cases. A second core requirement is the use of the same measure or access to the same kinds of data to make the comparative judgments. A third and perhaps less obvious requirement is the backing of a theoretical or conceptual scheme that might help explain and interpret any differences uncovered. The first of these requirements is considered here while the remaining two pivotal considerations are dealt with in the next section.

Selecting the family of cases for benchmarking needs to follow the goals of the research effort. If the goal is to place the data about a particular group or business in the context of other similar groups, then key intergroup parameters must be aligned. As an example, if a regional university wants to assess the academic publication performance of its staff, then the benchmarking partners should be other regional universities where staff have similar levels of resources and workloads. By way of contrast, if the point of the benchmarking exercise is aspirational, then the comparisons might be with better funded, larger and more prestigious institutions. In the latter case the benchmarking serves to identify structures and processes operating in the well-performed institutions that may be affecting the achievements of the regional case. Selection processes in benchmarking can be tied to similar considerations in the selection of examples for case study research. For example, Flyvbjerg (2006) identified the value of choosing typical cases versus outliers in building the understanding of a topic. In the present study the selection of cases for the benchmarking procedure can be described as seeking a small cohort of close affiliates that can provide enough diversity to explore the positioning of the motivations of Muslim tourists.

Tourists' Travel Motivation

Benchmarking requires a common way of assessing performance. Further, it is desirable if the assessment used has a conceptual background that can be employed to interpret the emphases observed. There have been various travel motivation theories that contribute to tourism research; most use psychographic, social psychological and sociological approaches. Some of the popular theories and models include Plog's (1974) psychocentric-allocentrism model, Dann's (1977) push and pull approach, Iso-Ahola's (1982) optimal arousal concept and Pearce's (2005b) TCP approach. Although push and pull theory is one of the most renowned approaches in understanding tourists' motivation, this is really a simple dichotomy emphasising internal drivers – that is social psychological motives – and contrasting these forces with the appeal of external destination features. Another theory, Plog's (1974) tourist typology, once common in early tourism textbooks, is a somewhat one-dimensional assessment built on data drawn only from the United States (Huang & Hsu, 2009). The arousal approach offered by Iso-Ahola (1982) proved challenging to assess in clear ways as his own autobiographical account of the work reveals (Iso-Ahola, 2011).

This chapter uses the TCP approach as it has been used consistently in academic and applied studies by a range of authors (Pearce, 2019). The validity of this approach has been tested in various tourist groups such as health tourists, backpackers, skiers and students to understand their motivation based on their travel experiences (Song & Bae, 2018; Pearce, 2022). The concept of the TCP proposes and finds consistent evidence that an individual's travel motives consist of core, middle and outer layer motives. The core motives include novelty, escape/relaxation and relationship. Middle layer motives typically comprise the desire to be in nature and indicate an interest in self-development, host-site involvement and self-actualisation. The outer and less important motives relate to nostalgia, status issues and isolation (Pearce, 2019). Importantly, the patterns change with more travel experience. All travellers pay attention to the core motives. Less experienced travelers emphasise all components while more experienced tourists give increasing priority to the middle layer motives and less to the outer level concerns.

As a theory within the study area of tourism, the TCP approach achieves several goals. These goals include being dynamic, flexible, sensitive to individual variation but offering integration with previous work and some predictive power for the future (Pearce, 1993; Smith et al., 2013). Five key points and assumptions underpin the contemporary TCP approach. First, there is an emphasis on change with increasing travel experience, making the core idea of the model dynamic rather than static. Second, rather than adopting a single trait approach such as arousal or anxiety, multiple co-existing motives are encapsulated in the travel career work. As a third feature the balance between a nomothetic and an ideographic approach can be addressed. It is possible to use the system to think about the motivational profile of an individual. The use of the work in this way may fit the needs of researchers conducting longitudinal work or case studies of a special traveller or tourist. More commonly though, a nomothetic approach is possible. By portraying means on the major factors it is possible to describe the broad motivational patterns of sub-groups of people.

There is a specific assumption that motivation can be sensibly measured with a set of diverse items. By building the original approach on over 140 items and then reducing them to a core of 74, the rich mix of drivers and aspirations that are needed to capture and characterise why people seek to travel are, arguably, adequately realised. That is, both the teleological (forward looking) goals of individuals as well as the potential deficits and inadequacies that characterise their world and produce the desire to be elsewhere find a place in the array of TCP items. Allied to this coverage, the results of the early work with the TCP revealed 14 consistent factors in these items; this consistent outcome assists researchers in succinctly describing the travel motive patterns of groups. A fifth point of interest lies in the credibility of a patterning approach with work being undertaken in neuroscience. Biological studies of motivation, most especially those that consider the brain and the activating of sensory systems, offer some consistency with the dynamic TCP work (see also Pearce, 2019). Basic emotional circuit systems in humans and primates are in accord with elements of the travel career work and include seeking novelty, play, stressing relationships and connectivity (Panksepp & Biven, 2012). The potential for a consistency with the neuroscience work is indeed credible. Nevertheless, as a tourism theory of social motivation the TCP work adopts the force field ideas as originally proposed by Lewin (1951). The field theory approach emphasises a pattern of motives that are constantly shaped by context and the individual's experience.

As the basis for the specific review and benchmarking goals of this chapter the basic TCP model, as updated and redrawn (see also Pearce, 2019), is provided as source of reference in Figure 4.1.

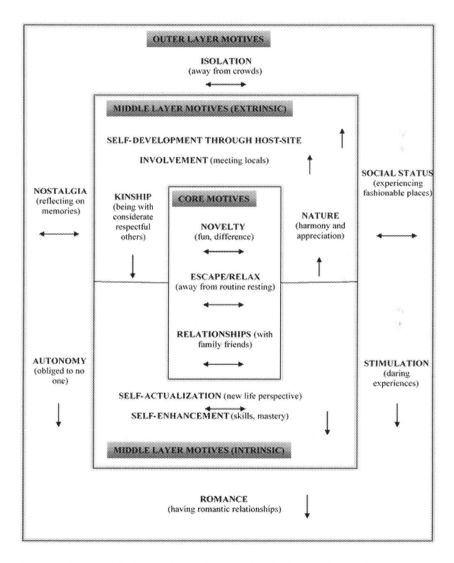

Figure 4.1 Core middle layer and outer layer motives depicted in the travel career pattern approach

Method

Case Selection

The studies that form the basis for the motivational benchmarking in this chapter are selected to represent measurements taken of Muslim tourists in South East Asia, specifically Malaysia and Indonesia, Chinese tourists, Korean tourists, a broad Asian sample and two samples of Western tourists. This succinct listing of studies thus provides Western samples, multiple Asian groups and nationalities as well as the central study of Muslim tourists from South East Asia. The cases thus provide a selection of a suitable diversity to encourage contextualisation and permit generalisation (cf. Eisenhardt & Graebner, 2007; Flyvbjerg, 2006). A succinct description of each sample and the relevant research context are provided as follows.

Pearce and Lee (2005)

The foundation study of the TCP work sought to understand pleasure travel motivation in a Western cultural context. Two approaches were used: interviews and surveys. The interviews were conducted to gain a broad overview concerning the TCP concept as well as to develop a strategic direction for the survey. The survey was distributed to people with a Western cultural background in Australia as the target participants. There were 1,012 participants involved in this study, consisting of 57% Australians, 22% from the United Kingdom and 21% from other Western countries. Data were collected at airports, coach terminals and major shopping centres. Respondents provided ratings of the importance of 74 items using a Likert scale. The results indicated 14 travel motive factors. Based on the level of importance, the factors were novelty, escape/relax, relationship (strengthen), autonomy, nature, self-development (host-site involvement), stimulation, self-development (personal development), relationship (security), self-actualisation, isolation, nostalgia, romance and recognition.

Pearce (2005b)

In a closely allied investigation of travel motivation of 824 South Korean tourists, again all 74 items and 14 core motive factors were applied. Data were collected in the three cities of Daegu, Daejon and Seoul, South Korea through utilising university and professional networks. Translation of the items into Korean and the back translation were employed to check for the exact meanings used in the Korean survey. The results were very similar to those obtained in the Pearce and Lee (2005) work. Novelty was ranked as the highest motive, followed by escape/relax, self-actualisation, nature, relationship, self-enhancement, romance, relationship-belonging, autonomy, self-development (host-site involvement), nostalgia, isolation and recognition.

Panchal and Pearce (2011)

For this application of the TCP work 319 travellers from Thailand (41.4%), the Philippines (33.2%) and India (25.4%) were studied. Data were gathered through a survey in the tourist areas, airports, and shopping centres in various cities of those three countries. A five-point Likert scale was employed in the survey. All the 14 motivation factors from the initial TCP study were applied. The authors however, added two motive items: 'to maintain my health' and 'to improve my health', which made up a fifteenth travel motivation interest area. Escape/relaxation and novelty were the most two important factors, tailed by nature, self-actualisation, health, isolation, self-development (host-site involvement), personal development, stimulation, strengthen relationship, secure relationship, autonomy, nostalgia, romance and recognition.

Li et al. (2015)

The motivations of Chinese tourists were of interest in this study. Data were collected using 71 motivation items on the five-point Likert scale. There were 640 respondents drawn from tourists visiting major sites and staying in hotels in Hangzhou. Differences among less experienced and more experienced tourists revealed the value of considering the amount of travel previously undertaken as a determinant of travel motive patterns rather than relying on the discriminatory power of age or gender. The overall findings showed that for the Chinese sample nature was viewed as the most important factor, followed by novelty, self-actualisation, self-development (host-site involvement), escape/relaxation, self-development (personal development), relationship strengthening, stimulation, isolation, nostalgia, relationship safety, autonomy, recognition and romance.

Oktadiana et al. (2017)

This research team used the TCP approach to study the travel motivation of Muslim tourists from Malaysia and Indonesia. In this work, 26 travel motives items were selected from the original 74 items used in Pearce and Lee's (2005) study, based on the two highest loading items from 13 core factors. One factor, romance, was excluded due to sensitivity issues about expressing the desire for intimate relationships in Muslim culture. Data were gathered from 356 valid respondents using a five-point Likert scale. Tourists were accessed through personal and professional networks, principally in Jakarta and Kuala Lumpur. Their study revealed that relationships (strengthening), nature and novelty were the top three most important travel motivations for the Muslim tourists. The other motivations included escape/relax, stimulation, relationship (security), self-development (host-site involvement), autonomy, isolation, self-development (personal development), self-actualisation, nostalgia and recognition.

Song and Bae (2018)

The travel motivation of international students coming to South Korea was explored using the original 14 factors and 74 motive items and measuring importance with a five-point Likert scale. The researchers surveyed 585 international students from China, Hong Kong, Taiwan, Japan, Southeast Asia, Russia, Europe, South America, North America, the Middle East, Africa and Oceania. Participants from China and Hong Kong made up 45.7% of the total. Their study showed that longer travel careers (experience) of international students were associated with higher internally oriented motives (e.g. personal development) in the middle layer motivation and shorter travel careers with higher external motives (e.g. host-site involvement). In general, the core travel motives of novelty, escape/relaxation and enhanced relationships ranked the highest. In order the other motives were ranked from valuing nature, personal development, self-actualisation, host-site involvement, autonomy, sense of belonging/security, isolation, nostalgia, romance, luxury and finally to recognition.

Agarwal and Pearce (2019)

The topic of repeat tourism to India from international tourists was the focus of this study. Data were collected using a five-point Likert scale questionnaire in six Indian tourist cities. There were 492 participants involved in this study. It is important to stress for later interpretation that this is a study of predominantly experienced Western travellers ($N = 392$), on their second or third trip to India, with a wide variety of other travel experiences. The other 100 tourists in this sample were repeat visitors from Asia. The participants who came for a business trip or had a family link in India were excluded. Following the work of Oktadiana et al. (2017), the researchers used 13 travel motive factors with 26 motive items. They study demonstrated that the core motives (novelty, escape/relaxation and relationships) were viewed as important for the repeat tourists. This was followed by relationship (security), nature, self-development (host-site involvement), self-development (personal development), self-actualisation, autonomy, isolation, nostalgia, stimulation and recognition.

Results and Discussion

The results from the multiple studies in this benchmarking appraisal are presented by considering the mean scores on the travel career pattern factors in three tables. The basis for the construction of these tables lies in the determination of a first set of factors from each case that can be identified as core factors. Expressed simply, core factors are a part of an identifiable cluster that are all given noticeably higher mean scores when compared to the other factors. The researchers' selection of the set of factors in the core was conceived as being analogous to the use of the screen test when deciding on the number of items to be extracted in factor analysis procedures (Child, 1970). Factors above the clear cut off point were in the core, while those below the cut-off point were not selected. Next, the researchers examined the remaining mean scores and identified a second cut off point in the array of the mean scores. Following the same logic, factors above a clear cut off point were selected as belonging to the middle layer of the travel career pattern and those below the clear cut off were identified as belonging to the outer core. It was this procedure that was followed in the original TCP work and enabled the portrayal of the factors and pattern produced in Figure 4.1 as portrayed previously.

By presenting the results of each study as motives belonging to the core, middle layer or outer layer of the TCP, the comparison between the Muslim motivation work and findings from other studies can be systematically examined. The discussion of the similarities and differences between the Muslim motivational emphases and that in the other studies follows each table. This material addresses directly the key question in the title of this chapter: Travel Motivation of Muslim Tourists: Are They Really Different? Table 4.1 provides the mean scores on the identified core factors in each study. In the subsequent Figure 4.2 the comparison of core motives between Muslim tourists and other groups is presented.

Table 4.1 Core level motives

	General Western[1]	General Western plus Asian[2]	General Asian[3]	International students to Korea[4]	Korean[5]	Chinese[6]	Southeast Asian Muslims[7]	N*
Novelty	4.23	4.05	4.19	4.11	3.99	4.10	4.07	7
Escape/Relaxation	3.84	–	4.23	4.04	3.93	3.89	3.92	6
Relationship (Strengthen)	3.72	3.95	–	3.72	–	–	4.28	4
Nature	–	3.79	–	–	3.79	4.27	4.13	4
Self-development (Host-site involvement)	–	3.88	–	–	–	3.90	–	2
Self-actualisation	–	–	–	–	3.84	3.91	–	2
Stimulation	–	3.73	–	–	–	–	–	1

Notes:
1 – Pearce and Lee (2005)
2 – Agarwal and Pearce (2019): No 'romance' factor
3 – Panchal and Pearce (2011)
4 – Song and Bae (2018): No 'stimulation' factor
5 – Pearce (2005b): Relationship (strengthen) was labelled as 'kinship'; self-development (personal development) was labelled 'self-enhancement'; relationship (security) was labelled 'Kinship-belonging'; recognition was labelled 'social status'
6 – Li et al. (2015)
7 – Oktadiana et al. (2017): No 'romance' factor
N* – the number of times the motive appears as a core level motive

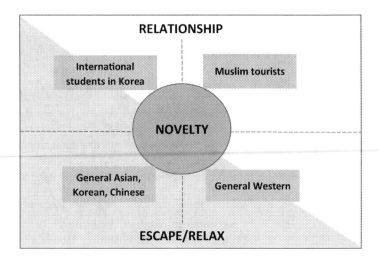

Figure 4.2 Comparison of core motives between the Muslim tourists and other groups

From the core motives, where the most common overall are novelty, escape/relaxation, relationship (strengthen) and nature, the Muslim tourists place relatively more emphasis on nature and strengthening relationships than do the other groups. There are commonalities here with the Chinese sample, most directly on the extra emphasis on nature as a core motive. Unlike the other Asian samples, the Muslim tourists stress strengthening relationships in the core of their holiday motivation patterns. It is notable, at a more general level, that the solid core of the original TCP work is reinforced by the composite findings across these studies. The importance of nature appears as another core candidate for some Asian samples as well as the experienced tourists repeating their travels to India, one quarter of whom are experienced Asian travellers. There are important cultural and religious consistencies that can be linked to this finding for the Muslim tourists and their differentiation from the Western samples. In the Qur'an there is an emphasis on appreciating nature and God's works. More specifically travel is portrayed as a useful and important pathway, to achieve a balanced and good life. According to multiple readings of the sacred text, travel is viewed predominantly as providing opportunities for socialisation and meeting other people as well as delighting in God's creations – viz. nature (Abu Hanifah, 2015; Zamani-Farahani & Eid, 2016). Thus, travel intention of the Muslims can be understood to include meeting friends and relatives and maintaining family ties, acquiring good health, gaining knowledge, helping community, learning about a community's conditions, seeing and appreciating the greatness of God's creation and nature and (separately to this study's interests) performing Haj or Umra (Halaltrip, n.d.). There is a consistency between these readings and the core motives reported in this benchmarking study.

The data for the middle level motives adds to this overall picture. These results are portrayed in Table 4.2.

From the middle level motives, the scores for the South East Asian Muslims are clustered in a tight bunch of results lying between the values 3.51 and 3.81. The results are very similar to the general Asian sample reported in the work of Panchal and Pearce (2011) and closely aligned with the largest sample, the general Western sample (Pearce & Lee, 2005). Following these results, it can be suggested that as well as being defined by an extended core of important motives, travel for the Muslims fits a broad swathe of moderately important motives, largely revolving around self-development, self-actualisation and building personal capacity to understand the world. Recourse to other studies

Table 4.2 Middle level motives

	General Western[1]	General Western plus Asian[2]	General Asian[3]	International students to Korea[4]	Korean[5]	Chinese[6]	Southeast Asian Muslims[7]	N*
Self-development (Personal development)	3.42	3.64	3.67	3.61	3.55	3.65	3.56	7
Relationship (Security)	3.26	–	3.58	3.21	3.53	3.17	3.74	6
Autonomy	3.65	3.68	3.50	–	3.37	–	3.61	5
Self-development (Host-site involvement)	3.44	–	3.69	3.48	3.37	–	3.69	5
Isolation	3.18	3.50	3.74	–	–	3.36	3.60	5
Self-actualisation	3.21	3.52	3.79	3.58	–	–	3.51	5
Stimulation	3.44	–	3.63	–	–	3.47	3.81	4
Nostalgia	–	3.57	–	–	3.36	3.22	–	3
Relationship (Strengthen)	–	–	3.59	–	3.67	3.51	–	3
Nature	3.58	–	3.79	3.70	–	–	–	3
Escape/Relaxation	–	3.61	–	–	–	–	–	1
Recognition	–	3.53	–	–	–	–	–	2
Romance	–	–	–	–	3.54	–	–	1
Health	–	–	3.75	–	–	–	–	1

Legend:

1 – Pearce and Lee (2005)

2 – Agarwal and Pearce (2019): No 'romance' factor

3 – Panchal and Pearce (2011)

4 – Song and Bae (2018): No 'stimulation' factor

5 – Pearce (2005b): Relationship (strengthen) was labelled as 'kinship'; self-development (personal development) was labelled 'self-enhancement'; relationship (security) was labelled 'kinship-belonging'; recognition was labelled "social status"

6 – Li et al. (2015)

7 – Oktadiana et al. (2017): No 'romance' factor

N* – the number of times the motive appears as a middle level motive and further interpretations of the Qur'an reinforce the validity of these findings. The value of travel for the enhancement of health and well-being, learning from the past, understanding cultural diversity, and the attainment of new knowledge have all been reported in previous work describing the incentives for Muslims to travel (Henderson, 2003; Jafari & Scott, 2014; Mohsin et al., 2016).

The outer layer of motives are those with the lowest set of mean scores for importance. In the foundation TCP work, it was demonstrated that these motives appeared to be recognised as somewhat important for inexperienced travellers but declined in importance for well-travelled tourists. In the general Asian group as well as in the Southeast Asian sample items pertaining to romance and potential sexual or intimate relationships were not included in the travel career survey content. The results for the outer layer motives are presented in Table 4.3.

The typical outer layer items of nostalgia and recognition are included in the South East Asian data, a finding consistent with the results from five other benchmarking partners. There were no clear common level outer layer motives for the repeat travellers to India (Agarwal & Pearce, 2019) and nostalgia and recognition were middle level motives for that group. Similarly, nostalgia appeared in the middle level motives for the Korean and Chinese samples so the Muslim sample who laced less emphasis on this factor was indeed a little

Table 4.3 Outer layer motives

	General Western[1]	General Western plus Asian[2]	General Asian[3]	International students to Korea[4]	Korean[5]	Chinese[6]	Southeast Asian Muslims[7]	N*
Recognition	2.37	–	2.93	2.56	3.18	3.03	3.07	6
Romance	2.83	–	3.00	2.66	–	2.87	–	4
Nostalgia	3.02	–	3.17	3.05	–	–	3.12	4
Isolation	–	–	–	3.11	3.28	–	–	2
Autonomy	–	–	–	3.29	–	3.03	–	2
Relationship (security)	–	3.39	–	–	–	–	–	1
Stimulation	–	–	–	–	3.27	–	–	1
Luxury	–	–	–	2.58	–	–	–	1

Legend:
1 – Pearce and Lee (2005)
2 – Agarwal and Pearce (2019): No 'romance' factor
3 – Panchal and Pearce (2011)
4 – Song and Bae (2018): No 'stimulation' factor
5 – Pearce (2005b): Relationship (strengthen) was labelled as 'kinship'; self-development (personal development) was labelled 'self-enhancement'; relationship (security) was labelled 'kinship-belonging'; recognition was labelled 'social status'
6 – Li et al. (2015)
7 – Oktadiana et al. (2017): No 'romance' factor
N*- the number of times the motive appears as an outer level motive

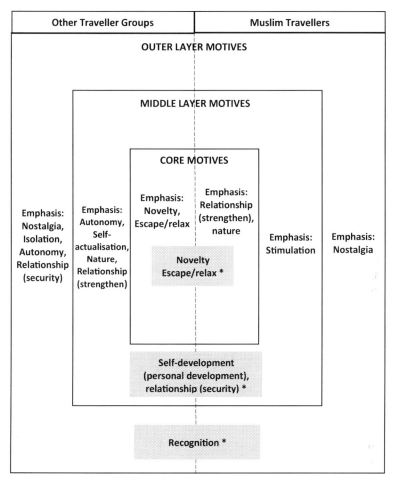

Note: * Similarities of travel motivation for all groups

Figure 4.3 A comparison of Muslim holiday travel motives with the common themes in Asian and Western samples

different to these North Eastern Asian groups. A visual portrayal of the main highlights from this benchmarking analysis is provided in Figure 4.3.

Conclusion and Implications

The value of the work is threefold. First, it is useful for all who study Muslim tourists to approach the topic of their interests with a clear view of what defines the group's key patterns of motives. Second, in the data employed, Muslim tourist groups from the two different nationalities of Malaysia and Indonesia are examined. Although previous work indicates some subtle variations between these nationality groups, the combined data show some clear patterns distinguishing their travel motives from a set of Western and other Asian communities. Of particular interest is the strong Qur'an linked perspective that travelling to enjoy nature and socialisation is a part of the distinctive core in the TCP work. The researchers believe this is a strong finding. Additionally, the suite of middle level motives unearthed through the benchmarking process indicates a slightly wider ambit of middle level motive forces for the Muslims than other groups. Again, some clear consistencies with previous studies and a faith-based emphasis concerning the self-development and learning opportunities possible through travel were identified. From these comparisons, it is possible to answer the core question of this chapter; Muslim tourists are not just like any other group. These differences lie not merely in their needs for halal food, prayer facilities and respect but also in the very suite of reasons that drive their holiday journeys.

Several implications flow from this kind of work. First, concerning theoretical implication, this study enriches the tourists' behaviour literature by providing an insight into Muslims' travel motivation, in comparison to the Western and Asian markets. It also reinforces the utility of the TCP work as a framework for providing integrated assessments of motivation among travel groups. For practical goals, it is potentially valuable for hospitality and travel operators to understand travel motivations of Muslims (a fast-growing market) to cater to their particular needs. As strengthening relationship and nature are viewed as very important motives by the Muslims, hospitality and travel operators may design a travel package such as a guided small Muslim group tour with a personalised Muslim friendly service to visit a destination. Another option is to offer Muslim guests a tour to a local community or a tourism village where they can meet the locals and learn about different cultures. The *Himalayan Trekkers' Nepal Special Muslim Tour* (https://himalayantrekkers.com/itinerary/nepal-special-muslim-tour) is a good example of a tour that offers a unique experience for the Muslim tourists. The tour provides natural and cultural experiences (core motive), an adventure of seeing the peaks of Eastern Nepal Himalayas (including Mount Everest) from 2,175 meters above sea level (middle layer motive), and a visit to historical monuments (outer layer motive).

It is important to note that Muslims are not all the same. This study only focuses on the Muslim tourists from two South East Asia's countries that together have the world's biggest Muslim population. Further study can include the comparison of Muslim tourists from other countries or regions such as the Middle East, Persia and Europe.

Acknowledgement

The authors would like to acknowledge Ding Xu (Carter) for assistance in assembling the data.

References

Abu Hanifah, A. B. (2015). *Islamic tourism: Brunei's conviction.* UNWTO regional seminar on the contribution of Islamic culture and its impact on the Asian tourism market. http://cf.cdn.unwto.org/sites/all/files/pdf/islamic_knowledge_heritage_tourism_brunei_darussalam.pdf

Agarwal, M., & Pearce, P. L. (2019, February 11–14). *Back to India again: Motivational insights from the travel career pattern approach* [Paper presentation]. 29th Annual Council for Australasian University Tourism and Hospitality Education Conference (CAUTHE): Sustainability of Tourism, Hospitality & Events in a Disruptive Digital Age, Cairns, QLD, Australia.

Bergin-Seers, S., & Mair, J. (2009). Emerging green tourists in Australia: Their behaviours and attitudes. *Tourism and Hospitality Research, 9*(2), 109–119. https://doi.org/10.1057/thr.2009.5

Blainey, G. (2013). *A very short history of the world* (rev ed.). Penguin.

Cernat, L., & Gourdon, J. (2012). Paths to success: Benchmarking cross-country sustainable tourism. *Tourism Management, 33*(5), 1044–1056. https://doi.org/10.1016/j.tourman.2011.12.007

Child, D. (1970). *The essentials of factor analysis.* Holt Rinehart and Winston.

Dann, G. M. S. (1977). Anomie, ego-enhancement and tourism. *Annals of Tourism Research, 4*(4), 184–194. https://doi.org/10.1016/0160-7383(77)90037-8

Doran, R., Larsen, S., & Wolff, K. (2015). Different but similar: Social comparison of travel motives among tourists. *International Journal of Tourism Research, 17*(6), 555–563. https://doi.org/10.1002/jtr.2023

Eisenhardt, K. M., & Graebner, M. E. (2007). Theory building from cases: Opportunities and challenges. *Academy of Management Journal, 50*(1), 25–32. https://doi.org/10.5465/amj.2007.24160888

Flyvbjerg, B. (2006). Five misunderstandings about case-study research. *Qualitative Inquiry, 12*(2), 219–245. https://doi.org/10.1177/1077800405284363

Fuchs, M. (2002). Destination benchmarking as a strategic management tool: The case of Tyrolean summer tourism. *Tourismus Journal, 6*(3), 291–320

Fuchs, M., & Weiermair, K. (2004). Destination benchmarking: An indicator-system's potential for exploring guest satisfaction. *Journal of Travel Research, 42*(3), 212–225. https://doi.org/10.1177/0047287503258827

Halaltrip. (n.d.). *Hadith on travel as well as the etiquettes and manners of travelling in Islam.* www.halaltrip.com/prayertimes/etiquettes

Henderson, J. C. (2003). Managing tourism and Islam in peninsular Malaysia. *Tourism Management, 24*(4), 447–456. https://doi.org/10.1016/S0261-5177(02)00106-1

Hermans, E. (2018). Benchmarking in tourism research. In R. Nunkoo (Ed.), *Handbook of research methods for tourism and hospitality management* (pp. 306–316). Edward Elgar Publishing.

Huang, S., & Hsu, C. H. C. (2009). Travel motivation: Linking theory to practice. *International Journal of Culture, Tourism and Hospitality Research, 3*(4), 287–295. https://doi.org/10.1108/17506180910994505

Huntington, S. P. (1993). *The third wave: Democratization in the late twentieth century* (Vol. 4). University of Oklahoma Press.

Iso-Ahola, S. E. (1982). Towards a social psychological theory of tourism motivation: A rejoinder. *Annals of Tourism Research, 9*(2), 256–262. https://doi.org/10.1016/0160-7383(82)90049-4

Iso-Ahola, S. E. (2011). Tourism as a social leisure behaviour. In P. L. Pearce (Ed.), *The study of tourism foundations from psychology* (Vol. 15, pp. 93–98). Pergamon.

Jafari, J., & Scott, N. (2014). Muslim world and its tourisms. *Annals of Tourism Research, 44,* 1–19. https://doi.org/10.1016/j.annals.2013.08.011

Johann, M., & Panchapakesan, P. (2016). Benchmarking holiday experience: The case of senior tourists. *Benchmarking: An International Journal, 23*(7), 1860–1875. https://doi.org/10.1108/BIJ-04-2015-0038

Kozak, M. (2002). Destination benchmarking. *Annals of Tourism Research, 29*(2), 497–519. https://doi.org/10.1016/S0160-7383(01)00072-X

Kumar, S., Kamble, S., & Roy, M. H. (2019). Twenty-five years of Benchmarking: An International Journal (BIJ): A bibliometric overview. *Benchmarking: An International Journal, 27*(2), 760–780. https://doi.org/10.1108/BIJ-07-2019-0314

Lewin, K. (1951). *Field theory in social science: Selected theoretical papers (Edited by Dorwin Cartwright.).* Harpers.

Li, H., Pearce, P. L., & Zhou, L. (2015). Documenting Chinese tourists' motivation patterns. In E. Wilson & M. Witsel (Eds.), *CAUTHE 2015: Rising tides and sea changes: Adaptation and innovation in tourism and hospitality* (pp. 235–246). School of Business and Tourism, Southern Cross University.

Ma'oz, M. (Ed.). (2009). *The meeting of civilizations: Muslim, Christian, and Jewish.* ISBS.

Mohsin, A., Ramli, N., & Alkhulayfi, B. A. (2016). Halal tourism: Emerging opportunities. *Tourism Management Perspectives, 19,* 137–143. https://doi.org/10.1016/j.tmp.2015.12.010

Morris, I. (2011). *Why the west rules for now: The patterns of history and what they reveal about the future.* Profile Books.

Oktadiana, H., Pearce, P. L., Pusiran, A. K., & Agarwal, M. (2017). Travel career patterns: The motivations of Indonesian and Malaysian Muslim tourists. *Tourism Culture & Communication, 17*(4), 231–248. https://doi.org/10.3727/109830417X15072926259360

Panchal, J., & Pearce, P. L. (2011). Health motives and the travel career pattern (TCP) model. *Asian Journal of Tourism and Hospitality Research, 5*(1), 32–44.

Panksepp, J., & Biven, L. (2012). *The archaeology of mind. Neuroevolutionary origins of human emotions.* W.W. Norton & company.

Pearce, P. L. (1993). Fundamentals of tourist motivation. In D. Pearce & R. Butler (Eds.), *Tourism research: Critiques and challenges* (pp. 85–105). Routledge.

Pearce, P. L. (2005a). Great divides or subtle contours? Contrasting British, North American/Canadian and European backpackers. In B. West (Ed.), *Down the road: Exploring backpacker and independent travel* (pp. 131–151). API Network.

Pearce, P. L. (2005b). *Tourist behaviour: Themes and conceptual schemes.* Channel View Publications.

Pearce, P. L. (2019). Dreaming and longing. In P. L. Pearce (Ed.), *Tourist behaviour. The essential companion* (pp. 20–40). Edward Elgar.

Pearce, P. L. (2022). The Ulysses factor revisited: Consolidating the travel career pattern approach to tourist motivation. In R. Sharpley (Ed.), *Routledge handbook of the tourist experience* (pp. 169–184). Routledge.

Pearce, P. L., & Benckendorff, P. (2006). Benchmarking, usable knowledge and tourist attractions. *Journal of Quality Assurance in Hospitality and Tourism, 7*(1/2), 29–52. https://doi.org/10.1300/J162v07n01_03

Pearce, P. L., & Lee, U-I. (2005). Developing the travel career approach to tourist motivation. *Journal of Travel Research, 43*(3), 226–237. https://doi.org/10.1177/0047287504272020

Plog, S. C. (1974). Why destination areas rise and fall in popularity. *Cornell Hotel and Restaurant Administration Quarterly, 14*(4), 55–58. https://doi.org/10.1177/001088047401400409

Smith, S. L., Xiao, H., Nunkoo, R., & Tukamushaba, E. K. (2013). Theory in hospitality, tourism, and leisure studies. *Journal of Hospitality Marketing & Management, 22*(8), 875–894. https://doi.org/10.1080/19368623.2013.771114

Song, H., & Bae, S. Y. (2018). Understanding the travel motivation and patterns of international students in Korea: Using the theory of travel career pattern. *Asia Pacific Journal of Tourism Research, 23*(2), 133–145. https://doi.org/10.1080/10941665.2017.1410193

Wöber, K. W. (2002). *Benchmarking in tourism and hospitality industries: The selection of benchmarking partners.* CABI.

Wöber, K. W., & Fesenmaier, D. R. (2004). A multi-criteria approach to destination benchmarking: A case study of state tourism advertising programs in the United States. *Journal of Travel & Tourism Marketing, 16*(2–3), 1–18. https://doi.org/10.1300/J073v16n02_01

Zamani-Farahania, H., & Eid, R. (2016). Muslim world: A study of tourism & pilgrimage among OIC member states. *Tourism Management Perspectives, 19*, 144–149. https://doi.org/10.1016/j.tmp.2015.12.009

Zekan, B., Önder, I., & Gunter, U. (2019). Benchmarking of Airbnb listings: How competitive is the sharing economy sector of European cities? *Tourism Economics, 25*(7), 1029–1046. https://doi.org/10.1177/1354816618814349

5 Exploring Turkish tourists' motivation and perception toward Muslim-friendly tourist destinations

Mohd Hafiz Hanafiah

Introduction

The size of the Muslim tourism market is expanding as a result of a growing Muslim population worldwide and increasing education and income levels (Jafari & Scott, 2014; Pew Research Center, 2017; Zamani-Farahani & Eid, 2016). Currently, the Muslim market is considered one of the world's most rapidly growing tourist markets (Mohsin et al., 2016; Seyfi & Hall, 2019). Based on the Crescent Rating Global Muslim Travel Index (GMTI) 2019 report, 200.3 million Muslim travellers contributed USD194 billion in global travel spend, attesting to its enormous potential (Travel News Digest, 2019). By 2026, the Halal travel sector's contribution to the global economy is expected to jump 35% to US$300 billion, up from US$220 billion in 2020. With the Muslim population being forecasted at a 1.5 percent growth rate compared to the non-Muslims (0.7% growth rate annually) (Pew Research Center, 2017), targeting Islamic tourists is increasingly important for tourism marketers. Subsequently, with the Muslim tourism market witnessing significant growth, tourism destinations need an appropriate strategy to cater to this prospective market.

Malaysia is one of the top Islamic tourism destinations in Asia (Jafari & Scott, 2014; Zamani-Farahani & Eid, 2016). Most of the Muslim tourists' market is from Jordan, Kuwait, Oman, United Arab Emirates, Syrian Arab Republic and Saudi Arabia. Through its Muslim-friendly tourism (MFT) marketing concept, Malaysia attracted 5.3 million Muslim tourists out of 26 million tourist arrivals in 2017 alone (Travel News Digest, 2019). As a predominantly Islamic country, Malaysia shares a common Islamic culture and tradition with Muslim travellers; they feel safer in terms of safety and security, Halal food, touristic activities and religiosity while visiting Malaysia (Ibrahim et al., 2009; Shafaei & Mohamed, 2017). Besides, Malaysia is also the top choice for Muslim tourists, especially those from Middle Eastern countries, due to the country's MFT facilities and wide availability of Halal food (Yusoff et al., 2010).

The Turkish outbound tourism market is steadily growing (Akay et al., 2017; Dogru & Sirakaya-Turk, 2018; Karadeniz, 2018; Katircioglu et al., 2018). Statistically speaking, Turkish tourists are travelling abroad more, according to the

DOI: 10.4324/9781003036296-7

Turkish Statistical Institute (Kultur, 2019). Over the first six months of 2018, the number of Turkish tourists travelling abroad rose 1.7 percent compared to the same period in 2017, reaching 4.26 million. In 2017, the total number of tourists travelling overseas reached 9.44 million (Kultur, 2019). The most popular destination for Turkish tourists was neighbouring Georgia, thanks to the significant effect of the visa exemption agreement between both countries (Baser, 2018), with more than a million (1,000,278) Turkish tourists traveling over the border to visit Georgia in 2017. Many Turkish tourists holiday in popular and well-known cities in Europe, while a growing number of Turkish people are taking an interest in Asia, the Pacific and other destinations. Nonetheless, only Iran and Azerbaijan are Islamic countries that are identified as preferred destinations (Kultur, 2019). Instead, in terms of Turkish tourist preferences, researchers claimed that they are more interested in city culture and sightseeing and shopping (Ozdipciner et al., 2010).

The challenges of Malaysia as a MFT destination for Turkish travellers

Although Islamic tourism has been widely promoted among Muslim countries (Jafari & Scott, 2014), Malaysia's acceptability as a preferred Islamic tourism destination among high-spending Muslim tourists is still limited (Rahman, 2014). There remains a gap to cover the factors influencing tourists to visit Malaysia as their preferred Islamic tourism destination. In terms of the inbound Islamic tourism market in Malaysia, most of the Muslim tourists are coming from Middle East countries such as Jordan, Kuwait, Oman, United Arab Emirates, Syrian Arab Republic and Saudi Arabia (Hassan et al., 2018; Salleh et al., 2010). Even though Malaysia is popular among Arab countries, Turkish tourists seemingly do not favour Malaysia as a leisure destination.

Statistically, Malaysia only received 12,775 Turkish tourists in 2013, although following the opening of the Malaysian Tourism Office in Istanbul the same year, the number of visitors increased by 62 percent in 2014 (Malay Mail, 2014). However, the number of Turkish tourists visiting Malaysia has since declined, with only 3,789 visiting in 2017 and 4,893 in 2018 (Kultur, 2019). Many reasons may be affecting the Turkish tourist pull factors, mainly due to connectivity issues and the two major air disasters involving flights MH370 to Beijing that disappeared and MH17, which crashed in Ukraine (West, 2014).

Many tourism studies conclude that a tourist's image of a destination is essential and that pull factors are therefore very decisive for destination choice (Prayag & Ryan, 2011; Yuan & McDonald, 1990). Therefore, it is vital to understand what Malaysia as an MFT destination needs to offer according to Turkish tourists' interests. Their perception needs to be explored in order to identify appropriate products and services to provide, which in return enhances the country's competitiveness as a preferred destination. As experience plays an essential role in determining tourist motivation, expectation and satisfaction, segmenting the visiting and non-visiting tourist perception could help tourism authorities better understand their specific travel motivation and perception. Such information is vital for them to strategise their tourism marketing plan.

This chapter assesses the motivating factors that influence visiting and non-visiting Turkish tourists' travelling behaviour, focusing on Malaysia as an MFT destination. The primary objective of this chapter is to deliberate on the Turkish tourists' push and pull motivation to travel abroad. In addition, this chapter also reports the expectations of outbound Turkish tourists on Malaysia as an MFT destination, and the Turkish tourists' attitude and behavioural intention towards MFT destinations are also deliberated.

Tourist behaviour

In successful destination marketing, understanding the expectations of tourists is essential to comprehend what factors affect their satisfaction levels during and after their holiday period. Tourist motivation can be conceptualised as the product of expectancy and valence (Hsu et al., 2010). Besides, motivation can be influenced by manipulating cues of an individual's expectation concerning the consequences of their action and the incentive value of the outcomes produced by the reaction (Hsu et al., 2010). It represents the psychological need to pursue a goal state. Interestingly, when tourists have high expectations, they are more willing to search for tour information, acquire knowledge regarding the destination culture and influence their travel motivation (Cahyanto et al., 2016; Money & Crotts, 2003).

Travel motivation has gained considerable attention from tourism academia since the 1960s to better understand and predict factors that influence travel decision-making (Hsu et al., 2010; Moutinho, 1987; Pearce, 2012; Wong et al., 2013). Vroom's (1964) expectancy model is prominent in explaining motivation, and several other motivation-based theories or models have been developed, including the push-pull and escape-seeking elements. Notably, the push and pull theory provides an essential theoretical framework to understand tourist behaviour (Moutinho, 1987; Yoon & Uysal, 2005). According to Yoon and Uysal (2005), tourist travel is mainly driven by two motivational aspects: push factors and pull factors.

The push factors refer to the psychological force influencing tourist choices about 'excitement' or 'relaxation'. People are driven by internal desires, such as personal escape, psychological or physical health, thrill and adventure, and social interactions (Moutinho, 1987). On the other hand, tourist behaviours are also pulled by external resources, such as natural or artificial attractions that a destination may possess (Moutinho, 1987). The pull factors include the external forces of the destination attributes, for example, the destination's environment or the country's culture. Basically, push forces are associated with 'considering whether to go' (i.e., the desire to travel), while the pull forces are associated with the decision of 'where to go' (i.e., the choice of destination) (Hsu et al., 2010).

Tourist attitude is a critical construct in understanding travel motivation and behaviour (Hsu et al., 2010). Ajzen and Fishbein (1977) suggest that motivation precedes attitude, and the former may influence the latter. Further, Hsu et al. (2010) propose that a tourist's attitude toward an object is determined by their felt needs and value system, highlighting the relationship between motivation and attitude. Tourist attitude or tourist behaviour frequently represent customers' conative loyalty. Since then, tourist loyalty has been treated as a crucial component for a destination's long-term viability or sustainability (Velázquez et al., 2011; Zhang et al., 2014). Measuring tourist loyalty can provide a better understanding of tourist retention (Eid, 2015). Furthermore, satisfied and loyal tourists are more likely to recommend friends, relatives or other potential visitors to a destination by acting as free word-of-mouth (WOM) advertising agents (Velázquez et al., 2011).

Muslim-friendly tourism (MFT)

Although only limited information is available on MFT characteristics, few studies try to define MFT, its practices and its various aspects in reference to the hospitality and tourism industry (see also Chapters 2 and 3). As per Jafari and Scott's (2014) and Mohsin et al's (2016) arguments, certain realities about Islam provide essential understandings of the rapid demands by the customers when it comes to the MFT market. For instance, while travelling to Muslim and non-Muslim majority destinations, Muslim travellers still practice their religion. Based on a study by Olya and Al-Ansi (2018) and Rasul (2019), the concepts of Halal and Haram have led Muslim travellers to be aware of the types of risks in using non-Halal products and services. Since the tourism and hospitality industry generally includes different types of products and services, i.e., food and beverages, accommodation, transportation and places and facilities of attractions, many non-Muslim stakeholders and policymakers may struggle to understand how to effectively start engaging with the Muslim market (Han et al., 2018).

Islamic travelling activities should reflect Shari'a law: mainly on the availability of Halal food, prayer rooms and the spa and gym facilities being separated between male and female (Jafari & Scott, 2014). Stephenson (2014) has classified the tangible and intangible forms of MFT elements. These elements include the principles of Halal tourism that affect the services available in the hospitality industry. In addition, it involves marketing, promotions, and other facilities available for the public, such as no gambling and casinos on the premises or even nightclubs. Therefore, the MFT elements include a destination's social environment, Muslim-friendly facilities, service quality and local behaviour (COMCEC, 2016).

Muslims' lives revolve around the concept of Halal and Haram. Halal means it is permissible for consumption by the Syariah law (Riaz & Chaundry, 2004; Hall & Prayag, 2020). Notably, consuming Halal foods cannot be separated from a part of a Muslim's life (El-Gohary, 2016; Riaz & Chaundry, 2004;

Hall & Prayag, 2020). Thus, it is essential to offer and make available Halal food and beverages. Halal certification is also vital to help ensure that food is safe to be consumed and gain Muslim consumers' trust (Hall & Prayag, 2020). According to Agriculture and Agri-Food Canada (2011), in non-Muslim majority countries, the concept of Halal foods remains overlooked. However, improvements in transportation and communication technologies and the globalisation of markets, trade and labour have all contributed to the supply of Halal food worldwide (Cwiertka & Walraven, 2002).

Looking at the demand side, the Muslim-friendly tourist seeks tourism and hospitality products and services that comply with Islamic Shari'a law. Muslim-friendly tourists prefer to visit alcohol- and gambling-free environments, in order to control sexual permissiveness and adhere to the Islamic dress code (Rasheed, 2018). To cater to the MFT market, such compliance plays an important role to attract Muslim visitors. Weidenfeld (2006) found that the tourism providers need to cater to Muslim tourists' elementary religious needs such as the prayer room, prayer mats and Halal foods. In addition, the provision of locations of mosques/prayer facilities at key tourist areas such as the tourist information centers, airports, hotels and parks would satisfy the Muslim tourists. Providing specific worship facilities for Muslim tourists may also encourage them to revisit a particular destination. Hence, destinations need to understand the needs and wants of the Muslim travellers if they intend to offer services to them (El-Gohary, 2016; Han & Hyun, 2017;Hall & Prayag, 2020).

The MFT element also includes Muslim tourists experience and satisfaction of tourism products and services (Han & Hyun, 2017; Rahman, 2014). MFT services and products have become necessary in places (e.g., airports, hotels, restaurants), and Muslim travellers expect to access these facilities in the countries they visit (Rahman et al., 2019). Liu et al. (2018) proposed that MFT destinations should offer Halal services (such as Halal food and beverages, sex-segregated swimming pools) and comfortable places for Muslims to perform their necessary religious activities.

The attitudes of the locals towards Muslim tourists also warrant attention (Henderson, 2016) as they help generate a positive destination image by creating positive word-of-mouth. As a preparation to entertain the Muslim market, MFT stakeholders (locals and hospitality staff) also need to understand MFT practices. Besides training, it is also commonplace for the MFT stakeholders (e.g., restaurants and hotels) to employ Muslim employees to ensure compliance (Liu et al., 2018). This practice is further supported by Mohsin et al. (2016), as the researchers claimed that Muslim tourists will feel more comfortable with people that follow the Islamic law in diet, attire and other customs.

Methodology

This chapter reports the extent to which Turkish tourists' motivation and expectation may affect their travel attitude and behaviour. The survey was developed for two different segments: visiting and non-visiting Turkish tourists. The survey examines Turkish tourists' demographic profile, expectation, motivational factors and attitude. The survey instruments were adapted from multiple studies (Cahyanto et al., 2016; Hsu et al., 2010; Wong et al., 2013; Zhang et al., 2014). The survey was translated to Turkish tourists by language professionals. A pilot survey was undertaken to ensure its validity and reliability. Based on the purposive sampling methodology, 409 responses were collected with 253 first time/repeat Turkish visitors (collected in Malaysia) and 156 Turkey citizens (non-visitor) collected in Istanbul.

Findings

Two hundred and fifty-three visiting Turkish tourists were interviewed. The majority of the respondents claimed that they are return visitors (64.8 percent) while 35.2 percent of them visited Malaysia for the first time. Most Turkish visitors spent less than two weeks in the country (96.8 percent), with 44.3 percent of them visiting Malaysia for leisure, while 22.3 percent were there because of the available heritage and cultural products. Of Turkish tourists interviewed, 38.3 percent claimed they visited Malaysia because it is a Muslim country. Nineteen percent were interested in natural beauty. Most of them opted to stay at 4- and 5-star hotels (84.6 percent). Social media was their main source of information (35.6 percent), while the availability of the Tourism Office in Esentepe, Istanbul, also boosted their motivation to visit Malaysia (26.5 percent).

This chapter assesses Turkish tourists' perception of Malaysia MFT destination attributes. They were asked about their cognitive (thinking) and affective (feeling) perceived value of Malaysia as an MFT destination based on the six-point Likert scales (Table 5.1). Most Turkish tourists possessed favourable cognitive and affective perceived behaviour towards Malaysia as an MFT

Table 5.1 Turkish tourists' perception of Malaysia as an MFT destination

	Cognitive evaluation	Mean	S.D.
1	Malaysia offers good value for the price.	5.32	.844
2	Malaysia MFT products and services provide a good deal compared to others.	5.37	.782
3	Malaysia MFT offers high-quality accommodation.	5.14	.710
4	Malaysia MFT offers plenty of Muslim facilities and services.	5.34	.723
5	Malaysia MFT offers high-quality personal safety and security.	5.35	.890
6	My overall image of Malaysia MFT products and services is positive.	5.18	.768
	Affective evaluation	**Mean**	**S.D.**
1	I like Malaysia MFT products and services more than other destinations.	5.18	.818
2	I am happy about my decision to visit Malaysia because of the availability of MFT products.	5.25	.722
3	I love travelling to Malaysia because of the availability of Muslim-friendly tourism products.	5.24	.790
4	The Islamic image of Malaysia MFT is consistent with my self-image.	5.17	.723
5	My Muslim friends thought highly of me when I visited Malaysia.	5.10	.890
6	Malaysia fits with my Muslim personality.	5.19	.765

destination. They have a positive image of Malaysia as an MFT destination and claimed it suits their Muslim personality.

Perception of Malaysia's MFT attributes were also appraised (Table 5.2). The MFT destination attributes assessed were the Muslim-friendly social environment, tourism facilities, Halal food and beverage and hotel services. From the descriptive analysis, Turkish tourists are satisfied with the Malaysian MFT hotel services

Table 5.2 Turkish tourists' perception of Malaysia MFT attributes

	MFT social environment	Mean	S.D.
1	The design and decoration of tourist places are Halal-friendly (e.g., paintings, pictures, architecture).	5.09	.828
2	The atmospherics of tourist places comply with Islamic rules.	4.95	.782
3	The Halal-friendly social environment of tourist places is comforting.	4.94	.777
4	My overall experiences with Halal-friendly social environments in tourist places are good.	4.89	.767
5	The social environment of tourist places is free of Haram items (e.g., nightclubs, red-light districts).	4.94	.720
6	The social environment of tourist places is safe and clean for Muslim travellers.	4.93	.723
7	At tourist sites, I enjoy a Halal-friendly social environment.	5.00	.890
	MFT facilities		
1	It is convenient to access a prayer room everywhere around tourist attractions.	4.90	.822
2	There is proper ablution (*wudu'*) facilities at tourism sites and public places.	4.88	.825
3	Separate prayer room facilities are offered to men/women in tourist places.	5.11	.782
4	Separate male and female Halal facilities are offered in tourist sites (e.g. spas, swimming pools, gyms).	4.93	.757
	Halal food and beverage		
1	Halal food outlets/restaurants in tourist sites display a Halal logo.	4.79	.794
2	No alcoholic drinks served in Halal restaurants.	5.00	.790
3	Halal food and beverage offered in tourist sites/places were clean, safe, and hygienic.	5.01	.723
4	Halal food providers in tourist sites are accredited with Halal certification.	4.76	.816
5	Availability of Halal food attracted me to visit tourist places.	4.92	.768
	MFT hotel services		
1	The hotel provides Halal food.	5.20	.922
2	Hotel room toilets are fitted with a hand shower bidet and Halal amenities products.	5.38	.843
3	The prayer room is available in the hotel.	5.35	.782
4	The hotel provides a dedicated place for prayer.	5.25	.818
5	Hotel local staff is well aware of Halal products and services.	5.30	.782
6	Hotel staff recognise and appreciate both Muslim and non-Muslim guests.	5.31	.790
7	In general, the Hotel staff had a good understanding of the Islamic and Halal rules.	5.22	.723

($M = 5.29$), probably due to their favourable selection of hotels (4- and 5-star hotels). Besides, the Malaysian social environment, facilities and Halal food and beverage availability were also other MFT attributes that they are satisfied with.

Turkish non-visiting tourists

One hundred and fifty-six Turkish non-visiting tourists participated in the survey. The female respondents accounted for 54 percent of the sample. The majority of respondents (68 percent) were aged between 26 and 49 years old. The majority of the respondents were married (65 percent) and just over half had a university degree or diploma (51 percent). Most of them earn between ฿1,001 to ฿10,000 per month (72 percent).

Table 5.3 reports Turkish non-visiting tourists' ($N = 156$) internal and external travel motivational factors. Focusing on the push attributes, looking for new experiences appeared to be the most crucial motive, triggering them to travel overseas. The self-exploration factor comprised the attributes relating to the desire to undertake travel activities that allow them to learn about a new culture, encounter the locals, learn their ways of life and meet with new people at the visited destination. Concerning the pull motivating factors, this study revealed various external factors. Accommodation quality and safety attributes together with natural attractions and value for money destinations are significant pull factors along with shopping and entertainment.

Table 5.4 reports on Turkish non-visiting tourists' perception of MFT attributes: brand awareness, quality, image and value. Seventeen items were adopted for this section. It appears that Turkish non-visiting tourists are aware of the MFT brand and brand quality. However, despite their awareness, they value MFT lowly and do not favour the MFT image. The Turkish non-visiting tourists also seem to have low expectations and perceptions of what MFT destinations have to offer.

Practical implications

This chapter focuses on the concept of MFT and aims to highlight the importance of MFT brand awareness, brand image, brand quality and brand value in

Table 5.3 Turkish tourists' travel motivational factors

Push Factors	Pull Factors
Learning a new culture	Accommodation facilities
Meeting with new people	Safety and security
Enjoying time with family	Familiar food
Enjoying life	Value for money
Visiting places outside Turkey	Natural attractions
Escape from routine	Tourist information centre
	Shopping facilities
	Entertainment

Table 5.4 Turkish non-visiting tourists' perception of Muslim-friendly tourism attributes

MFT brand awareness	Mean	S.D.
1 I have heard a lot of advertising promoting Muslim-friendly tourism.	4.12	.818
2 I have heard people talking about Muslim-friendly tourism.	4.15	.790
3 Muslim-friendly tourism is very famous among Turkish people.	4.17	.723
4 Muslim-friendly tourism destination has a positive reputation among Turkish people.	2.21	.833
MFT brand quality		
1 Muslim-friendly tourism offers high-quality accommodation.	3.21	.822
2 Muslim-friendly tourism offers plenty of Muslim facilities and services.	4.22	.790
3 Muslim-friendly tourism offers high-quality personal safety.	2.23	.723
MFT brand image		
1 Visiting Muslim-friendly tourism destinations reflects my Muslim personality.	2.12	.775
2 The image of a Muslim-friendly tourism destination is consistent with my own self-image.	2.13	.844
3 My friends would think highly of me if I visited a Muslim-friendly tourism destination.	2.17	.732
4 Muslim-friendly tourism fits with my personality.	2.22	.835
MFT brand value		
1 I will get much more than my money's worth by visiting a Muslim-friendly tourism destination.	2.19	.815
2 The costs of visiting Muslim-friendly tourism destinations are a bargain relative to the benefits I receive.	2.14	.723
3 Visiting Muslim-friendly tourism destinations is good value for money.	2.24	.711

explaining Turkish tourist behaviour. It also compares visiting and non-visiting Turkish tourist perceptions of MFT. Turkish tourists are not generic and mass travellers. Instead, they are experiential travellers and appear open to new ideas and flexible in decision-making. They are more at ease with having limited access to Halal facilities, but they look for destinations that adhere to their high standards and values.

From the perspective of the tourist market, this chapter focussed mainly on their personal motivation for travelling. Turkish and Middle-Eastern tourist behaviour appears considerably different. The latter prefer destinations that respect their cultural sensitivities, while the former want to explore the new and modern culture. Turkish visitors are motivated to visit Malaysia for the islands, nature and beauty, modest Islamic culture and Halal branded restaurants. All aspects of MFT attributes (destination's social environment, facilities, Halal food and beverages, service quality and local behaviour) are essential and need to be appropriately and timely delivered to satisfy tourists.

In contrast, the majority of non-visiting Turkish tourists seem willing and interested in MFT. However, they remain concerned with unattractive MFT products and services, especially their image and value. Perhaps, the terms Halal and Shari'a strike negative images and perceptions. Contrary to expectations, the MFT brand value and image are relatively low among Turkish tourists. Hence, rather than promoting Islamic tourism, destination marketers could highlight the Muslim-friendly brand as it is deemed much more friendly and acceptable. Nonetheless, these Turkish tourists are not bothered with MFT image and value, and tourism operators should be mindful of offering Islamic products.

Conclusion

This chapter has both academic and managerial importance. First, it explores Turkish visiting and non-visiting tourists' behaviour towards MFT destinations, products and services. This chapter is also one of the first to discuss the perceived value of MFT attributes from the visiting and non-visiting tourists' perspectives. Such insights should be of value to tourism authorities, industries and academics in Muslim and non-Muslim majority destinations.

Destination marketers need to decide whether Turkish travellers are the right MFT market for them, and there is a need to focus on the Muslim travellers' religious considerations based on different MFT market segments and motivations. Multiple brands and concepts were used to depict MFT. Concepts such as Halal tourism and Shariah compliance are popular terms. However, the MFT brand currently is widely used by various Muslim and non-Muslim destinations worldwide, thus potentially confusing the travel market in terms of the products on offer.

References

Agriculture and Agri-Food Canada. (2011). *Global Halal food market.* www.ats.agr.gc.ca/inter/4352-eng.pdf

Ajzen, I., & Fishbein, M. (1977). Attitude-behavior relations: A theoretical analysis and review of empirical research. *Psychological Bulletin, 84*(5), 888–918. https://doi.org/10.1037/0033-2909.84.5.888

Akay, G. H., Cifter, A., & Teke, O. (2017). Turkish tourism, exchange rates and income. *Tourism Economics, 23*(1), 66–77. https://doi.org/10.5367/te.2015.0497

Baser, G. (2018). Turkey's tourist profile: A document analysis for future implications. *Journal of Tourism and Hospitality Management, 6*(5), 222–239. https://doi.org/10.17265/2328-2169/2018.10.002

Cahyanto, I., Pennington-Gray, L., Thapa, B., Srinivasan, S., Villegas, J., Matyas, C., & Kiousis, S. (2016). Predicting information seeking regarding hurricane evacuation in the destination. *Tourism Management, 52*, 264–275. https://doi.org/10.1016/j.tourman.2015.06.014

COMCEC. (2016). *Muslim-friendly tourism: Understanding the demand and supply sides in the OIC member countries.* www.comcec.org/en/wp-content/uploads/2016/11/8-TUR-AR.pdf

Cwiertka, K., & Walraven, B. (Eds.). (2002). *Asian food: The global and the local.* Curzon Press.

Dogru, T., & Sirakaya-Turk, E. (2018). Modeling Turkish outbound tourism demand using a dynamic panel data approach. *Tourism and Hospitality Research, 18*(4), 411–414. https://doi.org/10.1177/1467358416663822

Eid, R. (2015). Integrating Muslim customer perceived value, satisfaction, loyalty and retention in the tourism industry: An empirical study. *International Journal of Tourism Research*, *17*(3), 249–260. https://doi.org/10.1002/jtr.1982

El-Gohary, H. (2016). Halal tourism, is it really Halal? *Tourism Management Perspectives*, *19*, 124–130. https://doi.org/10.1016/j.tmp.2015.12.013

Hall, C. M., & Prayag, G. (Eds.). (2020). *The Routledge handbook of halal hospitality and Islamic tourism*. Routledge.

Han, H., Al-Ansi, A., Olya, H., & Kim, W. (2018). Exploring halal-friendly destination attributes in South Korea: Perceptions and behaviors of Muslim travelers towards a non-Muslim destination. *Tourism Management*, *17*, 151–164. https://doi.org/10.1016/j.tourman.2018.10.010

Han, H., & Hyun, S. S. (2017). Impact of hotel-restaurant image and quality of physical environment, service, and food on satisfaction and intention. *International Journal of Hospitality Management*, *63*, 82–92. https://doi.org/10.1016/j.ijhm.2017.03.006

Hassan, M. G., Razalli, M. R., & Musa, U. F. (2018). A review of the challenges and prospects for Islamic tourism policies in Malaysia. *The Journal of Social Sciences Research*, *6*, 59–63. http://doi.org/10.32861/jssr.spi6.59.63

Henderson, J. C. (2016). Muslim travellers, tourism industry responses and the case of Japan. *Tourism Recreation Research*, *41*(3), 339–347. https://doi.org/10.1080/02508281.2016.12 15090

Hsu, C. H. C., Cai, L. A., & Li, M. (2010). Expectation, motivation, and attitude: A tourist behavioral model. *Journal of Travel Research*, *49*(3), 282–296. https://doi.org/10.1177/0047287509349266

Ibrahim, Z., Zahari, M. S., Sulaiman, M., Othman, Z., & Jusoff, K. (2009). Travelling pattern and preferences of the Arab tourists in Malaysian hotels. *International Journal of Business and Management*, *4*(7), 3–9.

Jafari, J., & Scott, N. (2014). Muslim world and its tourisms. *Annals of Tourism Research*, *44*, 1–19. https://doi.org/10.1016/j.annals.2013.08.011

Karadeniz, O. (2018). A general overview of Turkish tourism. *Journal of Human Sciences*, *15*(3), 1746–1755.

Katircioglu, S., Katircioğlu, S., & Altinay, M. (2018). Interactions between tourism and financial sector development: Evidence from Turkey. *The Service Industries Journal*, *38*(9–10), 519–542. https://doi.org/10.1080/02642069.2017.1406479

Kultur. (2019). *Tourism statistics*. www.kultur.gov.tr/EN-153017/tourism-statistics.html

Liu, Y. C., Li, I. J., Yen, S. Y., & Sher, P. J. (2018). What makes Muslim friendly tourism? An empirical study on destination image, tourist attitude and travel intention. *Advances in Management and Applied Economics*, *8*(5), 27–43.

Malay Mail. (2014, September 5). Malaysia set to be destination of choice for Turkish travellers, says Tourism Minister. *Life, Malay Mail*. www.malaymail.com/news/life/2014/09/05/msia-poised-to-be-destination-of-choice-among-turkish-travellers-mohamed-na/740191

Mohsin, A., Ramli, N., & Alkhulayfi, B. (2016). Halal tourism: Emerging opportunities. *Tourism Management Perspectives*, *19*, 137–143. https://doi.org/10.1016/j.tmp.2015.12.010

Money, R. B., & Crotts, J. C. (2003). The effect of uncertainty avoidance on information search, planning, and purchases of international travel vacations. *Tourism Management*, *24*(2), 191–202. https://doi.org/10.1016/S0261-5177(02)00057-2

Moutinho, L. (1987). Consumer behaviour in tourism. *European Journal of Marketing*, *21*(10), 5–44. https://doi.org/10.1108/EUM0000000004718

Olya, H. G., & Al-ansi, A. (2018). Risk assessment of Halal products and services: Implication for tourism industry. *Tourism Management*, *65*, 279–291. https://doi.org/10.1016/j.tourman.2017.10.015

Ozdipciner, N. S., Li, X., & Uysal, M. (2010). An examination of purchase decision-making criteria: A case of Turkey as a destination. *Journal of Hospitality Marketing & Management*, *19*(5), 514–527. https://doi.org/10.1080/19368623.2010.482850

Pearce, P. (2012). *The Ulysses factor: Evaluating visitors in tourist settings*. Springer Science & Business Media.

Pew Research Center. (2017). *Europe's growing Muslim population*. www.pewforum.org/2017/11/29/europes-growing-muslim-population/

Prayag, G., & Ryan, C. (2011). The relationship between the 'push' and 'pull' factors of a tourist destination: The role of nationality – an analytical qualitative research approach. *Current Issues in Tourism*, *14*(2), 121–143.

Rahman, M. K. (2014). Motivating factors of Islamic tourist's destination loyalty: An empirical investigation in Malaysia. *Journal of Tourism and Hospitality Management*, *2*(1), 63–77.

Rahman, M. K., Rana, M. S., Hoque, M. N., & Rahman, M. K. (2019). Brand perception of Halal tourism services and satisfaction: The mediating role of tourists' attitudes. *International Journal of Tourism Sciences*, *19*(1), 18–37. https://doi.org/10.1080/15980634.2019.1592987

Rasheed, S. (2018). Top 10 Muslim-friendly non-OIC-destinations. *HalalTrip*. www.Halaltrip.com/other/blog/10-muslim-friendly-non-oic-countries/

Rasul, T. (2019). The trends, opportunities and challenges of halal tourism: A systematic literature review. *Tourism Recreation Research*, *44*(4), 434–450. https://doi.org/10.1080/02508281.2019.1599532

Riaz, M. N., & Chaundry, M. M. (2004). *Halal food production*. CRC Press LLC.

Salleh, N. H. M., Othman, R., Noor, A. H. S. M., & Hasim, M. S. (2010). Malaysian tourism demand from the Middle East market: A preliminary analysis. *International Journal of West Asian Studies*, *2*(1), 37–52. https://doi.org/10.5895/ijwas.2010.03

Seyfi, S., & Hall, C. M. (2019). Deciphering Islamic theocracy and tourism: Conceptualization, context, and complexities. *International Journal of Tourism Research*, *21*(6), 735–746. https://doi.org/10.1002/jtr.2300

Shafaei, F., & Mohamed, B. (2017). Malaysia's branding as an Islamic tourism hub: An assessment. *Geografia-Malaysian Journal of Society and Space*, *11*(1), 97–106.

Stephenson, M. L. (2014). Deciphering 'Islamic hospitality': Developments, challenges and opportunities. *Tourism Management*, *40*, 155–164. https://doi.org/10.1016/j.tourman.2013.05.002

Travel News Digest. (2019, October 28). Malaysia retains the top position in the Global Muslim Travel Index 2019. *Travel News Digest*. www.mhtc.org.my/mhtc/2019/10/28/malaysia-retains-the-top-position-in-the-global-muslim-travel-index-2019/

Velázquez, B. M., Saura, I. G., & Molina, M. E. R. (2011). Conceptualising and measuring loyalty: Towards a conceptual model of tourist loyalty antecedents. *Journal of Vacation Marketing*, *17*(1), 65–81. https://doi.org/10.1177/1356766710391450

Vroom, V. H. (1964). *Work and motivation*. Wiley.

Weidenfeld, A. (2006). Religious needs in the hospitality industry. *Tourism and Hospitality Research*, *6*(2), 143–159. https://doi.org/10.1057/palgrave.thr.6040052

West, C. (2014, July 29). *Is there a future for Malaysia Airlines after flights MH370 and MH17? The Guardian*. www.theguardian.com/world/2014/jul/29/is-there-a-future-for-malaysia-airlines

Wong, M. M. C., Cheung, R., & Wan, C. (2013). A study on traveler expectation, motivation and attitude. *Contemporary Management Research*, *9*(2), 169–186. https://doi.org/10.7903/cmr.11023

Yoon, Y., & Uysal, M. (2005). An examination of the effects of motivation and satisfaction on destination loyalty: A structural model. *Tourism Management*, *26*(1), 45–56. https://doi.org/10.1016/j.tourman.2003.08.016

Yuan, S., & McDonald, C. (1990). Motivational determinates of international pleasure time. *Journal of Travel Research, 29*(1), 42–44. https://doi.org/10.1177/004728759002900109

Yusoff, F. M., Abdullah, F. S. C., & Alam, S. (2010). What really matters when choosing a hotel? The case of Middle East tourists in Kuala Lumpur, Malaysia. *Journal of Tourism, Hospitality and Culinary Arts, 2*(3), 53–62.

Zamani-Farahani, H., & Eid, R. (2016). Muslim world: A study of tourism & pilgrimage among OIC Member States. *Tourism Management Perspectives, 19*, 144–149. https://doi.org/10.1016/j.tmp.2015.12.009

Zhang, H., Fu, X., Cai, L. A., & Lu, L. (2014). Destination image and tourist loyalty: A meta-analysis. *Tourism Management, 40*, 213–223. https://doi.org/10.1016/j.tourman.2013.06.006

6 Tourism motives, tourism experience value and cultural change

A focus on Egyptian tourists

Omneya Mokhtar Yacout

Introduction

Understanding tourist behaviour and the reasons behind their travel choices have been major concerns of practitioners and academics for decades. Push and pull factors reflecting the demand and supply sides of tourism have been heavily investigated (e.g., Crompton, 1979). On one hand, push factors are socio-psychological motivations that encourage a person to travel; on the other, pull factors attract a person to a specific destination (Oh et al., 1995). While the former relates to travelers' needs and wants, the latter reflects the features, attractions and attributes of the destination itself.

Although push and pull factors have dominated the tourism literature for years, many researchers have tried to provide an understanding of the model by revisiting both push and pull factors. Concerning pull factors, destination attributes were traditionally studied as pull factors. Predictors of perceived value, identified in the literature, were mainly cognitive, and affective–hedonic factors have more often been ignored in research (Prebensen et al., 2013). This view was challenged as tourists report tangible direct functional benefits, as well as more abstract psychological and social benefits in their travel experiences (Klenosky, 2002). As such, experience value can be affective and cognitive, social and personal and active and reactive (Gallarza & Gil-Saura, 2006). Only a few studies have examined experience value with its different dimensions, however (e.g., Prebensen et al., 2013). Furthermore, the profiles of experiential users have not received enough attention from researchers (Wei & Tasci, 2017).

On the push side, research examining tourism motivation have also developed from efforts to identify travel motivations (e.g., Beard & Ragheb, 1983; Dann, 1977; Tasci & Ko, 2017) to research which attempts to understand factors explaining demographic differences in tourist motivations (e.g., Pearce, 1988; Pearce & Lee, 2005) to research concerned with examining tourism motivation as a reflection of identity development, maintenance or modification (Falk, 2006, 2009; Oyserman, 2009). Falk (2006) argues that identity attributes can be classified into 'big I identities' reflecting core identity attributes such as gender and ethnicity and 'small i identities' reflecting one's sense of being a member of a family or a valued employee. Falk (2006) notes that core

DOI: 10.4324/9781003036296-8

identity attributes have the potential to affect lower-order identity attributes and that the latter may be more prevalent in day-to-day activities or short visits such as visiting zoos and museums. Most of the identity-based motivation research was conducted in the context of short visits or day-to-day activities. Investigating it in a tourism context will enable a better understanding of identity as a primary source of motivation.

This research aims to identify motivation-based segments of Egyptian tourists and the differences in tourism experience value. Differences among segments concerning demographics will be also examined. The findings of this research can help academics and practitioners to understand the relationship between motivation and experience value, which is an under-investigated area of research inquiry (Pesonen, 2012; Prebensen et al., 2013). The research also contributes to the research in the field of tourism motivations by examining these motivations in a different culture. Prentice (2004) calls for greater attention to cultural variations in studying holiday motivations. Egypt, among other countries in the Middle East, has witnessed social and cultural changes with a strong impact on tourist motivations and behaviors. Such findings can help in understanding the tourism motivations of tourists where cultural and social changes have taken place. For practitioners, understanding tourist motivations is of great importance in framing appropriate product design and marketing (Prentice, 2004). Such understanding enhances awareness of customer needs, thus helps destination marketing organizations (DMOs) to offer more customized services, create more memorable customer experiences and obtain more repeat business (Huang & Hsu, 2009).

This chapter first presents a review of the literature related to experience value, motivation and the studies examining the relationship between them. The research methodology is then discussed followed by research findings, discussion and implications.

Literature review

Tourism motivation

Motivation is defined as the sum of biological and cultural forces that control behavior (Pearce, 2011). In the field of travel motivation, three main streams appear. The first stream attempted to answer the question 'what are the travel motivations?' Travel motivation was examined as one of the push variables that affect tourist behavior (Dann, 1977). Beard and Ragheb's (1983) *Leisure Motivation Scale* and Tasci and Ko's (2017) *general travel needs* belong to this stream of research.

The second stream focused on answering the question 'what factors explain differences in tourist motivations?' This stream included studies examining demographic differences, including Pearce's (1988) *Travel Career Ladder (TCL)*, and Pearce and Lee's (2005) *Travel Career Pattern (TCP)*. The third stream was concerned with answering the question of 'How an individual identity shapes his travel motivation'. This stream mainly relies on the work of Falk (2006, 2009) and Oyserman (2009) where both developed identity-based motivation models.

The first stream attempted to identify different tourism motivations. Tourist motivation is conceptualized as one of the push factors that affect tourist decisions. Crompton (1979) argues that tourist motives include escape, self-exploration and evaluation, relaxation, prestige, regression, enhancement of kinship relationships, facilitation of social interaction, novelty and education. Other motives are also identified in the literature such as relaxation (Uysal et al., 1996; Yoo et al., 2018), prestige (Figler et al., 1992; Uysal et al., 1996), health and fitness (Uysal et al., 1996), scenery and exotic experience (Yoo et al., 2018), adventure (Uysal et al., 1996), anomie/authenticity-seeking (Figler et al., 1992), wanderlust/exploring the unknown (Figler et al., 1992), feeling independent, study/work and vogue (Cavagnaro & Staffieri, 2015), cultural value and family togetherness (Bogari et al., 2004), meeting different people (Wong et al., 2018), culture (Yoo et al., 2018), self-actualization (Yoo et al., 2018), physical refreshment (Yoo et al., 2018) and pleasure (Yoo et al., 2018).

Beard and Ragheb (1983) developed the *Leisure Motivation Scale*, which includes an intellectual motive, a social motive, a competence-mastery motive and a stimulus avoidance motive reflecting escape and relaxation. Recently, Tasci and Ko (2017) have developed a parsimonious tool to measure general travel needs. The *Travel Needs Scale (TNS)* is comprised of self-actualization, social affiliation, arousal and escape.

The second stream of research examined factors that might explain differences in tourist motivations. Demographic variables and previous travel experience have been heavily investigated. Meng and Uysal (2008) report that female respondents had higher mean scores across all the motivation factors than did male respondents. However, the differences were not statistically significant at the 0.05 probability. Similarly, Jensen (2011) observes that females had higher ratings for four of the six motivational factors ('exploration', 'escape/relaxation', 'social relationship with family/friends' and 'appreciating famous sites/ heritages') than did their male counterparts. Furthermore, older travellers placed less importance on social relationships with family/friends and more emphasis on natural resources. Travellers with higher income and educational levels place more importance on 'natural resources' compared to those who are less educated and have lower income tourism. Jensen's (2011) findings also highlight the interaction among various demographic characteristics as he reports that young male travellers rate the 'prestige/impression' factor higher than females.

Pearce's (1988) *Travel Career Ladder (TCL)* views needs of travellers as a hierarchy, with the relaxation needs being at the lowest level, followed in order by safety/security needs, relationship needs, self-esteem and development needs and, finally, at the highest level, fulfillment needs. Travellers do not have only one level of travel motivation; instead, one set of needs in the ladder levels may be dominant. Later, Pearce and Lee (2005) developed the *Travel Career*

Pattern (TCP) where patterns and combinations of multiple motives are affected by previous travel experience and age. While self-development motivation is prevalent among people with high experience; stimulation, personal development, self-actualization, security, nostalgia, romance and recognition prevail among low experience travellers.

The second stream of research provides valuable insights regarding differences in tourism motivation among various demographic variables. It is worth noting that such differences are not only reflected in the type of travel motivation but also in its strength. Generally, females reported higher ratings than males for most of the tourism motivations examined (Jensen, 2011; Uysal et al., 1996; Meng & Uysal, 2008).

The third stream of research represents further development as it attempts to explain why individuals have different identities by relating it to an individual's identity. It integrates two research fields, identity and motivation. In this respect, the work of Oyserman (2009), and Falk (2006, 2009) shed some light on a deeper meaning of motivation. Oyserman (2009, 2015, 2019) and Oyserman and James (2011) argue that people prefer to act in ways that feel congruent with their identities whether personal or social. Garner et al. (2016) support this idea as they propose that visitors' motivations are often congruent with current and future self-conceptualizations. Oyserman (2009) note that these identities could be broad (such as gender or ethnicity) or narrow (such as a professor job). According to Oyserman (2009), broader identities (such as gender) are generally more psychologically salient and more likely to be situationally cued than others.

Meanwhile, Falk (2006) suggested that motivation is a complex sociological and psychological construct. Similar to Oyserman (2009), Falk (2006) notes that a sense of identity is a major source of motivation. Other sources include knowledge, experience, social relationships and expectations, the social and cultural meaning people attribute to the institution and personal interests.

Falk's (2009) study of museums distinguished between two sets of identity attributes that are likely to affect motivation. The first set includes what Falk (2009) called 'core identity' attributes or the 'big I identities'. These include gender, cultural or ethnic identity or one's core values, such as religious or sexual identity. The second set includes lower-order identities that have a great impact on day-to-day decision-making. They may include one's sense of being a member of a family, a good friend or even a valued employee. The 'little i identities' affect decisions such as going to a theme park. Later, Bond and Falk (2013) noted that 'big I identities' have the potential to affect the 'little i identities'.

Bond and Falk (2013) argued that tourism is a way through which an individual develops, maintains or reconfirms aspects of identity. Their model takes into consideration the multiplicity of roles and identities an individual may have throughout their life and the fact that some roles are stable while others are ephemeral. Bond and Falk (2013) also note that a change in the physical or social environment might lead to a reconstruction of identity. The identity-based model of motivation thus provides answers to the questions of 'why' individuals visit certain destinations, 'what' activities they make and 'how' they perceive the benefits that result from the tourism experience (Bond & Falk, 2013).

Falk (2009, p. 73) argued that museum visitor research emphasizing 'big I identities' such as demographic characteristics should be replaced with an emphasis on 'little i identities' reflected in behavioral and self-reported characteristics. Empirically, Falk (2006) reported five clusters of visitors: explorers; facilitators; professional hobbyists; experience seekers and spiritual pilgrims. Later, Falk (2009) developed the visitor's identity-related visit motivations, the series of specific reasons that visitors use to justify as well as organize their visit and ultimately use to make sense of their museum experience. However, Dawson and Jensen (2011) criticized Falk (2006) for deemphasizing demographics and for what they called a 'reductionist' approach to handle the visitor experience. They proposed combining demographic variables with other aspects of identity.

Relationship between tourism motivation and tourism experience value

Zeithaml (1988) defines customer perceived value as the consumer's overall assessment of the utility of a product based on the perceptions of what is received and what is given. These uni-dimensional customer value conceptualizations are simple, but they do not reflect the complexity of consumers' perceptions of value, which combines intangible, intrinsic and emotional aspects (Sánchez-Fernández & Iniesta-Bonillo, 2007). Similarly, Gallarza and Gil-Saura (2006) emphasize the importance of affective dimensions of the perceived value of destinations. Sheth et al. (1991) have developed a multidimensional conceptualization of consumption values. These values include the functional value that reflects utilitarian or physical performance, the emotional value reflecting product ability of the product or service to arouse feelings or affective states, the social value that is acquired from an alternative's association with a social group, the epistemic value obtained when the product arouses curiosity, provides novelty and/or satisfies a desire for knowledge and conditional value that occurs when there is a specific set of circumstances facing the choice maker. Empirical support for the multiple dimensions of consumer value is reported (e.g., Rageh et al., 2013; Sweeney & Soutar, 2001). Prebensen and Rosengren (2016) emphasize the existence of hedonic and utilitarian experience value in four different services in tourism. Sanchez et al. (2006) report that the perceived value of the purchase of a tourism product (including both consumption and purchase) includes six dimensions: (1) functional value of the travel agency (installations); (2) functional value of the contact personnel of the travel agency (professionalism); (3) functional value of the tourism package purchased (quality); (4) functional value price; (5) emotional value and (6) social value.

Only a limited number of studies have examined the relationship between motivation and tourism experience value, however. In their review of studies examining travel motivation research, Hsu et al. (2010) use the two terms 'tourist motivation' and 'tourist benefits' interchangeably. However, Pesonen (2012) stresses that the difference between the two concepts may not be clear. He uses motivation and benefits as two different concepts to reflect push and pull factors respectively. The rationale behind this distinction is that motivation resides inside of the individual regardless of the destination, while benefits reflect the tourist evaluation of destination-related attributes, and, thus, they are destination bound. Similarly, Paker and Vural (2016) use benefit segmentation to segment yachting tourists based on yachters' expectations from them. The corresponding demographic and motivation profiles were obtained. Prebensen et al. (2013) report that motivation affects tourists' experience value directly and indirectly through involvement.

Research method

The purpose of this research is to explore the tourism motivations of Egyptians and to examine how these segments differ concerning tourism experience values. To do this, a survey was developed and shared via an electronic link; the reliability and validity of research constructs were analyzed, and cluster analysis was performed.

Questionnaire design and measurement of research variables

The questionnaire used in this survey consists of three main sections: the travel needs section; the tourism experience value section and the demographics section. Respondents were required to recall a destination they visited and were satisfied with and then to answer the questions based on experience with this destination. The *Travel Needs Scale* by Tasci and Ko (2017) and the tourism value experience scale by Prebensen and Rosengren (2016) were used on a five-point Likert scale. The demographics section included questions that are related to age, gender, income, education and previous travel experience outside Egypt.

Data collection and sampling

An e-survey was sent via a link to a purposeful sample, with one condition for participation, which is a minimum age of 18 years old. The researcher used 24 data collectors who were mainly undergraduate and MBA students in the cities of Cairo, Alexandria, Damietta and Mansoura. The total number of responses was 497. The use of e-surveys can be both time and cost-efficient (Litvin & Kar, 2001). Nonetheless, sample bias remains a problem, and respondents might not represent the general population; there are also technical uncertainties, and the response rates are usually lower (Pan, 2010). As shown in Table 6.1, the percentage of females slightly exceeds that of males. Young respondents also exceed middle-aged and older respondents. Respondents whose income is less

Table 6.1 Descriptive statistics

Gender	F	%	Income in L.E.:	F	%
Males	230	46	Less than 5,000	278	55.9
Females	268	54	5,000–9,999	85	17.1
Travel experience			10,000–14,999	55	11.1
	F	%	15,000–19,999	32	6.4
Yes	258	52	20,000–24,999	7	1.4
No	239	48	25,000 or more	40	8
Age			**Marital status**		
	F	%		**F**	**%**
18–19	73	14.7	Single	287	57.7
20–24	144	29	Married	194	39
25–29	59	11.9	Divorced or		
30–34	94	18.9	widowed	16	3.2
35–39	43	8.7	**Education**		
40–44	40	8		**N**	**%**
45–49	33	6.6	Secondary school	7	1.4
50–54	7	1.4	University	490	98.6
55–59	2	.4			
60–65	2	.4			

than 5,000 Egyptian pounds reached 55.9%. The sample was also dominated by respondents who have obtained university education.

Reliability and validity of research variables

The convergent validity of the two research constructs was examined using exploratory factor analysis. The extraction method was *Principal Component Analysis* and the rotation method was *Varimax with Kaiser Normalization*. The average variance extracted (AVE) for the travel needs scale and tourism experience value was 65% and 66.7%, respectively. As shown in Tables 6.2 and 6.3, factor loadings were high for the dimensions of the two constructs, and no cross-loadings appeared in the analysis. For the travel needs scale, six factors appeared. Five of them were similar in terms of factor structure to those obtained by Tasci and Ko (2017). These variables included escape, self-actualization, arousal and novelty. Only two factors loaded on the variable private social affiliation. Conversely, seven variables loaded on what Tasci and Ko (2017) called public social affiliation. As shown in Table 6.2, alpha coefficients for five dimensions were above .67 except for the private social affiliation (alpha = .35), which was deleted from the analysis. Concerning the tourism experience value, the exploratory factor analysis revealed the existence of four factors. As shown in Table 6.3, high-reliability coefficients appeared for the four dimensions. The four dimensions are emotional value, value for money, functional value and social value.

Table 6.2 Factor analysis and alpha coefficients of the travel needs scale

	Public social affiliation Alpha = .86	Escape Alpha = .77	Self-actualization Alpha = .78	Arousal Alpha = .75	Novelty Alpha = .67	Private social affiliation Alpha = .35
To feel satisfied			.742			
To have self-actualization			.795			
To feel successful			.782			
To learn about other places					.799	
To learn about other people					.597	
To do and see new things					.731	
To be/spend time with family						.779
To be/spend time with friends						.601
To improve my relationships	.673					
To be around others similar to me	.516					
Become part of a group	.572					
To meet new people	.764					
To make new friends	.777					
To improve my social skills	.801					
To improve my social network	.808					
To feel excitement				.771		
To seek adrenaline rush				.790		
To feel emotionally charged				.705		
To be away from my everyday life		.709				
To feel detached from mundane tasks		.866				
To feel disconnected from my regular social circle		.703				
To get out of routine		.817				

Table 6.3 Factor analysis and alpha coefficients of the tourism experience value

	Emotional value Alpha = .81	Social value Alpha = .87	Functional value Alpha = .79	Value for money Alpha = .75
Value for money				.846
Suitable price				.860
Organized			.803	
Acceptable quality			.815	
Adventure feeling	.726			
Stable quality			.651	
Feel socially acceptable		.661		
Improve self-concept		.881		
Make others accept me		.899		
Genuine experience	.636			
Satisfies my curiosity	.595			
Impress others		.765		
Exciting place	.792			
Stimulates activity	.774			
Educational	.506			
Makes me happy	.599			

Cluster analysis

Cluster analysis (CA) is an exploratory data analysis tool for organizing data into clusters, as it maximizes the similarity of cases within each cluster and maximizes the dissimilarity between groups (Burns & Burns, 2008). Based on Hair et al. (1998), the research problem, the research objectives and the cluster variate were identified. The cluster variate is the set of variables representing the characteristics used to compare objects in the cluster analysis. The five travel motives identified previously are used as the cluster variate. Then, univariate and multivariate outliers were detected. Univariate outliers were identified by obtaining the standardized coefficients, and 16 univariate outliers were removed. The Mahalanobis test of distance was used to detect multivariate outliers by evaluating the position of each observation compared with the center of all observations on a set of variables (Hair et al., 1998). The significance levels for D2 were calculated and assorted ascendingly. Four cases with significance levels less than .001 were considered outliers and removed. The sample after removing outliers reached 477.

Standardization was not used since all variables were measured using the same scale (5-point Likert scale). Distance measures of similarity represent similarity as the proximity of observations to one another across the variables in the cluster variate (Hair et al., 1998). The squared Euclidean distance will be used. Cluster analysis is based on the assumptions of sample representativeness and the absence of multicollinearity (Hair et al., 1998). Since this study is exploratory and the sample size is small, the sample representativeness assumption is violated. For multicollinearity, variance inflation factor (VIF) was used (Meyers et al., 2016). VIFs of the five variables included in the cluster variate were less than ten, indicating an absence of multicollinearity (Norusis, 1990).

The hierarchical cluster analysis was used as a clustering algorithm due to the small size of the sample (Norusis, 1990). It starts with each case as a separate cluster – i.e. there are as many clusters as cases – and then combines the clusters sequentially, reducing the number of clusters at each step until only one cluster is left (Burns & Burns, 2008). Ward's method will be used since it measures the distance between two clusters as the sum of squares between the two clusters summed over all variables (Hair et al., 1998).

To determine how many clusters should be formed, Hair et al. (1998) argue that it would be best to develop several cluster solutions and then decide among the alternative solutions by using a priori criteria, practical judgment, common sense and theoretical foundations. The researcher tried three-, four- and five-factor solutions. A three-factor solution provided significant differences among groups. Finally, interpretation, labeling clusters and describing their profiles was conducted. To do this, ANOVA, Scheffe test and a comparison of means were performed (Table 6.4). A cross-tabulation of demographic variables and the three clusters was also performed (Table 6.5).

As shown in Table 6.4, there are significant differences among the three clusters for social motive, escape, arousal, self-actualization and novelty. Clusters also significantly vary for functional quality, social value and emotional value. Value for money was not significantly different among the three clusters. Table 6.5 also illustrates that the clusters varied significantly for demographic variables.

Cluster 1: $N = 91$. *The modests.* This group has lower means than clusters 2 and 3 in social motive, escape, arousal, self-actualization, novelty and social value. They have significantly lower means than the maximizers in functional and emotional values. The majority of this group includes married males from the ages of 20 to 49. The majority had previous foreign travel experience. Although some of the respondents reported income levels below 5,000 L.E, low -income respondents constituted less than 50% of the respondents in this cluster. The income levels seemed higher than those reported by the maximizers.

Cluster 2: $N = 246$. *The maximizers* are tourists who report significantly higher values for the five motives and three value dimensions. They are not significantly different from the other two groups in value for money, and they are not significantly different from group 3 in escape. Most of the respondents in this category are single females, with no foreign travel experience. Most of the respondents in this cluster are young travelers between the age of 18–34. Their income levels are mostly between 5,000 and 15,000 L.E.

Cluster 3: $N = 140$. *The balancers.* The means reported in this cluster are significantly higher than the modests and lower than the maximizers in social motive, arousal, self-actualization and novelty. They are not significantly different from maximizers in escape and functional quality; however, most of the respondents in this cluster were between the ages of 20–44. This cluster

Table 6.4 ANOVA and comparison of cluster means

Cluster		Social motive F = 108.15 Sig F = .000	Escape F = 13.49 Sig F = .000	Arousal F = 190.23 Sig F = .000	Self-actualization F = 295.14 Sig F = .000	Novelty F = 54.81 Sig F = .000	Value for money F = 1.19 Sig F = .306	Functional value F = 5.65 Sig F = .004	Social value F = 60.34 Sig F = .000	Emotional value F = 29.06 Sig F = .000
Modests N = 91	Mean	3.0251	4.2280	3.1136	2.6484	4.0330	3.8901	3.8864	2.6181	3.6000
Maximizers N = 246	Mean	4.0726	4.5569	4.4295	4.2106	4.6491	3.9959	4.1247	3.6169	4.0993
Balancers N = 140	Mean	3.4541	4.4625	4.0619	3.0405	4.2833	3.9143	4.0476	2.9982	3.7831
Total N = 477	Mean	3.6912	4.4665	4.0706	3.5691	4.4242	3.9518	4.0566	3.2448	3.9122

Table 6.5 Cross tabulation of the demographic variables and the three clusters

		Modests	*Maximizers*	*Balancers*
Age	18–19	8	52	11
	20–24	15	78	45
	25–29	9	32	15
	30–34	20	38	33
	35–39	14	13	15
	40–44	6	18	12
	45–49	15	12	5
	50–54	2	3	2
	55–59	1	0	1
	Above 60	1	0	1
Gender	Male	54	99	66
	Female	37	147	74
Marital status	Single	33	158	82
	Married	56	77	54
	Widowed or divorced	2	10	4
Travel experience	Yes	53	115	78
	No	38	130	62
Income	Less than 5000	39	155	73
	5000–9999	13	49	21
	10000–14999	13	23	18
	15000–19999	6	12	13
	20000–24999	1	2	4
	25000 and more	19	5	11

included a slightly higher percentage of single females who have previous foreign travel experience. The income level of most respondents was below 5,000 L.E., but higher income levels were also reported.

Discussion

The purpose of this research is to explore the tourism motivations of Egyptians, how it relates to tourism experience value and whether demographic differences exist in these motivations and tourism experience value. An electronic link was shared among respondents from four Egyptian governorates, and the total number of the sample reached 497 respondents. The exploratory factor analysis revealed that the *Travel Needs Scale* by Tasci and Ko (2017) and the *tourism experience value scale* by Prebensen and Rosengren (2016) were valid measures of the tourism motivations and the tourism experience value, respectively.

The cluster analysis conducted shows three findings that require some explanation from an identity-based motivation perspective. First, contrary to the contention of Falk (2006) that there are dominant motivations to visit museums, there is no distinct pattern of dominant motivation, and most respondents reported above-average ratings on different motives. The idea of having multiple motives has received considerable support in the field of psychology. For example, Kurzban and Aktipis' (2007) modularity theory in motivation argues that the mind consists of a set of informationally encapsulated systems or modules, which might be contradictory. In tourism, Pearce and Lee's (2005) *Travel Career Approach* supports the existence of multiple tourism motives that are affected by previous travel experience and age. The five motivations reported in the current study correspond to some extent to the novelty, escape, relationship and self-development reported by Pearce and Lee (2005).

Bond and Falk (2013) also note that, contrary to short visits, in tourism decisions individuals seek to satisfy multiple identity-related needs, and, in some cases, they are incorporated into a single experience. For tourists from low-income countries, tourism represents an experience that satisfies multiple motives, unlike tourists from high-income countries who might find satisfaction in non-travel related experiences. This effect is intensified in countries that have faced tremendous economic and social changes such as Egypt.

Second, when the hierarchical cluster analysis was used, and contrary to Falk (2006), the clusters did not vary for the type of tourism motive, they varied for the strength of the motive and the core identity attributes 'Big Is'. Maximizers reported higher values of the different tourism motives, and they were demographically distinct as they are mainly single young females who have no experience with foreign travel. Conversely, the modests, were mostly married males with higher income levels and foreign travel experience. The ratings of the third group, the balancers, were higher than those of modests and lower than those of maximizers. No significant differences between balancers and maximizers were reported in the escape motive. This cluster is different from maximizers as it included mostly young and middle-aged females who have previous foreign travel experience and an overall income level higher than that of maximizers. Gender differences were reported by Wei and Tasci (2017) who argue that emotion-based decision-makers are more likely to be females as they are more passionate about their travel needs than logic-based decision-makers. Such passion is also reflected in the type of tourism experience value they seek. Young, inexperienced females report higher tourism experience values than older females or males. Andreu et al. (2006) have reported that females had stronger motivations to travel than males and that the difference in motivation was only in magnitude and not type of motivation. Furthermore, it provides support for the finding of Uysal et al. (1996) who report no gender differences in the escape motive. For both age and experience differences, the findings provide support to Paris and Teye (2010) who have reported identifiable patterns of backpacker travel motivation, which were affected by previous travel experience and age, and it contradicts with the findings of Pearce and Lee (2005) who reported no differences in motivation for low versus high experienced tourists.

From an identity-based motivation perspective, these findings mean that the core identity attributes or the 'Big Is' as Falk (2006) called them are not only more salient, but they also affect to a great extent the 'small Is'. Thus, age, gender and marital status play a significant role in shaping the 'small Is', and the interaction between these 'Big Is' should not be ignored. This supports Oys-erman's (2009) perspective that broad identities (such as gender or ethnicity) affect narrow identities such as those surrounding profession.

Third, the findings provide support to the relationship between tourism motivation and tourism experience value previously reported by Prebensen et al. (2013). Maximizers reporting higher ratings of tourism motivations also reported higher ratings of the experiential tourism experience value dimensions. One interesting finding is the lack of significant differences among clusters in the value of money. This finding provides support for the experiential nature of the tourism experience. The two female-dominated clusters (the maximizers and the balancers) were significantly different from the male-dominated cluster (the modests) in terms of functional quality.

Conclusion and implications

From an academic perspective, the identity-based motivation model represents an avenue for a better understanding of motivation. Identities represent one of the important sources of motivation (Falk, 2006), yet it is essential to understand the type of identity prevalent in different consumption experiences. Small Is may be more salient in short visits such as visits to zoos, museums and aquariums. Conversely, Big Is may be more prevalent in longer visits where the tourist is trying to satisfy different goals at the same time. Furthermore, the examination of these identities cannot be separated from the socio-cultural context. This context shapes the role to be played by the identities. Thus, the roles played by a young single female in Egypt might be different from those played by a young single female in the USA. More cross-cultural research is required in this area to understand differences in identities and roles and how they affect tourism motivations.

From a practical point of view, this research provides practitioners with some guidelines that can be used in the segmentation and the design of the marketing mix for tourism experiences. Segments should be identified based on the magnitude of travel motivations, the demographic profile and the tourism experience profile of tourists. Travel packages should focus on the experiential aspects of the tourism experience with less emphasis put on pricing. These packages should be highly tailored to meet the travel needs of passionate female tourists.

Limitations

The first limitation relates to the sample. The sample used can be described as small, with an overrepresentation of females and young tourists. This might be attributed to the use of an e-survey where most of the responses come from young respondents who are more likely to use the internet. Including a higher percentage of older tourists may provide more insights on travel motivation and how it relates to tourism experience as, for example, Ryan and Glendon (1998) have reported differences in tourism experience value ratings of young and old tourists.

References

Andreu, L., Kozak, M., Avci, N., & Cifter, N. (2006). Market segmentation by motivations to travel: British tourists visiting Turkey. *Journal of Travel & Tourism Marketing, 19*(1), 1–14. https://doi.org/10.1300/J073v19n01_01

Beard, J. G., & Ragheb, M. G. (1983). Measuring leisure motivation. *Journal of Leisure Research, 15*(3), 219–228. https://doi.org/10.1080/00222216.1983.11969557

Bogari, N. B., Crowther, G., & Marr, N. (2004). Motivation for domestic tourism: A case study of the Kingdom of Saudi Arabia. In G. I. Crouch, R. R. Perdue, H. J. P. Immermans, & M. Uysal (Eds.), *Consumer psychology of tourism, hospitality and leisure* (Vol. 3, pp. 51–63). CABI.

Bond, N., & Falk, J. (2013). Tourism and identity-related motivations: Why am I here (and not there)? *International Journal of Tourism Research, 15*(5), 430–442. https://doi.org/10.1002/jtr.1886

Burns, R. P., & Burns, R. (2008). *Business research methods and statistics using SPSS*. Sage.

Cavagnaro, E., & Staffieri, S. (2015). A study of students' travellers values and needs in order to establish futures patterns and insights. *Journal of Tourism Futures, 1*(2), 94–107. https://doi.org/10.1108/JTF-12-2014-0013.

Crompton, J. L. (1979). Motivations for pleasure vacation. *Annals of Tourism Research, 6*(4), 408–424. https://doi.org/10.1016/0160-7383(79)90004-5

Dann, G. M. (1977). Anomie, ego-enhancement and tourism. *Annals of Tourism Research, 4*(4), 184–194. https://doi.org/10.1016/0160-7383(77)90037-8

Dawson, E., & Jensen, E. (2011). Towards a contextual turn in visitor studies: Evaluating visitor segmentation and identity-related motivations. *Visitor Studies, 14*(2), 127–140. https://doi.org/10.1080/10645578.2011.608001

Falk, J. H. (2006). An identity-centered approach to understanding museum learning. *Curator: The Museum Journal, 49*(2), 151–166. https://doi.org/10.1111/j.2151-6952.2006.tb00209.x

Falk, J. H. (2009). *Identity and the museum visitor experience*. Routledge.

Figler, M. H., Weinstein, A. R., Sollers, J. J., & Devan, B. D. (1992). Pleasure travel (tourist) motivation: A factor analytic approach. *Bulletin of the Psychonomic Society, 30*(2), 113–116. https://doi.org/10.3758/BF03330412

Gallarza, M. G., & Gil-Saura, G. (2006). Value dimensions, perceived value, satisfaction and loyalty: An investigation of university students' travel behaviour. *Tourism Management, 27*(3), 437–452. https://doi.org/10.1016/j.tourman.2004.12.002

Garner, J. K., Kaplan, A., & Pugh, K. (2016). Museums as contexts for transformative experiences and identity development. *Journal of Museum Education, 41*(4), 341–352. https://doi.org/10.1080/10598650.2016.1199343

Hair, J. S., Anderson, R., Tetham, R., & Black, W. (1998). *Multivariate data analysis* (5th ed.). Prentice-Hall.

Hsu, C. H., Cai, L. A., & Li, M. (2010). Expectation, motivation, and attitude: A tourist behavioral model. *Journal of Travel Research, 49*(3), 282–296. https://doi.org/10.1177/0047287509349266

Huang, S. S., & Hsu, C. H. (2009). Travel motivation: Linking theory to practice. *International Journal of Culture, Tourism and Hospitality Research, 3*(4), 287–295. https://doi.org/10.1108/17506180910994505

Jensen, J. M. (2011, November). The relationships between socio-demographic variables, travel motivations and subsequent choice of vacation. *2nd International Conference on Economics, Business and Management, 22*, 37–44.

Klenosky, D. (2002). The pull of tourism destinations: a means-end investigation. *Journal of Travel Research, 40*(4), 385–395. https://doi.org/10.1177/004728750204000405

Kurzban, R., & Aktipis, C. A. (2007). Modularity and the social mind: Are psychologists too self-ish? *Personality and Social Psychology Review, 11*(2), 131–149. https://doi.org/10.1177/1088868306294906

Litvin, S. W., & Kar, G. H. (2001). E-surveying for tourism research: Legitimate tool or a researcher's fantasy? *Journal of Travel Research, 39*(3), 308–314. https://doi.org/10.1177/004728750103900309

Meng, F., & Uysal, M. (2008). Effects of gender differences on perceptions of destination attributes, motivations, and travel values: An examination of a nature-based resort destination. *Journal of Sustainable Tourism, 16*(4), 445–466.

Meyers, L. S., Gamst, G., & Guarino, A. J. (2016). *Applied multivariate research: Design and interpretation* (3rd ed.). Sage Publications.

Norusis, M. J. (1990). *SPSS advanced statistics user's guide*. SPSS.

Oh, H. C., Uysal, M., & Weaver, P. A. (1995). Product bundles and market segments based on travel motivations: A canonical correlation approach. *International Journal of Hospitality Management, 14*(2), 123–137. https://doi.org/10.1016/0278-4319(95)00010-A

Oyserman, D. (2009). Identity-based motivation: Implications for action-readiness, procedural-readiness, and consumer behavior. *Journal of Consumer Psychology, 19*(3), 250–260. https://doi.org/10.1016/j.jcps.2009.05.008

Oyserman, D. (2015). Identity-based motivation. In R. Scott & S. Kosslyn (Eds.), *Emerging trends in the social and behavioral sciences: An interdisciplinary, searchable, and linkable resource* (pp. 1–11). Wiley.

Oyserman, D. (2019). The essentialized self: Implications for motivation and self-regulation. *Journal of Consumer Psychology, 29*(2), 336–343. https://doi.org/10.1002/jcpy.1093

Oyserman, D., & James, L. (2011). Possible identities. In S. Schwartz, K. Luyckx, & V. Vignoles (Eds.), *Handbook of identity theory and research* (pp. 117–145). Springer.

Paker, N., & Vural, C. A. (2016). Customer segmentation for marinas: Evaluating marinas as destinations. *Tourism Management, 56*, 156–171. https://doi.org/10.1016/j.tourman.2016.03.024

Pan, B. (2010). Online travel surveys and response patterns. *Journal of Travel Research, 49*(1), 121–135. https://doi.org/10.1177/0047287509336467

Paris, C. M., & Teye, V. (2010). Backpacker motivations: A travel career approach. *Journal of Hospitality Marketing & Management, 19*(3), 244–259. https://doi.org/10.1080/19368621003591350

Pearce, P. L. (1988). *The Ulysses factor: Evaluating visitors in tourist settings*. Springer.

Pearce, P. L. (2011). Travel motivation, benefits and constraints to destinations. In Y. Wang & A. Pizam (Eds.), *Destination marketing and management: Theories and applications* (pp. 39–52). CAB International.

Pearce, P. L., & Lee, U. I. (2005). Developing the travel career approach to tourist motivation. *Journal of Travel Research, 43*(3), 226–237. https://doi.org/10.1177/0047287504272020

Pesonen, J. A. (2012). Segmentation of rural tourists: Combining push and pull motivations. *Tourism and Hospitality Management, 18*(1), 69–82. https://doi.org/10.20867/thm.18.1.5

Prebensen, N. K., & Rosengren, S. (2016). Experience value as a function of hedonic and utilitarian dominant services. *International Journal of Contemporary Hospitality Management, 28*(1), 113–135. https://doi.org/10.1108/IJCHM-02-2014-0073

Prebensen, N. K., Woo, E., Chen, J. S., & Uysal, M. (2013). Motivation and involvement as antecedents of the perceived value of the destination experience. *Journal of Travel Research, 52*(2), 253–264. https://doi.org/10.1177/0047287512461181

Prentice, R. (2004). Tourist motivation and typologies. A companion to tourism. In A. A. Lew, C. M. Hall, & A. M. Williams (Eds.), *A companion to tourism* (pp. 261–279). Pergamon.

Rageh, A., Melewar, T. C., & Woodside, A. (2013). Using netnography research method to reveal the underlying dimensions of the customer/tourist experience. *Qualitative Market Research, 16*(2), 126–149. https://doi.org/10.1108/13522751311317558

Ryan, C., & Glendon, I. (1998). Application of leisure motivation scale to tourism. *Annals of Tourism Research, 25*(1), 169–184. https://doi.org/10.1016/S0160-7383(97)00066-2

Sanchez, J., Callarisa, L., Rodriguez, R. M., & Moliner, M. A. (2006). Perceived value of the purchase of a tourism product. *Tourism Management, 27*(3), 394–409. https://doi.org/10.1016/j.tourman.2004.11.007

Sánchez-Fernández, R., & Iniesta-Bonillo, M. Á. (2007). The concept of perceived value: A systematic review of the research. *Marketing Theory, 7*(4), 427–451. https://doi.org/10.1177/1470593107083165

Sheth, J. N., Newman, B. I., & Gross, B. L. (1991). *Consumption values and market choices: Theory and applications.* South-Western Publishing.

Sweeney, J. C., & Soutar, G. N. (2001). Consumer perceived value: The development of a multiple item scale. *Journal of Retailing, 77*(2), 203–220. https://doi.org/10.1016/S0022-4359(01)00041-0

Tasci, A. D., & Ko, Y. J. (2017). Travel needs revisited. *Journal of Vacation Marketing, 23*(1), 20–36. https://doi.org/10.1177/1356766715617499

Uysal, M., McGehee, N. G., & Loker-Murphy, L. (1996). The Australian international pleasure travel market: Motivations from a gendered perspective. *Journal of Tourism Studies, 7*(1), 45–57.

Wei, W., & Tasci, A. D. (2017). Antecedents and consequences of experiential versus utilitarian consumption in the travel context. *International Journal of Culture, Tourism and Hospitality Research, 11*(4), 500–551. https://doi.org/10.1108/IJCTHR-06-2017-0069

Wong, I. A., Law, R., & Zhao, X. (2018). Time-variant pleasure travel motivations and behaviors. *Journal of Travel Research, 57*(4), 437–452. https://doi.org/10.1177/0047287517705226

Yoo, C. K., Yoon, D., & Park, E. (2018). Tourist motivation: An integral approach to destination choices. *Tourism Review, 73*(2), 169–185. https://doi.org/10.1108/TR-04-2017-0085

Zeithaml, V. A. (1988). Consumer perceptions of price, quality, and value: A means-end model and synthesis of evidence. *Journal of Marketing, 52*(3), 2–22. https://doi.org/10.1177/002224298805200302

Part III

Pilgrimage and religious travel and tourism

7 A study on pre-trip experiences of Fijian pilgrims' Hajj performance

Farisha Nazmeen Nisha

Introduction

Religiously motivated travel, a traditional societal phenomenon, is regaining popularity in contemporary times, both in performance (growth in religious travellers) and in academia (increased multidisciplinary scholarly interest). Annually, around 300 to 330 million tourists make 600 million international sacred trips (UNWTO, 2014) and spend around US$18–20 billion (Tourism & More, 2014). The Hajj, an annual obligatory religious pilgrimage to Mecca (Esposito, 2011), is a prominent representation of religious tourism. Fijian Muslims represent one of the Muslim diasporas engaged in the Hajj trip, although they are a relatively small proportion of the massive Hajj population of millions.

This empirical study examined and drew new insights on Fijian Muslims' Hajj performance, a segment with little or no prior international travel experience. Additionally, in the Fijian context, outbound tourism – especially from a long-haul perspective – and religious tourism markets are inadequately researched, hence this chapter attempts to fill this literature gap. Extant Hajj studies (e.g. Buitelaar, 2018; McLoughlin, 2009a, 2009b, 2015) were positioned in a developed country or Western context; therefore, researching participants from a developing country like Fiji extends theoretical dimensions of the religiously motivated travel and Hajj phenomenon. Specifically, this study explored and discussed the pre-trip phase (fulfillment of conditions) of Fijian Muslims' Hajj performance. The pre-travel activities being discussed are financial arrangements, travel arrangement issues and concerns, intellectual preparations and farewell activities.

Understanding religious tourism

Since ancient times, travel has been an essential component of cosmopolitan religions, such as Islam, Christianity, Judaism, Buddhism and Hinduism (Rinschede, 1992; Tilson, 2005). The main travel motive was return to the origins of the religion and mankind and to understand their existence (Cohen, 2006; Kaelber, 2006; Vukonic, 1996). It is asserted that several contemporary

DOI: 10.4324/9781003036296-10

religious tourism destinations involve the sacred sites featured in global religions (Shackley, 2001; Stausberg, 2011; Timothy & Olsen, 2006). Through time, religious tourism sustained popularity and evolved into a greater segmented market (de la Torre et al., 2012). On that account, Ambroz and Ovsenik (2011) and Olsen and Timothy (2006) argued that a contemporary tourism trend was the desire to religiously explore life and seek answers for its existence. Also, the increased awareness and significance of religious heritage, sites, practices, traditions and activities are contributing to the religious tourism progression (UNWTO, 2011, 2014).

Religious tourism is characterised by the presence of religious components in tourism products and experiences including influencing tourist motivations and behaviours (Collins-Kreiner & Kliot, 2000; Domínguez & Alonso, 2018; Poria et al., 2003). It involves experiencing religious forms or products, induced through practices, traditions, art, culture, (heritage) architecture and seeking identification with the piety (Strategic Initiatives & Government Advisory (SIGA), 2012). Religious tourism can either be short-term involving a short travelling distance and length of stay or long-term encompassing a greater travelling distance and length of stay (Rinschede, 1992). Nolan and Nolan (1992) categorised religious tourism products as sacred sites, structures or objects consecrated mainly for religious activities to sustain historic or aesthetic significance. Some of the religious tourism activities include pilgrimages, festivals, faith-based events, missionary travel, retreats, youth camps and sacred site visits (Collins-Kreiner, 2010; Domínguez & Alonso, 2018; Griffin & Raj, 2017; Pintér, 2014).

Contemporary religious tourists are represented as pure (or secular) pilgrims, tourists who deem religion as their core travel motive, tourists who are religious but do not possess religion as an integral travel motive (rather it impacts their travel activities and behaviour) and any tourists attracted to religious cultures and sites (Collins-Kreiner, 2016; Durán-Sánchez et al., 2018; Olsen, 2013; Olsen & Timothy, 2006). Accordingly, it is argued that contemporary tourists' visits to sites of religious importance involve motives to fulfill both religious and non-religious needs (Shinde, 2015). However, religiously motivated tourists, such as pious pilgrims, are perceived to be more loyal and committed than leisure tourists due to their social 'sense of duty' (Abad-Galzacorta et al., 2016; Swarbrooke & Horner, 2016).

A religious journey: the Hajj performance

The Hajj is a prominent annual obligatory religious pilgrimage to Mecca, Saudi Arabia (Esposito, 2011). In 2019, approximately 2.49 million pilgrims performed Hajj (General Authority for Statistics, 2019), and this number is forecasted to reach 5 million pilgrims by 2025 (Gulf Research Center, 2018). The Hajj performance is perceived as the world's 'largest religious and social convention, bringing millions of people around the globe into one arena' (Alserhan, 2011, p. 129) at a specific period. As one of the five Islamic pillars, the Hajj is mandatory on every physically, mentally and financially abled adult Muslim (but females must be accompanied by a *Mahram* − permitted male kin) at least once in their lifetime (Buitelaar & Mols, 2015; Utomo et al., 2016). The preconditions of Hajj also requires pilgrims to arrange livelihood provisions for their dependents, settle debts, resolve differences with others and make atonements for wrongdoings (e.g. seeking forgiveness or repenting) (Joll, 2012; Maghniyyah, 1997; Raj, 2007; Timothy & Iverson, 2006). The Hajj is performed from the eighth until the twelfth of *Dhul-Hijjah* (twelfth Islamic month) (Peters, 1994; Sharma, 2013). It recognises Islamic historiography by commemorating and replicating events from the lives of Prophet Adam, Prophet Ibrahim, Prophet Ismail and Prophet Muhammed (McLoughlin, 2009a). Contemporary *Hajj* pilgrims imitate the physical and spiritual journey as performed by Prophet Muhammed (the last Islamic prophet).

The *Hajj* performance first involves pilgrims assuming *Ihram* state, which represents their ascetic appearances, with male pilgrims donning white unstitched clothing (Hillenbrand, 2015; Peters, 1994). Following this, pilgrims perform *Umrah*, which combines the *Tawaf* and *Say* rituals. *Tawaf* involves seven times counter-clockwise circumambulation of the *Kaaba* (house of *Allah*) (Baderoon, 2012; McLoughlin, 2015). *Say* is the act of making seven rounds between Safa and Marwah hills (Bianchi, 2013). It re-enacts Hazra's (Prophet Ibrahim's wife) search of water for baby Ismail (Islamic prophet) until *Zamzam* water (holiest water in Islam) emerges (Bianchi, 2013; Peters, 1994). The subsequent ritual of *Wuquf* officially commences the *Hajj*. Specifically from noon until sunset, pilgrims engage in a contemplative vigil through various religious acts (e.g. supplications, repentance, prayer performances) at the field of Arafah (Bianchi, 2013; Esposito, 2011; McLoughlin, 2009a, 2009b). Thereafter, pilgrims collect pebbles at Muzdalifah for the next ritual and spend a night at the open ground (Bianchi, 2013). For the final ritual, *Rami Jamrah*, pilgrims stay at the tent city of Mina for three days (Bianchi, 2013; Hillenbrand, 2015). They stone three pillars (*Jamrat*) representing Satan, whilst commemorating Prophet Ibrahim's refusal to obey Satan's temptations (Bianchi, 2013). The *Qurban* ritual on tenth *Dhul-Hijjah* involving animal sacrifice culminates the Hajj (Bianchi, 2013; Raj & Bozonelos, 2015). It re-enacts Prophet Ibrahim's sacrifice of Prophet Ismail to *Allah* who was later substituted by a ram. On Hajj conclusion, male pilgrims get bestowed with the title of Hajji and the females with *Hajjah* (Aziz, 2001).

The Hajj is incomparable to any other religious journey in Islam. It involves abundant devotions, which generates inner peace and refined moral values of pilgrims (Bianchi, 2013; Esposito, 2011; Timothy & Iverson, 2006). In religious essence, the Hajj represents self-sacrifice, especially of spirit, time, body, comfort, worldly relations, desires, pleasures and property or money, whilst being submissive towards *Allah* (Maududi, 1978; Raj, 2007; Vukonic, 1996). These attributes present the Hajj as a spiritually, physically and financially demanding Islamic worship. It is considered as the ultimate spiritual development of a Muslim and a lifetime achievement (Utomo et al., 2016). Muslims from diverse origins return to their religious homeland to perform Hajj (Baderoon, 2012; O'Connor, 2014; Buitelaar & Mols, 2015; McLoughlin, 2015). Thus, the Hajj reminds Muslims that they represent a single community, sharing a common historical and religious destiny (Bianchi, 2013; Hammoudi, 2006).

Islam in Fiji

The religion of Islam was introduced in Fiji through indentured Indian labourers, of whom some later settled as Fijian citizens (Al-Hilaly, 2011; Pandey, 2011). In the nineteenth century, Islamic practices were not freely executed due to strict conditions of the indentured labour system (Ali, 1979) and threats from religious tensions (Gillion, 1977; Rahman, 1993). Over time, Muslim communities prospered and strengthened their religious faith. *Da'wah* activities (missionary work by Islamic scholars) significantly reinforced the Muslim community. Establishment of religious and social infrastructures such as worship places (mosques/madrasas), religious organisations and Muslim schools further maintained and nurtured Islamic practices, while preserving Islamic identity in Fiji (Ali, 2004; Lal, 2009; Rahman, 1993). Thus, Islam in Fiji has become more institutionalised, with Muslims conforming to Islamic principles (e.g. regularly observing Islamic pillars – declaring faith, fasting, performing obligatory prayers, giving alms and undertaking Hajj), improving their educational status and acquiring political rights and equal status within Fijian society (Al-Hilaly, 2011; Miller, 2008). At the time of writing, Muslims, primarily represented by Fiji Indians, constitute about 6.3% of the Fijian population of 865,611, which makes them a religious minority group (FBoS, 2015; Nationmaster, 2016).

Method

Using a qualitative research inquiry, this study examined and discussed the pre-trip experiences of Fijian Muslims' Hajj performance. The use of an interpretative paradigm enabled generation of authentic and detailed accounts of these experiences, involving deciphering the research phenomena from participants' perspectives (Cavana et al., 2001; Taylor & Medina, 2011). Its subjective approach enabled free exploration of participants' interpretations, beliefs and views on pre-trip experiences of the Hajj performance from multifarious perspectives (Altinay et al., 2016; Gray, 2014). The study purposively selected and interviewed 25 Fijian Hajj pilgrims in Western and Central Fiji during the period of October 2017 to February 2018. Gatekeepers (well-known individuals in their communities) enabled access to the study participants. The diverse backgrounds of participants (e.g. life history, geographical, demographic and socio-economic status) generated multifarious perspectives of the research phenomenon, while minimising the risk of data generalisation. The qualitative interviews were semi-structured, which comprised themes and specific open-ended questions. These interviews were conducted face-to-face in local dialect (Fiji-Hindi or Urdu) and in participants' natural settings, which enabled obtaining first-hand knowledge from the participants. The interview responses were retained through permitted audio recording (and field notes were conducted when appropriate). After transcribing and translating data (in English language), the researcher employed thematic analysis to evaluate and explain research findings. Meaningful patterns in data involving key words, phrases, sentences, paragraphs or any other descriptive information were reviewed and categorised/coded. Consequently, related themes and ideas were generated, which guided the interpretations and discussions of findings.

Pre-trip phase of Fijian Muslims' Hajj performance

Financial arrangements

One of the Hajj performance requirements is to be financially secure (Buitelaar & Mols, 2015; Utomo et al., 2016). This study argues that Fijian Muslims employ various means to secure their Hajj expenditures. It found that several pilgrims used their retirement pension (Fiji National Provident Fund (FNPF)) to meet Hajj costs. This financial arrangement can also be deemed responsible for greater volume of Fijian pilgrims being elderly/retirees. However, some Fijian Muslims accumulate savings from their ongoing income to secure Hajj costs. It was elaborated that several pilgrims retained sufficient funds through many years of savings (involving working prolonged hours). Alternatively, some of the pilgrims secured funds by comprising their regular livelihood expenditures. For instance, P5's husband retained two years of his earnings to finance their Hajj, whilst having no secured home and leading a meagre livelihood from welfare provisions. In addition, certain financially constrained Fijian Muslims trade properties (e.g., house, land or vehicles) to settle their Hajj costs. For example, P9 revealed that his insufficient discretionary income and strong desire for Hajj pressed him to sell his vehicle to accumulate the required finance imminently. Contrarily, several working individuals willingly got demoted, took unpaid leave or work transfers to acquire needed time to accomplish Hajj. Hence, they diminished their economic status to fulfill their religious obligation. Nevertheless, some Fijian Muslim are able to prioritise both their economic status (career) and their religious obligation (Hajj performance). This study discovered that arrangements were made for the continuation of economic activities whilst these pilgrims performed Hajj. The arrangements included taking accumulated paid annual leave, arranging temporary job positions or supplying additional commercial produce (e.g. agricultural and homemade items).

In addition, philanthropic acts (either partial or full sponsorship) facilitated some of the Fijian Hajj accomplishments. Several pilgrims performed Hajj on other Muslims' (deceased or incapable) behalf, termed *Hajj Badal*. This Hajj is physically performed by another Muslim but symbolically represents accomplishment for the Muslim for whom this substitute pilgrimage was performed (Haq, 2014; Peters, 1994; Reda, 2016). Some of the pilgrims were charity or gift recipients such as of international religious organisations, Saudi Arabian government or Hajj travel agencies, which aimed to foster relationships with the Fijian Muslim communities. The study also recognised Fijian Muslim emigrants (friends and relatives) and their overseas descendants as the predominant Hajj sponsors. It was elaborated that often parents and children sponsored each other's Hajj. Nonetheless, related pilgrims acknowledged Hajj sponsorship as a great blessing, having facilitated a lifetime of religious obligation (or duty), which formerly was difficult or impossible to accomplish. For instance, P21, a financially distressed Muslim, disclosed that *Haijj* sponsorship (although it was a *Hajj Badal)* fulfilled his greatest desire of three decades.

However, the quality of life for several financially constrained individuals declined post-Hajj. Having exhausted most of the financial security measures, they were encountering financial challenges in their everyday lives. Welfare assistance, new occupations or retirees engaging in (self)employment were some of the attempts made in securing basic needs/livelihood afresh. The finding on self-sacrifice of regular needs and desires for accomplishing the Hajj (Maududi, 1978; Raj, 2007; Vukonic, 1996) implies that some of the Fijian Muslims prioritise their religious duty rather than a financially secured (secular) future. Thus, this travel attitude presented Fijian pilgrims as passionate religious tourists who possess a powerful sense of duty towards religion (Abad-Galzacorta et al., 2016; Swarbrooke & Horner, 2016).

Travel arrangement issues and concerns

The unavailability of local Hajj travel agencies in Fiji led to aspiring pilgrims' complete reliance on foreign travel agencies, specifically *Al-Marwah Travel Limited*, New Zealand and *Hayat International Travel & Tours Ltd.*, Australia. This supply constraint could be attributed to *Hajj* being a seasonal religious obligation (Peters, 1994; Sharma, 2013) and generation of small pilgrim volume from the Fijian market. Nonetheless, these two travel agencies annually offered approximately 80 *Hajj* packages each to Fijian Muslims (Ministry of Hajj and Umrah, 2018). The study also found that certain Fijian pilgrims perform *Hajj* directly with Australian or New Zealand groups. It was further revealed that the *Hajj* package selection was determined by the comfortability of products and services, costs, group leader expertise and experience, desired travel companions and the former pilgrims' word of mouth (WOM) recommendations. For instance, when selecting Hajj travel agencies P20 and her husband compared package prices, while P22 considered group leader familiarity and recommendations.

In addition, Hajj travel awareness was not widespread in Fijian Muslim communities. Participants revealed that the Hajj package promotions were restricted, with most of these activities (flyers, posters or verbal announcements) being executed at the Fiji Muslim League (the main Muslim organisation) managed mosques. Hence, individuals with little interaction with them were deprived of the required Hajj information and were compelled to engage further in acquiring needed resources for their Hajj preparations. Similarly, pilgrims from greater remote areas utilised additional resources, especially time and money, to secure Hajj participation. For example, P22 and her travel partners completed their Hajj travel requirements in several different locations due to the unavailability of related services in their residential locale. Other complexities of the Hajj travel arrangement process involved the delayed and lengthy Hajj confirmation process including rejection (incorrect or incomplete applications) and re-application of Hajj visas and submission of incorrect travel documents (airline ticket or passport exchange errors).

Intellectual preparation

Since Hajj is a once-in-a-lifetime obligation (Utomo et al., 2016), the Fijian pilgrims engaged in various intellectual preparations to enable its desirable accomplishment. They utilised diverse information sources to develop their knowledge, understanding and skills in performing Hajj. These information sources ranged from other individuals, travel agencies and their representatives, literature to digital mediums. The information sought was on the Hajj travel arrangements, ritual significances and processes, travel accessories and other performance related inquiries (e.g., life during Hajj). The study argued that WOM was the most prevalent and effective information source for Fijian pilgrims. It is stated that WOM plays an important role in travel decisions and risk aversion, especially when concerning less experienced travellers (Murphy et al., 2007). The current study discovered that pilgrims significantly considered their predecessors, Islamic scholars, relatives, colleagues, sponsors and travel agencies' recommendations, guidance and views to perform *Hajj*.

The preceding pilgrims' Hajj narratives substantially motivated and enhanced contemporary pilgrims' intentions, expectations and confidence to undertake Hajj. Several pilgrims aimed to replicate Hajj experiences of their predecessors. However, it was revealed that the differing Hajj guidance from different former pilgrims confused the contemporary pilgrims. This was attributed to the advancements in the Hajj travel requirements (e.g. immigration and health regulations or Hajj package options) (Back, 2015) and the annual development of the Hajj sites (e.g. logistics and facilities) (Reader, 2007). Accordingly, some of these pilgrims considered guidance from their recent predecessors as most effective.

Furthermore, several months before Hajj, Fijian Islamic scholars centered their talks on Hajj, its significance and the ritual procedures. However, it appeared that the extent of information depended on the scheduled durations and the ability to capture audiences' attention. Similarly, it was disclosed that pilgrims were guided in their Hajj preparations through seminars and preparatory classes conducted by the Hajj travel organisers. These activities provided former pilgrims' narratives, Hajj literature and travel accessory checklists to the intending pilgrims. However, certain pilgrims expressed dissatisfaction with the shorter timeframe of these seminars. Accordingly, pilgrims independently approached these organisers and utilised additional means (e.g. Islamic scholar guidance, Hajj literature) to further enlighten themselves on the Hajj performance activities.

Many Fijian Muslims employ traditional methods, such as using paper applications for a Hajj package (and visas) purchase and WOM strategies when preparing themselves for the Hajj, despite the availability of quicker digital options. This preference could be attributed to the scant use of digital mediums in rural areas, where these study participants were largely sourced from. However, few of the pilgrims found digital mediums beneficial in learning and understanding the Hajj performance procedures. Their digital activities included obtaining Hajj information (e.g. on ritual sites, demonstrations, logistics) from social media (e.g. Facebook, Twitter), Islamic websites/webpages and online videos (e.g. documentaries, lectures or ritual performance videos). For instance, P3, P4 and P15 used YouTube videos or religious organisational websites to seek information on certain Hajj rituals or activities (e.g. learning to wear *Ihram* or recite Hajj supplications).

Nonetheless, several pilgrims regularly practised Hajj rituals and associated worship activities to attain spiritual maturity prior to its participation. This finding demonstrated pilgrims' initial attempts in their overall spiritual development through the Hajj performance (Utomo et al., 2016). The current study further disclosed that some Fijian pilgrims fear forgetting the learnt procedures within the crowd of Hajj pilgrims (Alserhan, 2011). For instance, P17 mentioned that despite regular practice on Hajj rituals and associated supplications, she was worried that her nervousness in being at a new place and among many people would result in her forgetting everything. This perception highlighted destination risk and fear. However, some of these individuals addressed the constraint by retaining information in the form of books or storage files in their mobile phones. Through these sources, they intended to equip and reinforce their knowledge when required during the Hajj. Accordingly, these pilgrims' intrinsic efforts to combat perceived performance risk (and associated fears) exhibited religious passion.

Pilgrims' farewell

Fijian pilgrims' farewell rituals involve formal or informal religious and secular gatherings hosted by them or other individuals hosting them. It was highlighted that many distinctive well-wishers, both Muslims and non-Muslims, farewelled the pilgrims. This insight highlighted solidarity and positive interpersonal relationships in the Fijian communities. The study argued that the involvement in pre-Hajj gatherings spiritually and morally prepared Fijian pilgrims for the Hajj. These activities reinforced pilgrims' desire and enhanced their intellectual preparations. In another aspect, the Hajj farewell activities inspired pilgrims' well-wishers to accomplish this religious obligation. For instance, one of P22's well-wishers expressed her desire to prepare for her Hajj performance.

Reflecting on Joll (2012), Maghniyyah (1997) and Timothy and Iverson's (2006) works, the pre-Hajj activities involved Fijian pilgrims resolving differences and seeking forgiveness from others for their past misdeeds. The Fijian Hajj farewell activities also included presentation of (monetary/non-monetary) gifts to the pilgrims. However, the gift presenter also aimed to attain religious blessings associated with gift usage during the Hajj performance. Financially distressed pilgrims were highly considered gift recipients. It also disclosed that monetary gifts were predominantly provided by pilgrims' overseas relatives and companions. In another aspect, the study revealed that pilgrims were provided with resources (financial) to fulfil other individuals' requests and vows during Hajj. This finding indicated that both pilgrims and non-pilgrims desired spiritual merits from the Hajj performance.

In addition, fellow Fijian Muslims considered that intending pilgrims were more blessed and closer to *Allah* than any other Muslims. As such, pilgrims were numerously requested to make supplications for others during Hajj. Alternatively, the supplications offered for successful Hajj accomplishment and safe return increased pilgrims' confidence to undertake the religious task. For instance, P12 stated that since he was offered supplications from others, he was hopeful to successfully fulfill his life's ambition, that is, to accomplish the Hajj. These supplications for pilgrims were predominantly attributed to the anticipated difficulties in the Hajj performance, particularly relating to the past tragedies such as stampedes and the extreme environment leading to poor health (e.g. exhaustion) (Clingingsmith et al., 2009; France-Presse, 2015; McLoughlin, 2015; Taylor, 2011). However, Fijian pilgrims' religious beliefs were strong as they proceeded with their journey despite being apprehensive.

Thus, the Hajj farewell activities, imposing profound emotional impacts, were regarded blessed and meritorious by all the attendees. This was attributed to Hajj being a lifetime obligation, for which the majority of Fijian Muslims made massive sacrifices when addressing the performance constraints. Also, the privilege of Fijian pilgrims from a small geographical location engaging in the global massive pilgrimage to a long-haul destination, Saudi Arabia, led to a prominent communal affair locally.

Summary and conclusion

Using a qualitative research design that was based on an interpretive paradigm, this empirical study generated insights on Fijian Muslims' pre-travel experiences of the Hajj performance. Pilgrims' perceptions emphasised on Hajj preparation aspects of financial arrangements, travel arrangement issues and concerns, intellectual preparations and farewell activities. The majority of Fijian pilgrims made massive financial sacrifices to acquire required funds to accomplish Hajj. Certain financial arrangements included the use of retirement pensions, accumulated savings of many years, trade of properties or relinquished potential earnings to fulfill their religious obligation, while also compromising their quality of living standards. Several financially distressed pilgrims took a fresh start in securing their livelihoods after returning from the Hajj. Alternatively, some of the pilgrims made arrangements to maintain economic activities in their absence when accomplishing Hajj. Philanthropic acts (partial or full sponsorship) effectuated several Fijian pilgrims' Hajj. In addition, some of the issues or concerns raised by Fijian pilgrims concerning their Hajj travel arrangements included limited Hajj travel agency choices, lack of travel awareness, inconvenient geographical locations and the delayed and lengthy Hajj confirmation process. Nevertheless, diverse methods guided pilgrims' intellectual preparations for the Hajj performance, with WOM method being the predominant choice. The ultimate pre-trip activity was the pilgrims' farewell, which was a prominent community affair. Thus, the pre-Hajj activities generated various exchanges such as in intellectual, social, economic, psychological and spiritual contexts for the Fijian pilgrims.

This study makes contributions to the fields of religious tourism and Muslim travel, particularly from the perspectives of pilgrims and within the Fijian context. It drew insights on Fijians as consumers of international tourism, thus showcasing an emerging tourist generating market (but long-haul and small), centering on religious tourism (pilgrimage). Nonetheless, this study benefits many stakeholders who lack substantial information on religious tourism and Hajj pilgrimage in particular, in the Fijian context on which little previous research has been conducted.

References

Abad-Galzacorta, M., Guereño-Omil, B., Makua, A., Iriberri, J. L., & Santomà, R. (2016). Pilgrimage as tourism experience: The case of the Ignatian way. *International Journal of Religious Tourism and Pilgrimage, 4*(4), 48–66.

Al-Hilaly, T. A.-D. (2011). Islam in Australia, New Zealand and the neighbouring islands. In I. E. Hareir & E. H. R. M'Baye (Eds.), *The different aspects of Islamic culture: The spread of Islam throughout the world* (pp. 831–854). United Nations Educational, Scientific and Cultural Organization (UNESCO).

Ali, A. (1979). Girmit – The indenture experience in Fiji. *Bulletin of the Fiji Museum*, No. 5.

Ali, J. (2004). Islam and Muslims in Fiji. *Journal of Muslim Minority Affairs, 24*(1), 141–154. https://doi.org/10.1080/1360200042000212241

Alserhan, B. A. (2011). *The principles of Islamic marketing*. Gower.

Altinay, L., Paraskevas, A., & Jang, S. S. (2016). *Planning research in hospitality and tourism* (2nd ed.). Routledge.

Ambroz, M., & Ovsenik, R. (2011). Tourist origin and spiritual motives. *Journal of Contemporary Management Issues, 16*(2), 71–86.

Aziz, H. (2001). The journey: An overview of tourism and travel in the Arab/Islamic context. In D. Harrison (Ed.), *Tourism and the less developed world: Issues and case studies* (pp. 151–159). CABI Publishing.

Back, I. (2015). From West Africa to Mecca and Jerusalem: The Tijāniyya on the Hajj routes. *The Journal of the Middle East and Africa, 6*(1), 1–15. https://doi.org/10.1080/21520844.2015.1026243

Baderoon, G. (2012). 'The sea inside us': Narrating self, gender, place and history in South African memories of the Hajj. *Social Dynamics, 38*(2), 237–252. https://doi.org/10.1080/02533952.2012.724249

Bianchi, R. R. (2013). *Islamic globalization: Pilgrimage, capitalism, democracy, and diplomacy.* World Scientific Publishing Co.

Buitelaar, M. (2018). Moved by Mecca: The meanings of the Hajj for present day Dutch Muslims. In I. Flaskerud & R. J. Natvig (Eds.), *Muslim pilgrimage in Europe* (pp. 29–42). Routledge.

Buitelaar, M., & Mols, L. (2015). Introduction. In L. Mols & M. Buitelaar (Eds.), *Hajj: Global interactions through pilgrimage* (pp. 1–8). Sidestone Press.

Cavana, R. Y., Delahaye, B. L., & Sekaran, U. (2001). *Applied business research: Qualitative and quantitative methods.* Wiley.

Clingingsmith, D., Khwaj, A. I., & Kremer, M. (2009). Estimating the impact of the Hajj: Religion and tolerance in Islam's global gathering. *Quarterly Journal of Economics, 124*(3), 1133–1170. https://doi.org/10.1162/qjec.2009.124.3.1133

Cohen, E. (2006). Religious tourism as an educational experience. In D. H. Olsen & D. Timothy (Eds.), *Tourism, religion and spiritual journeys* (pp. 78–93). Routledge.

Collins-Kreiner, N. (2010). Researching pilgrimage: Continuity and transformations. *Annals of Tourism Research, 37*(2), 440–456. https://doi.org/10.1016/j.annals.2009.10.016

Collins-Kreiner, N. (2016). The lifecycle of concepts: The case of 'Pilgrimage Tourism'. *Tourism Geographies, 18*(3), 322–334. https://doi.org/10.1080/14616688.2016.1155077

Collins-Kreiner, N., & Kliot, N. (2000). Pilgrimage tourism in the Holy Land: The behavioural characteristics of Christian pilgrims. *GeoJournal, 50*(1), 55–67. https://doi.org/10.1023/A:1007154929681

de la Torre, G. M. V., Naranjo, L. M. P., & Cárdenas, R. M. (2012). Life-cycle stages in religious tourism development: A comparison of case studies. *Cuadernos de Turismo, 30*, 241–266.

Domínguez, M. d. M. R., & Alonso, M. V. (2018). Religious tourism in Galicia: The case of El Camino de Santiago. In J. Álvarez-García, M. d. l. C. d. R. Rama, & M. Gómez-Ullate (Eds.), *Handbook of research on socio-economic impacts of religious tourism and pilgrimage* (pp. 86–103). IGI Global.

Durán-Sánchez, A., Río-Rama, M. D. L. C. D., Oliveira, C., & Álvarez-García, J. (2018). Religious tourism and pilgrimage: Study of academic publications in Scopus. In J. Álvarez-García, M. D. L. C. D. R. Rama, & M. Gómez-Ullate (Eds.), *Handbook of research on socio-economic impacts of religious tourism and pilgrimage* (pp. 1–18). IGI Global.

Esposito, J. L. (2011). *What everyone needs to know about Islam.* Oxford University Press.

FBoS. (2015). Population and labour force estimates of 2014. *Statistical News, 99.* Fiji Bureau of Statistics.

France-Presse, A. (2015, October 20). 2015 hajj stampede deadliest ever as foreign governments put toll at 1,849. *The Guardian.* www.theguardian.com/world/2015/oct/20/2015-hajj-stampede-deadliest-ever-as-foreign-governments-put-toll-at-1849

General Authority for Statistics. (2019). *Hajj statistics: 2019–2014.* Ministry of Economy and Planning, Saudi Arabia.

Gillion, K. L. (1977). *The Fiji Indians: Challenge to European dominance, 1920–1946.* Australian National University Press.

Gray, D. E. (2014). *Doing research in the real world* (3rd ed.). SAGE.

Griffin, K., & Raj, R. (2017). The importance of religious tourism and pilgrimage: Reflecting on definitions, motives and data. *International Journal of Religious Tourism and Pilgrimages Today, 5*(3), 2–9. https://doi.org/10.21427/D7242Z

Gulf Research Center. (2018). *Kingdom of Saudi Arabia: Public investment fund & tourism*. Gulf Research Center.

Hammoudi, A. (2006). *A season in Mecca: Narrative of a pilgrimage*. Polity Press.

Haq, M. I. U. (2014). *Companion of Hajj: Your step by step guide to perform Hajj correctly*. Xlibris.

Hillenbrand, C. (2015). *Introduction to Islam: Beliefs and practices in historical perspective*. Hames & Hudson.

Joll, C. M. (2012). *Muslim merit-making in Thailand's far-south*. Springer.

Kaelber, L. (2006). Paradigms of travel: From medieval pilgrimage to the postmodern virtual tour. In D. H. Olsen & D. Timothy (Eds.), *Tourism, religion and spiritual journeys* (pp. 49–53). Routledge.

Lal, B. V. (2009). Indo-Fijians: Roots and routes. In R. Rai & P. Reeves (Eds.), *The South Asian diaspora: Transnational networks and changing identities* (pp. 89–107). Routledge.

Maghniyyah, M. J. (1997). *The Hajj: According to five schools of Islamic law*. Department of Translation and Publication, Islamic Culture and Relations Organization.

Maududi, S. A. A. l. (1978). *Fundamentals of Islam*. Islamic Publications Ltd.

McLoughlin, S. (2009a). Contesting Muslim pilgrimage: British-Pakistani identities, sacred journeys to Makkah and Madinah, and the global postmodern. In V. S. Kalra (Ed.), *The Pakistani diaspora: Culture, conflict and change* (pp. 278–316). Oxford University Press.

McLoughlin, S. (2009b). Holy places, contested spaces: British – Pakistani accounts of pilgrimage to Makkah and Madinah. In P. Hopkins & R. Gale (Eds.), *Muslims in Britain: Race, place and identities* (pp. 132–149). Edinburgh University Press.

McLoughlin, S. (2015). Pilgrimage, performativity, and British Muslims: Scripted and unscripted accounts of the Hajj and Umra. In L. Mols & M. Buitelaar (Eds.), *Hajj: Global interactions through pilgrimage* (pp. 41–64). Slidestone Press.

Miller, K. C. (2008). *A community of sentiment: Indo-Fijian music and identity discourse in Fiji and its diaspora* [PhD Dissertation, University of California]. www.proquest.com/openview/0 4428a15660736e007d419a00fbbfa66/1?pq-origsite=gscholar&cbl=18750

Ministry of Hajj and Umrah. (2018). *Companies & tourism agencies for overseas pilgrims*. www. haj.gov.sa/english/Hajj/TourismAgencies/ Pages/ tur keylowlist.aspx

Murphy, L., Mascardo, G., & Benckendorff, P. (2007). Exploring word-of-mouth influences on travel decisions: Friends and relatives vs. other travellers. *International Journal of Consumer Studies*, *31*(5), 517–527. https://doi.org/10.1111/j.1470-6431.2007. 00608.x

Nationmaster. (2016). *Fiji religion stats*. www.nationmaster.com/country-info/profiles/Fiji/ Religion

Nolan, M. L., & Nolan, S. (1992). Religious sites as tourism attractions in Europe. *Annals of Tourism Research*, *19*(1), 68–78. https://doi.org/10.1016/0160-7383(92)90107-Z

O'Connor, P. (2014). Hong Kong Muslims on Hajj: Rhythms of the Pilgrimage 2.0 and experiences of spirituality among twenty-first century global cities. *Journal of Muslim Minority Affairs*, *34*(3), 315–329. https://doi.org/10.1080/13602004.2014.939557

Olsen, D. H. (2013). A scalar comparison of motivations and expectations of experience within the religious tourism market. *International Journal of Religious Tourism and Pilgrimage*, *1*(1), 41–61.

Olsen, D. H., & Timothy, D. J. (2006). Tourism and religious journeys. In D. H. Olsen & D. Timothy (Eds.), *Tourism, religion and spiritual journeys* (pp. 1–22). Routledge.

Pandey, A. (2011). Indo-Fijians and their success story in Fiji. In A. Dubey (Ed.), *Indian diaspora: Contributions to their new home* (pp. 347–365). MD Publications Pvt Ltd.

Peters, F. E. (1994). *The Hajj: The Muslim pilgrimage to Mecca and the holy places.* Princeton University Press.

Pintér, A. R. (2014). *Religious tourism in Mecca, Saudi Arabia* [Bachelor of Arts thesis]. Budapest Business School. http://dolgozattar.repozitorium.uni-bge.hu/1065/1/Szakdolgozat%20 Pint%C3%A9r%20Anna%20Rita.pdf

Poria, Y., Butler, R., & Airey, D. (2003). Tourism, religion and religiosity: A holy mess. *Current Issues in Tourism, 6*(4), 340–363. https://doi.org/10.1080/13683500308667960

Rahman, M. F. (1993). Prospects for Islam in Fiji. *Research Journal, 2*(7), 43–58.

Raj, R. (2007). Case Study 1: The festival of sacrifice and travellers to the city of heaven (Makkah). In R. Raj & N. D. Morpeth (Eds.), *Religious tourism and pilgrimage festivals management: An international perspective* (pp. 127–139). CABI International.

Raj, R., & Bozonelos, D. (2015). Pilgrimage experience and consumption of travel to the city of Makkah for Hajj ritual. *International Journal of Religious Tourism and Pilgrimage, 3*(1), 38–45.

Reader, I. (2007). Pilgrimage growth in the modern world: Meanings and implications. *Religion, 37*(3), 210–229. https://doi.org/10.1016/j.religion.2007.06.009

Reda, O. M. (2016). Mobile ad hoc networks group mobility models of Hajj crowd dynamics. *International Journal of Applied Engineering Research, 11*(22), 10772–10778.

Rinschede, G. (1992). Forms of religious tourism. *Annals of Tourism Research, 19*, 51–67. https://doi.org/10.1016/0160-7383(92)90106-Y

Shackley, M. (2001). *Managing sacred sites: Service provision and visitor experience.* Thomson Learning.

Sharma, V. (2013). Faith tourism: For a healthy environment and a more sensitive world. *International Journal of Religious Tourism and Pilgrimage, 1*(1), 15–23. https://doi.org/10.21427/D7772J

Shinde, K. (2015). Religious tourism and religious tolerance: Insights from pilgrimage sites in India. *Tourism Review, 70*(3), 179–196. https://doi.org/10.1108/TR-10-2013-0056

Stausberg, M. (2011). *Religion and tourism: Crossroads, destinations, and encounters.* Routledge.

Strategic Initiatives & Government Advisory (SIGA). (2012, April). *Diverse beliefs: Tourism of faith. Religious travel gains ground.* https://ficci.in/spdocumen t/20207/diverse-beliefs-tourism-of-faith.pdf

Swarbrooke, J., & Horner, S. (2016). *Consumer behaviour in tourism* (3rd ed.). Routledge.

Taylor, P. C., & Medina, M. (2011). Educational research paradigms: From positivism to pluralism. *College Research Journal, 1*(1), 1–16.

Taylor, R. M. (2011). Holy movement and holy place: Christian pilgrimage and the Hajj. *Dialog: A Journal of Theology, 50*(3), 262–270. https://doi.org/10.1111/j.1540-6385.2011.00626.x

Tilson, D. J. (2005). Religious-spiritual tourism and promotional campaigning: A church-state partnership for St. James and Spain. *Journal of Hospitality & Leisure Marketing, 12*(1–2), 9–40. https://doi.org/10.1300/J150v12n01_03

Timothy, D. J., & Iverson, T. (2006). Tourism and Islam: Considerations of culture and duty. In D. H. Olsen & D. Timothy (Eds.), *Tourism, religion and spiritual journeys* (pp. 186–206). Routledge.

Timothy, D. J., & Olsen, D. H. (2006). *Tourism, religion and spiritual journeys.* Routledge.

Tourism & More. (2014). *The importance of the religious tourism market.* www.tourismandmore.com/tidbits/the-importance-of-the-religious-tourism-market/

UNWTO. (2011). *Religious tourism in Asia and the Pacific.* UNWTO.

UNWTO. (2014). *Tourism can protect and promote religious heritage.* www.unwto.org/archive/
europe/press-release/2014-12-10/tourism-can-protect-and-promote-religious-heritage

Utomo, S., Scott, N., & Jin, X. (2016, February 8–11). *Hajj outcomes: A review of the literature*
(pp. 314–330). [Paper presentation]. Council for Australasian Tourism and Hospitality
Education (CAUTHE), Conference Proceedings, Sydney.

Vukonic, B. (1996). *Tourism and religion.* Pergamon.

8 Material Religion in Twelver Shiite Pilgrimage

Resources, values, and dynamics in contemporary Mashhad

Rasool Akbari

Introduction: The 'Holy' City of Mashhad

Mashhad, in northeastern Iran, is the capital of the Razavī Khorāsān Province and one of the most popular pilgrimage destinations in the Twelver Shiite geography (Seyfi & Hall, 2018). As it is already reflected in the place-name Mashhad, which literally means 'place of martyrdom' for its association with the Shrine of Imam Reza (the eighth Imam for Twelver Shiite Muslims), the historical macro-scene of the city has made an impact on its sociocultural dynamics. Being the second largest and most populous city in contemporary Iran after Tehran the capital, Mashhad is commonly known to be the modern development of Noqān near Sanābād in the Ṭūs region, located in the Greater Khorāsān district on the Silk Road (Durand-Guédy, 2015). The city has been a popular destination for pilgrimage throughout the ages for Shia pilgrims. Mashhad is visited annually by over 36 million pilgrims and travelers including approximately 4 million foreign tourists and pilgrims, which carries profound economic, sociocultural, and environmental consequences for the whole region, as well as (geo)political implications at both national and transnational levels (Seyfi & Hall, 2018, 2019). This has led to the growing significance of the shrine city on the travel map of contemporary Islam.

Numerous Persian and several international studies have already examined the historical, archeological, architectural, geographical, political, psychological, sociological, anthropological, and economic as well as touristic and even theological dimensions of pilgrimage and the Shrine in Mashhad (see Yousofi et al., 2013). In the existing literature on pilgrimage and tourism in the Mashhad context, one particularly salient element has been the dualities or complexities within the religious and nonreligious aspects of travel (e.g., Khamsy & Vossughi, 2018; Olya, 2018). Nevertheless, scant attention has been paid to understanding such sociocultural ambivalences of pilgrimage in Mashhad within the framework of religious studies to include micro and macro levels of analyses that can offer the possibility of greater insight into forms of cultural life that are labeled as 'religion'.

DOI: 10.4324/9781003036296-11

Study Design: Approaching Twelver Shiite Pilgrimage in Mashhad

In light of the 'cultural turns' in the study of religion (Lynch, 2012), this chapter argues that a cultural approach can examine the dynamics of pilgrimage as religion at concurrent intersections of the scared on the one hand and the human on the other. On this basis, presumably such concepts as dimensionality, materiality, and relationality that are salient features in the cultural dynamics of religion within human society can help better explain the complexities of religious and nonreligious elements in the contemporary Mashhad's pilgrimage field.

First, pilgrimage seems to be embodied at not only ritual and doctrine aspects of religion that have commonly been addressed in the existing literature but also at such multiple 'dimensions of the sacred' as particularly theorized by Smart (1996). Hence, the intricacies of faith tourism in Mashhad can be rooted in the multidimensionality of pilgrim attitudes and behaviors in their cultural milieus. Moreover, a growing trend in current religious studies is the attempt to deal with the role of materiality in religions. In this context, 'material religion' offers an analytical framework for understanding materialization as the embodiment, emplacement, and enactment of not only religious belief and experience but also all religion dimensions, 'as there is no such thing as an immaterial religion. . . . Religion is unable to do without things, places, or bodies, nor may it operate without theories about materiality' (Meyer et al., 2010, p. 210). In this regard, among the living denominations of Islam, materiality of religion seems to be particularly featured in Twelver Shiism, with a plentiful reservoir of places, personages, myths, objects, and practices; so much that the devotional acts in this madhab are even sometimes dismissed as 'paganism', 'idolatry' or 'polytheism' by a number of ultraconservative and Islamist movements (Bianchi, 2013). Additionally, a number of Sunni schools, particularly Wahhabism, reject as untrue the Twelver Shiites belief that the veneration of saints and theirs shrines can mediate between Allah and humans (Nasr, 2006). This intrareligious clash can display divergences between contested Islamic theologies of humanity–divinity relations. Therefore, the relational, dimensional materialities of religion seem to offer a helpful point of departure that must be considered sufficiently when it comes to understanding the complexities of pilgrimage.

Based on such a conceptual triangulation, the present study aims to address the cultural intricacies of Islamic travel in the contemporary field of Mashhad. This research objective is pursued by not only marshaling evidence of material artifacts utilized in the ritualistic procedures of Imam Reza Shrine pilgrimage but also by exploring the multidimensional materiality of its

"lived religion" (McGuire, 2008) at the complex intersection of doctrine, ritual, narrative, ethics, law, institution, location, space, time, aesthetics, economy and politics. In other words, the materiality of Twelver pilgrimage cannot be merely allocated to the things and practices that have to function as symbols to be interpreted for the religious meanings they hold or only considered as the product of the cultures and disciplines of power and not even simply ascribed a phenomenological aspect with religious elements imbued with human experience and cognition (Hazard, 2013). Instead, materiality of pilgrimage in the present case studied in the Twelver context of Mashhad can be approached as a multidimensional 'assemblage' with hybrid formations of tangible and intangible resources and multifold values in the setting of relations among human and non-human agents. According to the state-of-the-art for material religion, 'a shift in the study of materiality from primary attention to production, form, style, and artistic intention' towards understanding the meanings of objects entails a consideration of 'different cultures of materiality' with a concentration on the 'lives of objects . . . in relation to audiences or users by tracing their social careers, the places they go and the different ways they are put to use' (Meyer et al., 2010, p. 209). This is corroborated in existing research in terms of materializing the local circulation and adaptation of 'a matrix or network of components' consisting of 'people, divine beings or forces, institutions, things, places, and communities' (Insoll, 2009), as well as the 'cultural construction of materiality in relational structure' (Pels, 2008).

Although such a relational element in the dimensional materiality of religion can shed some light on the cultural complexities of Twelver Shiite pilgrimage culture, a theoretical foundation is required for describing, explaining, and interpreting ambivalent dynamics of the sacred and the social. With a focus on the relational feature of pilgrimage religiosity, Müller (2017) has conducted fieldwork research on the 'religious endowment' of *Vaqf* in the context of the Imam Reza Shrine in Mashhad. The theoretical framework of 'Socio-Cosmic Fields' that Müller (2017) has adopted from the German ethnologist Hardenberg (2015) can be a useful conceptual tool for the present research at both descriptive and analytical steps to categorize and better understand the dimensions and typologies of materiality and further address questions surrounding the complex dynamics of "valuation" involved in the "production, distribution, and consumption" of the dimensional material assemblages.

Apart from the triangulated conceptualizations of dimensionality, materiality, and relationality, mainly through Smart (1996) and Hardenberg (2015), the present chapter also applies methodological triangulation (Denzin, 1970) in a qualitative research approach that includes semi-structured interviews, participant observation, and document analysis (Flick, 2018). Hence, the qualitative data collection comprises of participant observation in various locations, practices, and events within the Imam Reza Shrine zone and its nearby bazaars in Mashhad, semi-structured interviews with institutional and vernacular human actors in the field, as well as analytical documentation of relevant artifacts of objects and printed and digital materials gained from the research settings. The fieldwork was conducted in the period from August 2019 to September 2020, which created a large and convergent interview data collected through snowballing sampling as well as the expansion of the researcher's existing connections and previous knowledge and familiarities with the field through his professional work at the central administration of the Imam Reza Shrine called the Āstān Qods Razavī (AQR) (literally, the Sacred Threshold of Imam Reza).

The primary informants whose 'native interpretations' (Geertz, 1966) are finally used for descriptive analysis in this chapter include AQR officials (*karkonān*), shrine-servants (*khoddām*), pilgrims (*zowwār*), and members from the Islamic City Council of Mashhad, as well as salespersons from the bazaar (*bāzārī*). In addition, this study has secondary informants among the Iranian clerical and political figures (*rohānīyūn va sīyāsīyūn*) whose stories have been adapted from public lectures and mass media. Throughout this research, all participant names have been anonymized by pseudonyms to protect confidentiality; except for the names of commonly known public figures. Even though the research participants come from different backgrounds in terms of ethnicity, religiosity type, social class, education, and gender, what unites them is their comparable and contrastable personal and institutional attitudes when it comes to the multidimensional dynamics of Twelver Shiite pilgrimage materiality in contemporary Mashhad. Therefore, the main selection criteria of primary and secondary interviews for analysis have been the significance of the informants' experiences and interpretations in relation to the topic under study. In what follows, the descriptive data are presented as macro-scene and micro-scene findings on the question of how dimensional, material, and relational elements in Twelver Shiite pilgrimage create cultural complexities in terms of religious and nonreligious aspects of travel.

Macro-scene: Post-revolutionary Cultures of Pilgrimage in Mashhad

It is important and relevant in the present chapter to consider at least briefly the macro-scene of urban development as well as Shrine administration in Mashhad's pilgrimage landscape, which brings us to the contemporary post-revolutionary condition with its complex cultures of pilgrimage. In the early centuries, the organization of the 'Holy Shrine' was small and its endowments were a few; therefore, a doorkeeper, sometimes even a woman caretaker, used to be in charge of the affairs of the tomb building, so they would stay at the tomb during the day and then close the doors at night and return to their own place of residence. Later, the people who were called *Naqīb* (from among the *Sādāt* descendant of Prophet Muhammad or among the local scholars and elders) were in charge of managing the Shrine (Birjandi & Naseri, 2012). In the face of countless foreign invasions and national turbulences, the protection of the mausoleum of Imam Reza became possible particularly by the patronage works of benefactors such as the Timurid ruler Shāhrukh in the 15th century CE and his reportedly 'pious' wife Gowharshād who sponsored the construction of a cathedral mosque as well as Islamic chapels or prayer rooms within the Shrine yard for scholarly purposes and spiritual practices (Manz, 2007).

With the spread of the Twelver Shiite religion in Iran and particularly its formal political institution during and after the Safavid, the Shrine organization became increasingly important because of its ever-growing endowments due to its exalted place among the Shiites who formed the great majority of the Iranian population. For this reason, the administration and management of this complex was expanded and assigned to a particular Shrine custodian called *mutawallī bāshī* working under the control of the king who intervened directly in the allocation of the Shrine resources (Birjandi & Naseri, 2012). The governorship of Khorāsān by a member of royal family during the Qajar reign (1909–1925) was later merged with the prominent and moneymaking function of the *mutawallī bāshī*, who was in charge of the Shrine treasures.

During the course of the 20th century, Mashhad grew to become the second most populous Persian metropolis with its far-reaching influences on the economic as well as sociopolitical dynamics of Iran. Particularly based on its unique access to the massive revenue amounts of *vaqf* or donations made by local as well as national, regional, and international pilgrims, the AQR as the central administration of the Shrine has increasingly gained a crucial political and economic authority in Iran and in the Muslim World. As part of their so-called modernization plan, the Pahlavi monarchs (1925–1979) ordered the transformation of the Mashhad urban landscape. It is often said that relying largely on the iron fist power of the AQR as well as the booming oil money of 1974, Mohammad Reza, the Pahlavi king from 1941 until the year 1979 of the Islamic Revolution, had the ambitious plan to make Mashhad the most important and most modern pilgrimage center of the Muslim World (Bosworth, 2007). The Pahlavi expansion programs were met by a storm of protests and disagreements from the prevailing public opinion – largely shaped by the clerical institutions and seminaries as well as the bazaar activists who had an important mobilization role throughout the Islamic Revolution against the Shah. They mainly considered the Pahlavi development plans as a secularizing mission to desacralize Mashhad and to control revolutionary movements rooted in the religious circles and seminaries as well as the bazaar.

After the overthrow of the Pahlavi dynasty in 1979, the renovation project of the Shrine complex was halted shortly for both financial as well as cultural-ideological reasons, including most importantly the general economic depression of the post-revolutionary era worsened by the prolonged Iran-Iraq War (1980–1988), as well as the alleged ideals of the Islamic Revolution to return the public properties to the people, to avoid luxurious lifestyles that were against Islamic values, and to care for the religiosity and spirituality of the nation. This attitude is documented in an early revolutionary interview of the ayatollah Abbās Vāez-Tabasī (1983), the Shrine custodian appointed by Imam Khomeini since the beginning of the Islamic Revolution in 1979 until his death in 2016. 'The AQR was an organization to serve the [Pahlavi] regime at material as well as spiritual and intellectual aspects', says the ayatollah, 'to use the huge capitals of the Shrine for propaganda against underlying religious beliefs . . . and to develop the surface decorations of the Shrine at the cost of their missions against Islamic programs' (Vāez-Tabasī, 1983). He then explains the revolutionary mission of the AQR to be 'the fulfillment of the material and spiritual as well as intellectual needs of the oppressed nation' and to use the Shrine endowment resources for 'charity support for the poor', 'construction of mosques and religious buildings', 'mass housing projects', 'building community hospital and drugstore', 'development of economic and agricultural infrastructures', as well as 'cultural' activities such as 'the establishment of a university for Islamic sciences and an enormous library to keep and spread intellectual capitals' (Vāez-Tabasī, 1983).

Such ideals held by the custodian ayatollah four decades ago seem to have prevailed as post-revolutionary values for the AQR. One research informant who currently works for the Organization of Shrine Territory Development at AQR [Sādeq], believes that the perspective behind the 'strategic planning in the Islamic Revolution differs essentially from that of the Pahlavi'. According to Sādeq's interpretation, the Pahlavi had 'a secular expansionist view based on their materialistic ideology' focused primarily on 'financial gains from Mashhad pilgrimage' with an aim to 'transform the holy city into a tourist destination'; therefore, they 'destroyed the Shrine neighborhood' and 'applied force' against the local settlers and businesses. Sādeq believes that the post-revolutionary understanding of development correlates with the terms in Article 3 of the Constitution Law; i.e. the duty for the Islamic Republic government of Iran to direct all its resources for 'the creation of a favorable environment for the growth of moral virtues based on faith and piety and the struggle against all forms of vice and corruption' (Islamic Parliament Research Center, 2004). Sādeq emphasizes that the development planning for the Shrine of Imam Reza after the revolution has 'exactly' been founded on such 'values and missions' to construct new prayer rooms, mosques, and yards in order to improve the infrastructure and all facilities needed by the people who want to 'fulfill their pilgrimage duties and practice their pious religiosity'. He refers to such a development as a 'paradigm shift in governing Mashhad as a pilgrimage destination on the basis pure of Islamic teachings'.

Today, outside the Shrine building complex and its surrounding neighborhood, when it comes to the rather non-religious touristic tendencies of the pilgrims, Mashhad offers a variety of options with regard to the entertainment industry. Several suburban area provide typical attractions apart from the Shrine pilgrimage and historical sites for visitors of Mashhad to spend some time for leisure. Some of the visitor offerings include the natural landscape; Mashhad cuisine (based on various types of Persian kebabs); recreational centers such as water parks (some of the largest in the Middle East); and old and modern shopping malls offering quality saffron and precious blue stone of turquoise as specialist souvenir of the Khorāsān region. Local basket-weaving and colorful designs of Persian carpets and rugs are also among the most important handicraft products of this region. Nonetheless, a number of controversial discussions led by authoritative clerical figures still raise issues as to whether Mashhad's 'holy city' identity can be amalgamated with non-religious and 'profane' activities and locations of 'worldly' and 'luxurious fun'. According to the Imam of Friday Prayer in Mashhad, ayatollah Alam al-Hodā, who is appointed to this clerical-political position by the Supreme Leader and acts as a frontline con-servative player in the Mashhad field, 'the people of this city are not citizens but neighbors of Imam Reza; and the pilgrims of this Imam are not to be consid-ered as tourists who want to have fun in this city' (The Islamic Republic News Agency (IRNA), 2019). He continues,

> some people who have the idea of developing tourist places in this city and have created facilities in the green areas of this city, which have failed and been humiliated even now [referring to the financial breakdown of a tourism development center in Mashhad's green suburbs], because they wanted to change the identity of this city from pilgrimage to tourism, and Imam Reza beats them because he does not like the change of identity of this city.
>
> (IRNA, 2019)

Nevertheless, a member of the City Council sees no paradoxes between the sacred and secular identities of Mashhad. As a PhD in urban planning, he believes that, while the 'pilgrimage identity' of Mashhad is a dominant marker, the city's both religious and nonreligious touristic 'potentials must be liber-ated' and proportionately exploited for reinvigorating and strengthening the whole region's economy. At the same time, however, another member of the Council who comes from an engineering background at university and holds more traditional and revolutionary perspectives acknowledges the importance of finding ways to improve and stabilize local economies and businesses with-out 'endangering the religious identity of the City of Imam Reza'. In his inter-pretation, if this 'holy identity' is not 'preserved', the whole 'social and cultural capitals' of the city will be jeopardized. In addition, he regrets the 'failure to provide a comprehensive plan for sustainable development' of the city's pil-grimage horizon as 'cultural economy'.

Underlining cultural contingency in contemporary society, there are social scientists who suggest that the term 'culture' should always be used in plu-ral (Hardenberg et al., 2017, p. 17) as 'contested systems of meaning, learnt, shared and negotiated in various ways'. On this basis, the post-revolutionary culture[s] of pilgrimage in contemporary Mashhad seems to be characterized by mixed valuations of both sacred and profane elements as they relate to the materialized visibility of religion. The interpretations narrated here from local institutional actors in the field can bring into attention the micro-scene complexities of pilgrimage and travel; particularly with regard to the socio-spatial and material dimensions which embody the visibility of religion in Iran an Islamic state. In this sense, the religious and ideological investment of the political system in the Twelver Shiite Islam – specified in Article 12 of the Constitution as 'official religion' in an 'eternally immutable' manner (Islamic Parliament Research Center, 2004) – seems to have blurred the bounda-ries of the sacred and the society further and created more complexities and ambivalences.

Micro-scene: Dimensions of Material Religion in Mashhad Pilgrimage

Participant observation in different locations and events at three layers of the Shrine, the surrounding Bazaar, and the city tourism landscapes reveals various dimensions of the pilgrimage materiality. According to the Smartian anatomy, different dimensions of religion are mutually interconnected or dialectically interactive. Although each of the dimensions of religion may exist independently or can be discerned in other domains of human culture, they are clustered into an interactive complex 'whole', and it is in this sense that we can speak usefully of a 'religion' (Strenski, 2015).

In the setting of the Shrine interior and open spaces, doctrinal and narrative religion have been materialized in the form of countless copies of not only the Qur'an but also various books of prayer and supplication (often attributed to Twelver Shiite Imams), with Persian and even sometimes English and Urdu translations, mostly published by the AQR publishing company (*Behnashr*) and distributed widely free for access everywhere within the Shrine interior areas and its courtyards. The same publications outside the Shrine zone are distributed for purchase consumption as some believers consider the AQR brand as carrying a blessed association. Numerous objects are used at the aesthetic dimension for interior and exterior design of the Shrine and its different courts, yards, and mosques; from the golden and silver tomb frame itself, to the different types of cloths, stones, tiles, carpets, glasses, lamps, colors, papers, posters, scents, and sounds; and even the pigeons. Moreover, there are several things that are particularly employed for ritual purposes. However, for the faithful community, it is difficult and irrelevant to separate the aesthetic functions of material objects in the Shrine from their ritual or legal functions. One important reason can be that materialized religion enacts a variety of religious experiences at the emotional dimension. According to one volunteer servant wearing a formal black garment, 'everything in the Shrine is attached to the holiness of the atmosphere which is blessed by the living presence of the martyred Imam; there is nothing impure in this sanctuary'.

Especially after the Revolution, the AQR has purchased, introduced, and installed several electronic and digital as well as technological devices and machineries to improve a multitude of services and tasks e.g., religious and cultural performance, cleaning, security, and maintenance practices at the Shrine complex. In many cases, the people working with those gadgets also venerate their materiality as an embodiment of service to the Imam and the pilgrims. Nonetheless, there have always been different degrees of controversial debates whether, what types, and how far technological devices can be introduced to the Shrine, as new gadgets are often thought to desacralize the spaces and change or challenge traditional procedures. One AQR official said, for instance, how in the face of the COVID-19 pandemic, the observation of sanitation protocols and health measures has turned out to be a serious challenge to meet, with grave concerns over the use of hygiene products and sanitizing devices for cleaning and disinfecting the 'holy spaces that are conventionally believed to be pure'.

Outside, many such Shrine items and salvation-goods are often produced and distributed by AQR related companies or other corporate businesses carrying its logo brand not only to attract faith travel buyers but also to win a quality market share in the region and at the national as well as exportation level. Apart from the AQR Agricultural and Gardening as well as Dairy Productions, the traditional Nan-e-Razavi have been producing a diversity of bakery products since the 1960s with a huge development project after the Revolution and its nationwide distribution has run over a hundred kiosks in Mashhad. More recently, the AQR Institute for Artistic Creations has opened several pilgrimage souvenir and gift shops especially in the Shrine neighborhood to supply decorative, crystal, pottery, stone, ceramic, embossed, and painting products on Islamic and Twelver Shiite motifs as well as Islamic Revolutionary themes. Many casual interviewees at those shops and department stores seemed to be satisfied with their purchase by both material quality and design of the products and more particularly 'the blessed element in the goods carrying Imam Reza's holy name'. More middle-class buyers are seen in the rather stylish artistic gift shops while the casual middle and lower-class customers often flock the AQR bakery and dairy products in its department and grocery stores – both for their consumption during their stay in Mashhad or as a souvenir to take for their relatives back home 'to share the blessing (*barekat*) of Imam Reza's food'.

Additionally, in the surrounding Bazaar, old and modern markets offer various kinds of religious and nonreligious goods, from shroud, evil eye, rosary, prayer soil (*mohr*), prayer blanket (*sajjādeh*), hijab (*chādor*), headscarf (*maqnaeh*), rings and jewelry, and holy shrine perfume (*atr-e haram*), to spice, saffron, barberry, nuts and dried fruit, *nabāt* candy, and toys for kids. Most of the shopping, particularly at AQR stores, seems to happen after the pilgrimage visitation of the Shrine, as if in the gesture of a post-liminal rite (Van Gennep, 1960). Ali, a young salesman at a famous saffron shop who is also a university graduate in accounting explains that many pilgrims believe 'their pilgrimage will not be completely accepted by Imam Reza' if they do not buy souvenirs for their relatives back home. He thinks there is no death for pilgrimage business as there is no end for the Imam's blessings. However, another seller, Mostafā, who is a middle-aged man working at a souvenir shop, complains that the AQR chain stores have caused the private businesses to suffer. 'Of course, people prefer to buy religious souvenirs with an Imam Reza logo', he explains cheerlessly, 'because they imagine that they will receive more *barekat*'. Having said that, Mostafā concludes, 'God is great and we hope Imam Reza himself will help us'.

Mahdī, a 22--year-old university student of sport sciences, who works in his father's rings and jewelry store, regrets that his family business is not profitable enough and says how he is taking lifeguarding courses to get a certificate and find a job in a water park. 'I don't understand why there should be a problem if you come to visit Imam Reza and also enjoy your free time with family and friends in a water park, or go to cinema'. His father, a tall man in his 60s, frowns at him, 'Of course there is a problem! You want to swim, you can go to the North [of Iran] at beach. Clearly, man travels to Mashhad to visit Imam Reza and pray! Not to have fun!' The debate soon takes a political turn as Mahdī and his father seem to disagree over the role of the clerical institution in Iranian society. Mahdī makes a loud comment in the end, 'It is all about business! Āstān [i.e. AQR] makes charity money, but also sells cakes and cookies. You are selling rings to Imam Reza's pilgrims. Others and I want to have a swimming business. So, what's the problem?!' 'But we do religious job to sell souvenirs. It is not a shame!' his father responds quickly.

Many non-AQR shops also sell tickets to touristic attractions of the city, including discount coupons for the water and amusement parks. Davood, a young man with a university education in geography who works for a governmental office in Tehran, tells me when I meet him after a prayer in the Shrine that he travels 'to see Imam Reza' at least once a year and spends about a week in a government hotel with his family. Davood emphasizes that Mashhad is 'a mixed pilgrimage and tour city' where he always plans to do several activities in addition to the Shrine pilgrimage; including visiting relatives in Mashhad, going to the green suburbs, and enjoying their time in water amusement parks. When I ask him what he thinks is the significance of material culture in the Shrine architectures, the rituals, and the souvenirs and if religion needs those objects and things, he answers that 'we love our Imams and although they do not need these decorations their shrines deserve to be magnificent; and we buy material souvenirs for our relative with a hope that they will receive their share of the *barekat* of *zīyārat* (pilgrimage)'.

For Meyer et al. (2010, p. 209), the material study of religion deals with the functions of 'bodies, things, places, and practices' and investigates them 'all within the network of relations that make the sacred a social reality'. The data collected in this research demonstrates how the things, places, and practices in Twelver Shiite pilgrimage cultures can be categorized into the Smartian 'dimensions of the sacred'. To cut a long story short, the doctrine and narrative dimensions play mostly an 'attitudinal' function to justify not only the 'holiness' of the 'martyred Imam' (*al-Imām al-Shahīd*, as the Shiite supplication texts read) but also the faithful veneration of his Shrine as a materialized 'part of paradise on earth' (*qet'e-yee az behesht*, according to popular religious culture and narrative). At the ritual and emotional dimensions, countless Shiite devotional practices are associated with the pilgrimage act to embody and enhance religious experience, e.g. from prayer, to charity, to souvenir purchases. The Islamic Republic claims to invest in the material development of the Shrine complex and related infrastructure with a mission to improve the moral and ethical dimensions of religiosity among the nation. This can in itself reflect not only the ideological and political aspects of pilgrimage but also highlight the significance of the institutional element that hierarchizes religious experience and practice. The legal or *fiqhi* dimension of Shiite Islam is apparently merged with the role of the clerical institution to be enacted in spatial sanctions and sensitivities with regard to the Shrine's 'holy territory', which is also expanded to include the whole city and the region, where for instance it is exclusively prohibited to hold music concerts. And finally, the aesthetic dimension is most vividly reflected at the material diversities of things, practices and places associated with Twelver Shiite pilgrimage and Shrines.

Discussion: Mashhad as a Socio-cosmic Field

When it comes to the material culture of salvation-goods and souvenir purchases, or the production, distribution, and consumption of material objects in association with pilgrimage practice, the boundaries between the religious and nonreligious seem to have become significantly blurred. Moreover, one out of three pilgrims in the Shrine the researcher talked to thought it is a 'distraction' and a 'disgrace' to travel to Mashhad with an aim to 'waste their time in the water parks' instead of a 'devoted attention to the martyred Imam'. Nonetheless, outside the Shrine setting, particularly in the bazaar, only one out of five considered it 'not a good idea' to 'confuse' the religious identity of Mashhad's pilgrimage with nonreligious practices such as 'excessive shopping in modern markets' or doing 'leisure activities'. Although such observations can create ambivalent dualities for approaching religious travel, this chapter argues that an attention to the dimensional, material, and relational dynamics of religion as a cultural system of meanings (Geertz, 1966) can facilitate our understanding of those complexities.

In light of a variety of 'cultural turns' (Bachmann-Medick, 2016) in social sciences since at least the 1970s, Hardenberg et al. (2017) coin the term 'Resource Turn'. In this context, 'resources' are tangible and intangible means that create, maintain or change relationships. Hardenberg et al. (2017, p. 19) emphasize, however, that 'a strict dichotomy between tangible and intangible has to be avoided, because human beings themselves are part of the tangible world'. Accordingly, resources can be seen as embedded in cultural systems of action and meaning where value is attributed to resources and 'specific ways' are defined for using them (Hardenberg et al., 2017). In addition, by expanding Bourdieu's concept of the 'field' (Bourdieu & Wacquant, 1992) as a sociocultural 'space of action', Hardenberg (2015) has introduced 'socio-cosmic fields' characterized by two different kinds of relations 'between human actors' and 'between human and non-human actors'. According to this typology, society is not to be considered as something distinctly unique to humans 'but as part of a larger cosmos with which people entertain various relations in different contexts of life' (Hardenberg, 2015). As a result, 'resources' are conceptually expanded 'as an analytical category' not only to include the conventional tangible aspects of life and existence but also to cover the more intangible dimensions of culture. Therefore, for Hardenberg (2015, p. xxx), resources are embedded into both social and cosmic spheres, and 'defined by similar actions but different relations'.

Drawing on Hardenberg's (2015, 2017) conceptualizations, we can approach Mashhad as a socio-cosmic field where the pilgrimage dynamics occur in the context of relations 'between human actors' and 'between human and non-human actors'. On this basis, Mashhad's pilgrimage field is a sociocultural 'space of action' where the multidimensional materializations of Twelver Shiism are enacted by multiple actors. The tangible and intangible resources in Mash-had's pilgrimage tend to overlap with the dimensional materialities of doctrine, narrative, ritual, ethics, law, emotion, institution, etc. that are utilized by the human agents to 'create, maintain or change relationships'. As it has been seen in the collected data, human agency includes not only the institutional actors such as the AQR organization, the custodian, the Friday prayer imam, or the officials but also the pilgrims and the salespeople as independent individuals. These actors position themselves in a mixed field of socio-cosmic relations, with not only human but also non-human actors. This duality of relations in the field can be a cause for complexities in understanding the religious and nonreligious elements in Twelver Shiite pilgrimage. For example, the late custodian of the Shrine or the Friday prayer Imam reveal in their verbal expressions how they find themselves in relations not only with the pilgrims and the nation at the social sphere but also with cosmic actors of religion, i.e., Allah and the Imam Reza. Similarly, the salespeople and the pilgrims are positioned in social relations with other human actors, i.e., pilgrims, colleagues, and community, as well as the cosmic actors of religion, i.e., Allah and the Imam Reza.

In addition, Hardenberg (2017) argues that the social and the cosmic fields of action are connected by 'certain values' that in their view form valued relations, i.e., relations structured by values. These valued relations are extended to various (non)human beings 'recognized as agents of the socio-cosmos'. By adopting two possible variations of 'value pluralism' and 'value monism' from Robbins (2013), Hardenberg (2017) demonstrates that the social and cosmic fields are simultaneously 'separate' and 'undifferentiated'. Accordingly, at least two 'monist' and 'pluralist' tendencies exist in the value relations of all societies. Hence, the two social and cosmic spheres are either (1) separated and 'experienced as distinct areas of action' determined by their own specific values that might even be essentially different from or in conflict with each other, or (2) connected with a 'paramount value' that dominates all relations and subordinates all other values.

Based on the findings of the present study, while some actors interpret the valued relations of pilgrimage in monistic and undifferentiated ways, others experience value pluralism in pilgrimage relationality and separate the two spheres of the social and the cosmic multidimensional materiality. For instance, actors with a monistic perspective disapprove of the possibility to materialize intangible religious resources or values and as a result tend to reject much of the material culture in pilgrimage and instead prioritize or hierarchize moral and spiritual dimensions of religiosity as paramount values. On the contrary, the pluralists, who prefer to separate conflicting spheres of values in social and cosmic realms, do not repudiate one value at the cost of the other; so, for example, they accept materiality as a possibility at multidimensional levels of pilgrimage religiosity. Apparently, when it comes to the complexities of religious and leisure activities, value monists consider tourism development as a threat to the pilgrimage identity of Mashhad and define the materiality of Twelver Shiite culture in exclusively cosmic, doctrinal, or legal sense, whereas the pluralists tend to valuate both pilgrimage and touristic dimensions of Mashhad's identity as potentials for urban development and promote the materiality of Twelver culture at various dimensional levels. In consequence, various institutional and individual actors with monistic and pluralist preferences and choices in the socio-cosmic field of Mashhad finally create, sustain, and change different types of relations at both humanity-humanity and humanity-divinity layers. These micro-scene sociocultural diversities are translated into ambivalences and complexities in the macro-scene of pilgrimage cultures within the Mashhad socio-cosmic field of action.

Conclusion

From a religious studies perspective, the present chapter applied a conceptual triangulation of dimensionality, materiality, and relationality in an attempt to better understand the dualities of religious and nonreligious elements in contemporary Twelver Shiite pilgrimage in Mashhad. Based on the analysis of data collected from triangulated field observation, interviews, and artifact sources, it has been demonstrated that the intricacies of pilgrimage cultures in Mashhad are grounded in the different valuation behaviors of the institutional and individual actors in the production, distribution, and consumption processes of religiosity. Drawing on Hardenberg's (2017) theories, it can be concluded that Mashhad functions as a socio-cosmic field or space for action where different actors with their divergent value monistic and pluralist tendencies enact and materialize various dimensions of religion, i.e., in this case, pilgrimage religiosity. Such divergent valuation preferences and choices by the actors in the field will ultimately create, maintain, and alter a diversity of relations at social as well as cosmic spheres. The ambivalences or complexities of Mashhad's pilgrimage landscape can be better understood through such cultural analysis of religiosities in contemporary society.

References

Bachmann-Medick, D. (2016). *Cultural turns: New orientations in the study of culture* (A. Blauhut, Trans). De Gruyter.

Bianchi, R. (2013). *Islamic globalization: Pilgrimage, capitalism, democracy, and diplomacy.* World Scientific.

Birjandi, Z. A., & Naseri, A. (2012). The effect of the functions of the custodians of Astan Qods Razavi on Shiite culture (Case study: Qajar era). *Quarterly Research Journal of Islamic History, 6*(1), 77–107. [Persian].

Bosworth, E. (Ed.). (2007). *Historic cities of the Islamic world.* Brill.

Bourdieu, P., & Wacquant, L. (1992). *An invitation to reflexive sociology*. University of Chicago Press.

Denzin, N. K. (Ed.). (1970). *Sociological methods: A sourcebook*. Routledge.

Durand-Guédy, D. (2015). Pre-Mongol Khurasan: A historical introduction. In R. Rante (Ed.), *Greater Khorasan: History, geography, archaeology and material culture* (pp. 1–8). De Gruyter.

Flick, U. (2018). *An introduction to qualitative research* (6th ed.). Sage.

Geertz, C. (1966). Religion as a cultural system. In M. Banton (Ed.), *Anthropological approaches to the study of religion* (pp. 1–46). Tavistock Publications.

Hardenberg, R. (2015). Beyond economy and religion: Resources and socio-cosmic fields in Odisha, India. *Religion and Society: Advances in Research, 7*(1), 83–96. https://doi.org/10.3167/arrs.2016.070106

Hardenberg, R. (2017). Introduction: The study of socio-cosmic fields. In R. Hardenberg (Ed.), *Approaching ritual economy: Socio-cosmic fields in globalized contexts* (pp. 7–36). Universität Tübingen.

Hardenberg, R., Bartelheim, M., & Staecker, J. (2017). The 'resource turn': A sociocultural perspective on resources. In A. K. Scholz, M. Bartelheim, R. Hardenberg, & J. Staecker (Eds.), *Resource cultures: Sociocultural dynamics and the use of resources – theories, methods, perspectives* (pp. 13–24). Universität Tübingen.

Hazard, S. (2013). The material turn in the study of religion. *Religion and Society, 4*(1), 58–78. https://doi.org/10.3167/arrs.2013.040104

Insoll, T. (2009). Materiality, belief, ritual-archaeology and material religion: An introduction. *Material Religion, 5*(3), 260–264. https://doi.org/10.2752/175183409X12550007729824

Islamic Parliament Research Center. (2004). *Iran constitution*. https://rc.majlis.ir/fa/law/show/133730

The Islamic Republic News Agency (IRNA). (2019). *The axis of Mashhad city should be the development of pilgrimage*. www.irna.ir/news/83548792 [Persian].

Khamsy, N., & Vossughi, F. (2018). The mutual relationship between women's pilgrimage tourism and the religious city: A case study of Mashhad, Iran. In S. Seyfi & C. M. Hall (Eds.), *Tourism in Iran: Challenges, development and issues* (pp. 84–98). Routledge.

Lynch, G. (2012). Living with two cultural turns: The case of the study of religion. In S. Roseneil & S. Frosh (Eds.), *Social research after the cultural turn* (pp. 73–92). Palgrave Macmillan.

Manz, B. F. (2007). *Power, politics and religion in Timurid Iran*. Cambridge University Press.

McGuire, M. (2008). *Lived religion: Faith and practice in everyday life*. Oxford University Press.

Meyer, B., Morgan, D., Paine, C., & Plate, S. B. (2010). The origin and mission of material religion. *Religion, 40*(3), 207–211. https://doi.org/10.1016/j.religion.2010.01.010

Müller, R. (2017). 'Write *Vaqf*, read paradise'. Emām Rezā's religious endowment in the socio-cosmic field of Mashhad, Iran. In R. Hardenberg (Ed.), *Approaching ritual economy: Socio-cosmic fields in globalized contexts* (pp. 135–158). Universität Tübingen.

Nasr, V. (2006). *The Shia revival: How conflicts within Islam will shape the future*. W.W. Norton & Company.

Olya, H. G. T. (2018). Mass faith tourism and life satisfaction of residents: Evidence from Mashhad, Iran. In S. Seyfi & C. M. Hall (Eds.), *Tourism in Iran: Challenges, development and issues* (pp. 99–110). Routledge.

Pels, P. (2008). The modern fear of matter: Reflections on the Protestantism of Victorian science. *Material Religion, 4*(3), 264–283. https://doi.org/10.2752/175183408X376656

Robbins, J. (2013). Monism, pluralism and the structure of value relations: A Dumontian contribution to the contemporary study of value. *HAU: Journal of Ethnographic Theory, 3*(1), 99–115.

Seyfi, S., & Hall, C. M. (Eds.). (2018). *Tourism in Iran: Challenges, development and issues.* Routledge.

Seyfi, S., & Hall, C. M. (2019). Deciphering Islamic theocracy and tourism: Conceptualization, context, and complexities. *International Journal of Tourism Research, 21*(6), 735–746. https://doi.org/10.1002/jtr.2300

Smart, N. (1996). *Dimensions of the sacred: An anatomy of the world's beliefs.* University of California Press.

Strenski, I. (2015). *Understanding theories of religion: An introduction* (2nd ed.). Wiley Blackwell.

Vāez-Tabasī, A. (1983). Interview. *Pasdar-e Eslam 19*, 24–27. [Persian].

Van Gennep, A. (1960). *The rites of passage.* University of Chicago Press.

Yousofi, A., Ouraie, G. S., Kohansal, A., & Mocrizadeh, F. (2013). Empirical phenomenology of pilgrimage to Imam Reza's shrine in Mashhad. *Iranian Social Studies, 6*(3–4), 180–198. [Persian].

9 An ethnographic study of lived experiences of Iranian Arba'een foot-pilgrims in Iraq

Zohair Siyamiyan Gorji, Abolfazl Siyamiyan Gorji and Seyedasaad Hosseini

Introduction

Religious tourism is one of the oldest forms of tourism that, in the modern age, continues to have a substantial market (George, 2014). Individuals visit a religious site to confirm, deepen, or reflect on their faith. In addition, religious visitors travel to see religious attractions such as mosques, cathedrals, statues, and temples, or to participate in an annual religious event (Nikjoo et al., 2020). According to Stausberg (2011), religious tourism includes pilgrimages, retreats, conferences, seminars, and festivals. Raj and Griffin (2015, p. 14) defined religious tourism as "a variety of spiritual places and related services visited for both secular and religious purposes". Religious tourism is not just a spiritual vocation, but it also has a significant economic component. As a result, religious tourism has emerged as a new market segment in the tourist industry (George, 2014). Religious tourism is motivated by a combination of cultural, traditional, secular, and spiritual elements that lead to a travel decision (Raj et al., 2015), and many UNESCO World Heritage List sites have a religious or spiritual connection (Adie & Hall, 2017; Adie, 2019).

Many pilgrims and tourists visit religious destinations every year, including Lourdes in France, Canterbury in England, Czestochowa in Poland, Fatima in Portugal, Saint Peter's in the Vatican, Jerusalem in Palestine and Israel, and Mecca and Medina in Saudi Arabia. Some religious symbols and rituals are more sacred than others. The reason for this lies in the context of the formation of the religious memory of this community and the different readings of various religious symbols in different periods of history (Bod, 2019) as well as the growth in secular interest in non-religious spiritual experiences. However, there are other important religious sites, and the foot journey to the shrine of Imam Hussain in Iraq is arguably the largest neglected pilgrimage market for those that travel on foot (Nikjoo et al., 2021).

The uprising of Imam Hussain and various readings of the Ashura account throughout history have given it and the Ashura storytelling a vivid narrative, and this dynamic can be seen in the specific mourning ritual of Karbala and Arba'een. The substance of Shiite social and political life was formed on the basis of a movement directed against political hegemonic power. At the same

DOI: 10.4324/9781003036296-12

time, the Third Imam of the Shiites holds a special place in their hearts as a fighter and insurrectionary leader and has long served as a source of motivation for their protest movements. The participation of millions of Shia Muslims of pilgrims in Karbala in the Arba'een walk on this day has meant that it has become established as the largest annual public gathering of Shia Muslims in the world (BBC, 2014). Huge crowds of pilgrims, mostly from the Shia community of Iran, Pakistan, India, Saudi Arabia, Azerbaijan, Lebanon, Turkey, Kuwait, Afghanistan, Bahrain, and Syria, come to Iraq at the end of the 40-day mourning period after Ashura in Arba'een to commemorate the martyrdom of the third Shia Imam; Imam Hossein. Imam Hossein, who was one of the grandsons of Prophet Mohamad killed in 61 AH (680 AD) in battle with Yazid I (Nikjoo et al., 2020). The Arba'een ritual has only become more popular after being restricted during Saddam Hussein's rule and since revived after the fall of Saddam in 2003.

While foot pilgrimage is well researched in Western countries, there are few studies that focus on religious goals especially in the Middle Eastern context (Blacker, 1984; Murray & Graham, 1997; Reader, 2007; González & Medina, 2003; Kim et al., 2016; Husein, 2018; Seyfi & Hall, 2019; Nikjoo et al., 2020, 2021). The aim of this chapter is to investigate the motivations and experiences of pilgrims walking on their journey to Imam Hussain's shrine in Karbala, the world's largest, yet overlooked, foot-pilgrimage market. The chapter begins with a review of the literature on the Karbala pilgrimage and provides contextual background on foot-pilgrimage. This is followed by the study's methodologies, results, and discussion before conclusion drawn.

Literature review

Religious tourism and Islam

Pilgrimage is one of the oldest and most significant human movements in the world. According to Cazaux (2011) pilgrimages are transformational in that pilgrims seek inner changes such as miracles, enlightenment, knowledge, closer connections with supernatural powers, and a better sense of self-mastery. Tourism has traditionally been closely linked to religion, which serves as a strong motivator for travellers. Religious sites are a source of attraction for travellers (Timothy & Olsen, 2006). Moreover, religious organizations increase people's confidence in the power of the sacred by creating collective realities (Albayrak et al., 2018). According to Terzidou et al. (2018), they can influence pilgrims' motivation to attend by spreading miraculous places and fueling them through ideological interpretations of religious texts and collective stories. Blackwell (2007) notes that religious tourism is described as a trip to specific tourist towns where travelers experience religious events, including art, culture, traditions, and architecture. Religious tourism is one of the oldest forms of tourism and represents a significant, expanding, growing, and more diverse sector of the global tourism business (Rinschede, 1992; Sharpley, 2009) and includes a wide variety of spiritual sites and locations, as well as related services, that are utilized for both secular and religious purposes and experiences (Morinis, 1992; Raj et al., 2015).

History is replete with examples of the connection between religion and travel. Pilgrimages are practiced by virtually all the world's major religions. Regardless of religion, pilgrimages are becoming increasingly popular, despite the secular nature of many modern countries. Religion has a great impact on the daily lives of Muslims. Islam has over one and a half billion followers, making it one of the largest religions in the world. Muslims are mainly native to the Middle East, where the religion originated before spreading to Africa and Southeast Asia (Esposito, 1999).

In Islam pilgrimage involves an obligation to wander and is one of the five pillars of Islam, along with belief in God and the Prophet Muhammad, prayer, fasting, and almsgiving. Kessler (1992) argued that *ziyarat* is a type of voluntary pilgrimage travel that illustrates the spatially distinct traditions of Islam and refers to pilgrimage to locations associated with Muhammad, his family (including the Shia Imams), and other venerated figures in Islam. Muslims, according to the Quran, should travel to enjoy the beauty of God's creation and to visit their friends and relatives (see also Chapters 1 and 2, this volume). The Kaaba in Mecca is the holiest site in Islam. Another holy city for Muslims is Jerusalem, which is also a holy place for Christians and Jews. Shiite Muslims on the other hand, consider Karbala in Iraq as one of the holiest places in the world (Iliev, 2020).

Since the late 1980s, pilgrimage has gained greater academic attention from a tourism perspective (Coleman & Elsner, 1995). Reader (2007) examined the rise of modern pilgrimage and asserts that personal motives for participating in pilgrimages vary regardless of religious background. In Islam, the Hajj journey is considered one of the most significant pilgrimage phenomena in the world with millions now making the journey each year (Kamali, 1996). During the rituals associated with the Hajj, Muslims repeat various supplications and prayers to Allah. Those who consider themselves religious tourists or pilgrims visiting holy sites also often have a strong attachment to these places and destinations. Consequently, religious tourism can have an impact on the economic and cultural growth of places that have significant religious elements (Kim et al., 2020).

Shiite pilgrimage and Karbala

Shia Muslims, the second largest group in Islam, accept the centrality of Mecca and the Hajj but take a different approach to pilgrimage rituals and sites than Sunni Muslims. To understand contemporary Shiites, we must return to the formative battle of Karbala in 680, where one of Muhammad's grandsons (Hussain) was killed by the Umayyads. Accordingly, Shia pilgrimages to such places as Karbala, Najaf, Mashhad, and others that are associated with the battle and Imam Hussain, which are now mainly in Iran and Iraq, are considered almost as important as Mecca because they contain the tombs of the Imams and their descendants (Imam Zadeh) (Seyfi & Hall, 2018).

Pilgrims who complete these pilgrimages are given the title *Karbalaei*, which is the Shia equivalent of *Hajji* (Nikjoo et al., 2020). Along with the current geopolitical changes in the Middle East (Hall & Seyfi, 2020), the Shia pilgrimage is undergoing significant changes, especially in the pilgrimage centers in present-day Iran and Iraq. After the Iran-Iraq war – which effectively banned Iranians from visiting holy sites in Iraq – and the fall of Saddam Hussein, many Iranians are now making a trip to traditional Shiite centers in Iraq. The visits are not only encouraged but also supported and organized by the Iranian government, such as the hub of the festival at Arba'een, in Karbala. This pilgrimage is currently the largest religious gathering in the world. Every year on the 10th of Muharram (the first lunar month) as Ashura (the holiday that celebrates the prophet Moses crossing of the Red Sea) and 40 days later, on the 20th of Safar (the second lunar month), Arba'een (literally '40') is commemorated (Jonathan et al., 2018). Shia Muslims observe Arba'een in commemoration of the Battle of Karbala with different religious rituals at their homes. Mourning assemblies are held from the first Muharram to the day of Arba'een, a 40-day period commemorating the martyrdom of Imam Hussain. Pilgrims travel to Karbala from Iraq, Iran, and other parts of the world, resting in tents along the way. Some pilgrims even travel on foot from Azerbaijan, Georgia, and Pakistan. Charities, mosques, and religious organizations set up booths to ensure that no traveller goes hungry. Thousands of Iraqi military and special police units are deployed to protect pilgrims along the routes. Pilgrims of different genders and ages take part in the pilgrimage (*meshaya*). Female *zawars* wear black *abayas* (long robes), while the men wear white/black long robes. People often organize large marches in cities around the world on this day to symbolize the permanence of Hussain's revolution and to show their support for social justice, compassion and dignity. Arba'een Day is now one of the largest annual peaceful gatherings in the world and continues to grow each year.

Methodology

The interpretive paradigm and thematic analysis approach were used to conduct this research because of its qualitative, reflective, and interpretive nature and its commitment to understanding the nature of activists' shared experiences. One of the authors joined other pilgrims who were walking the 78 km distance from Najaf to Karbala to better understand the motivations and intentions of the pilgrims to participate in the pilgrimage despite the extreme danger. He observed and interviewed the pilgrims using ethnographic research methods. Ethnography is a qualitative set of research methods used by anthropologists and other social scientists to comprehensively and qualitatively capture the lived and embodied experience of research subjects. This visit lasted five days and included social interaction between

one of the researchers and other visitors. The author collected data during
the visit to gain a conceptual understanding of Arba'een and then contacted
foot pilgrims who can communicate in Persian. Forty-seven people were
asked to participate in the interviews, and forty of them agreed. Seventeen
females and twenty-three males were interviewed. Before each interview
began, the interviewer informed interviewees that their voices would be
recorded for research purposes, and all participants gave their consent. The
interviewer assured participants that their identities would be kept confi-
dential and questioned the participants about their reasons for travelling
to Karbala, their narratives of the journey, their emotions and feelings, the
reasons for determining this number of pilgrims, and the hospitality of the
Iraqis. Each interview lasted about 35 minutes on average. Thematic analysis was used to analyze the interviews in an iterative process. In this step,
we identified and labeled concepts that emerged from the data. To avoid
bias in the coding process and to increase confidence, the authors met and
discussed codes in the open and axial coding process. The data were then
organized into major themes and the specific comments of the interviewees
were matched.

Research findings and discussion

In this study, four underlying themes are identified: expected guerdon (reward);
embodied experience; guest experience; and lived time.

Expected Guerdon

One of the reasons some people decide to participate in the Arba'een foot-pilgrimage is a vow to walk and request to meet their needs and wishes. Indeed,
the "vows" and "wishes" are some of the drivers of these trips. The pilgrim
walk is a way to achieve these vows, because it is believed that when enduring
the hardships and difficulties of travelling along this path Imam Hussein will
help pilgrims to achieve individual aspirations. This is commented on by an
interviewee who argued that participation in the foot-pilgrimage ritual will
lead to them meeting their wishes:

> I couldn't get pregnant. I used to go to some doctors and took medicine.
> but the result didn't satisfy me. I was getting depressed, so decided to walk
> to Arba'een, that maybe Imam helps me and my wishes come true.
>
> (interview #23)

In other words, the pilgrim endures the hardship of the route in exchange
for what they think is desirable. Intentions such as healing the sick, having
children, marrying a beloved, getting a money-making job, gaining virtue, and migration were common thoughts commented on by many foot-
pilgrims. Another interviewee expressed that participating in walking with

the hope of a miracle in their life is common among many pilgrims. He commented:

> I'm walking on foot for the sake of my ill father to be healed by Imam. My father is bedridden in the hospital. He has cancer. He is suffering from that cancerous gland. Doctors told us there is no way to get better except a miracle. I'm not the only one that comes with this hope, many people on the route have the same wish.
>
> (interview #2)

The healing experiences along the route of Karbala represent the factors of sacredness linked to the journey. Hassner (2003) considered healing as one of the functions that characterize a sacred site. Besides, Husein (2018) reported the healing experiences that happened for some Zawars as they were walking on the path, noting that foot-pilgrims deeply believe in that miracle.

Embodied experience

Embodied experiences are related to the physical experiencing of walking on a sacred route. Some participants expressed that by enduring the challenges of the Karbala path they can attain spiritual refinement and inner purity by identifying with their Imam on Ashura Day. Many of the interviewees stated that "love of Imam" helps them to tolerate the suffering and desolation of walking along the path. This "redemptive suffering" also raised their passion and eagerness to continue the sacred and spiritual journey. One of the interviews indicates their experience as follows:

> This path is nearly 80 kilometers and for many of us, this is too much. However, we feel it hurting in our body or on our knees, but a hidden power, a hidden hand is pulling us to go forward, and says to us that move, take the steps, come, I'm waiting for you.
>
> (interview #8)

Nikjoo et al. (2020, 2021) argue that enduring hardships on the Karbala path can be explained as a form of behavior attachment by foot-pilgrims, as they believe that they are invited to this sacred journey by Imam Hussein. Therefore, there is a sense of satisfaction with suffering pain among Arba'een foot-pilgrims as it justifies the deliberate nature of their actions (Nikjoo et al., 2020).

This is echoed by another interviewee:

> Depending on my schedule, this route takes from two days to four days. A path that, due to its length, I never feel fatigued. My body may be tired at times, but it is an enjoyable hardship to see the love. A spiritual trip with many hardships but full of love for Imam Hussein.
>
> (interview #5)

Guest experience

The dominant aspect of Iraqi's hospitality during the walk experience manifests the distinctive form of hospitality known as "Arab hospitality" or "karam al-arab," which is a traditional virtue in which the guests are welcomed (Shryock, 2004; Hall et al., 2020). However, in 2019 the generous hospitality of Iraqi people during the Arba'een pilgrimage has been registered to UNESCO's prestigious heritage list titled: "Provision of services and hospitality during the Arba'in (Arba'een) visitation" (Teymoori, 2019). All participators commented on the hospitality; one of the respondents stated:

> Along the entire journey, one finds tents [called *mawqibs*] established by the locals to serve the *zowar* [visitors] of Imam Hussain. Furthermore, there is some accommodation to rest, take shower, and eat food. Some local are ready to massage your feet and legs. So how much money should you take with you to pay for this wonderful hospitality?
>
> (interview #17)

It is echoed by another interviewee:

> It's notable the way Iraqian behave with us as a guest on Arba'een. During this period Iraqi people host and will welcome to everyone . . . there is no price for food and places to sleep and rest . . . all locals open their homes. Iraqi people welcome everyone . . . I can say that even Iraqians have redefined the whole meaning of hospitality, where a host takes pride in servicing guests who really are random people to him . . . an elderly Iraqi man grabbed me from the crowd and sat me on a bench . . . he began removing my shoes and socks for me, then started to polishing my shoes for God's sake and respect to Imam Husein pilgrims.
>
> (interview #12)

Among Muslim people there is a consensus that being hospitable and generous toward guests is an integral part of faith in Islam (Hall & Prayag, 2020). It can be seen in Qur'an as well as a considerable number of *ahadith* such as the content in the Surat Hud (69 and 78) and LI-Surahtal-Thariat (24–27), which comprise evidence in the Islamic faith about the importance of serving, hospitality, and honoring guests (Sobh et al., 2013). Hence, this type of home hospitality comprises a lived experience for our interviewees.

Lived time (temporality)

From a phenomenological perspective, the concept of time and space is considered as the time and space of inner lived experience or "intentionality" (Im & Jun, 2015). Im and Jun (2015) also state that, although human bodies inhabit time and space, they do not just exist in time and space. Indeed, these two concepts are lived and experienced, and individuals are moving in time and space. The bodies of those who were questioned along the way exist in time and space. "Lived time (temporality)" is a subjective term that refers to the lived experience time of a circumstance that is provided to a person. As a result, pilgrims to Karbala perceive the passage of time in different ways depending on their circumstances. The respondents' lived experience of time's notion of a "period-machine" is the time of daily life they encountered before travelling on the journey to Karbala. A respondent made the following observation:

> The entire 24 hours of a day I was always working, my mind always was busy about the challenges in my personal life, I even forgot what was the meaning of rest. I lived alone and immersed myself in my career . . . but now I am away from the boring daily grind and this is why I feel so excited.
>
> (interview #19)

Our respondents believe that the feeling of forgetting the routine life motivated them to revisit the shrine and the path. Three of them echoed the same perspective word-for-word:

> Every year after getting back [home], I wait for the next Arba'een. I count down day by day and wish whether I can come again.
>
> (interview #11, 12, 23).+

Indeed, the interviewees were of the belief that the "temporality" has made good sense to them. This was echoed by another respondent:

> This is the first time that I decided to go on the Arba'een walk. I had no idea of what awaited me, just heard that the feeling is inexplicable. When the time arrived, the feeling was incredible. It's like a few days when you can forget about life, time, work and all worldly concerns. And, they were right; I wanted more of the experience. The feeling was different. I hadn't felt it in years.
>
> (interview #16)

Conclusion

Religious tourism is one of the oldest types of tourism. Pilgrims travelled into sacred places even before existence of the holy books such as the Holy Bible and Quran (Timothy & Olsen, 2006). In Islam, Muslims are encouraged to take religious travels to see the world (Luz, 2020; see Chapters 1 and 2, this volume). Millions of travellers, predominantly Shia, travel to Karbala each year to visit the shrine of Imam Hussein, where the Prophet Mohammed's grandson is buried. During this pilgrimage commemoration which is called Arba'een (Arabic for 'forty'), Zowars from countries such as Iran, Pakistan, Lebanon, Afghanistan, India, Azerbaijan, and Armenia, take the steps toward this city. The Arba'een journey has dramatically increased in recent decades among faithful Shiite Muslims in Iran, particularly those who support the Islamic Republic's ideology (Nikjoo et al., 2020). Considering such popularity, this chapter adopts a phenomenological approach which sought to uncover the lived experiences of the Iranians' foot-pilgrims of Arba'een.

According to the interviews and their coding, four overall dimensions were extracted as the main context of the lived experience: lived time (temporality); expected guerdon; embodied experience; and guest experience. According to the empirical findings, pilgrims were pulled by an ongoing religious custom related to the Shia branch and the battle of Karbala. Indeed, as has long been noted in the literature on pilgrim's movements and mobilities, pilgrim's motivations are both sacred and secular (Smith, 1992). However, between these two points of the scale can be seen numerous secular/religious combinations of religious tourism (Qurashi, 2017). As such, their lived experiences and motivations of Arba'een foot-pilgrims have sacramental source intentions that are rooted in religious rituals.

References

Adie, B. A. (2019). *World Heritage and tourism: Marketing and management.* Routledge.

Adie, B. A., & Hall, C. M. (2017). Who visits World Heritage? A comparative analysis of three cultural sites. *Journal of Heritage Tourism, 12*(1), 67–80. https://doi.org/10.1080/17 43873X.2016.1151429

Albayrak, T., Herstein, R., Caber, M., Drori, N., Bideci, M., & Berger, R. (2018). Exploring religious tourist experiences in Jerusalem: The intersection of Abrahamic religions. *Tourism Management, 69*, 285–296. https://doi.org/10.1016/j.tourman.2018.06.022

BBC (2014, December 14). *Shia pilgrims flock to Karbala for Arba'een climax.* www.bbc.com/news/world-middle-east-30462820

Blacker, C. (1984). The religious traveller in the Edo period. *Modern Asian Studies, 18*(4), 593–608. https://doi.org/10.1017/S0026749X00016310

Blackwell, R. (2007). Motivations for religious tourism, pilgrimage, festivals and events. In R. Raj & N. D. Morpeth (Eds.), *Religious tourism and pilgrimage festivals management: An international perspective* (pp. 35–47). CAB International.

Bod, M. (2019). Mega event of Arba'een, a manifestation of religious tourism. *Journal of Art and Civilization of the Orient, 7*(23), 5–14. https://doi.org/10.22034/jaco.2020.83915

Cazaux, F. (2011). To be a pilgrim: A contested identity on Saint James' Way. *Tourism: An International Interdisciplinary Journal, 59*(3), 353–367.

Coleman, S., & Elsner, J. (1995). *Pilgrimage: Past and present in the world religions.* Harvard University Press.

Esposito, J. L. (1999). *The Islamic threat: Myth or reality?* (3rd ed.). Oxford University Press.

George, R. (2014). *Marketing tourism in South Africa* (5th ed.). Oxford University Press.

González, R., & Medina, J. (2003). Cultural tourism and urban management in northwestern Spain: The pilgrimage to Santiago de Compostela. *Tourism Geographies, 5*(4), 446–460. https://doi.org/10.1080/1461668032000129164

Hall, C. M., & Prayag, G. (Eds.). (2020). *The Routledge handbook of Halal hospitality and Islamic tourism.* Routledge.

Hall, C. M., Razak, N. H. A., & Prayag, G. (2020). Introduction to Halal hospitality and Islamic tourism. In C. M. Hall & G. Prayag (Eds.), *The Routledge handbook of Halal hospitality and Islamic tourism* (pp. 1–18). Routledge.

Hall, C. M., & Seyfi, S. (Eds.). (2020). *Cultural and heritage tourism in the Middle East and North Africa: Complexities, management and practices.* Routledge.

Hassner, R. E. (2003). "To halve and to hold": Conflicts over sacred space and the problem of indivisibility. *Security Studies, 12*(4), 1–33. https://doi.org/10.1080/09636410390447617

Husein, U. M. (2018). A phenomenological study of Arba'een foot pilgrimage in Iraq. *Tourism Management Perspectives, 26*, 9–19. https://doi.org/10.1016/j.tmp.2017.11.015

Iliev, D. (2020). The evolution of religious tourism: Concept, segmentation and development of new identities. *Journal of Hospitality and Tourism Management, 45*, 131–140. https://doi.org/10.1016/j.jhtm.2020.07.012

Im, K. M., & Jun, J. (2015). The meaning of learning on the Camino de Santiago pilgrimage. *Australian Journal of Adult Learning, 55*(2), 329–349.

Jonathan, A., Widjaja, P., & Husein, F. (2018). Fostering religious exclusivism and political pluralism in Indonesia through interfaith-based student community. *KnE Social Sciences, 3*(5), 53–70. https://doi.org/10.18502/kss.v3i5.2325

Kamali, M. H. (1996). Methodological issues in Islamic jurisprudence. *Arab Law Quarterly, 11*, 3–33.

Kessler, L. D. (1992). Missionaries and Chinese nationalism: Devolution at a Southern Presbyterian Mission in Jiangsu. *Republican China, 17*(2), 52–76. https://doi.org/10.1080/08932344.1992.11720198

Kim, B., Kim, S. S., & King, B. (2016). The sacred and the profane: Identifying pilgrim traveler value orientations using means-end theory. *Tourism Management, 56*, 142–155. https://doi.org/10.1016/j.tourman.2016.04.003

Kim, B., Kim, S. S., & King, B. (2020). Religious tourism studies: Evolution, progress, and future prospects. *Tourism Recreation Research, 45*(2), 185–203. https://doi.org/10.1080/02508281.2019.1664084

Luz, N. (2020). Pilgrimage and religious tourism in Islam. *Annals of Tourism Research, 82*, 102915. https://doi.org/10.1016/j.annals.2020.102915

Morinis, E. A. (1992). Introduction: The territory of the anthropology of pilgrimage. In E. A. Morinis (Ed.), *Sacred journeys: The anthropology of pilgrimage* (pp. 1–28). Greenwood Press.

Murray, M., & Graham, B. (1997). Exploring the dialectics of route-based tourism: The *Camino de Santiago. Tourism Management, 18*(8), 513–524. https://doi.org/10.1016/S0261-5177(97)00075-7

Nikjoo, A., Razavizadeh, N., & Di Giovine, M. A. (2021). What draws Shia Muslims to an insecure pilgrimage? The Iranian journey to Arba'een, Iraq during the presence of ISIS. *Journal of Tourism and Cultural Change, 19*(5), 606–627. https://doi.org/10.1080/14766825.2020.1797062

Nikjoo, A., Sharifi-Tehrani, M., Karoubi, M., & Siyamiyan, A. (2020). From attachment to a sacred figure to loyalty to a sacred route: The walking pilgrimage of Arba'een. *Religions, 11*(3), 145. https://doi.org/10.3390/rel11030145

Qurashi, J. (2017). Commodification of Islamic religious tourism: From spiritual to touristic experience. *International Journal of Religious Tourism and Pilgrimage, 5*(1), 89–104.

Raj, R., & Griffin, K. (2015). Introduction to sacred or secular journeys. In R. Raj & K. Griffin (Eds.), *Religious tourism and pilgrimage management: An international perspective* (pp. 1–15). CAB International.

Raj, R., Griffin, K., & Blackwell, R. (2015). Motivations for religious tourism, pilgrimage, festivals and events. In R. Raj & K. Griffin (Eds.), *Religious tourism and pilgrimage management: An international perspective* (pp. 103–117). CAB International.

Reader, I. (2007). Pilgrimage growth in the modern world: Meanings and implications. *Religion, 37*(3), 210–229. https://doi.org/10.1016/j.religion.2007.06.009

Rinschede, G. (1992). Forms of religious tourism. *Annals of Tourism Research, 19*(1), 51–67. https://doi.org/10.1016/0160-7383(92)90106-Y

Seyfi, S., & Hall, C. M. (Eds.). (2018). *Tourism in Iran: Challenges, development and issues.* Routledge.

Seyfi, S., & Hall, C. M. (2019). Deciphering Islamic theocracy and tourism: Conceptualization, context, and complexities. *International Journal of Tourism Research, 21*(6), 735–746. https://doi.org/10.1002/jtr.2300

Sharpley, R. (2009). Tourism, religion and spirituality. In M. Robinson & T. Jamal (Eds.), *The Sage handbook of tourism studies* (pp. 237–253). Sage.

Shryock, A. (2004). The new Jordanian hospitality: House, host, and guest in the culture of public display. *Comparative Studies in Society and History, 46*(1), 35–62. https://doi.org/10.1017/S0010417504000039

Smith, V. L. (1992). Introduction: The quest in guest. *Annals of Tourism Research, 19*(1), 1–17. https://doi.org/10.1016/0160-7383(92)90103-V

Sobh, R., Belk, R. W., & Wilson, J. A. (2013). Islamic Arab hospitality and multiculturalism. *Marketing Theory, 13*(4), 443–463. https://doi.org/10.1177/1470593113499695

Stausberg, M. (2011). The Bologna process and the study of religion\s in (Western) Europe. *Religion, 41*(2), 187–207. https://doi.org/10.1080/0048721X.2011.586259

Terzidou, M., Scarles, C., & Saunders, M. N. (2018). The complexities of religious tourism motivations: Sacred places, vows and visions. *Annals of Tourism Research, 70*, 54–65. https://doi.org/10.1016/j.annals.2018.02.011

Teymoori, A. (2019, December 14). The generous hospitality of Iraqi people during the Arba'een pilgrimage has been added to UNESCO's prestigious heritage list. *Ijtihad Network.* http://ijtihadnet.com/Arba'een-hospitality-gains-unesco-heritage-status/

Timothy, D., & Olsen, D. (Eds.). (2006). *Tourism, religion and spiritual journeys.* Routledge.

Part IV

Women's travel

10 Complexities of women solo travelling in a conservative post-Soviet Muslim society

The case of Uzbek women

Abolfazl Siyamiyan Gorji, Seyedasaad Hosseini, Fernando Almeida Garcia and Rafael Cortes Macias

Introduction

Travel means different things to different people. Many people travel for pleasure, while others travel for adventure and to experience new things. Either way, an important component is that travel has the potential to change people's lives in a variety of ways (Wilson & Harris, 2006). When people decide to travel, they face constraints, that is, factors that limit their ability to participate in leisure activities even though they have the freedom and desire to do so (Raymore, 2002). Moreover, as tourism is a cultural and social phenomenon, the traveller's experience as a socially structured factor shaped by cultural norms affects their gender (Seow & Brown, 2018). The challenges to gender equality have arisen in every aspect of our lives. The focus is on gender equality in areas such as education, status, awareness, and access to socio-economic opportunities. Gender has also entered the realm of leisure. Leisure time has long been segregated by gender, with women disadvantaged in terms of leisure opportunities. Travel restrictions differ regarding social background or gender norms that influence opportunity and actions (Jackson, 1988). Consequently, as with many leisure activities, access to travel and tourism is not evenly distributed across social groups, including other classes and genders (especially women) (Hosseini et al., 2021).

Prior to the mid-twentieth century, long-distance leisure and travel were reserved only for wealthier, upper-class men and women (Harris & Wilson, 2007). In addition, women travelling alone were deemed unsuitable by society. Following World War II, massive social transformations occurred, resulting in changing social conditions and structural circumstances for women. Gender equality has now resulted in a significant increase in female employment among emerging and developing countries. Women's travel opportunities are expanding as their economic empowerment grows, and an increasing number of females have recently begun to travel independently in search of freedom, independence, and empowerment (Elliot, 2015). The growing trend of female travel has attracted the attention of scholars (Wilson & Harris, 2006; Wilson & Little, 2008; Jordan & Aitchison, 2008; Seow & Brown, 2018; Yang

DOI: 10.4324/9781003036296-14

et al., 2018a, 2018b; Nikjoo et al., 2021; Hosseini et al., 2021) who examine various aspects of the female solo travel experience, including the meanings associated with their experiences. There are a number of studies and reviews on gender, women, and travel restrictions (Yang & Tavakoli, 2016; Yang et al., 2017). Nevertheless, many studies on gender and tourism focus on Western countries with conservative Muslim societies being overlooked (Seyfi & Hall, 2019). According to Cohen and Cohen (2015), while solo travellers share some characteristics, the interpretation of tourism in developing regions such as the Middle East and Muslim countries differs significantly from that of the West. Therefore, more research is needed on the differences in tourism studies from these emerging regions.

According to Tavakoli and Mura (2021), throughout history, social, cultural, and religious variables have limited the tourist mobility of Muslim women. However, in recent years, Muslim travellers have become a growing segment of tourism, whether they travel for work or leisure with friends, family, or alone. For example, in 2018, the number of Muslim female travellers was estimated at 63 million, accounting for 45 percent of all Muslim travellers. While there are some studies and reviews on gender, women, and travel restrictions, the specific travel restrictions for Muslim women travellers need further analysis and study. Additionally, there is a lack of studies investigating the travel constraints of the growing women traveller's segment, in new independent post-soviet countries in central Asia. Overall, there are some important considerations that direct the focus of the current study to Uzbek women travellers. First, by focusing on a relatively unknown market segment (Muslim women in Central Asia), the study adds a specific perspective to the existing body of knowledge on leisure and travel constraints in general and on women's leisure and travel constraints in particular. Second, this study uses leisure travel as an example to investigate how one's gender plays a role in travel decisions and to what extent these factors are perceived as constraints. Third, this study adds to the existing body of knowledge by not only providing an overview of the existing literature on Muslim women's travel restrictions but also critically evaluating it to highlight areas for future focus.

Solo female travel and restriction on leisure

Tourism perceptions have shifted over the course of the twenty-first century. Nowadays, people want to travel not only to see places but also to learn about new cultures and have new experiences. The concept of solo travel is one such example of a new travel trend that is constantly evolving (Spreitzhöfer, 2008). Solo travellers make up an increasingly large proportion of the rapidly growing international tourism market (Dempsey, 2015). Solo travellers have a variety of motives, including resilience, exploration, autonomy, lack of a travel companion, spontaneity, prestige, and loneliness (Mehmetoglu et al., 2001). Larsen et al. (2009) found that the travel goals and travel behaviours of solo travellers differ from those of mass visitors (see also Larsen, 2014). The solo traveller has the freedom to go wherever they want and participate in the activities they want to (Kozak, 2010). Since tourism is a social and cultural phenomenon, tourists' experiences are influenced by their genders as a socially structured component influenced by cultural norms (Henderson & Gibson, 2013). Changes in socioeconomic levels, along with the development of democracy and gender equality, have led to an increase in the number of women participating in leisure activities (Wilson & Little, 2005). As a consequence, solo travel by women has increased substantially (Jordan & Gibson, 2005; Jordan & Aitchison, 2008; Seow & Brown, 2018). Meanwhile, women's main goals for solo travel are to challenge themselves, feel independent, and meet new people (Jordan & Gibson, 2005; Wilson & Harris, 2006). According to Wilson and Harris (2006), females who travel alone have the opportunity to reevaluate how they view life and society, including their own relationships with others. Women travellers who are confident enough to solo travel, in quest of adventure, social contact, education, and self-knowledge tend to feel more autonomous (Hosseini et al., 2021). However, despite female solo travellers, many leisure spaces are still primarily dominated by men (Hall & Page, 2016; Khan, 2017).

The progress of travel is accompanied by new obstacles to overcome. Travel restrictions are defined as 'those barriers or blockages that inhibit continued use of a recreation service' (Backman & Crompton, 1989, p. 59). In leisure research, restrictions are seen as limiting the formation of leisure preferences and inhibiting participation and enjoyment (Jackson et al., 1993; Hung & Petrick, 2012). Many scholars have addressed the issue of constraints in recreation studies. Wilson and Little (2005) state that, in some societies, recreational opportunities were separated by gender because gender can be a barrier when making travel arrangements and decisions. Gender differences in travel restrictions are understood as an expression of the unequal distribution of power relations in a patriarchal society. According to Hung and Petrick (2010), constraints are characteristics that impede travel; affect women's ability to initiate, sustain, or enhance travel; and/or negatively affect the quality of travel. Wilson and Little (2005) argue that, while women are free to travel, they may be restrained by social and gendered environments. Brown and Osman (2017) emphasize that from the past to the present women face gender barriers in their pursuit of leisure experiences. This situation varies in different parts of the world, and women are still restrained by cultural norms and gender norms. Furthermore, women's social roles and their gendered position as 'women' have severely limited their access to leisure activities over the past decade (Jackson & Henderson, 1995). For example, societal expectations of women are related to the traditional image of marriage and children, which emphasizes women's primary duties as family preservers and caretakers of their husbands and children (Cambronero-Saiz, 2013).

Travellers are usually victims of violent crime because they are careless, ignorant, and unfamiliar with the area. Nonetheless, women are likely to be easier targets because they are more visible when alone (Lepp & Gibson, 2003) and they are often exposed to gendered threats (Karagöz et al., 2020) ranging from unwanted attention to physical attacks (Wantono & McKercher, 2020). Both gender and risk perceptions impact travel decisions (Hall & Page, 2016). There-fore, women unconsciously learn to fear strangers, avoid going to certain areas alone (Wilson & Little, 2008), avoid certain times of day (Yang et al., 2018a, 2018b), or select same-sex groups when meeting new people (Wantono & McKercher, 2020), which leads them to be restricted (Wilson & Little, 2008). Moreover, risk-taking is associated with masculinity, whereas risk management is associated with femininity, especially in patriarchal systems dominated by fear and social control, where female travel behavior is judged by appropriateness.

Asian Muslim female solo travellers

Research has tended to focus on the limitations experienced by Western women more than Asian Muslim female solo travellers. However, exceptions include recent studies by researchers on the impact of Asian cultural norms on women's travel behavior (Yang & Tavakoli, 2016; Yang et al., 2018a, 2018b; Seow & Brown, 2018). Compared to Western and Asian women, Muslim women are portrayed as fragile and dependent (Seyfi & Hall, 2018; Seyfi et al., 2020). One of the challenges for Muslim female travellers is planning to travel alone or in an all-female group, as they must obtain permission from their legal guardians. According to Islamic rules, an unmarried girl (under 18) must seek permission from her guardian, while a married woman needs official permission from her husband (Tavakoli & Mura, 2021). This rule may differ from country to coun-try, depending on how Islamic rules are implemented and the socio-cultural context (e.g., family, community, city) to which a woman belongs. As such, these constraints can exist at four different levels, namely two at a micro-level (individual, family) and two at a macro level (national and international) (Tava-koli & Mura, 2021). Nevertheless, this view is contradicted by the finding of an increase in female solo travellers from Muslim countries (Hosseini et al., 2021). This suggests that Muslim travellers are resisting pressures placed on them to conform to socio-cultural norms of expected female behavior, as reflected in two studies by Nikjoo et al. (2021) and Hosseini et al. (2021). While studies and reviews on gender, women, and travel constraints have been conducted, the specific travel constraints pertaining to Muslim women travellers need fur-ther analysis and investigation. Therefore, in this study, we highlight the con-straints Uzbek women face on solo travel.

Study context

In a modern context, Central Asia includes five former Soviet republics of Uzbekistan, Kyrgyzstan, Tajikistan, Kazakhstan, and Turkmenistan (Lee et al., 2012). We adopted this definition of Central Asia in this chapter. Uzbekistan (officially Republic of Uzbekistan) is a landlocked country located in this region and is famous for its diverse range of tourism attractions and resources such as the Silk Road. Among 7,500 historic sites, 5 properties are registered in UNESCO's

World Heritage List (WHL), namely, Itchan Kala, Historic Centre of Bukhara, Samarkand – Crossroad of Cultures and Historic Centre of Shakhrisabz, including Western Tien-Shan as a natural heritage (UNESCO, 2021), which are the main historical tourist hubs. Based on a report in 2018 published by the World Travel and Tourism Council (WTTC), Uzbekistan is ranked 146th in tourism and is expected to continue its growth to 118th (WTTC, 2018).

In 1992, Uzbektourism was established by the government of Uzbekistan as its national tourism company (Fayzullaev et al., 2021). Despite the wealth of tourism sources, the flow of domestic tourism such as family travel is not well established. On the other hand, while women are near 50 percent of the country's population (World Bank, 2020), structural reasons lead Uzbek women not to engage in tourism leisure activities.

In the Central Asian region, Uzbekistan is the only state that doesn't have a law on equal rights and opportunities for men and women (Matvienko, 2019a, 2019b). According to statistics, Uzbekistan takes 127th place in terms of the gender equality index scoring 70.63, while the average global score is 74.71 (World Bank, 2019). Besides, there is poor representation of women in decision-making policies. Their share in the leadership of state bodies and large organization of Uzbekistan is 1.7 percent, and in the managerial staff is also below 2 percent (Matvienko, 2019a). However, gender equity is improving in the country, but more reforms are needed in other sectors. In order to achieve this goal, in recent years, some decrees, resolutions, and laws were confirmed in relation to women's labour rights and entrepreneurship, participation in competitions and admission to higher education institutions, guarantees of equal rights and opportunities, protection from oppression and violence, and procedures for gender and legal regulatory examination. In addition, 14 regional and 203 district Women's Public Councils were established to increase the confidence of women in their place in society. Some women also serve in high level positions such as Tanzila Kamalovna Narbaeva, who has been the chairperson of the Senate of Uzbekistan since 2019. Furthermore, women's share in the parliament is 32 percent, and in the Upper House of the Oliy Majlis it is 22 out of 100 senators, and in the legislative chamber it is 18 out of 150.

Method

The authors adopted an interpretive paradigm and the qualitative approach in which data was derived from five focus groups. Interviews were conducted in May and June 2021 in Tashkent-Uzbekistan. All respondents were university students and with a snowball sampling were invited to participate in the investigation. Since the study followed the concept of 'data saturation', theoretical saturation has been achieved after 16 interviews, which means that no more new data were observed. Questions were framed according to the study objectives. The lead author conducted each of the semi-structured interviews. All interviews were recorded with an electronic recorder with the permission of the participant and lasted from 25 to 50 minutes. Interviews were conducted in

English; hence, after ending the discussions, transcribed files were sent to the respondents to ensure the accuracy of the interview, and so that respondents remain anonymous, pseudonyms have been used to maintain their identity. Each of the authors independently repeatedly read line-by-line the transcribed interviews to identify codes and themes based on Charmaz's (2006) guidelines. After consecutive discussions, the final themes were categorized.

Research findings and discussion

Analysis identified three major themes: (i) individually-perceived constraints; (ii) family-related constraints; and (iii) gendered-imposed constraints.

Level 1: individually-perceived constraints

Fear and safety

Compared to men, women are more concerned about their safety and security when travelling. Almost all those interviewed mentioned 'fear' and 'safety' as a crucial travel constraint. One of the interviewees noted that safety was one of her main anxieties:

> I am deeply concerned about my personal safety. To tell the truth, if I felt safe, I would travel alone right now . . . I always think about the time that something bad happened to me like a sexual attack, what can I do then? How can I keep my head up! How can I look my parents, friends, relatives' eyes.

This was also echoed by another participant:

> Solo travelling will involve too much risk for me. I'm not sure if I can overcome my fears . . . the bad thing also is that there is nobody experienced such a trip as this to ask how they solve it.

The issue of safety creates fear in our respondents which stops them from travelling. In particular, women are afraid of being injured or attacked by men while travelling. Indeed, it was crucial for the Uzbek women to ensure safety before being confident to embark on any leisure activity. In this respect, a number of studies have highlighted how women's fear leads them to not engaging in solo travel. In their study, Whyte and Shaw (1994) found that the fear of violence affected negatively on their involvement in and enjoyment of leisure activities. Wilson and Little (2008, p. 167) labelled the lack of safety as the 'geography of women's travel fears'. However, it is interesting to note that Hosseini et al. (2021) declared that, in Muslim societies, such as Iran, women perceived safety in a different way than women in Western countries.

LACK OF PERSONAL SKILLS

The lack of the needed skills was one of the main constraints identified by females in this study. The interviewees remarked that because of not having experiences, they did not know how, when, and where they should go on a trip and manage the upcoming challenge. They were also concerned about the way of overcoming unpredictable events during travel. As one of the interviewees puts it clearly:

> let's think that there is no barrier on my way of travel alone, but I don't know anything about this type of trip. I have no information about that.

It was echoed by another respondent:

> I think that solo travelling needs some specific skills and abilities. Some skills like time managing, budget controlling, map reading, solving challenges and problems.

Prior empirical investigations have discovered that women reported the lack of skills as a constraint in the stage pf pre-travel (Henderson et al., 1995; Henderson, 1997; Jackson & Rucks, 1995; Gilbert & Hudson, 2000). Mei and Lantai (2018) stress that the lack of skills can be categorized in intrapersonal and intrinsic constraints, the barrier in which women reject participation in solo travelling. In this respect, some needed skills for solo travelling can be developed through training or sharing knowledge. Also, interpersonal barriers like the lack of skills can be mitigated through short-term travelling (Lai et al., 2013; Lin et al., 2017).

Level 2: family-related constraints

Giving permission

It would not be normal for many of the Uzbek's parents to let their girls experience solo travel. In the view of nearly all our interviewees, approving such a request from their family will definitely be denied by them. One of the respondents commented:

> Not only my parents, I know that approximately all of my friends' family don't let the single girls go on a trip, not only the solo travelling, but also a group of girls.

Our respondents believe that the attitude of their family toward this style of trip is totally negative and if they do that, indeed, they pass the 'red lines'. This was noted by a respondent:

> I have always wanted to go on a trip with myself. For me, it is like a dream to be a solo traveller. . . . My parents won't allow me to go travel alone.

They always simply say "No, you can't go, we don't allow you to go travelling with yourself, don't talk about that again".

Another respondent gave more details about the position of parents in the Uzbek culture, where children must show respect to them by following all of parents' wishes:

> Here, we must respect our parents by following all of the things that they say to us. In our culture, parents have the top position. The children must not do anything against their will, we must take it, not leave it.

Family and adherence to the authority of elders are a crucial part of Muslim societies, thus family permission is significant and unquestionable (Nikjoo et al., 2021; Hosseini et al., 2021). Respecting elders has long been a custom, while standing against their orders is considered disrespectful (Wantono & Mckercher, 2020). A modern, more gender equitable, style of life can be seen only in urban middle-class families, as most of the Uzbek families stay patriarchal. The dominant aspect of these families is having a hierarchical structure in which all members are well-aware of their own roles. The father/husband is considered as the head of the family who has an indisputable prestige and the main role in the decision-making process. The main duty of the father is controlling, monitoring, and leading. Then, the role of the mother/wife take a subordinate position (Saifnazarov et al., 2021).

THE ROLE OF FAMILY MEMBERS

Besides the parents, other constraints were related to the attitude of the rest of the family members. We found that there is another restriction for those respondents who also have elder brothers. Some interviewees were of the belief that their brothers obstructed them when they were convincing their parents to give their permission. For instance, one of the respondents remarked:

> In our culture, where there is an elder brother, it means that there is another father in the home. I always argue with my brother to not make a dam on my way.

This was echoed by another respondent:

> It is on my nerves that I should also talk to my elderly brother in this respect. It is ridiculous, even my father allows me, my brother not helping me for experiencing solo travelling. He several times has said that I will do whatever that lead you not to go solo travelling.

Historically, in central-Asian countries, particularly in Uzbekistan, culture has been formed along patrilineal principles, with status kin relationships among members defined by gender and birth order age. The terminology of kinship is quite complicated. There are various words for patrilineal and matrilineal uncles and aunts, as well as older and younger brothers and sisters (Tokhtak-hodjaeva, 1997). Women should gain permission from guardians before they participate in any outdoor activities (Hosseini et al., 2021). Hence, Uzbek women are confined in a cultural-social bubble, therefore, their desire for alone travel is constrained by a series of certain cultural family relationship requirements.

Level 3: gendered-imposed constraints

Gender labels: solo travelling is a masculine thing

In the eyes of most of the interviewees, solo travel is not acceptable because of cultural norms. Our sample believe that in a patriarchal-Islamic society like Uzbekistan, it would not be easy to change the individuals' attitude toward a female solo traveller. The respondents also mentioned that even if some changes occur in terms of social norms in the future, the negative attitude about solo travellers will remain for years. This was noted by a respondent:

> We are living in a restricted society, the society where women are known as the second sex. We can make our future scheme. Nor now, neither in the near future.

Another interviewee expressed that:

> People think that travel for women is not essential. They say that why a girl should not go and travel.

The respondents' expressions provide clues of the gender-based barriers that single women will face when solo travelling in Uzbekistan. In some conservative Muslim societies women are not allowed to go on a trip (Nikjoo et al., 2021). Indeed, women in such countries are intensely limited to participating in leisure activities (Shahvali et al., 2016; Tavakoli & Mura, 2021; Hosseini et al., 2021). For instance, the role of women is limited to bringing up children, caring for their husbands, and doing chores. Gender norms also influence the judgment of alone travelling in religious/conservative countries. It means that if individuals see a single solo girl traveller, they put an obscene phrase/label on the women. Our respondents referenced to the constraints of labeling. Examples of their comments included:

> One of the main reasons that I avoid alone travel is about the bad thing that people will say behind girl traveller. I'm ashamed even of mentions that words.

Another interviewee expressed that:

> My biggest concern about solo travelling is about the people's word. They cannot accept that a girl can travel alone while doing nothing bad. I mean, a girl can alone travel and be a chaste girl, but many people think that she is not a lady.

Early marriage

Another dominant theme that was seen through the interviews identified the marriage age for the women. The interviewees expressed that in Uzbekistan it is expected that girls get married when they are in their early twenties. Examples of their comments included:

> When we are in the age of 21 or 22, our culture pushed us to get married as soon as possible, our traditions ask us to be a mother or a wife rather than an independent girl. When there is a single girl above the age of her mid-twenties is called 'old maids', which is deemed extremely derogatory in our eyes, while there is not a similar kind of phrase for a single boy.

Another girl mentioned:

> The age for solo travel starts above of 18 in most countries, but here this age instead of experiencing novel things like solo travelling, we must get married.

Women in many Muslim countries have long taken the Muslim role of a woman as wife and mother (Ulko, 2017). With respect to the cultural norms in Uzbek society, girls are being encouraged to adhere to their values as a good daughter, subservient wife, and a strong mother. Thus, this leads to early marriage in this country and answers why Uzbekistan is characterized by an early age of marriage for women (22.7 years), although more urbanized women prefer to postpone it (Pirjanovna & Bekmuratovih, 2021).

Conclusion

Many women, especially those who reside in non-Western cultures, encounter difficulties to being involved in leisure activities such as travel (Henderson et al., 1996; Koca et al., 2009). The objectives of this study were to explore the travel constraints facing women in solo travel in Uzbekistan, a Muslim post-Soviet country. The results of this study highlighted that Uzbek women face many barriers in their freedom to travel. Three types of constraints such as (i) individually perceived constraints; (ii) family-related constraints; and (iii) gendered-imposed constraints) were identified.

While the first theme (i.e., fear and safety, lack of skills) includes intrapersonal constraints, the second and third themes highlight the role of social-structural norms (i.e., family approval, family member's relationship, gender labels) that affect females' ability to travel. Indeed, these identified codes are rooted in the culture and society in which our respondents are raised. The dominant cultural model regarding females and travel in Uzbekistan was that women should not travel alone. Indeed, another interesting finding of this study is the gendered perception of solo travelling; in other words, this relates to the concept of 'solo travelling' and whether the women can choose this style of travelling. In a patriarchal society, while males are perceived to be 'hard', females are 'soft' (Ashmore & Del Boca, 1986). In such a conservative society, travel norms are considered in favour of men. Therefore, it can be concluded that the thought of 'solo travelling is a masculine thing' comes from this attitude. Besides, good daughters are those who show concern about family relationships, spend time with family, and adhere to the family rules and social norms. As the findings reflected, the majority of respondents were of the belief that their family holding a negative attitude towards female solo travel constrains them in this respect.

This study represents the first empirical findings on the travel constraints of the growing solo travellers segment, in new independent post-Soviet countries in Central Asia. While understanding the importance of adopting theoretical frameworks in investigation, the authors decided not to tie the findings in this study to only Crawford et al's (1991) seminal leisure constraints model. This is because, as some scholars emphasize, the hierarchical constraints model would not have allowed the authors to depict the complexity of the samples' lives (Shahvali et al., 2016). Due to the context of this study, which included females from a different cultural/social context, this decision was correct as the findings shed light on how Uzbek women with various demographic profiles perceived the barriers to solo travel. This would not have been possible if the sample were asked to highlight a list of barriers and challenges taken from prior studies. All in all, this study contributed to the tourism literature by showing how women in central Asia's society encounter barriers in leisure activities such as solo travelling.

References

Ashmore, R. D., & Del Boca, F. K. (1986). Toward a social psychology of female-male relations. In R. D. Ashmore & F. K. Del Boca (Eds.), *The social psychology of female-male relations: A critical analysis of central concepts* (pp. 1–17). Academic Press.

Backman, S. J., & Crompton, J. L. (1989). Discriminating between continuers and discontinuers of two public leisure services. *Journal of Park and Recreation Administration*, 7(4), 56–71.

Cambronero-Saiz, B. (2013). Gender policies and advertising and marketing practices that affect women's health. *Global Health Action*, 6(1), 20372. https://doi.org/10.3402/gha.v6i0.20372

Charmaz, K. (2006). *Constructing grounded theory: A practical guide through qualitative analysis.* Sage.

Cohen, E., & Cohen, S. A. (2015). Tourism mobilities from emerging world regions: A response to commentaries. *Current Issues in Tourism, 18*(1), 68–69. https://doi.org/10.1080/13683500.2014.956705

Crawford, D. W., Jackson, E. L., & Godbey, G. (1991). A hierarchical model of leisure constraints. *Leisure Sciences, 13*(4), 309–320. https://doi.org/10.1080/01490409109513147

Dempsey, C. (2015, October 16). Visa global travel intention study 2015. In *PATA conference. Auckland, New Zealand*. PATA.

Elliot, M. (2015, March 5). Solo female travels on the rise in Southeast Asia. *Travel Daily Media.* www.traveldailymedia.com/218965/solo-female-travel-on-the-risein-southeast-asia

Fayzullaev, K., Cassel, S. H., & Brandt, D. (2021). Destination image in Uzbekistan–heritage of the Silk Road and nature experience as the core of an evolving Post Soviet identity. *The Service Industries Journal, 41*(7–8), 446–461. https://doi.org/10.1080/02642069.2018.1519551

Gilbert, D., & Hudson, S. (2000). Tourism demand constraints: A skiing participation. *Annals of Tourism Research, 27*(4), 906–925. https://doi.org/10.1016/S0160-7383(99)00110-3

Hall, C. M., & Page, S. (2016). *Geography of tourism and recreation* (4th ed.). Routledge.

Harris, C., & Wilson, E. (2007). Travelling beyond the boundaries of constraint: Women, travel and empowerment. In A. Pritchard, N. Morgan, I. Ateljevic, & C. Harris (Eds.), *Tourism and gender: Embodiment, sensuality and experience* (pp. 235–250). CABI.

Henderson, K. A. (1997). A critique of constraints theory: A response. *Journal of Leisure Research, 29*(4), 453–457. https://doi.org/10.1080/00222216.1997.11949808

Henderson, K. A., Bedini, L. A., Hecht, L., & Schuler, R. (1995). Women with physical disabilities and the negotiation of leisure constraints. *Leisure Studies, 14*(1), 17–31. https://doi.org/10.1080/02614369500390021

Henderson, K. A., Bialeschki, M. D., Shaw, S. M., & Freysinger, V. J. (1996). *Both gains and gaps: Feminist perspectives on women's leisure.* Venture Publishing.

Henderson, K. A., & Gibson, H. J. (2013). An integrative review of women, gender, and leisure: Increasing complexities. *Journal of Leisure Research, 45*(2), 115–135. https://doi.org/10.18666/jlr-2013-v45-i2-3008

Hosseini, S., Macias, R. C., & Garcia, F. A. (2021). The exploration of Iranian solo female travellers' experiences. *International Journal of Tourism Research.* https://doi.org/10.1002/jtr.2498

Hung, K., & Petrick, J. F. (2010). Developing a measurement scale for constraints to cruising. *Annals of Tourism Research, 37*(1), 206–228. https://doi.org/10.1016/j.annals.2009.09.002

Hung, K., & Petrick, J. F. (2012). Testing the effects of congruity, travel constraints, and self-efficacy on travel intentions: An alternative decision-making model. *Tourism Management, 33*(4), 855–867. https://doi.org/10.1016/j.tourman.2011.09.007

Jackson, E. L. (1988). Leisure constraints: A survey of past research. *Leisure Sciences, 10*(3), 203–215. https://doi.org/10.1080/01490408809512190

Jackson, E. L., Crawford, D. W., & Godbey, G. (1993). Negotiation of leisure constraints. *Leisure Sciences, 15*(1), 1–11. https://doi.org/10.1080/01490409309513182

Jackson, E. L., & Henderson, K. A. (1995). Gender-based analysis of leisure constraints. *Leisure Sciences, 17*(1), 31–51. https://doi.org/10.1080/01490409509513241

Jackson, E. L., & Rucks, V. C. (1995). Negotiation of leisure constraints by junior-high and high-school students: An exploratory study. *Journal of Leisure Research, 27*(1), 85–105. https://doi.org/10.1080/00222216.1995.11969978

Jordan, F., & Aitchison, C. (2008). Tourism and the sexualisation of the gaze: Solo female tourists' experiences of gendered power, surveillance and embodiment. *Leisure Studies*, *27*(3), 329–349. https://doi.org/10.1080/02614360802125080

Jordan, F., & Gibson, H. (2005). "We're not stupid . . . But we'll not stay home either": Experiences of solo women travelers. *Tourism Review International*, *9*(2), 195–211. https://doi.org/10.3727/154427205774791663

Karagöz, D., Işık, C., Dogru, T., & Zhang, L. (2021). Solo female travel risks, anxiety and travel intentions: Examining the moderating role of online psychological-social support. *Current Issues in Tourism*, *24*(11), 1595–1612. https://doi.org/10.1080/13683500.2020.1816929

Khan, M. J., Chelliah, S., & Ahmed, S. (2017). Factors influencing destination image and visit intention among young women travellers: Role of travel motivation, perceived risks, and travel constraints. *Asia Pacific Journal of Tourism Research*, *22*(11), 1139–1155. https://doi.org/10.1080/10941665.2017.1374985

Koca, C., Henderson, K. A., Asci, F. H., & Bulgu, N. (2009). Constraints to leisure-time physical activity and negotiation strategies in Turkish women. *Journal of Leisure Research*, *41*(2), 225–251. https://doi.org/10.1080/00222216.2009.11950167

Kozak, M. (2010). Holiday taking decisions – The role of spouses. *Tourism*, *31*(4), 489–494. https://doi.org/10.1016/j.tourman.2010.01.014

Lai, C., Li, X. R., & Harrill, R. (2013). Chinese outbound tourists' perceived constraints to visiting the United States. *Tourism Management*, *37*(8), 136–146. https://doi.org/10.1016/j.tourman.2013.01.014

Larsen, J. (2014). The tourist gaze 1.0, 2.0, and 3.0. In A. A. Lew, C. M. Hall, & A. M. Williams (Eds.), *The Wiley Blackwell companion to tourism* (pp. 304–313). John Wiley & Sons.

Larsen, S., Brun, W., & Øgaard, T. (2009). What tourists worry about: Construction of a scale measuring tourist worries. *Tourism Management*, *30*(2), 260–265. https://doi.org/10.1016/j.tourman.2008.06.004

Lee, C. K., Kang, S., Reisinger, Y., & Kim, N. (2012). Incongruence in destination image: Central Asia region. *Tourism Geographies*, *14*(4), 599–624. https://doi.org/10.1080/14616688.2012.647325

Lepp, A., & Gibson, H. (2003). Tourist roles, perceived risk and international tourism. *Annals of Tourism Research*, *30*(3), 606–624. https://doi.org/10.1016/S0160-7383(03)00024-0

Lin, P. M. C., Zhang, H. Q., Gu, Q., & Peng, K.-L. (2017). To go or not to go: Travel constraints and attractiveness of travel affecting outbound Chinese tourists to Japan. *Journal of Travel & Tourism Marketing*, *34*(9), 1184–1197. http://dx.doi.org/10.1080/10548408.2017.1327392

Matvienko, I. (2019a, March 11). Uzbekistan: Women are less paid, less educated, less equal. *Central Asian Bureau for Analytical Reporting*. https://cabar.asia/en/uzbekistan-women-are-less-paid-less-educated-less-equal

Matvienko, I. (2019b, May 7). Uzbekistan: On the way to equality. *Central Asian Bureau for Analytical Reporting*. https://cabar.asia/en/uzbekistan-on-the-way-to-equality

Mehmetoglu, M., Dann, G. M., & Larsen, S. (2001). Solitary travellers in the Norwegian Lofoten Islands: Why do people travel on their own? *Scandinavian Journal of Hospitality and Tourism*, *1*(1), 19–37. https://doi.org/10.1080/15022250127794

Mei, X. Y., & Lantai, T. (2018). Understanding travel constraints: An exploratory study of mainland Chinese international students (MCIS) in Norway. *Tourism Management Perspectives*, *28*, 1–9. https://doi.org/10.1016/j.tmp.2018.07.003

Nikjoo, A., Markwell, K., Nikbin, M., & Hernández-Lara, A. B. (2021). The flag-bearers of change in a patriarchal Muslim society: Narratives of Iranian solo female travelers on Instagram. *Tourism Management Perspectives, 38*, 100817. https://doi.org/10.1016/j. tmp.2021.100817

Pirjanovna, S. Z., & Bekmuratovih, U. B. (2021). Characteristic of the social status of women in Uzbekistan. *International Journal of Development and Public Policy, 1*(5), 94–97.

Raymore, L. A. (2002). Facilitators to leisure. *Journal of Leisure Research, 34*(1), 37–51. https://doi.org/10.1080/00222216.2002.11949959

Saifnazarov, I., Mukhtarov, A., Ernazarov, D., & Mirakbarova, D. (2021). Implementing the principle of gender equality in a balance of secularism and religiosity. *Linguistics and Culture Review, 5*(S4), 761–779. https://doi.org/10.21744/lingcure.v5nS4.1720

Seow, D., & Brown, L. (2018). The solo female Asian tourist. *Current Issues in Tourism, 21*(10), 1187–1206. https://doi.org/10.1080/13683500.2017.1423283

Seyfi, S., & Hall, C. M. (Eds.). (2018). *Tourism in Iran: Challenges, development and issues.* Routledge.

Seyfi, S., & Hall, C. M. (2019). Deciphering Islamic theocracy and tourism: Conceptualization, context, and complexities. *International Journal of Tourism Research, 21*(6), 735–746. https://doi.org/10.1002/jtr.2300

Seyfi, S., Hall, C. M., & Vo-Thanh, T. (2020). The gendered effects of statecraft on women in tourism: Economic sanctions, women's disempowerment and sustainability? *Journal of Sustainable Tourism.* https://doi.org/10.1080/09669582.2020.1850749

Shahvali, M., Shahvali, R., & Kerstetter, D. (2016). Women's travel constraints in a unique context. In M. Kozak & N. Kozak (Eds.), *Tourist behaviour: An international perspective* (pp. 16–25). CAB International.

Spreitzhöfer, G. (2008). Zwischen Khao San und Lonely Planet: Aspekte der postmodernen Backpacking-Identität in Südostasien. *Austrian Journal of South-East Asian Studies, 1*(2), 140–161.

Tavakoli, R., & Mura, P. (2021). Muslim women travellers' constraints: A critical review. In N. S. Valek & H. Almuhrzi (Eds.), *Women in tourism in Asian Muslim countries* (pp. 25–40). Springer.

Tokhtakhodjaeva, M. (1997). Society and family in Uzbekistan. *Polish Sociological Review, 18*, 149–165.

Ulko, A. (2017). *Uzbekistan. Culture smart!: The essential guide to customs & culture.* Kuperard.

United Nations Educational, Scientific and Cultural Organization (UNESCO). (2021). *Uzbekistan (Republic of).* https://whc.unesco.org/en/statesparties/uz

Wantono, A., & McKercher, B. (2020). Backpacking and risk perception: The case of solo Asian women. *Tourism Recreation Research, 45*(1), 19–29. https://doi.org/10.1080/02508 281.2019.1636180

Whyte, L. B., & Shaw, S. M. (1994). Women's leisure: An exploratory study of fear of violence as a leisure constraint. *Journal of Applied Recreation Research, 19*(1), 5–21.

Wilson, E., & Harris, C. (2006). Meaningful travel: Women, independent travel and the search for self and meaning. *Tourism: An International Interdisciplinary Journal, 54*(2), 161–172.

Wilson, E., & Little, D. E. (2005). A "relative escape"? The impact of constraints on women who travel solo. *Tourism Review International, 9*(2), 155–175. https://doi. org/10.3727/154427205774791672

Wilson, E., & Little, D. E. (2008). The solo female travel experience: Exploring the 'geography of women's fear'. *Current Issues in Tourism, 11*(2), 167–186. https://doi.org/10.2167/ cit342.0

World Bank. (2019). *Women, business and the law 2019: A decade of reform.* https://open knowledge.worldbank.org/bitstream/handle/10986/31327/WBL2019.pdf

World Bank. (2020). *Population, female – Uzbekistan.* https://data.worldbank.org/indicator/ SP.POP.TOTL.FE.IN?locations=UZ

World Travel and Tourism Council (WTTC). (2018). *Travel and tourism economic impact 2018 Uzbekistan.* WTTC.

Yang, E. C. L., Khoo-Lattimore, C., & Arcodia, C. (2017). A systematic literature review of risk and gender research in tourism. *Tourism Management, 58,* 89–100. https://doi. org/10.1016/j.tourman.2016.10.011

Yang, E. C. L., Khoo-Lattimore, C., & Arcodia, C. (2018a). Constructing space and self through risk taking: A case of Asian solo female travelers. *Journal of Travel Research, 57*(2), 260–272. https://doi.org/10.1177/0047287517692447

Yang, E. C. L., Khoo-Lattimore, C., & Arcodia, C. (2018b). Power and empowerment: How Asian solo female travellers perceive and negotiate risks. *Tourism Management, 68,* 32–45. https://doi.org/10.1016/j.tourman.2018.02.017

Yang, E. C. L., & Tavakoli, R. (2016). 'Doing' tourism gender research in Asia: An analysis of authorship, research topic and methodology. In C. Khoo-Lattimore & P. Mura (Eds.), *Asian genders in tourism* (pp. 23–39). Channel View Publications.

11 The Silent and Unseen

Two examples of women's restricted travel in Pakistan

*Tazayian Sayira, Hazel Andrews and
Qurat-ul-Ann Ayesha*

Introduction

This chapter is a comparative study of women's travel patterns and roles in the tourism and hospitality industry in two cities in Pakistan, a Muslim majority country. In less developed countries it is often the case that women bear the burden of poverty more than men due to existing conditions of gender inequality. Much of the literature that has discussed gender and tourism has highlighted empowerment for women (Cole, 2007) as well as issues of economic inequality (Jucan & Jucan, 2013; Cole & Morgan, 2010; Cole, 2018). However, little of this literature has considered the situation of women in areas that are under crises. Crises is used here to mean conditions that have arisen due to, for example, human negligence, conflicts, errors, and/or failures in established systems (Jha, 2010). These are referred to as anthropogenic crises as opposed to those that might be termed natural crises for example an earthquake or tsunami. When a major anthropogenic crisis occurs, this has severe ramifications for human populations as people may be displaced and left with few or none of the basic means for survival. This chapter builds on the previous work of Sayira and Andrews (2016, 2019) to highlight the experiences of women as both producers of tourism and as travellers and tourists in an area considered as having been under crises, that of Chilas in northern Pakistan. It compares the findings from Chilas to data collected in the city of Abbottabad, which has experienced fewer problems than Chilas and has a more established tourism sector.

The chapter focuses on Pakistan because of government initiatives to promote tourism and increase the number of international visits to the country. Before the outbreak of COVID-19 and the global pandemic of 2020, these efforts were beginning to have some effect. For example, the UK-based newspaper the *Independent* reported in 2019 that Pakistan would be among one of the top destinations for international tourists in 2020. This repositioning of Pakistan in the market is needed to challenge the country's characterisation as a place of violent conflict in the form of terrorist attacks (Usmani, 2017; Briam, 2017).

The focus on women is because of the role they play in supporting the development of tourism in a patriarchal socio-cultural setting in which

DOI: 10.4324/9781003036296-15

women's roles and movements are often strictly controlled (Sayira, 2015). As the United Nations World Tourism Organization (UNWTO) and Entity for Gender Equality and the Empowerment of Women's (UN Women) (2010) *Global Report on Women in Tourism* showed, 50% of the tourism and hospitality sectors' workforce worldwide were women. The second edition of the report in 2019 (UNWTO, 2019) showed this figure had grown to 54%. In relation to Pakistan, the 2019 document reported that, based on information supplied by the International Labour Organization (ILO) (2018), women's earnings as a percentage of men's in the broader economy were 60.87%. In the food and accommodation sector (which is used as a proxy for tourism employment) it is 102.19%, a difference of 41.3%. As such, understanding the role that women play in contributing to the construction of contemporary tourism practices in Pakistan is important for understanding what issues women face in relation to achieving empowerment through tourism, as empowerment can only be achieved if problems can be overcome. Furthermore, in terms of power relations there is an interesting dichotomy to note when women who cannot enjoy freedom of movement (which is understood here as the ability to make autonomous decisions about where one goes and with whom and when one travels) are working behind the scenes to facilitate the enjoyment of the freedom of movement for other women – and men – in the form of both domestic and international tourists.

This chapter provides additional context to the relationship between Muslim women and travel in Pakistan by considering not only their part in the provision of tourism and hospitality but also how they themselves travel. The chapter will discuss the limitations placed on women travellers (which is predominately for the purpose of visiting friends and relatives (VFR) or taking day trips) by highlighting issues relating to the laws of Mahram and Na-Mahram. These two codes of practice restrict who women can be alone with, which in terms of travel means they must always be escorted by an 'appropriate' person.

Discussion proceeds in the following way: It begins by highlighting some of the key themes to have emerged in the tourism literature about women and gender equality. As shall be noted, the focus has been on women's work in tourism. This chapter will mainly focus on inequalities in women's travel. It will begin by briefly outlining some general issues of travel for Muslim women before outlining the research context and data collection. This will be followed by a discussion of the two case study sites and will draw out the similarities and differences in experiences between the women in both locations.

Women, Tourism, and Equality

Although there is now a growing literature on issues of gender in tourism studies, some of which includes research in Muslim countries (Jafari & Scott, 2014), much research is dominated by male perspectives, and where women are considered there has been a tendency to focus on economic development and sex tourism (Pritchard & Morgan, 2000; Pritchard, 2014). Other studies have examined questions of inequality (Jucan & Jucan, 2013; Cole & Morgan, 2010; Cole, 2018). As Pritchard and Morgan (2000, p. 887), noted 'there is a prevailing male bias in tourism research where no allowance is made for gender difference, subsuming female behaviour into that of the dominant male pattern'. What appears to be the absence of women and their voices in some tourism research could be, in part, due to their exclusion, at times, from tourism activities because of the local socio-cultural and religious conditions under which they live (Shakeela & Cooper, 2009). However, there are notable exceptions, and the work of Cole (2007) has been at the forefront of drawing attention to women's roles in tourism and issues of inequality. Similarly, Gentry (2007) highlights the connection between economic independence with women's equality with reference to the tourism industry. Further, the Indian-based NGO Equitable Tourism Options (Equation) (2007) notes that in developing countries women's engagement in tourism is an extension of their domestic labour and that they work in low skilled and low paid jobs in positions that are seen as stereotypically 'female' such as housekeeping, catering, and front-desk. In addition, they claim

> The role of women in informal tourism settings such as running home-stay facilities, restaurants and shacks, crafts and handicrafts, handloom, small shops and street vending is significant. But these roles and activities . . . are treated as invisible or taken for granted.
>
> (Equation, 2007, p. 4)

The issues discussed thus far in relation to women as workers in tourism finds resonance in the settings under consideration in this chapter. The role of women as producers of tourism in the form of providing services, such as, for example, washing hotel laundry, making and sometimes selling handicrafts as tourism souvenirs (although selling is usually undertaken by men), is familiar in both Chilas and Abbottabad. It is also the case that in both places this work by women is frequently unpaid and unacknowledged because it is seen as part of their existing domestic duties. The inequality that the women face is in part due to the socio-cultural circumstances of the patriarchal system in which they live. The previous discussion briefly highlights some of the questions of gender inequality in tourism work; what is less well-rehearsed in the academic literature are questions of inequality relating to women's travel, which are especially pertinent in a Muslim majority country like Pakistan where women's movements are restricted and where the dissonance between those women who can and cannot freely travel becomes apparent.

Travel for Muslim Women

Before proceeding to discuss the research findings we wish to provide a brief outline of Islamic teachings about travel for Muslim women. Islam allows both men and women equally to travel to gain knowledge. In Islamic teachings the Prophet Muhammad undertook the greatest journeys [*pbuh*], along with his family and his companions to seek and spread knowledge. This approach continues in the present day with one of the many aims of travel being to learn and receive reminders of previous lessons. The command to travel appears in several places in the Qur'an. For example, the Qur'an says, '(O Muhammad *pbuh*): Travel in the land and see what the end of those was who rejected truth' (Al-Qur'an: Al-An'aam 6:11). In another chapter, Allah says, 'Say to them (O Muhammad *pbuh*): Travel in the land and see how has been the end of the Mujrimoon (criminals)' (Al-Qur'an: Al-Naml 27:69).

In the Muslim world tourism is often associated with a religious visit to Saudi Arabia for Hajj – which involves visiting Makkah at a specific time of year – and Umrah, which involves visiting Makkah any time of the year (Jafari & Scott, 2014). Other aims to travel in Islam include moving around or immigrating for the purpose of spreading knowledge and

> travelling to ponder the wonders of Allah's creation and to enjoy the beauty of this great universe, so that it will make the human soul develop strong faith in the oneness of Allah and will help one to fulfil the obligations of life. Relaxation is essential to enable one to strive hard after that.
>
> (Al-Qur'an: al-'Ankaboot 29:20)

In the Qur'an Allah says: 'Travel in the land and see how (Allah) originated the creation, and then Allah will bring forth the creation of the Hereafter (i.e. resurrection after death)' (Al-Qur'an: al-'Ankaboot 29:20).

Islamically, then, Muslim women can seek education, travel, and work as can men. However, in some Muslim majority countries including Pakistan,

> women must receive consent from their husbands, fathers or brothers [*mahram*] in order to do something outside their house . . . the conduct of Muslim women is very much controlled, in part because of the focus on maintaining family honor and a good reputation, and to avoid the negative consequences of shame.
>
> (Al Mazro'ei, 2010, p. 8)

The mention of honour killings highlights the very serious consequences for women in Pakistan should they fail to comply (see for example Hadi, 2017). Previous research that has examined gender issues in tourism in relation to Pakistan concluded that women face a lack of recognition for their role in tourism (Sayira, 2015). In addition, the research also identified that women's movements as tourists/travellers were also, as Al Mazro'ei (2010) points out, and noted by Sayira (2015) and Sayira and Andrews (2016, 2019), strictly controlled.

Under a patriarchal social system, which also permits polygamy, such as in Pakistan, there is a lack of gender equality. The situation for women is made more precarious because, as Hadi (2017, p. 300) notes, 'killing in the name of honor is getting its justification from patriarchy social norms and values prevalent in Pakistan'. Honour killings refer to the idea that 'women's bodies are associated with the honor of the family. In order to protect this honor, men feels entitled to regulate and direct women's sexuality and their way of living' (Hadi, 2017, p. 299). Research by the Thomson Reuters Foundation (TrustLaw, 2011) also notes that honour killings account for the deaths of over 1,000 women and girls a year in Pakistan. Further, Hadi (2017) claims that 90% of women are said to endure domestic violence. Later work by the Thomson Reuters foundation (2018) reports Pakistan as the sixth most dangerous country in the world for women. In addition, the country is ranked 'third-to-last (151st) on the 2020 Global Gender Gap Index' (World Economic Forum, 2019, p. 32).

The degree to which many women in Pakistan live in such an unequal world and in the shadow of violence, especially in relation to freedoms that many other women take for granted, is illustrated by a tragic case in May 2020, in North Waziristan in Khyber Pakhtunkhwa province. In this instance two young women aged 16 and 18 were shot dead by members of their own family under the guise of 'honour killings' because they had been videoed outside their home with a man who was not a member of their family (Jozuka & Saifi, 2020). Although not unique to the country, such murders are regularly reported in Pakistan despite changes to the law following the killing of the social media star Qandeel Baloch by her brother in 2016 (Reuters News Agency, 2019). These changes were not the first to have been enacted in Pakistan following the introduction of legislation in 2004, which made honour killings a punishable offence. Honour killings in Pakistan now carry a life sentence. However, most murders go unreported as they are concealed by family members as suicides or natural deaths. This broad understanding about restrictions on women's freedoms in Pakistan provides the backdrop for the case studies being discussed in this chapter. The next section provides the background to the case study sites and the data collection methods.

Research Methods

Chilas is situated on the ancient Silk Road, now part of the Karakoram Highway, on the banks of the Indus River in the territory of Gilgit-Baltistan, North Pakistan. It is connected to the Chinese cities of Kashghar and Tashkuragan via the Gilgit, Sust and Khunjerab Passes. Chilas can also be accessed from the Kaghan Valley, passing over the Babusar Pass. The highway also provides links to main tourist destinations including Babusar Pass, K2, Gilgit, Hunza, and Kailash Chitral, and tourists must pass through Chilas on their way to these places.

Chilas is surrounded by some of the highest mountain ranges in the world, i.e., Karakoram, Himalayas, Pamirs, and Hindu Kush, with 120 peaks of an average height of 6,000m, along with the world's second and ninth highest peaks, K2 (8,611m) and Nanga Parbat, also known as the 'killer mountain'

(8,125m) (Sayira, 2015). It is known for its ancient rock art and petroglyphs. Despite the tourism potential and movement of tourists along the Karakoram Highway, Chilas is yet to develop sustainable visitor numbers and the place remains a tourism area in development.

The local demographics in Chilas can be linked to the lack of tourism development. The area is one characterised by depopulation, especially of men between the ages of 18 and 55, as they have immigrated to other parts of Pakistan and overseas to seek education and employment. Therefore, the Chilassi community mainly consists of older men, women, and children. The community also operates a system of Biyaak and Zeeto Kalak. These are local customs whereby local elder male members of the community, along with younger local policemen, form a jury that ensures that local customs and traditions including no interaction with *na-mahram* women and restrictions on women's movement outside of their homes are maintained. In addition, most domestic duties are the preserve of women, which further serves to bind them to the home. As such, in Chilas, women are not seen very often outside of their houses (Sayira, 2015; Sayira & Andrews, 2016, 2019).

The research was devised to directly access the women in a way that allows them to give expression to their own thoughts and feelings, in their own words, about their experiences of tourism and travel. As such it has taken the form of field research that has adopted qualitative techniques in the form of semi-structured interviews, as well as periods of participant and non-participant observation (see Sayira, 2015 for more details). The research was initially focussed on Chilas and conducted over a period of six months during 2010, 2011, and 2012. During this fieldwork one of the authors (Sayira) was able to engage directly with women living in Chilas and to speak to them about their lives, some of which was related to tourism. She also had direct experience of women's tourism related hospitality work (Sayira, 2015). Another author (Ayesha) made a follow-up visit in 2019 to assess how the situation had evolved since Sayira's last visit in 2012. During the 2019 visit Ayesha also conducted some semi-structured interviews. In addition, based on her established links with the community, Sayira also conducted semi-structured interviews in 2019 via telephone and other social media.

Chilas is in a remote part of Pakistan where many traditional cultural and religious values are still practiced, which have a strong influence on women's lives. Therefore, it was decided that to get a broader picture of the relationship between women and tourism in Pakistan it was necessary to obtain the perspectives from women based in a different part of the country. Abbottabad was chosen, in part, as a convenience sample as this is where Ayesha lives and works. Through her employment in a museum, she was already in contact with women working in tourism-related activities, as well as those who are not directly connected to the tourism sector.

Compared to neighbouring cities, Abbottabad is a quiet and peaceful town, in the province of Khyber Pakhtun Khwa (KPK). It is a gateway to other famous tourist destinations further to the north in Pakistan (Dawn, 2011). The city is in a mountainous area and, like Chilas, is situated on the Ancient Silk Road. Abbottabad is known as the 'city of schools' due to its high standards of education. The city's favourable climate – especially during the summer months – and its natural setting has seen it labelled as a 'tourist heaven' and it attracts many tourists.

Twenty-two people from Chilas and Abbottabad were interviewed in 2019. Of these, 6 were from Chilas of which 4 were women and 2 were men; 16 were from Abbottabad, four of whom were men and twelve were women. The data from these interviews were used to 'update' data from Chilas collected in the earlier visits as well as allowing a comparison with women's experiences in Abbottabad.

The respondents ranged in age between 18 and 70. All interviews were conducted in Urdu and Hindko. Interviews lasted between 45 and 60 minutes per person. The interviews were electronically recorded, apart from those conducted via social media for which handwritten notes were taken. Both Ayesha and Sayira translated their respective interviews and the transcripts were then discussed and cross-checked for consistency in meaning across the translations. Two focus group sessions were planned in 2020 to gain the voices of more interlocutors, but only the one in Abbottabad could take place. The focus group planned for Chilas was cancelled due to COVID-19 lockdown restrictions.

The 2020 focus group questions in Abbottabad were based on how women participated in tourism, how taking part in tourism has reshaped their lives as well as investigating their own travel patterns and ability to undertake solo travel for leisure purposes. All the research was conducted within ethical guidelines of informed consent and assurances of confidentiality. To this end, none of the interviewees is identified by name, and no specific location outside of the main research areas is given that would allow participants to be identified.

Abbottabad and Chilas were chosen for this research because the former had faced similar natural and anthropogenic crises to Chilas, along with strict socio-cultural codes of conduct embedded in traditional practices. Since the early 1990s government initiatives to promote tourism, along with positive media promotion and the increase in domestic tourism Abbottabad, has seen many changes. This had been aided by the launch (1995–1996) of a helicopter service to promote tourism in Abbottabad by the Pakistan International Airline and which was extended to the other northern areas (Ahmed, 2019). These changes brought positive impacts to the socio-cultural milieu in Abbottabad in general, but especially for women. For example, the literacy rate among women has increased, and more women are seen working outside their homes employed in non-domestic activities. Few honour killings are recorded; this is most likely due to the fear of consequences should a report be made, rather than such murders not happening. Indeed, writing in the *Guardian* newspaper, Baloch (2019) reports on the threats received by those who try to draw attention to the practice.

Findings

Discussion

This section draws on all the research conducted in the two sites to compare the experiences of and freedom of movement in relation to tourism for women in both places. We begin with Chilas.

The Women of Chilas: Ghosts and Hosts

As noted, despite the tourism potential of Chilas it is yet to see a sustained increase in visitor numbers. This in part can be attributed to the strict local laws and customs of the area that restrict contact with outsiders (Sayira, 2015). The situation is further exacerbated by the lack of skilled communication media and an overall unfavourable place image (Sayira & Andrews, 2016). The movement of women outside of their immediate home environment is still frowned upon by the majority of Chilassi people. This prevailing attitude makes domestic tourism in the form of VFR an uncomfortable experience for those women from outside of the area (Sayira, 2015).

The lack of women's visible presence in the community has seen them labelled by one male journalist from Abbottabad as 'ghost women'. As both Sayira and Ayesha noticed in their respective visits, the presence of women can be felt, but overall, they are unseen. This is even though women are involved in the production of the tourism that exists in the area. For example, women provide services in terms of cooking, laundry, washing-up – for which they receive no direct financial payment – to local tourist resorts where male members of their family work. Further, the women make souvenirs and entertain visitors but only within their own homes, ensuring the *purdah* tradition remains intact. They also cook for tourists who are invited to their homes by the men of the household. However, on the whole they work behind the scenes and do not consider what they do in relation to tourism to be a job but rather a part of their duties supporting male members of their family in their work (Sayira, 2015). In addition, when friends and relatives from other parts of the country visit Chilas, the women are expected to also service their needs and attend to existing domestic duties in the family home. Such visits can last for three days to three months. Given the work that the women do to support tourism activities, the research data leads us to conclude that Chilassi women are ghosts and hosts at the same time.

When interviewing the women in Chilas they were asked not only about what work they did to support tourism but also their own experiences of travel. One interviewee shared that she had visited her cousin's house in Peshawar – another city in the KPK province – and had stayed for two days. Another respondent said she only took part in some day trips to nearby valleys, but this was only when accompanied by her husband on his yearly return trips from working overseas. The idea of travelling for leisure purposes is not a concept that the women interviewed recognised since it is men who decide where and when women (and children) can go. As one interlocutor, a woman aged 49 who runs an in-house shop for female customers explained, Chilassi women do not travel just for the purpose of leisure and recreation 'even to next door and you are talking about sair spata [travel for leisure']". Another woman (a housewife, aged 26) concurred saying that Chilassi women were subjected to restrictions based on living in a patriarchal system that meant women felt 'bound inside their houses' and 'the cost of going out is to risk your life [due to the honour based system]'. She went on to say that she wished she could be like the 'confident female tourists' she sees during her stays in Babusar, a valley where Chilassi women migrate to graze their livestock during the summer. Similar views were expressed by other women in both periods of data collection. By seeing other women as tourists, the women interviewees felt inspired to also want to travel.

Hence travel for tourism, apart from VFR (which is accompanied by a male relative) or the occasional supervised day trip, is uncommon for Chilassi women. The only other reason women are permitted to be outside the home is for grazing livestock during women-only hours in nearby farms during which times men's presence is prohibited. The restrictions on freedom of movement are in stark contrast to the behaviour of tourists who visit Chilas. Indeed, tourists and visitors freely roam around. As one male Chilassi interviewee observed, 'the rules and regulations about tourism, tourists, dress code in South [part of Pakistan] can't be applied to us' (Sayira, 2015, p. 186).

However, there were expressions of hope for change. These were based on the Pakistani Government's plans to construct the Diamer Basha Dam. It is hoped that this large construction project and the accompanying financial investment in the area will bring prosperity to the region. It is anticipated that the dam would become a site for tourism activity and that in turn this would generate more employment opportunities for women outside of their homes and further afford them chances to engage more with people outside of the area. It is hoped that the construction of the dam would provide opportunities for women's empowerment in all its forms (see Schevyens, 2002) leading to greater gender equality. According to one of the Chilassi women (a housewife, aged 26) with the 'empowerment of local women the pattern of male dominance could be minimised'.

Abbottabad: Women Are Seen but Not Always Heard

In a similar way to Chilas, in Abbottabad women play an important yet often unacknowledged role in travel and tourism providing direct services and products to tourists and tourism and hospitality businesses. As one businesswoman explained, 'women work from home [in activities] ranging from making souvenirs such as wooden utensils and decorative items, knitted, woven stuff, to making snacks for local shops and restaurants to sell to customers'. In addition, many of the women interviewed acknowledged that they were the sole income earners for their households. This was, however, problematic in that, as one interlocutor explained, 'it is considered as bringing shame to the family by accepting they [women] earn to feed their families'. Further, the tourism-related work that the women undertook was not necessarily seen as acceptable as one male interviewee explained, 'the only respectable job for women is to do is teaching in an all-girls' setting'.

The experience of travelling outside of the home for women in Abbottabad is different from that of Chilas. In Abbottabad, although there is still adherence to cultural values that restrict women's movements, there are women who enjoy a greater sense of freedom. Migrants from other parts of Pakistan have brought changes to the socio-cultural milieu of the city mainly in terms of women's views on working outside the home. Indeed, women undertake paid employment in tourism and hospitality, as well as having the freedom to travel for leisure. Both Sayira and Ayesha noted an increased number of women working and travelling alone since the city has seen an increase in tourism numbers.

The interviewees in Abbottabad can be categorised into two groups. One group is from a part of Abbottabad that is known as 'town' and the other group from what is called 'Abbottabad city'. The latter is newly built and mainly occupied by migrants from elsewhere in Pakistan. There were different experiences of women's freedoms depending on which area of the city the respondents came from. For those women who lived in 'town' the majority advised that they were only able to make family visits on special occasions, for example, two Eids a year or to go and stay with their parents for a few days once or twice a year. Day trips were mentioned by two interviewees who once or twice a year visit Islamabad and/or nearby villages and farms just for leisure purposes. The restrictions were tighter for women under the age of 30 as it was not considered to be acceptable for them to go out of their houses unless for work or education purposes or essential visits to doctors, and these outings were under strict guidelines from the male head of the family.

In contrast, women from Abbottabad city who are working in tourism and tourism related educational institutes stated that they have travelled to several other cities in Pakistan, and two mentioned overseas trips for work. However, these 'freedoms' had consequences in that some of the women said they had been abandoned by their families or divorced by their husbands. In addition, although the situation was more favourable compared to 'town' and Chilas for women's freedoms a woman out on her own is still frowned upon and they run the risk of verbal abuse, being called 'prostitutes' or taunted as 'divorcees'. As one female teacher aged 36 explained,

> no matter how educated you are . . . going out for travel without mahram, even if it is work related, is not the norm and is stigmatised . . . you have to be ready for bullying and harassment upon your return . . . and worse, in some cases.

As one woman aged 30 who works from home explained, for women to be 'stepping outside their house for work is taken as challenging men's power and we can't afford that'. Further, as another woman (aged 39) who also works in education discussed,

> we are so dominated by men that talking about women's rights or becoming financially independent is associated with mental illness where you are known as *pagal* and *maghaz phiri* [terms used in Urdu to describe someone as mentally unstable or psychotic] . . . and you are considered a bad influence on other obedient and innocent wives.

Women travelling for leisure is still a 'taboo subject' in Abbottabad. However, the increase in tourist numbers to the city has begun to slowly change attitudes and, although it is not without problems, women do travel for work purposes without a *mahram*. As one of the women teachers said, the

> trend of women travelling on their own is increasing . . . the urban community is becoming more accepting [of women travelling] . . . over the last couple of years a significant number of female staff have visited foreign countries for research and study related purposes. . . . [However], for leisure it is still uncommon for a single woman to travel abroad.

Conclusion

This chapter has explored issues relating to freedom of movement and women's travel patterns in two locations in Pakistan. It provides an understanding of how some Muslim women in the country see themselves and their abilities to travel in relation to tourism and hospitality activities. In the case of Chilas women are working in tourism and hospitality, but their work is mainly conducted within their own homes. The women contribute to the production of tourism by providing souvenirs in the form of handicrafts and other hospitality related services. Most of this work is behind the scenes, and the women's labour is unacknowledged as going beyond their existing domestic duties, it is also unpaid. In Abbottabad women have a more active role in tourism in terms of providing direct and indirect services. Here the women have more of a 'public profile' as tourists and migrants from other parts of Pakistan have brought different ideas and approaches to the role of women in society. Although the women who do engage in work outside of the home still face problems in trying to assert their independence, there is nevertheless a feeling that greater exposure to ideas from outside the city has been liberating for local women, and some are becoming more financially independent. However, there is a marked difference of experiences between those who live in 'town' and those who live in 'Abbottabad city'. In terms of financial stability and independence, Chilassi women, by contrast, are still dependent on male relatives. They are unable to negotiate their own income for the work they do because they are prohibited from speaking to men outside of their household. While some women are gaining financial independence in parts of Abbottabad, they are also gaining more freedom of movement and some of the women spoke of the ability to travel without *mahram*. This relaxation in approach was again attributed to the outside influences of tourists and migrants coming to Abbottabad. In Chilas, women's travel is still strictly controlled under the *purdah* tradition and the requirement for *mahram*.

The situation in Abbottabad offers some hope for the improvement of women's lives in that in some circumstances they are afforded more freedoms and tourism has had a positive role to play in this. As noted, women do travel, but overall, in Chilas and Abbottabad, their movements are restricted. The irony is that in both places the silent and unseen women whose lives are controlled by men work to serve the needs of those who enjoy greater freedoms, thus throwing not only gender inequality into stark relief but also that of inequalities between the toured and the tourees.

References

Ahmed, T. (2019). Choppers to take tourists to northern areas – Operators to get licenses as part of new aviation policy. *The Express Tribune*. https://tribune.com.pk/story/1928108/choppers-take-tourists-northern-areas

Al Mazro'ei, L. (2010). *The experiences of Muslim women employed in the tourism industry: The case of Oman* [Master's thesis, University of Waterloo]. https://pdfs.semanticscholar.org/1da2/581a3f29c0e5d424c523ec2c33a0c9fa116d.pdf

Baloch, S. M. (2019, May 17). Pakistan authorities record a dozen cases of 'honour' killing in a fortnight. *The Guardian*. www.theguardian.com/global-development/2019/may/17/pakistan-authorities-record-a-dozen-cases-of-honour-killing-in-a-fortnight

Briam, K. M. (2017). *Managing cultural tourism in a post-conflict region – The Kurdistan Federal region of Iraq* [Doctoral dissertation, University of Nottingham].

Cole, S. (2007). Entrepreneurship and empowerment: Considering the barriers – a case study from Indonesia. *Tourism: An International Interdisciplinary Journal, 55*(4), 461–473.

Cole, S. (Ed.). (2018). *Gender equality and tourism: Beyond empowerment*. CABI.

Cole, S., & Morgan, N. (2010). Introduction: Tourism and inequality. In S. Cole & N. Morgan (Eds.), *Tourism and inequality: Problems and prospects* (pp. xvii–xxv). CABI.

Dawn. (2011, May 15). *Hope for bumper tourist season in Abbottabad*. www.dawn.com/news/628877/hopes-for-bumper-tourist-season-in-abbottabad

Equitable Tourism Options (Equation). (2007). *Women in tourism realities, dilemmas and opportunities*. www.scribd.com/doc/30326203/Women-in-Tourism-Realities-Dilemmas-and-Opportunities#download

Gentry, K. M. (2007). Belizean women and tourism work: Opportunity or impediment? *Annals of Tourism Research, 34*(2), 477–496. https://doi.org/10.1016/j.annals.2006.11.003

Hadi, A. (2017). Patriarchy and gender-based violence in Pakistan. *European Journal of Social Sciences Education and Research, 10*(2), 297–304.

International Labour Organization (ILO). (2018). *Social finance annual report*. ILO.

Jafari, J., & Scott, N. (2014). Muslim world and its tourisms. *Annals of Tourism Research, 44*, 1–19. https://doi.org/10.1016/j.annals.2013.08.011

Jha, M. K. (2010). Natural and anthropogenic disasters: An overview. In M. K. Jha (Ed.), *Natural and anthropogenic disasters: Vulnerability, preparedness and mitigation* (pp. 1–16). Capital Publishing Company.

Jozuka, E., & Saifi, S. (2020, May 18). Two Pakistani women murdered in so-called honor killing after a leaked video circulates online. *CNN*. https://cnnphilippines.com/world/2020/5/18/two-women-pakistan-honor-killing.html?fbclid=IwAR1osjhR0TJw HaRRtSWLa0XZ84IJCIfasflDDcYrR-DFnqYNmW9m69m1AX4

Jucan, M. S., & Jucan, C. N. (2013). Gender trends in tourism destination. *Procedia – Social and Behavioural Sciences, 92*, 437–444. https://doi.org/10.1016/j.sbspro.2013.08.698

Pritchard, A. (2014). Gender and feminist perspectives in tourism research. In A. Lew, C. M. Hall, & A. Williams (Eds.), *The Wiley Blackwell companion to tourism* (pp. 314–324). Wiley.

Pritchard, A., & Morgan, N. J. (2000). Privileging the male gaze: Gendered tourism landscapes. *Annals of Tourism Research, 27*(4), 884–905. https://doi.org/10.1016/S0160-7383(99)00113-9

Rueters News Agency. (2019). Qandeel Baloch: Pakistan social media star's brother gets life for her 'honour' murder. *The Telegraph*. www.telegraph.co.uk/news/2019/09/27/pakistan-social-media-stars-brother-gets-life-honour-murder

Sayira, T. (2015). *Tourism development and women in under crises destinations: A case study of Chilas, Pakistan* [Doctoral dissertation, John Moores University]. https://ethos.bl.uk/OrderDetails.do?uin=uk.bl.ethos.697487

Sayira, T., & Andrews, H. (2016). Impacts of crises and communication media on place image: A case study of Chilas, Pakistan. *Journal of Destination Marketing and Management, 5*(4), 351–360. https://doi.org/10.1016/j.jdmm.2016.09.010

Sayira, T., & Andrews, H. (2019). Tourism in Chilas, Pakistan: Destination under crisis. In R. K. Isaac, E. Çakmak, & R. Butler (Eds.), *Tourism and hospitality in conflict-ridden destinations* (pp. 104–117). Routledge.

Schevyens, R. (2002). *Tourism for development: Empowering communities*. Prentice Hall.

Shakeela, A., & Cooper, C. (2009). Human resource issues in a small island setting the case of the Maldivian tourism industry. *Tourism Recreation Research, 34*(1), 67–78. https://doi.org/10.1080/02508281.2009.11081576

The Independent. (2019, December 2). *This is where the experts recommend for travel next year, from Egypt to Pakistan*. www.independent.co.uk/travel/news-and-advice/holiday-predictions-trends-egypt-peru-experts-copenhagen-pakistan-a9225001.html

Thomson Reuters Foundation. (2018, June 26). *Factbox: Which are the world's 10 most dangerous countries for women?* www.reuters.com/article/us-women-dangerous-poll-factbox-idUSKBN1JM01Z

TrustLaw. (2011, June 16). Factbox: The world's most dangerous countries for women. *Reuters*. www.reuters.com/article/us-women-danger-factbox-idUSTRE75E32A20110615

United Nations World Tourism Organisation (UNWTO) and Entity for Gender Equality and the Empowerment of Women (UN Women). (2010). *Global report on women in tourism*. UNWTO & UN Women. www.e-unwto.org/doi/pdf/10.18111/9789284413737

United Nations World Tourism Organisation (UNWTO). (2019). *Global report on women in tourism: 2nd edition*. UNWTO. www.e-unwto.org/doi/epdf/10.18111/9789284420384

Usmani, Z. (2017). Pakistan suicide bombing attacks: Most authentic count of suicide bombing attacks in Pakistan (1995–2016). *Kaggle*. www.kaggle.com/zusmani/pakistansuicideattacks

World Economic Forum. (2019). *Global gender gap report 2020*. http://www3.weforum.org/docs/WEF_GGGR_2020.pdf

12 The travel pattern and experiences of Turkish female outbound tourists

İsmail Kervankiran, Ayla Deniz and Kübra İlban

Introduction

Modern Turkish history has often been viewed as the 'conflict between two Turkeys'; that is, a division highlighting either Turkey as a secularist and progressive nation or as an Islamic and conservative one (Yavuz, 2019). This dual structure that distinguishes Turkey from many other Muslim countries has become the dominant element of the formation of daily life from the foundation of the country until today. Therefore, as in many social phenomena, in order to understand the behavior of participation in tourism, it is necessary to progress on the basis of this dual structure for a deeper understanding.

Within this context, since secularity was accepted as one of the founding principles during the establishment of the Turkish Republic, many regulations were made in accordance with this principle. Hence, the reflection of religion in daily life was intervened by secular regime. Although some of these principles were maintained when there was the transition to multi-party democracy in the 1950s, newly founded parties included religious symbols in public discourse to get the votes of conservative elements in society. With the 1980 military coup, Turkish-Islamic synthesis unifying Turkish national ties with Islamic identity emerged, and to make this structure even stronger, the Directorate of Religious Affairs (Diyanet), the most competent institution in religious service, was founded (Öztürk & Gözaydın, 2018; Yavuz, 2019).

Since the 1990s, this structure has made itself stronger through forming an identity comprised of national and religious symbols, spreading its ideas via mass media and printed works and developing close relationships with the Anatolian bourgeoisie (Yavuz, 2019). On account of this power, the ruling party, known for its Islamic policies, has shaped the Turkish political life since the beginning of the 2000s. Therefore, although secularists played an important role in the foundation of the country, the effectiveness of the conservatives in the government of the country has increased over time. Nonetheless, as the opposition of secularists to the conservative lifestyle has continued, conservatives have started to adopt the various practices peculiar to the lifestyles of secularists. How then have these changes in the political-economic structure of the country affected tourism in Turkey?

DOI: 10.4324/9781003036296-16

In 1972, the development of domestic tourism was provided through setting up planned organized tourism regions. The fact that these policies became successful especially in the south and west coast cities ensured that more comprehensive tourism promotion laws were made in 1982. This was, at the same time, the beginning of neoliberal policies in tourism in as much as the state directly built and ran touristic premises itself in previous periods, it supported the private sector to develop tourism after that period. However, the policies until those periods were suitable for the holiday style of the secularists. Both the power of the secularists in state and their accumulation of multiple capitals being sufficient to invest in tourism historically contributed to that fact. In the meantime, that hotels were very expensive for family holidays in these periods made the way for the creation of new holiday concepts, and in 1985, with an amendment to the law, a legal framework was provided for the building of timeshare properties.

Built especially for secularists preferring coastal tourism, timeshare properties were started to be built with a new concept in Anatolian cities with thermal springs by conservative entrepreneurs. In these facilities, separate pools were built in accordance with the demands of these conservative families and the holiday concept was established in the consumption practices of conservatives. This enterprise took off very rapidly and conservative hotels were built in classical holiday routes in the beginning of the 2000s. These hotels have also become the places people from Arabic countries prefer. As of 2018, there are 63 hotels with a halal certificate and many more serve with the concept of halal tourism without the certificate. On the other hand, especially after Turkey became a candidate country for EU membership, European tourists and the ones from former Union of Soviet Socialist Republics (USSR) preferred the country as their primary holiday route, which caused hundreds of touristic facilities to be built for these millions of tourists. The hotels secularists prefer are the ones tourists from Europe stay at. In this regard the tourist habitus of secularists and conservatives are quite separate.

As can be seen, the development of the political–economic structure of Turkey and the construction of tourism for secular and conservative tourists are quite related to each other. The real issue that has affected tourism practices recently is that economic capital, which was in the hands of secularists, has changed hands for the last 30 years, and a new market organization consisting of conservative capitalists has emerged. The domination of conservatives in daily life has caused secularists to feel inclined to go to places where the likelihood of meeting them is low. Conservatives who have the economic capital but have not been able to break the power of secularists stemming from their cultural capital have started to imitate their lifestyles after a while. In this way, the holiday styles of secularists have turned into a way for conservatives to gain cultural capital. Conservatives have also diversified their travel routes not only to show their financial capital but also to enrich their cultural capital through international tourism. Even the ones who cannot afford this encourage their children to go abroad for holidays to have the same effect. In this way, they transform their capital and habitus. As a matter of fact, the emergence of travel agencies selling international holiday packages in Anatolian cities and the increase in the news about foreign travel in Islamic media are all about this. What should not be forgotten among these developments is that the tourism practices of secularists have not regressed with the participation of conservatives in tourism. On the contrary, the variation in the style of the two groups' concepts of holiday has enabled the tourism market to become varied, developed and spread spatially. Therefore, in consumption culture created by this new touristic activity, what then is the place of women?

According to data from the Turkish Statistical Institute (TurkStat; 2018), female outbound tourists are a quarter of male outbound tourists in Turkey. However, despite this inequality, especially since the beginning of the 2000s, the number of women travelling abroad has increased rapidly. Between 2003–2018, the number of women travelling internationally quadrupled, and the visited countries became more varied (see also Chapter 13, this volume). Among this increase, what role women play in the formation of touristic practices and what effect differentiation of women has on the structure of foreign travel are not known. This study criticizes the invisibility of the differentiation of this basic lifestyle that determines the life of women in touristic literature and claims that one needs to focus on women experiences for a deep academic understanding and an effective tourism planning. In this context, the development of touristic activities in the consumption practices of women identifying themselves as secular or conservative has been presented comparatively.

Muslim travel market

There are many factors affecting tourism consumption and tourist behavior (Shaw et al., 2000). Although in literature there are studies revealing that demand for travelling, direction of tourist flows and tourism consumption in Muslim countries are affected by religious factors (Digance, 2006; Eid & El-Gohary, 2015; Fischer, 2011; Henderson, 2016; Jafari & Scott, 2014; Ritter, 1975; Ryan, 2016; Scott & Jafari, 2010; Timothy & Iverson, 2006; Seyfi & Hall, 2019), it is obvious that Muslims' tourism consumption culture is not only affected by religious factors (Dluzewska, 2008; Stodolska & Livengood, 2006; Taheri, 2016), but there are also other factors affecting it (Hall & Prayag, 2020).

In this heterogeneous structure, travel market in Islamic countries has been undergoing important changes. The most important indication of this change is the increase in the number of Muslims travelling to different countries for holidays. This increase includes not only pilgrimage but also travels to non-Muslim countries. Therefore, tourism operators develop different practices toward tourists with different profiles from these countries. Travels from Islamic countries to other countries of the world are expected to increase in the future due to the reasons such as population increase, increased economic wealth, change in consumption culture, development of technology, increase in social activism and developed travel awareness. This situation also demonstrates that discussions will continue as to how the relationship between tourism and the Muslim world will develop, how tourism will keep pace with the Muslim world (Vukonić, 2010), how tourism experiences will be reflected in social relationships and consumption culture in Islamic countries and, as a result, how social categories will be formed.

Gender and travel behavior

All these tendencies and related discussions get complicated in tourists' behavior. The main factor determining this behavior is gender. As a matter of fact, in the studies carried out it has been revealed that gender affects individuals' travels considerably, and generally there are more restrictors for women (Crawford & Godbey, 1987; Wilson & Little, 2008). Despite this, it is a fact that there has been a rise in female tourists and even women travelling alone in recent years. This has enabled the tourism market for women to gain importance in the global economy, and thus, the studies about the experiences of women tourists have increased in the tourism literature (Carvalho et al., 2014; Chiang & Jogaratnam, 2006; Jordan & Aitchison, 2008; Jordan & Gibson, 2005; McNamara & Prideaux, 2010; Wilson & Harris, 2006; Wilson & Little, 2008; Yang et al., 2018). In addition to these studies, there are also ones that deal with the general travel view of women (Bhimji, 2008; Fendt & Wilson, 2012; Green & Singleton, 2006; Khan, 2011; Laing & Frost, 2017; Stark & Meschik, 2018). In these studies, such issues as adversities faced by women in their travels, strategies to deal with difficulties, the effects of bad experiences on travelling behavior, risk in women's spare time activities and safety situations and adventure stories are dealt with. However, there is a lack of detailed information and survey on tourism experiences of women participating in it (Kaba & Emekli, 2018), and this lack is even more evident in Islamic countries. In this study, to make a contribution to fill this deficiency and in reference to Bourdieu (1986), the course of the journey women with financial capital take in order to reach cultural capital is shared. Furthermore, the experiences women have during these travels from their habitus is also discussed.

A trajectory of female travel in Turkey

The reason why Turkey was chosen as the study field is that it is possible to observe the difference among women in the country, because Turkey has a different structure than other Islamic countries. Travels for tourism in Turkey – where the social structure is not homogeneous and where there are two different structures (conservative and secular) whose consumption culture, lifestyle, behavior patterns and choices are different – have a more distinctive profile than other Islamic countries, where Islamic rules are more dominant and that are more traditional. In other words, tourism consumption culture in Turkey differs from approaches that are conceptualized like 'Islamic tourism' or 'Halal tourism' in the literature and have distinctive dynamics. As a result, this difference in Turkey affects the tourism behavior of the women in the country in different ways, which makes it a very interesting research topic.

1990s: differing routes

The 1990s were the years during which Turkey's international expansion policy started to affect tourism as well. However, in this period, among women tourists, secularists were more observable. It is clear that this situation is due to the secularist policies to encourage women to participate in the public domain more (Göle, 1997). Therefore, secular women could obtain financial and social support to travel more rapidly than conservatives. In addition, financial resources conservative women could use independently were more limited, and teachings of their communities about not spending money except for basic needs for individual security used to affect their lives more.

In the 1990s, there were two primary destinations secular women were inclined to visit (Figure 12.1), European countries and the USA, where secular lifestyle is widespread. However, two routes were set up for conservatives through travel agencies under the influence of political Islam, which started to rise in this period: Holy places (especially Mecca and Medina, Saudi Arabia) and the Balkan states carrying traces of the Ottoman period (especially Bosnia-Herzegovina). Therefore, the first destinations of conservative women were places where the Islamic way of living was widespread and thus provided 'Halal tourism' facilities. Among these countries, the ones who went to holy places were generally elderly women who wanted to do their religious duty while the others who went to the Balkan states were relatively educated and young women. Therefore, cultural and geographical proximity affected conservative women's choice of destination.

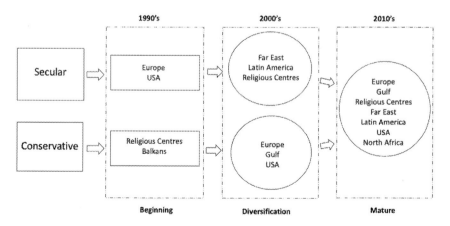

Figure 12.1 Destination choices of women by decade

2000s: routes becoming varied

In the 2000s, there was a variety of places that women preferred for tourism. Such factors as the increase in Turkey-based flights to different destinations, agreements with many countries for visa-free travels and agreements to increase cooperation among countries (e.g., education, business, culture and art) were influential in this tourism mobility. In addition, secularists were inclined to travel to farther places and ones not known previously. The women who went to the Far East and Latin America also tended to travel to holy places. However, their difference from the conservatives was that they preferred these places for completely cultural reasons, not for religious purposes. Another important point is that secular women whose participation in the workforce was higher went on overseas business trips more and started to combine these trips with touristic activities.

In the same period, conservative women inclined toward Europe's developed countries. Particularly countries such as Germany, France and Italy were the most preferred ones by these women. The reason for this was they had relatives there and they started to visit them. However, wealthier conservative women who got rich in this period started to travel to Gulf countries where a lot of luxury consumption items were sold for shopping and to the USA for cultural tourism.

2010: converging routes

There seemed to be a convergence in the destinations secular and conservative women preferred for travel in the 2000s. Even new routes like North Africa were added to the tourism preferences of women. The reasons for this convergence were various since the cultural capital women obtain in a certain period increases through experiencing new destinations. The presentation of different destinations on social media also contributes to rapid popularity and even becomes an indication of social class, creating an interest in destinations not experienced before. Furthermore, travelling alone or regular travel as lifestyle practices that have become widespread among young secular women affect other women as well because they have started to provide information other women need through travel channels they create on YouTube.

What increased the outbound travel of conservatives is rapid development of holiday concepts catering to them worldwide. Surveys carried out in different countries reveal that this tourism concept boosts customer satisfaction and his/her desire to participate in tourism (Han et al., 2019; Henderson, 2016). This situation has contributed to the extension of the tourism market. Within this extension, travel agencies were set up in many cities in Turkey, and they started to prepare holiday packages on the basis of the needs of women living in those places. This made it easier for conservative women who used to travel with their families to travel as groups of women and, later, on their own. Owing to this, family visits, which were the first among the reasons for women's foreign travel previously, were replaced with travel, entertainment, sports and cultural activities (TurkStat, 2018). However, even in this period, people's travels to holy places for reasons other than worshipping were criticized by the president.

Study design and data collection

During the data gathering period of the study, in order to make women's experiences visible and include more of their voices in the study, a semi-structured interview technique, a qualitative research methodology, was employed. First, women with an experience of foreign travel were reached through the Internet on different platforms. In the following stage, interviews were held with other interviewees as a result of snowball sampling. Therefore, in reaching participants, purposeful and multiple snowball sampling led to 30 different women living in different cities being interviewed face-to-face or by phone.

Most of the participants are university graduates and work in paid employment. This situation is compatible with the data TurkStat (2018) has on women tourists going abroad (70%). On the other hand, the education level of women defining themselves as secular (17) is higher than that of women defining themselves as conservative (13). In addition, the age of first foreign travel of the former is lower than that of the latter and the frequency of foreign travel of the former is more than that of the latter. This situation clearly indicates that whether women are secular or conservative affects the formation of tourism practices.

The interviews held with the participants occurred from March to May 2019. The interviews lasted 50–75 minutes. The interviews were recorded with the consent of the participants. Then, sound recordings were analyzed and, through MAXQDA, content analysis was done. To understand the significance of the data in the general structure of tourism practices in Turkey, women directors of the two travel agencies with their headquarters in İstanbul and Ankara and branches in many cities in the country were interviewed. In this way, the views of both tourism service suppliers and the ones taking part in tourism were included in the study.

Findings

Changing tourism consumption culture

Preparation for holiday

In this part of the study, questions as to how women plan going abroad, how they organize it and the choice of accommodation are discussed. It is seen in

Table 12.1 Profile of participants

	Age	Education	Employment status	Marital status	City	Identity	Age at first travel	Travel frequency
P1	25	Bachelor	Private sector employee	Single	Ankara	Secular	20	Once a month
P2	31	Bachelor	Civil servant	Single	İstanbul	Secular	6	Once a month
P3	42	High school	Unemployed	Married	İzmir	Secular	25	Once a quarter
P4	50	Master	Retired	Single	Ankara	Conservative	5	Semi-annually
P5	29	Master	Civil servant	Single	Konya	Conservative	23	Biennially
P6	42	Bachelor	Private sector employee	Single	İstanbul	Conservative	28	Once a quarter
P7	36	High school	Employer	Single	Ankara	Conservative	32	Twice a month
P8	38	Bachelor	Private sector employee	Single	Antalya	Secular	22	Twice a month
P9	44	High school	Private sector employee	Married	İstanbul	Conservative	27	Once a quarter
P10	34	Master	Private sector employee	Single	Eskişehir	Conservative	19	Once a quarter
P11	39	Master	Civil servant	Married	Eskişehir	Conservative	31	Once a quarter
P12	25	Bachelor	Private sector employee	Single	İstanbul	Conservative	21	Biennially
P13	37	Bachelor	Private sector employee	Single	İstanbul	Secular	37	Once a quarter
P14	24	Bachelor	Unemployed	Single	İzmir	Conservative	18	Semi-annually
P15	27	Master	Student	Single	Eskişehir	Secular	20	Semi-annually
P16	25	Bachelor	Unemployed	Single	İstanbul	Secular	6	Once a quarter
P17	31	Doctorate	Civil servant	Single	Isparta	Secular	27	Semi-annually
P18	34	Master	Civil servant	Single	Isparta	Secular	32	Once a year
P19	26	Master	Private sector employee	Single	İzmir	Secular	23	Once a year
P20	30	Master	Private sector employee	Single	İstanbul	Secular	25	Once a quarter
P21	32	Bachelor	Private sector employee	Single	İstanbul	Secular	6	Once a quarter
P22	38	Bachelor	Private sector employee	Single	İstanbul	Secular	23	Once a year
P23	36	Master	Private sector employee	Married	İzmit	Secular	24	Semi-annually
P24	38	Master	Private sector employee	Single	İstanbul	Secular	26	Once a quarter
P25	35	High school	Employer	Married	Isparta	Conservative	29	Triennial
P26	43	Bachelor	Civil servant	Single	Isparta	Conservative	40	Once a year
P27	29	Bachelor	Private sector employee	Single	İstanbul	Secular	13	Once a month
P28	46	Doctorate	Civil servant	Married	Elazığ	Conservative	33	Once a year
P29	27	Master	Private sector employee	Single	Kayseri	Conservative	20	Once a quarter
P30	29	Master	Private sector employee	Single	Bursa	Secular	11	Once a month

the scope of the study that secular women plan their holidays by themselves dealing with all the details as they want to travel independently:

> I make a plan as I please. Since I make the plan on my own, I can make up my mind about the slightest change including the place I will go immediately.
>
> (K2)

On the other hand, conservatives go abroad through tourism agencies. In this way, conservative women overcome any security problem they might face during their travel and find food according to their beliefs easily since most of these women's not knowing a foreign language causes them to experience communication problems:

> I work it out through travel agencies. That is, I work with them because I have a language problem. I can't travel alone, either.
>
> (K4)

Accommodation styles of secular and conservative women change based on the way they travel. Secular women tend to find cheap accommodation that they can stay at for a long time. Therefore, their demand for using their financial resources effectively affects their choice of accommodation. In addition, their wish to have closer relationships with the people in the places they go to, and thus, develop their cultural capital, too, affects this choice:

> If I go alone, I stay at a hostel. The price is quite reasonable. The best thing about staying there is you can make friends and improve your language.
>
> (K3)

Conservative women, however, make a different choice from secular women by preferring hotels with relatively higher accommodation fees. As a matter of fact, travel agencies these women prefer arrange accommodation as well. However, even if they travel independently, their accommodation preferences may not change:

> I can no longer stay at a hostel. It is not suitable for me to travel with a back-pack. I'm a bit conservative. Maybe it is something related to my conservatism.
>
> (K4)

As can be seen, preparation processes for a holiday differ between secular and conservative women. The places women go to and why are explained in three sub-periods. Nonetheless, it should be recognized that travel routes in one period are not eliminated from the preference list. On the contrary, in addition to the existing routes, new ones are added, and thus women experience greater variety in their destinations.

Diversification of tourism experiences

In this part of the study, experiences of women travelling to foreign countries and contributions of travels to women's lifestyles and social relationships are evaluated. As a result of the interviews, although the effects of social and human differences mentioned in the previous part on travel experiences could be observed, meaning attributed to consumption cultures, practices and consumption by women is changing rapidly. Even though they have different lifestyles, women generally want to have a delightful and unforgettable experience while consuming something.

Having an experience is basically comprised of five different dimensions, that is, sensory, emotional, intellectual, behavioral and relational dimensions (Schmitt, 1999). The fact that travels nowadays are more active, original, interesting, adventurous and informative than traditional mass tourism (Hall, 2007) enriches and diversifies tourist experiences. Given the versatile dimension of the experience, the concept of tourism experience is complex and hard to define. Women travellers who adopt a conservative view of the world in Turkey look for places, food and environments belonging to their own culture in their first travels. They prefer experiencing different places and food in the following ones. This supports the previously mentioned view about the convergence of travels of secular and conservative women:

> I was more conservative in my initial travels. I didn't have any choice of food except for my culture. I got worried about whether I would be able to find a Turkish restaurant in the country I went to. My worries got disappeared in the following travels. Now I want to experience the cuisine of the country I went to and this makes me very happy.
>
> (K28)

While Otto and Ritchie (1996) describe the tourist experience as a subjective mental situation felt by the participants during the service, Tung and Ritchie (2011) describes it as a meaningful experience remembered and restructured by the tourist. Pine and Gilmore (1999) stated that experience is not only offering a service but also creating an unforgettable and unique activity. That's why 'unforgettable' experiences instead of 'standard' ones have been considered more important for the tourism industry nowadays (Kim & Ritchie, 2014). As a result, tourist experience has become one of the crucial research topics in tourism (Chandralal & Valenzuela, 2015; Çetin & Bilgihan, 2014; Quan & Wang, 2004; Seyfi et al., 2020; Rasoolimanesh et al., 2021; Sthapit & Coudounaris, 2018; Tung & Ritchie, 2011; Uriely, 2005; Zhang et al., 2017). In new generation tourism perception, approaches encouraging individualism and experiential practices become prominent. This situation has changed the position of modern tourists from 'glance collector' to 'experience hunter' (Kaba & Emekli, 2018). As a result of this, women interviewed want to live a different tourism experience by touching the lives of people in the places they go to instead of watching the environment, culture and people there:

> My dream has been travelling all over the world since my childhood. I don't like travelling aimlessly like Instagram phenomenon. I am curious about the culture, life and geography of the place I travel to. Having contact with people and watching their lives affect me. I'm a doctor and I want to learn about the local cures they have.
>
> (K18)

As can be seen, the participant emphasizes that travelling enables her to have experiences that enrich her knowledge. It is already known that with changing economic, social and political conditions, women travel for independence, sociability, and learning, and a desire to discover them and travelling strengthen these feelings (Kaba & Emekli, 2018). As Wilson (2004) suggests, nowadays courageous, self-confident and adventurous women travel independently, Yang et al. (2017) also states that women have more opportunity and choice about travelling and suggests that women take part in travelling more in order to be stronger. What participants say supports this:

> I think travelling is an experience which frees women and helps them feel stronger. There are no more borders. You can go to a place you don't know without needing anyone, being afraid and by organizing everything on your own. As women travel, their points of view change.
>
> (K8)

> Touristic travels have contributed a lot to my self-confidence because you are free. There is no one you depend on. I didn't want to be alone but I realized that I don't need anybody to travel and that I can accomplish a lot of things. I had a boyfriend who didn't want me to travel. We broke up due to this. Your perspectives, targets and dreams change during travels. You see different cultures. When you see all of these, you develop yourselves and always want better. That is, you view the world more favorably and positively.
>
> (K14)

Although participation of women in tourism differs spatially and structurally in Turkey historically, all women obtain similar experiences in travels. The common point of all travels for women is that they become stronger through travelling. The most important element boosting this strengthening is that women avoid control mechanisms by travelling in groups. Women who get out of this control, that is, who in a way can change their habits, do lots of things that they did not have the courage to do in daily life in Turkey. Among them drinking alcohol, wearing short dresses, taking part in different art activities, travelling together and staying with them in the same room could be included. The reason for secular women to have these experiences abroad is the political and social structure of Turkey nowadays. In a way, their going abroad is an escape from the conservatives' control. What is interesting is that conservative women do so to escape from other conservative women's control.

Conclusion

Turkey has increasingly adopt consumption-oriented culture as a result of its communication and interaction with modern societies. Touristic travels have contributed considerably to Turkey's integration to modern consumption culture more rapidly than other Islamic countries.

In this study, the travelling practices of secular and conservative women in Turkey were discussed and highlighted that travel experiences affected their lives in a positive way and that their travel routes and ways to plan them changed in time due to this. In a way, women who started to differ in many ways from each other began to get similar in terms of travel practices. More specifically, there is an increase in the cultural capital of all women through travels, tourism consumption is enriched through travels becoming continuous and the tourism market is diversified in the same way. Women's getting free via travels not only makes them similar but also causes their habitus to change. It is already known that habitus is not fixed or permanent, and it might change in unexpected situations or in a long historical period and is the reason why habitus forms group culture and societies as well as individual history. Therefore, it has been revealed in this study that its settling in a tourism practice and consumption culture that did not exist before has a potential to transform secularists and conservatives in Turkey by affecting them.

References

Bhimji, F. (2008). Cosmopolitan belonging and diaspora: Second-generation British Muslim women travelling to South Asia. *Citizenship Studies*, *12*(4), 413–427. https://doi.org/10.1080/13621020802184259

Bourdieu, P. (1986). The forms of capital. In J. G. Richardson (Ed.), *Handbook of theory and research for the sociology of education* (pp. 241–258). Greenwood.

Carvalho, G., Baptista, M., & Costa, C. (2014). Women travelling alone: Prospects on gender and tourism experiences. *Revista Turismo & Desenvolvimento*, *5*(21), 31–32.

Cetin, G., & Bilgihan, A. (2014). Components of cultural tourists' experiences in destinations. *Current Issues in Tourism, 19*(2), 137–154. *https://doi.org/10.1080/13683500.2014.994595*

Chandralal, L., & Valenzuela, F. R. (2015). Memorable tourism experiences: Scale development. *Contemporary Management Research*, *11*(3), 291–310. https://doi.org/10.7903/cmr.13822

Chiang, C., & Jogaratnam, G. (2006). Why do women travel solo for purposes of leisure? *Journal of Vacation Marketing, 12*(1), 59–70. https://doi.org/10.1177/1356766706059041

Crawford, D., & Godbey, G. (1987). Reconceptualizing barriers to family leisure. *Leisure Sciences, 9*(2), 119–127. https://doi.org/10.1080/01490408709512151

Digance, J. (2006). Religious and secular pilgrimage: Journeys redolent with meaning. In D. J. Timothy & D. H. Olsen (Eds.), *Tourism, religion and spiritual journeys* (pp. 36–48). Routledge.

Dluzewska, A. (2008). The influence of religion on global and local conflict in tourism: Case studies in Muslim countries, In P. M. Burns & M. Novelli (Eds.), *Tourism development growth, myths and inequalities* (pp. 52–67). CABI.

Eid, R., & El-Gohary, H. (2015). The role of Islamic religiosity on the relationship between perceived value and tourist satisfaction. *Tourism Management, 46*, 477–488. https://doi.org/10.1016/j.tourman.2014.08.003

Fendt, L. S., & Wilson, E. (2012). 'I just push through the barriers because I live for surfing': How women negotiate their constraints to surf tourism. *Annals of Leisure Research, 15*(1), 4–18. https://doi.org/10.1080/11745398.2012.670960

Fischer, J. (2011). *The halal frontier: Muslim consumers in a globalised market.* Palgrave Macmillan.

Göle, N. (1997). Secularism and Islamism in Turkey: The making of elites and counter-elites. *Middle East Journal, 51*(1), 46–58. www.jstor.org/stable/4329022

Green, E., & Singleton, C. (2006). Risky bodies at leisure: Young women negotiating space and place. *Sociology, 40*(5), 853–871. https://doi.org/10.1177/0038038506067510

Hall, C. M. (2007). Response to Yeoman et al: The fakery of 'The authentic tourist'. *Tourism Management, 28*(4), 1139–1140. https://doi.org/10.1016/j.tourman.2006.09.008

Hall, C. M., & Prayag, G. (Eds.). (2020). *The Routledge handbook of halal hospitality and Islamic tourism.* Routledge.

Han, H., Al-Ansi, A., Koseoglu, M. A., Lin, P. M. C., Park, J., Yu, J., & Kim, W. (2019). Halal tourism: Travel motivators and customer retention. *Journal of Travel & Tourism Marketing, 36*(9), 1012–1024. https://doi.org/10.1080/10548408.2019.1683483

Henderson, J. C. (2016). Muslim travelers, tourism industry responses and the case of Japan. *Tourism Recreation Research, 41*(3), 339–347. https://doi.org/10.1080/02508281.2016.1215090

Jafari, J., & Scott, N. (2014). Muslim world and its tourisms. *Annals of Tourism Research, 44*, 1–19. https://doi.org/10.1016/j.annals.2013.08.011

Jordan, F., & Aitchison, C. (2008). Tourism and the sexualisation of the gaze: Solo female tourists. Experiences of gendered power, surveillance and embodiment. *Leisure Studies, 27*(3), 32–349. https://doi.org/10.1016/j.annals.2013.08.011

Jordan, F., & Gibson, H. (2005). "We're not stupid . . . But we'll not stay home either": Experiences of solo women travelers. *Tourism Review International, 9*(2), 195–211. https://doi.org/10.3727/154427205774791663

Kaba, B., & Emekli, G. (2018). Turizmde Yükselen Bir Eğilim: Yalnız Seyahat Eden Kadın Gezginler: Türkiye Örneği. (A rising trend in tourism: Solo women travelers: The case of Turkey). *Aegean Geographical Journal, 27*(2), 111–126.

Khan, S. (2011). Gendered leisure: Are women more constrained in travel for leisure? *Tourismos: An International Multidisciplinary Journal of Tourism, 6*(1), 105–121.

Kim, J. H., & Ritchie, J. B. (2014). Cross-cultural validation of a memorable tourism experience scale (MTES). *Journal of Travel Research, 53*(3), 323–335. https://doi.org/10.1177/0047287513496468

Laing, J., & Frost, W. (2017). Journeys of well-being: Women's travel narratives of transformation and self-discovery in Italy. *Tourism Management, 62*, 110–119. https://doi.org/10.1016/j.tourman.2017.04.004

McNamara, K., & Prideaux, B. (2010). A typology of solo independent women travellers. *International Journal of Tourism Research, 12*(3), 253–264. https://doi.org/10.1002/jtr.751

Otto, J. E., & Ritchie, J. (1996). The service experience in tourism. *Tourism Management, 17*, 165–174. https://doi.org/10.1016/0261-5177(96)00003-9

Öztürk, A. E., & Gözaydın, İ. (2018). A frame for Turkey's foreign policy via the Diyanet in the Balkans. *Journal of Muslims in Europe 7*(3), 331–350.

Pine, B. J., & Gilmore, J. H. (1999). *The experience economy: Work is theatre & every business a stage.* Harvard Business School Press.

Quan, S., & Wang, N. (2004). Towards a structural model of the tourist experience: An illustration from food experiences in tourism. *Tourism Management, 25*(3), 297–305. https://doi.org/10.1016/S0261-5177(03)00130-4

Rasoolimanesh, S. M., Seyfi, S., Hall, C. M., & Hatamifar, P. (2021). Understanding memorable tourism experiences and behavioural intentions of heritage tourists. *Journal of Destination Marketing & Management, 21*, 100621. https://doi.org/10.1016/j.jdmm.2021.100621

Ritter, W. (1975). Recreation and tourism in the Islamic countries. *Ekistics, 40*, 149–152.

Ryan, C. (2016). Halal tourism. *Tourism Management Perspectives, 19*, 121–123. https://doi.org/10.1016/j.tmp.2015.12.014

Schmitt, B. (1999). Experiential marketing. *Journal of Marketing Management, 15*(1–3), 53–67. https://doi.org/10.1362/026725799784870496

Scott, N., & Jafari, J. (Eds.). (2010). *Tourism in the Muslim world.* Emerald Group.

Seyfi, S., & Hall, C. M. (2019). Deciphering Islamic theocracy and tourism: Conceptualization, context, and complexities. *International Journal of Tourism Research, 21*(6), 735–746. https://doi.org/10.1002/jtr.2300

Seyfi, S., Hall, C. M., & Rasoolimanesh, S. M. (2020). Exploring memorable cultural tourism experiences. *Journal of Heritage Tourism, 15*(3), 341–357. https://doi.org/10.1080/1743873X.2019.1639717

Shaw, G., Agarwal, S., & Bull, P. (2000). Tourism consumption and tourist behaviour: A British perspective. *Tourism Geographies, 2*(3), 264–289. https://doi.org/10.1080/14616680050082526

Stark, J., & Meschik, M. (2018). Women's everyday mobility: Frightening situations and their impacts on travel behaviour. *Transportation Research Part F: Traffic Psychology and Behaviour, 54*, 311–323. https://doi.org/10.1016/j.trf.2018.02.017

Sthapit, E., & Coudounaris, D. N. (2018). Memorable tourism experiences: Antecedents and outcomes. *Scandinavian Journal of Hospitality and Tourism, 18*(1), 72–94. https://doi.org/10.1080/15022250.2017.1287003

Stodolska, M., & Livengood, J. (2006). The influence of religion on the leisure behaviour of immigrant Muslims in the United States. *Journal of Leisure Studies, 38*(3), 293–320. https://doi.org/10.1080/00222216.2006.11950080

Taheri, B. (2016). Emotional connection, materialism, and religiosity: An Islamic tourism experience. *Journal of Travel & Tourism Marketing, 33*(7), 1011–1027. https://doi.org/10.1080/10548408.2015.1078761

Timothy, D., & Iverson, T. (2006). Tourism and Islam considerations of culture and duty. In D. Timothy & D. Olsen (Eds.), *Tourism, religion and spiritual journeys* (pp. 186–205). Routledge.

Tung, V. W. S., & Ritchie, J. B. (2011). Exploring the essence of memorable tourism experiences. *Annals of Tourism Research, 38*(4), 1367–1386. https://doi.org/10.1016/j.annals.2011.03.009

Turkish Statistical Institute (Turkstat). (2018). *Tourism statistics.* Ankara.

Uriely, N. (2005). The tourist experience: Conceptual developments. *Annals of Tourism Research, 32*(1), 199–216. https://doi.org/10.1016/j.annals.2004.07.008

Vukonić, B. (2010). Do we always understand each other? In N. Scott & J. Jafari (Eds.), *Tourism in the Muslim world* (pp. 31–45). Emerald Group.

Wilson, E., & Harris, C. (2006). Meaningful travel: Women, independent travel and the search for self and meaning. *Tourism: An International Interdisciplinary Journal, 54*(2), 161–172.

Wilson, E., & Little, D. (2008). The solo female travel experience: Exploring the geography of women's fear. *Current Issues in Tourism, 11*(2), 167–186. https://doi.org/10.2167/cit342.0

Wilson, E. C. (2004). *A journey of her own?: The impact of constraints on women's solo travel* [Doctoral thesis]. Griffith University.

Yang, E. C. L., Khoo-Lattimore, C., & Arcodia, C. (2017). A systematic literature review of risk and gender research in tourism. *Tourism Management, 58*, 89–100. https://doi.org/10.1016/j.tourman.2016.10.011

Yang, E. C. L., Khoo-Lattimore, C., & Arcodia, C. (2018). Constructing space and self through risk taking: A case of Asian solo female travelers. *Journal of Travel Research, 57*(2), 260–272. https://doi.org/10.1177/0047287517692447

Yavuz, H. K. (2019). Understanding Turkish secularism in the 21th century: A contextual roadmap. *Southeast European and Black Sea Studies, 19*(1), 55–78. https://doi.org/10.1080/14683857.2019.1576367

Zhang, H., Wu, Y., & Buhalis, D. (2017). A model of perceived image, memorable tourism experiences and revisit intention. *Journal of Destination Marketing & Management, 8*, 326–336. https://doi.org/10.1016/j.jdmm.2017.06.004

13 The travel motivations and experiences of Turkish solo women travellers

Gözde Emekli, İlkay Südaş and Bahar Kaba

Introduction

"It sometimes seems as if all the world is on the move" says (Urry, 2007, p. 3). Here, the expression "all the world" includes all different social groups with diverse motivations and reasons to move. Unlike the relatively easier mobility of international tourists, lifestyle migrants, international investors or highly skilled migrants due to their priviledged position within their own social contexts; for some other groups such as asylum seekers, refugees, and those in pursuit of better employment, mobility is an obligation and can even be a burden. Different types of mobility and how and why they occur in a certain society cannot be understood regardless of its actors' social status. In a Western context, Sager (2006, p. 482) states that mobility is one of the aspects of the freedom and concludes that "it is a widespread idea in the Western world that much of what is experienced as freedom lies in motion". From this point of view, mobility in a modern and individual society can be considered as a means to fulfill personal needs such as recreation and self-realization. Thus, sense of freedom is closely related to being mobile. If mobility refers to an understanding of freedom in the Western world, it is not surprising that all types of tourism-informed mobilities from annual holidays to long-term lifestyle migrations predomiantly stem from Western countries. The top-ranking countries that generate the greatest tourism expenditures, for instance, are mostly from the Western world. This is the case not only in terms of the short-term mobility such as mass tourism flows or solo travels but also in terms of long-term or permanent movements such as the lifestyle migration of Europeans and Americans to well-established coastal tourism destinations. Generally speaking, pleasure mobility at diverse geographical and temporal scales is a Western cultural practice. "However, emerging economies in Asia, Central and Eastern Europe, the Middle East, Africa and Latin America have shown fast growth over recent years" (UNWTO, 2018, p. 14) and as stated by the UNWTO (2018, p. 14) "Europe still remains the world's largest source region for outbound tourism, generating almost half of the world's international arrivals".

Travel and mobility have become increasingly everyday practice for many in developed countries and the elite in developing countries (Cohen et al., 2013).

DOI: 10.4324/9781003036296-17

In other words, for many people, "being on the move or road" has become a preferred "way of life" that they will return to whenever the opportunity presents itself (Westerhausen, 2002). These preferences lead to a lifestyle travel concept that is defined by Cohen (2010, 2011) as a phenomenon that illustrates a de-differentiation of everyday life and tourist experiences. For the lifestyle traveller, mobility within places and mobility between places are equivalent to freedom and lifestyle, travel provides the freedom to break free of routine and settlement in order to sustain a lifestyle based on change, novelty and progression (Anderson & Erskine, 2014). The relationship between lifestyle and mobility is linked in the work of Benson and O'Reilly (2009), under the title of "*lifestyle migration*". Searching for an alternative way of life (Benson & O'Reilly, 2009), searching for self (Cohen, 2010, 2011), and searching for happiness are the main motivations for such mobility.

Independent or solo travel is a growing lifstyle tourism segment (Bianchi, 2016), largely driven by a desire to understand how these individuals incorporate their travelling experiences into their own conception of self-identity (Davidson, 2005, p. 31). Women solo travellers are a distinct group among the tourist typologies, and the Turkish women solo travellers are a more specific subgroup from a non-Western culture and, more specifically, often from an Islamic context. This research aims at understanding the voices of solo woman travellers from a Muslim majority liberal country, Turkey. Thus, by focusing on Turkish women solo travellers' travel motivations and experiences and the constraints that they encounter during their travels, the research makes an original contribution to the related literature.

Women solo travellers: motivations, benefits, and constraints

Today, with changing social-political conditions, women have increasingly been active in the participation and consumption of travel in addition to working in the tourism industry and are recognized as a growing force within the tourism industry (McNamara & Prideaux, 2010; Pereira & Silva, 2018). "Women are grasping the opportunity to be tourists in their own right; for their own pleasure and satisfaction, breaking away from their hybrid identities of, 'the wife', 'mother', 'girlfriend' or the 'housewife'" (Myers, 2010, p. 16), and they increasingly prefer to travel alone rather than with family, friends, husband, or tours (Chiang & Jogaratnam, 2006). According to Bond (1997, p. 3) "solo woman travellers are not loners; they are bold, confident, gutsy adventurers" and do not wait for or depend upon a husband, friend, or tour. They travel independently (Wilson, 2004). These women define themselves as distinct from mass tourists, and the desire to tie in with local people is a part of being a solo women traveller (Cockburn-Wootten et al., 2006).

As a growing trend globally, "solo women travel" has been examined from several different perspectives. For example, researchers have shed light on *experiences* (McArthur, 1999; Wilson & Little, 2008; Jordan & Aitchison, 2008;

Myers, 2010), *motivations* (Wilson & Harris, 2006; Chiang & Jogaratnam, 2006; McNamara & Prideaux, 2010), *constraints* (Wilson, 2004), *safety or risk perception* (Ahokas, 2017; Toh et al., 2017; Valaja, 2018), and *risk-taking behavior* (Awang & Toh, 2018; Yang et al., 2018) of women related to solo travel, and they generally focus on Western (Chiang & Jogaratnam, 2006; McNamara & Prideaux, 2010; Wilson & Little, 2008) and previously Asian women (Toh et al., 2017; Seow & Brown, 2018; Yang et al., 2018; Thomas & Mura, 2018; Awang & Toh, 2018). According to these studies, there are diverse travelling motivations. Bond (1997) showed that the search for adventure, social inter-action, education, and self-understanding are significant. The search for new experiences, escape, comfort, sociability, self-esteem, self-empowerment, and increased self-confidence have also been found to be important factors (Chiang & Jogaratnam, 2006; Wilson & Harris, 2006). Yinghua (2016) revealed the role of social media tools that could motivate women to travel. Ahokas (2017) indicated the role of introducing different cultures and reating relationships as motivations. Seow and Brown (2018) showed that motivations were multifaceted ranging from the ability to be free and flexible, escape from personal lives at home, to the absence of travel companions.

There are various constraints before or during their travels too (Jordan & Gibson, 2005; Wilson & Little, 2008; Ahokas, 2017; Toh et al., 2017; Seow & Brown, 2018; Valaja, 2018). Travel constraints refer to "factors that inhibit continued travel, cause inability to begin travel, result in the inability to maintain or increase frequency of travel" (Khan et al., 2017, p. 1142) and may lead to negative effects on the quality of the travel experience. According to Wilson and Little (2008), some women perceive certain travel destinations to be limiting and risky. Fear especially makes women worried about attacks and sexual harassment during their solo travelling, and the male gaze sometimes limits their travel choices as well as interactions with locals (Wilson & Little, 2008; Su & Wu, 2020). Research about Asian solo travellers by Seow and Brown (2018) showed that sexualized male attention was an important constraint faced by participants on their travels. Besides, Wilson and Little (2005) found that solo woman travellers encounter *socio-cultural* (the influence of social expectations, others' perceptions toward their travel), *personal* (women's self-perceptions, beliefs, and emotions such as fear and loneliness), *practical* (lack of time, money, local knowledge of the destination), and *spatial* (limit and restrict women's freedom and movements within tourist destinations) constraints. To deal with constraints, women mostly adopted resistant practices such as "not visiting destinations perceived as unsafe" or "left places where they felt to be in danger", "avoiding isolated places and not going out during night", "dressing modestly", "creating relationships" or "pretending to be married", "behaved according to local female norms", "remained aware at all times", "avoiding alcohol and drugs", and "hiding their bodies in public tourism spaces" (Wilson & Little, 2008; Jordan & Aitchison, 2008; Ahokas, 2017; Thomas & Mura, 2018; Yang et al., 2018).

Women's solo travel research samples are generally drawn from Australian, American, British, and Canadian women. In other words, solo woman travellers are predominantly Westerners (Wilson & Little, 2005). However, in recent years research has expanded to include solo women from Asia (Toh et al., 2017; Yang et al., 2018; Seow & Brown, 2018; Awang & Toh, 2018; Thomas & Mura, 2018). Before presenting the findings on the Turkish case, contextual information will be given about Turkey as a Muslim country and the changing recreational habits of Turkish society.

Study background: Turkey – a distinct Muslim country?

Turkey has a Muslim-majority population of 83 million. A strong tradition of secularization makes this country unique in aspect of the evolution of cultural values when compared to the other Muslim countries. Modernization, secularization, and a gender equality-based civil code resulted in a distinctive socio-cultural context among the Muslim societies, especially in aspect of the social status of women. The social environment in Turkey is one of the more liberal ones for women when compared to many other Muslim societies as a result of the secular state structure and social life since the early 1920s. The Turkish Republic established a secular system based on French system of *laïcité* and took the Swiss civil code as a model; men and women were equalized in aspect of civil rights such as accessing public education, political participation, employment, and property. However, since the 2000s Turkey has been under the rule of a political Islamist party; it is still a secular state and a candidate country for the European Union. Though it is a reductionist description, Turkey is seen as a bridge between "East" and "West", between the "Muslim world" and "Europe". It is a Western-oriented and politically stable Middle Eastern country with strong ties to Europe. Turkey is far from being a stereotypical Muslim country. Traditional cultural norms and the conservative way of life are significant and visible in the social landscape; however, they are not the main determinants that shape the daily life of individuals, especially in the big cities.

One of the main instruments to "modernize" Turkey has been the development of tourism. At the end of the Ottoman Empire and the early years of Turkey as a modern nation state, it was not possible to mention the tourism sector in a western sense (Özgüç, 2017). Turkey was not significant until the late 20th century as either a destination or as a tourist generating country. After the intensive efforts to develop tourism for long decades, particularly during the 1980s, Turkey has become one of the top ten destination countries in the world today. In the Southern/Mediterranean European tourism region, it ranked third after Spain and Italy in 2017 (UNWTO, 2018). While Turkey is well known as a destination country, what is less known is its position as a tourist sending country. Especially since the early 2000s, there is a considerable growth in outbound and domestic tourism as well. The recreational habits and holiday preferences of Turkish society are in the process of change, therefore it is significant to understand the emerging women's mobility in Turkey. As Sezgin (1987) states

> political, social, economic and cultural revolutions, the establishment of secular education, progress in transportation and communication, attempts to integrate to the capitalist markets resulted in leaving the centuries-old traditional lifestyle behind and a transition to an urban lifestyle. This change towards a modern lifestyle, socio-cultural progress and especially women's rights were adopted initially by the bureaucrats and the military officers whom were accredited to Anatolian cities. Significance of gender difference disappeared and state ceremonies changed into ballroom parties in western style. Acceptance of western lifestyle spread especially among the economically advanced parts of the society.
>
> (Sezgin, 1987, p. 50)

This top-to-down modernization in Turkey led to a miscellaneous social change and development of new habits and needs in aspects of recreation too. Sezgin (1987) attracts attention to the relationship between the improvements in income and educational level with the changing recreational needs in the Turkish context. In today's Turkey, recreational demand is increasing and holiday preferences are changing both among more secular and also conservative groups (Karakaya, 2015; Başarangil, 2019). The results of some surveys to determine the holiday habits and preferences of the Turkish society indicate that a vacation at least once a year has become a part of the life of the majority (around 60 per cent) of Turkish people. A cooperative survey of Google and The Nielsen Company in 2009 based on a sample of 1,008 Turkish citizens from 14 cities found that 56 per cent of the population goes on a holiday. 95 per cent of the population prefers spending their holidays in Turkey, and 44 per cent prefers coastal destinations based on 3S. Another survey in the same year, conducted by Millward Brown based on a sample of 510 participants from eight big cities found that 58 per cent of the population have a holiday at least once a year. On the other hand, Growth for Knowledge (GfK) conducted a survey in 16 cities of Turkey in 2010 and found that 61 per cent of the Turkish people plan to have a holiday in a year (Turizm Dünyasi, 2009; Cumhuriyet, 2010; NTV, 2010).

While most people prefer to be with their families or partners, there is a growing share of independent travellers. According to the Turkish Statistical Institute (2019), the number of domestic trips has increased to 78.2 million. While visiting relatives and friends is still a very strong motivation for travelling (64.9%), 30 per cent of the Turkish population travelled for pleasure, health and holiday purposes in 2019. Outbound tourism is also in a growing trend. The number of Turkish citizens travelling abroad grew from 5.3 million to 16.3 million since 2000. The number of international departures by Turkish citizens has doubled since 1995, from 3.9 million to 8.4 million in 2018. European countries rank the top in the destination of Turkish outbound tourists. Outbound tourism flows are increasing year by year despite the compulsory *departure stamp fee* every Turkish citizen has to pay just before leaving the country and Turkish citizens often being subject to long and heavy visa procedures by the state authorities of developed countries. However, participation in leisure travel is not as common a practice as it is in the Western societies, yet, both domestically and internationally, Turkish society is becoming more and more mobile for tourism purposes, in a way that can be observed in any modernizing society.

Within this general picture of changing recreational character of Turkish society, a distinct tourist group is the *solo woman travellers*. Many highly educated, wealthy Turkish women, especially from the metropolitan areas, tend to travel abroad independently. The possibility of such travels by women indicates the crucial role of the secular state and relatively liberal social environment. However, it does not mean that Turkish women are completely exempt from the peer pressure of the patriarchal mentality.

In Turkey, women are at a more disadvantaged position from birth, when compared to men (Özaydınlık, 2014). This social position is shaped according to the locations where women live, dominating ideology or political environment in the county, religion, and socio-economic class. For example, patriarchal structure and religion have more effect on everyday practices of women who live in socially conservative parts of Turkey or rural areas and they have more limited access to education, work and social opportunities than women who live in urban areas. However, gender roles and traditions are quite significant in the regulation of social relations, and written rules of law are based on equality. Under such legal basis, Turkish women officially have all types of freedom. This is not comparable, for instance, with Saudi Arabia, where women did not even have the right to obtain a driving license until 2017; Iran, where married women need official permission from their husbands to travel abroad; or Afghanistan, where women cannot go out without a male accompanying them. These are only some examples of how *mobility of women* is restricted in Muslim countries, *legally* or *culturally*. Not only in the relatively liberal ones such as Turkey and Tunisia but also in more conservative ones such as Saudi Arabia, Iran, or Afghanistan. The territorial limits of women and their freedom of mobility in Muslim countries is still a vital issue that necessitates the questioning of patriarchal ideology.

Research methodology

This research aimed to understand the travel motivations and experiences and the constraints encountered by Turkish solo woman travellers. What does solo travel mean for them? What kind of constraints do they encounter before or during their travels? How do they cope with these constraints and what benefits does solo travelling provide them? A qualitative research process was followed by the nature and purpose of the subject. The qualitative method, as Seow and Brown (2018) stated, can help understand the experiences of female travellers and allows participants to express themselves freely on a potentially sensitive topic. In-depth interviews were conducted with 15 participants who were selected by the purposeful and snowball sampling methods to broaden the demographic diversity of the participants. Participants were reached via an Instagram platform called *gezginkadinlar* [*womantravellers*] with 73,300 followers. They were interviewed provided that they resided in Turkey and have travelled solo at least more than once to a foreign country (participant details are listed in Table 13.1). Ten of the interviews were performed via Skype and Facetime, while the others were conducted face to face. The interview form consisted of the one formed by Wilson (2004). The list of questions asked was as follows:

1) How many times have you travelled solo in total? Which destinations have you visited?
2) What has motivated you to travel solo?
3) When you think of the word "travel", in particular "solo travel", what does it mean for you? What word comes to your mind?
4) What is your general opinion about "solo female travellers" like yourself?
5) What kind of constraints or challenges do you encounter before and during your solo travel? How do you deal with these difficulties?
6) Do you feel anxious before or during your travels; if so, why?
7) What benefits does solo travel provide for you?

Destinations

The preferred destination countries by Turkish women are predominantly European. This is in parallel with the preferences of Turkish outbound tourists. In 2018, for instance, 14.7 per cent of all international departures were

Table 13.1 Characteristics of participants

Participant	Age	Residence place	Marital status	Education	Occupation
1	63	Izmir	single	bachelor	retired
2	38	Izmir	single	bachelor	teacher
3	40	Istanbul	single	bachelor	public relations specialist
4	40	Izmir	single	bachelor	nurse
5	53	Izmir	non-single	bachelor	teacher
6	51	Izmir	single	bachelor	academician
7	56	Izmir	single	high school	retired
8	27	Izmir	non-single	bachelor	postgraduate student
9	38	Istanbul	non-single	bachelor	marketing staff
10	34	Istanbul	single	bachelor	marketing staff
11	35	Edirne	single	bachelor	teacher
12	21	Afyon	single	high school	student
13	30	Istanbul	non-single	bachelor	engineer
14	46	Mugla	single	bachelor	director
15	22	Manisa	single	high school	student

to a European destination. This figure does not include the departures to Bulgaria and Greece with specific cultural-historical connections with Turkey. When the shares of these two European countries are added, Europe received 37 per cent of all departures from Turkey. Turkey has diverse and long-standing connections with Europe. It is not surprising that European destinations are top ranking ones for Turkish outbound flows because of many reasons such as migration networks, tourism, or trade. But what is also found among the woman travellers is that a strong sense of *safety* is attributed to European countries. For example, a recent study by Ying et al. (2017) that was conducted in a Muslim majority country, Malaysia, also indicated that the main concern of Malaysian women linked to solo travel is safety. Besides European countries, they visited some other destinations in Asian, African, or Middle Eastern countries much less in number when compared to European countries.

Motivations and meanings

The need for freedom and independence appears to be the most important motivation for solo travelling. In this section, the participants were asked what motivates them. It is also possible to catch the individualistic sensuosities in some participants' words. For example,

> As I said before, freedom, the greatest reason is freedom in my choices. I can stay in a place as long as I want. And I can travel as much as I want. For example, if you have a friend with you, you depend on him/her and make common decisions. For instance, when you visit a place, you want to stay for two days but your friend wants to keep for one day. So, you can make better decisions when you are alone.
>
> (P 11, 35)

The desire to *meet new people* emerged as another significant motivation. Most of the participants mentioned that travelling without companions gave them a chance to interact with the locals and other travellers, as participant 9 stated (38):

> Well, when you travel alone, you communicate more with local people. It does not just have to be local. You communicate more with other travellers like you. That is also a reason why I love travelling alone. If you have someone with you, no matter how much you communicate with others, your priority is the person or persons on your side.

The desire to *learn, self-discovery*, and *to be on your own* were also among other motivating factors:

> I am generally a compatible person, but my energy is sometimes too high for my friends because I love learning and research. That's why it's

hard for them to keep up with me. That is an obstacle for me. Because I go somewhere to explore the streets instead of sitting in a cafe for five hours.

(P 2, 38)

Sometimes I want to be alone. Because I'm always with people, it's like a retreat for me. Also, my boyfriend doesn't so much love touristic places, but I like touristic places because I have a travel blog.

(P 8, 27)

Lastly, two participants stated that they were motivated by the *desire for risk-taking:*

Nobody wants to come to places where I go because I go to hazardous places.

(P 7, 56)

I take a little risk on my trips. But my other friends or my partner do not want to take that risk.

(P 5, 53)

The participants were asked to explain what solo travel meant to them. Similar to motivations, almost all participants stated *freedom* as the main connotation that had the highest frequency in their words, following *self-discovery, meeting new people, and learning excitement and pleasure,* which were also cited as the meaning of solo travel by many participants. Solo travels give the chance to explore a new place and culture, for example:

When you travel with someone, no matter what happens, its enjoyment and expectations always are included in the journey. But when you are alone, what you want to do or see at that moment, you have the luxury to spare time for it. So, it is much more exciting for me to do this exploration alone.

(P 9, 38)

To be able to plan travel on my own and be alone are a pleasure for me.

(P 4, 40)

During the interviews, participants tended to name themselves as powerful and courageous women with a discourse bearing the traces of self-actualization and confidence:

I love all of them. I know a lot of women traveling alone like me, our paths cross in some way, we find each other. When I meet solo woman travellers, I think of that there is a confident and courageous woman.

(P 8, 27)

I can say that women are stronger than men; women are much stronger in every sense. Even if men travel alone, they never stay alone. Either they find a friend or a girlfriend and travel together. But women are not like this, they are able to travel on their own. As a woman, it makes me proud to see that women can do everything.

(P 3, 40)

Constraints

A perceived danger related to certain destinations played a significant role in destination choice and resulted in significant socio-spatial constraints. Most of the participants stated that they were confined to choose a destination because of security concerns and fear of harassment. Such an attitude is valid in aspect of time, not only space. Some of the interviewees narrated that they had to restrict their movements at certain times of the day, especially during nights.

I choose destinations beforehand, I usually try to go to places where I can feel safe but, of course, none of us will know what happens in an hour.

(P 2, 38)

A woman's outfits and style of dress may also become an issue during travels (Wilson & Little, 2008; Yang et al., 2018), especially in Islamic destinations such as Egypt (Brown & Osman, 2017). The obligation of choosing "the dress to be worn in a certain destination" is a limiting factor for woman travellers, as stated in the following examples:

For example, when you are alone, you wear clothes that you want to wear, doubtfully. When you are with your friends and wearing a mini you are exposed to less verbal harassment. I think your dresses draw attention when you are alone.

(P 12, 21)

According to the destination I will go to, I have some confusion like "Should I take this dress with me or not?" Since I'm a woman, I have a concern about dress. Probably, a man has not such a concern. For example, in my Africa travel, I experienced it such as to wear or not wear. It's a limiting thing. But there is nothing to do; you have to get into the society which you go and somehow you should not draw too much attention.

(P 4, 40)

Others' perception and reactions were cited by three participants as a socio-spatial constraints that influenced their access to solo travel. There are demotivating approaches. One participant noted the feeling of restriction by reactions of local people in the destination visited. Even before their travel, women encounter negative critiques from their own social environment in Turkey about the risks of travelling as a single woman:

> There is generally a perception related to being on your own as a white woman in Arab countries. There is a perception that a white woman is explicit and we can approach her more defiantly.
>
> (P 9, 38)

> There are the reactions of people around you like "don't do this because something bad might happen" or "what kind of safety precaution do you have if someone tries to abduct you and do something to you? How will you save yourself?"
>
> (P 5, 53)

Some women develop behaviors like going out with others, for example with those they meet during their travel in order to deal with such constraints, while some travel regardless. As expressed by participant 3 (40):

> All in all, everything can really happen to people in life, everywhere, for example, something even can happen more frequently in Turkey. Of course, it is risk-taking. But life is a risk. You have to take this risk to live and experience life.

There are also *personal constraints* that emerged as the second category. Some women cited that they felt stress and emotional fatigue because of being alone for a long time:

> When you are alone, your attention can easily disperse, and you can get tired. That was difficult for me. You can get lost on your own, and that can give rise to stress. There are lots of distresses of being alone.
>
> (P 8, 27)

> The stress of watching my stuff leads to tension and that makes me tense. I get angry when I am under stress. I start to tease people when I get angry. Such a cycle occurs. Apart from that, also a certain sensitivity that stems from being alone. I miss my family more when I am alone. If I have some-one with me, it feels like I can travel for five years.
>
> (P 10, 34)

Another common constraining factor for women was *economic* concerns:

> The challenges that I face are generally economical. You can guess that financing travel is difficult in today's conditions. I am paying attention to

how I can arrange the budget and stay the cheapest price in the places where I travel. I try to pick up cheap flight tickets.

(P 11, 35)

The possibility of finding a cheap place is hard in some destinations. I try to solve it with couch-surfing.

(P 1, 63)

As shown by these two participants' narratives, trying to find cheap flight tickets, resorting to suitable accommodation options (e.g., hostels, couch-surfing) were among the participants' strategies to deal with economic constraints.

Bureaucratic factors were also expressed by two participants as a constraint. For instance, participant 2 (38) mentioned that she had a visa problem:

The biggest challenge I have experienced is about the visa. Although I work as a government officer for a long time, I do not have a green passport. Each time, these visa procedures; documents, making an appointment make me stress.

Because Turkey is not an EU member country, Turkish citizens do not have the right of freedom of mobility within EU borders. They are subjected to detailed Schengen visa application procedures, including justifying their reason for visiting, having proof of sufficient financial resources, arranging their accommodation before their travel, proof of health insurance and a guarantee of their return by a flight ticket. Other Western countries such as the USA, UK or Australia also have different and difficult visa regimes for non-western visitors like Turks. This procedure may take weeks and may have a negative effect on travel motivation. A specific type of passport, called a "green passport", may only be issued for the senior state officers of Turkey whose owners only then acquire the right to freedom of mobility within EU. However, the number of green passport holders is very limited in Turkey.

Many of the participants reported that they somehow felt fear before and during their travels. *Fear of harassment* was pointed out as a striking reason. Other reasons of negative feelings included a possibility of an attack and unsecure situation. While the fear of being sexually harassed may be gender-specific; being in an unsecure situation or a possible attack, missing a plane or a bus sound as more neutral reasons of fear.

I felt worried in Cambodia. Once I was worried because I was the only female passenger on a bus. On the bus, there was a driver, an assistant driver and me. I was really worried there. I thought, they would do harassment to me or abduct.

(P 3, 40)

> There were times when I felt anxious. For example, I had a transfer in Doha and had a long waiting period. So, I wanted to walk around in the city, but I had a bias about it. Because I was dressed short and I was concerned about whether I could walk around the city safely.
>
> (P 4, 40)

Participants were also asked to explain what *benefits* solo travel brought to them. Answers generally coincide with the connotations and motivations of solo travelling. *Sociality* was stated by participants as the main benefit of solo travel. Besides, *self-confidence and empowerment, learning, freedom,* and *self-discovery* were expressed as the other benefits.

> Firstly, it lets me to gain my self-confidence. In foreign countries, standing on my own feet and taking matters into account with own hands are an incredibly big satisfaction. Also, solo travel sets me free; I can communicate with other people/locals comfortably. I use websites where I can communicate with locals such as couch-surfing and inter-nations. During my solo travel, I come across other solo travellers. Sometimes we walk around for a few hours together. I'm able to be more socially with locals and other travellers.
>
> (P 4, 40)

Discussion and conclusions

Turkish solo woman travellers are mostly single, highly educated, economically independent, and living in the big cities and western parts of Turkey. They mostly travelled to countries in Europe such as Germany, Austria, Italy, and Belgium. Images of Europe as a "safe place" and "geographic proximity" to Turkey are the main factors in choosing destinations. In addition to European countries, solo women travellers also have travel experiences to countries of Asia, Africa, South America, and North America. Some of them quit their job after these travels and became travel bloggers via social media platforms that enable Internet users to collaborate, communicate, and publish original content such as blogs, videos, wikis, reviews, or photos (Hays et al., 2013; Yinghua, 2016).

One of the main aims of this research was to find out what motivates Turkish women to travel solo and results indicated that there are lots of factors affecting them choosing to travel alone: The desire for *freedom and independence, meeting new people, learning, self-discovery, loneliness,* and *risk-taking*. In this context, this research supports the results of previous studies (Bond, 1997; McArthur, 1999; Gibson & Jordan, 1998; Wilson & Harris, 2006; Chiang & Jogaratnam, 2006; Ahokas, 2017; Seow & Brown, 2018). The motivations reported here show that these women's requirements and expectations differ from mass tourists. When these requirements and expectations are considered, it can be said that Turkish solo woman travellers reflect Cohen's (2010) post-modern tourist-traveller, who cares about taking risks, adventure, novelty, and independence (Wilson, 2004).

The research demonstrated that *socio-spatial constraints* were significant issue faced by solo woman travellers. For instance, they felt confined in destination choice because of security concerns, fear of harassment, others' reactions, comments or negative approaches. In this context, this study supports research by Wilson and Little (2008), Carvalho et al. (2014), Awang and Toh (2018), and Seow and Brown (2018). The findings also indicate that *personal factors* such as stress and emotional fatigue from being alone for a long time are significant. *Economic factors* were the other central constraints faced by solo woman travellers. Thus, our findings on the Turkish case support Wilson and Little's (2005) assertion that solo woman travellers encounter a combination of personal, socio-cultural, spatial, and practical constraints before and during their travels. They develop various strategies in order to negotiate economic constraints, such as chasing cheap flight tickets and resorting to accommodation options such as hostels and couch-surfing. These strategies also reflect the findings of McNamara and Prideaux (2010) and McArthur (1999), who found that solo woman travellers mostly stayed in low-cost hostels. However, the research showed that Turkish solo women travellers also faced *bureaucratic constraints*.

Despite these constraints, the literature emphasizes that solo travel contributes to women's feelings of "freedom" (Gibson & Jordan, 1998; Wilson & Harris, 2006) and "self-confidence" (Gibson & Jordan, 1998; McArthur, 1999; Wilson & Harris, 2006) and provide a space for learning, self-reflection, and self-development (Jordan & Gibson, 2005). To a certain extent, our research supports these findings. The self-attribution of Turkish women as *powerful* and *courageous* suggests that travelling independently provides a way to overcome socio-cultural gender roles that affect women's lives and construct their social identity by travelling independently.

Turkish solo woman travellers share a similar pattern with their western counterparts, in terms of motivations and constraints. However, the origin country might be a factor determining the attributes toward woman travellers in the destinations visited. Few studies focused on Asian cases, (e.g., Yang et al., 2018; Seow & Brown, 2018; Osman et al., 2019) for example, mentioned that being Asian has created a constraint for solo female travellers. The Turkish case also showed that being a female traveller from a Muslim country in non-western destinations could cause more social-spatial constraint than in a western one. The constraints and their reasons changed according to the destination; however, it can be said that a common limitation of solo travel is more simply about being a woman. Turkish women as solo travellers from a secular Muslim country feel social pressure both in their immediate environment and in the wider society due to their travelling choices. Research by Kaba and Emekli (2018) stated that relatively underdeveloped and rural regions of Turkey were perceived as risky by solo woman travellers due to the gender-based risks, male gaze, and negative reactions by others. The authors of this study found that Turkish solo woman travellers receive negative reactions from their families and friends too. These are generally expressed through demotivating words before they travel as travelling independently is a behavior that clashes with expected gender roles. Nonetheless, possible obstacles to travel for Turkish women are only *socio-cultural*, not *legal*, thus they are challengeable and changing. As long as they have the financial capacity and desire, Turkish women have the freedom of all types of mobility, which must be the right of all women in other Muslim-majority countries too.

References

Ahokas, S. (2017). *Safety of female travellers* [Bachelor's thesis, Haaga-Helia University of Applied Sciences]. www.theseus.fi/bitstream/handle/10024/129998/Ahokas_Salla.pdf?sequence=1&isAllowed=

Anderson, J., & Erskine, K. (2014). Tropophilia: A study of people, place and lifestyle travel. *Mobilities*, *9*(1), 130–145. https://doi.org/10.1080/17450101.2012.743702

Awang, K. V., & Toh, J. Y. (2018). A review on Malaysian women's leisure and perceptions towards solo travelling. *International Journal of Engineering & Technology*, *7*(3.25), 139–142.

Başarangil, İ. (2019). Sosyal Medyanın Tatil Tercihlerine Etkisi: Kırklareli Üniversitesi Turizm Fakültesi Öğrencileri Üzerine Bir Araştırma [The effect of social media on holiday preferences: A study on Kırklareli University Tourism Faculty Students]. *Journal of Tourism and Gastronomy Studies*, *7*(2), 839–852. https://doi.org/10.21325/jotags.2019.395

Benson, M., & O'Reilly, K. (2009). Migration and the search for a better way of life: A critical exploration of lifestyle migration. *The Sociological Review*, *57*(4), 608–625. https://doi.org/10.1111/j.1467-954X.2009.01864.x

Bianchi, C. (2016). Solo holiday travellers: Motivators and drivers of satisfaction and dissatisfaction. *International Journal of Tourism Research*, *18*(2), 197–208. https://doi.org/10.1002/jtr.2049

Bond, M. (1997). Women travellers: A new growth market. *Pacific Asia Travel Association*. www.hotel-online.com/News/PressReleases/PataWomenTravellers_Nov1997.html

Brown, L., & Osman, H. (2017). The female tourist experience in Egypt as an Islamic destination. *Annals of Tourism Research*, *63*, 12–22. https://doi.org/10.1016/j.annals.2016.12.005

Carvalho, G., Baptista, M. M., & Costa, C. (2014). Women travelling alone: Prospects on gender and tourism experiences. *Revista Turismo & Desenvolvimento*, *21–22*(5), 31–32.

Chiang, C., & Jogaratnam, G. (2006). Why do women travel solo for purposes of leisure? *Journal of Vacation Marketing*, *12*(1), 59–70. https://doi.org/10.1177/1356766706059041

Cockburn-Wootten, C., Friend, L., & McIntosh, A. (2006). A discourse analysis of representational spaces: Writings of women independent traveller. *Tourism: An International Interdisciplinary Journal*, *54*(1), 7–16.

Cohen, S. A. (2010). Personal identity (de)formation among lifestyle travellers: A double-edged sword? *Leisure Studies*, *29*(3), 289–301. https://doi.org/10.1080/02614360903434100

Cohen, S. A. (2011). Lifestyle travellers: Backpacking as a way of life. *Annals of Tourism Research*, *38*(4), 1535–1555. https://doi.org/10.1016/j.annals.2011.02.002

Cohen, S. A., Duncan, T., & Thulemark, M. (2013). Introducing lifestyle mobilities. In T. Duncan, S. A. Cohen, & M. Thulemark (Eds.), *Lifestyle mobilities: Intersections of travel, leisure and migration* (pp. 1–18). Ashgate.

Cumhuriyet. (2010, September 9). *Türk halkı tatilde deniz, güneş ve kumu tercih ediyor* [Turkish People prefers sea, sun and sand for holiday]. www.cumhuriyet.com.tr/haber/turk-halki-tatilde-deniz-gunes-ve-kumu-tercih-ediyor-176784

Davidson, K. (2005). Alternative India: Transgressive spaces. In A. Jaworski & A. Pritchard (Eds.), *Discourse, communication and tourism* (pp. 28–52). Channel View.

Gibson, H., & Jordan, F. (1998, October 26–30). *Shirley Valentine lives! The experiences of solo women travellers* [Paper presentation]. The Fifth Congress of the World Leisure and Recreation Association, Brazil.

Hays, S., Page, S. J, & Buhalis, D. (2013). Social media as a destination marketing tool: Its use by national tourism organizations. *Current Issues in Tourism, 16*(3), 211–239. https://doi.org/10.1080/13683500.2012.662215

Hubbard, B. (2019, February 13). Apple and Google urged to dump Saudi app that lets men track women. *The New York Times.* www.nytimes.com/2019/02/13/world/middleeast/saudi-arabia-app-women.html

Jordan, F., & Aitchison, C. (2008). Tourism and the sexualisation of the gaze: Solo female tourists' experiences of gendered power, surveillance and embodiment. *Leisure Studies, 27*(3), 329–349. https://doi.org/10.1080/02614360802125080

Jordan, F., & Gibson, H. (2005). "We're not stupid . . . but we'll not stay home either": Experiences of solo women travelers. *Tourism Review International, 9*(2), 195–212. https://doi.org/10.3727/154427205774791663

Kaba, B., & Emekli, G. (2018). A rising trend in tourism: Solo women travelers (the case of Turkey). *Aegean Geographical Journal, 27*(2), 111–126.

Karakaya, H. (2015). *Türkiye'de dindar burjuva ve kadın* [Religious bourgeois and woman in Turkey] [Unpublished doctoral dissertation]. Atatürk University Institute of Social Sciences.

Khan, M. J., Chelliah, S., & Ahmed, S. (2017). Factors influencing destination image and visit intention among young women travellers: Role of travel motivation, perceived risks, and travel constraints. *Asia Pacific Journal of Tourism Research, 22*(11), 1139–1155. https://doi.org/10.1080/10941665.2017.1374985

McArthur, M. (1999). *Out of place: Gender, identity, and space, and the experiences of contemporary solo women travellers* [Unpublished master's thesis, Trent University].

McNamara, K. E., & Prideaux, B. (2010). A typology of solo independent women travellers. *International Journal of Tourism Research, 12*(3), 253–264. https://doi.org/10.1002/jtr.751

Myers, L. M. (2010). *Women's independent travel experiences in New Zealand* [Doctoral thesis, University of Sunderland]. https://sure.sunderland.ac.uk/id/eprint/3308/1/Women%E2%80%99s_Independent_Travel_Experiences.pdf

NTV. (2010, May 20). *İşte Türklerin tatil alışkanlıkları* [Holiday habits of Turks]. www.ntv.com.tr/yasam/iste-turklerin-tatil-aliskanliklari,45k8lIAlxkOrS5EdFFgeOg

Osman, H., Brown, L., & Phung, T. M. T. (2019). The travel motivations and experiences of female Vietnamese solo travellers. *Tourist Studies, 20*(2), 248–267. https://doi.org/10.1177/1468797619878307

Özaydınlık, K. (2014). Toplumsal Cinsiyet Temelinde Türkiye'de Kadın ve Eğitim [Women and education in Turkey on the basis of gender]. *Sosyal Politika Çalışmaları Dergisi, 14*(33), 93–112.

Özgüç, N. (2017). *Turizm Coğrafyası: Özellikler ve Bölgeler* [Tourism geography: Features and regions]. Çantay Kitabevi.

Pereira, A., & Silva, C. (2018). Women solo travellers: Motivations and experiences. *Milenium, 2*(6), 99–106. https://doi.org/10.29352/mill0206.09.00165

Sager, T. (2006). Freedom as mobility: Implications of the distinction between actual and potential travelling. *Mobilities, 1*(3), 465–488. https://doi.org/10.1080/17450100600902420

Seow, D., & Brown, L. (2018). The solo female Asian tourist. *Current Issues in Tourism, 21*(10), 1187–1206. https://doi.org/10.1080/13683500.2017.1423283

Sezgin, S. (1987). *Türk Toplumunun Rekreasyon Alışkanlıkları: İstanbul Örneği*. [Recreational habits of Turkish people: The Istanbul pattern] [Unpublished doctoral dissertation, Mimar Sinan Üniversitesi].

Su, C. P., & Wu, T. C. (2020). The dark side of solo female travel: Negative encounters with male strangers. *Leisure Sciences*, *42*(3–4), 375–392. https://doi.org/10.1080/01490 400.2020.1712277

Thomas, T. K., & Mura, P. (2018). The 'normality of unsafety'- foreign solo female travellers in India. *Tourism Recreation Research*, *44*(1), 33–40. https://doi.org/10.1080/025082 81.2018.1494872

Toh, J. Y., Awang, K. W., & Bojei, J. (2017). Generation Y Malaysian women's perception towards solo travel. *Asia- Pacific Journal of Innovation in Hospitality and Tourism*, *6*(2), 45–54.

Turizm Dünyasi. (2009). *Google, Türkiye'nin Tatil Tercihlerini Araştırdı* [Google research on the vacation preferences of Turkey]. http://turizmdunyasi.com.tr/uncategorized/ google-turkiyenin-tatil-tercihlerini-aratyrdy/

Turkish Statistical Institute (Turkstat). (2019). *Tourism statistics*. Ankara.

UNWTO. (2018). *Tourism highlights: 2018 edition*. www.e-unwto.org/doi/pdf/10.18111/ 9789284419876

Urry, J. (2007). *Mobilities*. Polity Press.

Valaja, E. (2018). *Solo female travellers' risk perceptions and risk reduction strategies – As expressed in online travel blog narratives* [Master's thesis, Lund University]. https://lup.lub.lu.se/ student-papers/search/publication/8947243

Westerhausen, K. (2002). *Beyond the beach: An ethnography of modern travellers in Asia*. White Lotus Press.

Wilson, E., & Harris, C. (2006). Meaningful travel: Women, independent travel and the search for self and meaning. *Tourism: An International Interdisciplinary Journal*, *54*(2), 161–172.

Wilson, E., & Little, D. E. (2005). A "relative escape"? The impact of constraints on women who travel solo. *Tourism Review International*, *9*(2), 155–174. https://doi.org/10.3727/ 154427205774791672

Wilson, E., & Little, D. E. (2008). The solo female travel experience: Exploring the 'geography of women's fear. *Current Issues in Tourism*, *11*(2), 167–186. https://doi.org/10.2167/ cit342.0

Wilson, E. C. (2004). *A journey of her own? The impact of constraints on women's solo travel* [Doctoral thesis, Griffith University].

Yang, E. C. L., Khoo, L. C., & Arcodia, C. (2018). Constructing space and self through risk taking: A case of Asian solo female travelers. *Journal of Travel Research*, *57*(2), 260–272. https://doi.org/10.1177/0047287517692447

Ying, T., Khairil, W. A., & Jamil, B. (2017). Generation Y Malaysian women's perception towards solo travel. *Asia-Pacific Journal of Innovation in Hospitality and Tourism*, *6*(2), 45–54.

Yinghua, L. (2016). *Gender equality in tourism-The solo female travel experience* [paper presentation]. Tourism students virtual conference, University of Lincoln. www.travel-confer ence.co.uk/commentries.php?paper=332#.WzIaOKf7TIU

Part V

Interrelationships between consumers and business

14 Muslims' perspectives on tourism boycotts – a complicated relationship

Ismail Shaheer and Neil Carr

Introduction

People have boycotted tourism destinations since at least the 1940s on the grounds of ethics and morality (Shaheer et al., 2018). Many people have and continue to call for boycotts against tourism destinations, as is evident from a quick search of the Internet (including social media platforms). Despite this, relatively few studies have examined the destinations that are boycotted and the reasons why these destinations have become the target of a boycott (Shaheer et al., 2018; Seyfi & Hall, 2020; Shaheer et al., 2019).

Boycotts, directly and indirectly, have adverse impacts on tourism destinations. However, this issue has received relatively little attention (Seyfi & Hall, 2020). Those studies that have been conducted provide a Western-skewed view. It is essential to explore boycotts from diverse viewpoints that encompass different political ideologies and religious philosophies, and western and non-western, and developed and developing nations' perspectives to enable development of a richer understanding of boycotting behaviour and the associated implications.

There are limited studies that particularly address Muslims boycotting products and businesses. This neglect is particularly true for Muslim perspectives on boycotting tourism products and destinations. This is despite the fact that Muslim travellers represent a fast-growing market that has attracted the attention of many tourism destinations and whose outbound travel expenditure was predicted to reach US$ 274 billion by 2023 before the COVID-19 global pandemic (Thompson Reuters & Dinar Standard, 2018). The rationale behind the prediction remains valid, suggesting it will still happen, though potentially at a later date. Thus, the significance of the Muslim travel market warrants understanding of boycott behaviour by Muslims targeting tourism products and/or destinations.

While there is consensus that the ethics and morality of different religious groups overlap (Neusner & Chilton, 2008), they each have particular values that mandate and direct the way of life of their followers. In this regard, Muslims as a global community have risen to address and criticise issues that concern them, such as the Prophet Mohamed's cartoon controversy. The Danish

DOI: 10.4324/9781003036296-19

Newspaper Jyllands-Posten daily posted cartoon caricatures of the Prophet Mohamed in 2005, which outraged Muslims and led to many global protests (Maamoun & Aggarwal, 2008). In this regard, how are tourism boycotts and other protests influenced by ethics and morality dictated from Islam? Using the theory of planned behaviour (TPB) (Ajzen, 1991), this chapter aims to explore the behavioural intention of Muslims boycotting tourism products and destinations. This will enable tourism providers and destination management organisations serving – or seeking to serve – the Muslim market to address and/or avoid issues that may lead to a boycott as well as mitigate the impact of boycott calls from Muslim travellers. This work is situated within the realisation that the Muslim community is diverse rather than a homogenous group (Akbarzadeh & Smith, 2005). Indeed, although Muslims are united by their faith, multiple denominations, including Sunni, Shiite, and Khawari, exist under the umbrella of Islam. In addition to the religious diversity across the branches of Islam, differences across Muslim communities are related to ethnicity and nationality.

Consumer boycotts

Boycotts have emerged as a strategic tool used by consumers and interest groups to encourage countries, organisations and individuals to cease/modify behaviour and practices perceived as unethical (Trentmann, 2019). Boycotts have become a bargaining chip for people to exercise their sovereignty through their money (Smith, 1990), using them as a currency. Boycotts have been increasingly used in modern history to fight against issues such as human rights violations (e.g., militant governments), international land rights, sovereignty and imperial power, social justice, environmental violations, and animal rights (Trentmann, 2019).

A boycott is understood to involve people abstaining from doing business with the boycott target as a result of egregious behaviour by or within the target (John & Klein, 2003). The application of boycotts in a tourism context implies "a refusal to travel to a destination or attraction or use the services of particular tourism-related companies" (Seyfi & Hall, 2020, p. 80). In addition, Friedman's (1985) definition of surrogate boycotts is useful here. Boycotts against a party to induce change in the behaviour of a second party as the actual target is perceived to be unaffected to direct action is known as a surrogate boycott (Friedman, 1985). In most instances, tourism boycotts are observed as surrogate boycotts.

Tourism destinations are boycotted for various reasons (Shaheer et al., 2019), similar to other products and services (see Friedman, 1985). According to research undertaken by Shaheer et al. (2019), destinations are boycotted for violations of human rights, political conflicts between countries, and animal welfare concerns.

The unacceptability of the egregious behaviour of destinations that motivates people to call for boycotts may be perceived differently across communities. For example, the consumption of certain animals (e.g., dogs) is acceptable in some, though increasingly few, Asian communities. At the same time, this is observed to be animal abuse and cruelty in many Western countries (Carr, 2014). Similarly, many religions agree on what is ethical and moral. However, there are variations to what is acceptable. This difference is a function of the place-specificity of socio-cultural norms and values (Akbarzadeh & Smith, 2005). Religion is closely related to these norms and values, and is, therefore, an important institution that defines acceptable behaviour. Thus, religions can influence people to participate in boycotts. Consequently, people may boycott a destination for mistreating the members of their religion or engaging in a behaviour that negatively impacts their religion.

Religion and boycotts

People sometimes take part in protests and undertake action to demonstrate their displeasure with perceived wrongdoings against their religion (Abosag & Farah, 2014; Basedau et al., 2017). Such protests or expressions can take many forms, from violent to non-violent actions. For example, Marshall (2013) reported that Buddhists in Myanmar boycotted Muslim businesses, identifying it is a means to protect their religion. A boycott is used as a form of non-violent action by members of religious faiths to punish businesses, communities, and destinations that are perceived to have engaged in unacceptable behaviour (Abosag & Farah, 2014; Al-Hyari et al., 2012). For instance, Malykhina (2009) reports that in the United States of America, Christian groups called for a boycott of Gap, explaining that the business downplays Christianity's teachings.

A religious-based boycott is claimed to be more damaging and persistent (Abosag & Farah, 2014). According to Ysseldyk et al. (2010), this is because members of religious groups have stronger bonds and influence and can therefore ensure boycotts persist for a longer period. Religion-based boycotts capitalise on religious teachings and scriptures to justify a boycott and influence members of the same religion (Muhamad et al., 2019). This influence can be argued to have the objective of defending the religion or its members from the actions of others. Hoffmann's (2013) argument about proximity being an important motivator for boycott participation is particularly useful in this context. He argues that geographical and cultural proximity can be factors that influence boycott participation. Thus, having membership to the same religion can be an important proximity that encourages people to boycott in the name of religion. This is irrespective of whether the individuals are directly impacted by the boycotted activity/destination or are geographically close to the people or destination affected. Consequently, shared cultural agents such as religion can be said to bring a group of people together for collective action such as boycotts (Oliver & Marwell, 1992).

Muslims have participated in many boycotts over the years, using religion as a lens (Maamoun & Aggarwal, 2008; Muhamad et al., 2019). One of the most popular boycott movements organised and participated in by Muslims is the *Boycott, Divestment, and Sanctions* (BDS) movement against Israel (Bakan &

Abu-Laban, 2009). Izberk-Bilgin (2012) notes that Muslims often use 'consumer jihad' to denote Muslims' rejection of businesses and brands in the name of religion. The premise of the boycotts is argued from the perspective of defending Islam and Muslims across the world. For instance, there were calls for a boycott of British products by Muslims after the British Government awarded the Knight Bachelor title to Salman Rushdie, whom some Muslims believed had offended Islam and the Prophet Mohamed when he published his book, *The Satanic Verses* (Hoyle, 2007). Although there is a body of work that has studied religious-based boycotts of products and businesses by Muslims (Al-Hyari et al., 2012; Jevtic, 2009), there is a dearth of studies that directly address Muslims boycotting tourism products or destinations. Therefore, this chapter aims to explore religious-based tourism boycotts from the perspective of Muslims.

Theoretical framework

The theory of planned behaviour (TPB) of Ajzen (1991) is a popular lens through which to look when seeking to understand how one's beliefs are linked to behaviour. TPB has been extensively used in studies across a range of different disciplines, including tourism (Aish et al., 2013; Chen & Tung, 2014). TPB was developed by Ajzen (1991) as an expanded version of the theory of reasoned action (TRA) (Fishbein & Ajzen, 1975). The theory is based on the recognition that the closest determinant of behaviour is the behavioural intention, which is an individual's perceived likelihood of performing a behaviour. When TRA was initially proposed, Fishbein and Ajzen (1975) identified two independent constructs, namely attitudes and subjective norms that can be used to predict the dependent variable intention. Attitude is a person's evaluation of the outcome of behaviour, whereas the subjective norm explains the perceived social pressure to perform or not to perform an action. Later, Ajzen (1991) added perceived behavioural control (i.e., one's view of their degree of control over a behaviour) as another construct and named it TPB. Ajzen (1991, p. 188) stated that "the more favourable the attitude and subjective norm with respect to a behaviour and the greater the perceived behavioural control (self-efficacy), the stronger should be an individual's intention to perform the behaviour under consideration". Ajzen's (1991) conclusion was that although individual variables (attitudes, subjective norms, and behavioural control) can be used to test TPB; collectively, these variables provide a better predictor of behavioural intention.

Methods

As noted earlier, the existing literature on Muslims and tourism boycotts is limited. When a phenomenon that is being investigated is not well understood, a qualitative approach is more appropriate and will provide rich insights (Creswell, 2009). Thus, this study takes a qualitative approach to gain a deeper understanding of Muslim perspectives about tourism boycotts. A decision was made to include Muslims from as many countries as possible to obtain diverse perspectives (Matthews, 2018).

Data was collected from 29 Muslims based in 10 countries between 15 June and 7 July 2020. Interviewees were from countries where the perception of the population identifying as Muslim differs significantly. For instance, Iran is identified as a country with a 99.4% Muslim population, while Nigeria has a 49.6% Muslim population (see Table 14.1; World Population Review, 2020).

Participants for the study were identified through a snowball sampling approach. A snowball sampling approach was particularly important as the subject of religion is a sensitive topic, and potential participants may decline to speak to a stranger (Dunlap et al., 1990). Sensitive topics require trust, which results in the participants being comfortable to speak to researchers (Mealer & Jones, 2014). The inclusion criteria for the study was that the participants identify themselves as a Muslim, taking into consideration that the Muslim community is diverse (Akbarzadeh & Smith, 2005). Moreover, participants were not asked to identify any further information about their religious beliefs (e.g., Shia, Sunni, conservative, liberal).

Data was collected using semi-structured interviews through phone, email/text, and face-to-face interviews, depending on the preferences of respondents and their accessibility. The text/email data collection method required contacting some of the participants more than once to clarify and elaborate on their responses. The flexible data collection process was necessary given that participants were located in different parts of the world. The line of questioning was specific to religiously influenced boycotts to get the perspective of Muslims about boycotts. Table 14.1 provides a breakdown of the participants and the data collection method.

Table 14.1 Characteristics of participants and data collection method

Country	Gender		Data collection method			Percentage of Muslims in the country*
	Men	Women	Phone	Text/email	Face-to-face interview	
Indonesia	3	2	1	4		87.20%
Nigeria	3	2	1	4		49.60%
Malaysia	2			1	1	61.30%
Egypt	1	1	1		1	92.35%
Thailand	1	1		2		4.30%
Iran		2			2	99.40%
United Kingdom	1		1			6.30%
Maldives	3	2	4	1		98.4%
Pakistan	2	1			3	96.50%
India	2			2		14.20%

* World Population Review, 2020.

The locals' view of the percentage of Muslims in the country may have minor differences to the percentage reported here.

Thematic analysis was employed to analyse the data. Walters (2016) states thematic analysis is a rigorous means of analysing data, especially for unpacking latent cultural meanings. Given that participants were spread across ten countries and there were many references to cultural contexts (both directly and indirectly), thematic analysis was the ideal data analysis method for this study. Furthermore, an inductive approach was utilised to generate the themes, relying minimally on pre-existing literature (Patton, 1990).

Findings and discussion

Analysis of the data revealed 13 sub-themes. These themes are categorised according to the three variables (principal themes) that predict the intention to boycott based on the TPB, as depicted in Figure 14.1. Participants' references to the mistreatment of Muslims in destinations varied from physical assault to discrimination. Furthermore, even though questioning was based on tourism products (e.g., destinations, travel companies, hotels), most of the time, the responses referred to destinations.

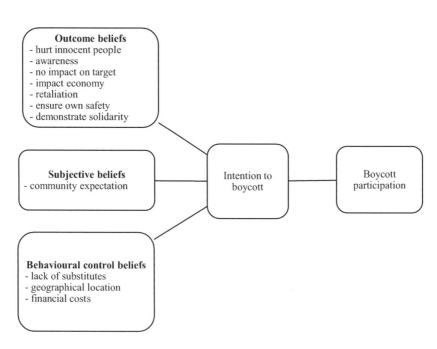

Figure 14.1 Themes categorised according to TPB

Outcome beliefs

The participants' attitudes towards intention to boycott depend on outcome beliefs, which is an evaluation of the boycott leading to either a positive or negative result. Overall the findings show that respondents identified four positive and three negative outcomes associated with participating in a tourism boycott.

Some participants stated that a tourism boycott is likely to hurt innocent people in the destination (McDowell, 1993). Given the interlinked and globalised nature of the tourism industry, an impact on the tourism system may be experienced by many people. Participants particularly stressed a whole country should not be penalised for any act of a group of people.

> Every country has good people and bad people . . . if I boycott it may end up hurting innocent people . . . I am sure everybody in a country does not hate us [Muslims]. Also, what about companies in my country who do business with them, their business will also [be] impact[ed].
>
> (Pakistan)

A tourism boycott is likely to lead to economic hardships for many people in destinations (Holden, 2005). It can also further isolate the destination, rather than lead to healthy negotiations to cease the egregious behaviour that lead to the boycott calls in the first place. One participant (Iranian) sums up this viewpoint, "rather than boycott, in my opinion, Muslims should visit those destinations and create an opportunity to discuss and raise awareness. Sometimes these conflicts could be because of lot of misunderstanding". This view alludes to the notion of tourism being a vehicle for understanding and peace (Higgins-Desbiolles, 2006).

Iranian participants echoed the sentiment that tourism boycotts can hurt innocent people, sharing their own experience of being under international sanctions (see Seyfi & Hall, 2020). This is reflective of past experience from subsequent boycotts influencing the outcome beliefs.

> We have been boycotted and sanctioned by the international community for our governments' action. Our people, my family, have suffered as a result, so I don't think we should punish a whole country.
>
> (Iran)

Two Maldivian participants shared a similar consideration, linking past experience to the evaluation of the outcome beliefs.

> I have been to Sri Lanka many times, met many Buddhists who are good people. . . . Although there are handful of Buddhists who are reported in the media to have been violent towards Muslims, it's not all of them. . . . What about Muslims in Sri Lanka, it [boycott] will affect them too.
>
> (Maldives)

This observation demonstrates that even in a religiously-motivated boycott, people are willing to look past religion when deciding whether to boycott.

For some participants, the impact of a boycott is meant to create or raise awareness of the plight of Muslims. They identified that a boycott is a tool that can be used as a weapon by the weak and disadvantaged (Scott, 1985). Highlighting and bringing international attention to how Muslims are mistreated in some countries is one of the reasons Muslim stage protests in general and boycotts in particular (Jevtic, 2009). This is based on the idea that protests help create awareness for the protest cause (Branton et al., 2015). The goal of attempting to create awareness indicates that people may not necessarily intend to boycott but may use boycott as a platform to raise awareness, particularly as it may lead to media attention. Consequently, media attention can be problematic for destinations as it will lead to negative destination images, especially if the boycott gains momentum (Marshall, 2002). These views are highlighted in the following response from a Malaysian participant:

> Don't think boycotts will necessarily impact the tourist arrivals. We don't even know how many people will actually boycott – enough to have an impact. For me, the important thing is it creates awareness. Hopefully, in time positive change will come too.

Only a few participants noted that boycotting will show solidarity within the Muslim community and provide moral support for Muslims struggling with injustices. The idea of Muslims as one community is manifested in the concept of "Ummah" (i.e., as one community, irrespective of transnational borders) (Akram, 2007). These religious teachings can be a powerful reason to support a boycott (Gardberg & Newburry, 2010). This view was echoed by an Indonesian respondent, "I cannot claim it [boycott] to be effective but at least this will help support the persecuted". Similarly, a Thai respondent stated, "It's important to show solidarity for Muslims. . . . Boycott is a way to signal that".

The majority of participants were aware that a boycott might never have an impact on the destination. In this context, they stressed how conflicts and maltreatment of Muslims in some societies are linked to macro-environmental factors such as geopolitics (Morey & Yaqin, 2011). However, participants may be confused between the success and impact of a boycott, where success refers to the achieving of objectives, and impact is the resulting effect of the boycott (Pruitt & Friedman, 1986). In other words, a boycott may have an impact without being a *success*, as narrowly defined. Tourism boycotts are often proxies that are used to influence change in the macro-environmental factors that triggered the boycott. An example of this was the boycott of South Africa in the 1960s, which aimed to change the policies towards the black community (Clark & Worger, 2016). However, in many cases, boycotts can be an expression of retaliation to express anger. Such boycotts can have a cathartic effect (Huefner & Hunt, 2000), even knowing that it may never impact the target. This was recognised by an Indonesian respondent who stated, "Boycotting a destination (or country) won't make any change as long as the real problems [political and religious conflicts] were not resolved".

Only a few participants stated that tourism boycotts would have an impact on the target destinations. The reference to impact was not specific to tourist arrivals. Rather, it also included people forming negative perceptions about the destination. These findings are reflective of previous studies that identified how boycotts might have diverse impacts on a destination. For example, a boycott of Arizona tourism cost the economy US$140 million (Reuters, 2010). Furthermore, the tourism boycott of Myanmar popularised the negative image of the "land of fear" associated with the destination (Pilger, 2000). These views were highlighted by a Nigerian respondent who stated that destination boycotts "will affect their economy. This will help stop maltreatment of Muslims". In comparison, a Maldivian respondent stated that in the face of a boycott

> people might still continue to go, but you know, people will think negatively of these destinations. How they are treating people. For example, my perception about India have changed because of how they are trying to revoke citizenship of Muslims. But I still go to India.

Some participants offered an alternative view, suggesting that boycotts may be effective in the long-run in changing the behaviour that triggered the boycott. However, such a scenario is possible only if the boycott gains momentum and persists long enough to impact the destination and influence change (Marshall, 2002). Even then, other factors may have to be considered if the boycott is to influence change. For instance, the boycott of Israel by the BDS movement (Chaitin et al., 2017) has existed since the 1940s but has resulted in no *expected* consolation for the boycotters (Seyfi & Hall, 2020). Reflective of this view, one participant stated:

> Not all Muslims will boycott. Global tourism is large. The percent of Muslims who will boycott will definitely be infinitesimal to the population of tourists globally. . . . It won't make impact in making countries accountable for maltreating Muslims but it can have a good effect on Behavioural change over time.
>
> (Nigeria)

A few participants explained that boycotts of destinations could further worsen the situation for Muslims as it might lead to retaliation. They particularly specified how this might be the case in communities where Muslims are a minority and disadvantaged. A Maldivian participant used a workplace example to explain the reasoning,

> we hear a lot about how people do not report workplace harassment as it may lead to more trouble for the victim. In some communities, Muslims

may be in a similar situation without much power, and it is better not to welcome more trouble.

In addition, a Nigerian respondent said, "the more tourism boycotts, the more the violence and mistreatment towards Muslims".

Respondents from Indonesia and Malaysia explained that they boycott some destinations to ensure their safety and avoid anxiety. Their reasoning is based on their religious identity, which they felt made them a target while travelling. Einashe (2017) reports how Muslims are reluctant to travel to the United States due to "fears of what might happen when they travel or arrive there". Blackwood's (2015) research on Muslims' negative experiences at airports after 9/11 provides further evidence about why Muslims may be reluctant to visit particular destinations and subsequently boycott them to ensure their wellbeing.

> For me, one of the most important outcomes of the boycott is that I can ensure my own safety. Why should I go to a country where I have to fear for my own safety?
>
> (Indonesia)

Subjective beliefs

Only one subjective belief was identified in this study, but it is, nonetheless, clearly an important one.

More than half of the respondents stated that there is an expectation from the Muslim community to voice anger against and concern about destinations that have been reported to mistreat Muslims. This expectation is related to the earlier discussion of showing solidarity with Muslims across the world (Farook, 2007). Being a Muslim creates a religious membership, often leading to an expectation that Muslims will support activities that are conducted in the name of religion, such as the boycott of a tourism destination.

> There is a very strong expectation when Muslims are suffering in any corner of the world, we as a community should raise our voice. We do that in collecting charity of people in Syria, we protest on the street to raise awareness for the way Palestinians are treated. When there is a global boycott against a destination that have been wrongdoing Muslims, it's no different. It is expected we as a community should participate.
>
> (Maldives)

> There is the concept of Muslim brotherhood and Ummah . . . as a community, collectively we should protest and participate in any non-violent activities for the way Muslims are treated.
>
> (Malaysia)

Religious membership is identified as a significant factor in influencing behaviour (Minton & Kahle, 2017). This argument does not only apply to Islam. Rather other religions such as Christianity and Hinduism, also influence behaviour based on a person's religiosity (e.g., Parboteeah et al., 2009).

Behavioural control beliefs

Behavioural control beliefs refer to the expected barriers in participating in boycotts (Armitage & Conner, 1999). Participants identified three factors that they perceived to control their participation in boycotts. While there is a financial consideration associated with all of the behaviour controlling factors, specific focus was provided on geographical location and lack of substitute destinations.

Many respondents identified the lack of substitutes as a hurdle for boycotting destinations. They argued that boycotting destinations is not comparable to other products that could have many substitutes. Even in boycotts associated with other types of products (e.g., toothpaste), Sen et al. (2001) identified that lack of substitutes is a challenge for people to participate in boycotts. In this regard, destinations might be less impacted as a result of boycotts due to an absence of alternatives.

> Boycotting a country is difficult. Our holidays are a combination of medicals and holiday, and we usually go to India or Sri Lanka. If I was to boycott them [India and Sri Lanka] based on how some Buddhists are treating Muslims or how Modi's [Indian Prime Minister Narendra Modi] administration is alleged to treat Muslims, where can I go? It's not like there is other options.
>
> (Maldives)

Some participants stated that geographical location is a limitation when thinking about boycotting destinations. The following quote also highlights how different ideologies across Islamic factions can lead to Muslims boycotting other Muslim countries. This observation relates to the diversities within religions, and the importance of having the flexibility to accommodate different perspectives when using a blanket reference to a religion in research. Furthermore, it relates to the argument in the introduction about how Muslims can be a very diverse group of people, depending on factors such as where they come from (Akbarzadeh & Smith, 2005) and which branch of Islam they belong to (Maréchal & Zemni, 2013).

> I am a Shia Muslim and most of the Middle Eastern countries don't really like us. My husband was physically beaten in Saudi Arabia because he is Shia. I wish I could boycott all these countries [Middle East], but unfortunately, we have limited choice in terms of countries that are close to Iran.
>
> (Iran)

Financial costs were identified by respondents as an influence on participation in boycotts. This was directly linked to geographical location, with it being potentially costly to boycott a destination that is geographically near and then having to travel to a destination that is further away. This situation is similar to the boycotting of products that have a lower price compared to the available substitutes (Sen et al., 2001). Earlier studies (e.g., John & Klein, 2003) also found that in some instances there could be a financial cost for boycotters associated with boycotting products. In some studies, it is identified as a social dilemma (Sen et al., 2001) for boycott participants as it involves the question of spending more money to buy a substitute versus losing face with the community that expects the person's support for the boycott. This dilemma is exemplified by the following respondent:

> India and Sri Lanka are the most popular destinations for Maldivians to go during holidays, as you will know, just one hour flying time. Based on media reports of how Muslims are treated there [India and Sri Lanka] should I boycott them [India and Sri Lanka]? That means I will have to spend almost twice the money for a single ticket to go to the next nearest countries which are Malaysia and Singapore or maybe even Thailand.
>
> (Maldives)

Having a financial burden associated with participating in boycotts may deter many people from doing so (John & Klein, 2003). However, this becomes a question of how strongly people believe and invest in religiously influenced boycotts for the betterment of other Muslims.

Conclusion

Tourism boycotts will continue to be employed by people to punish and express their displeasure with destinations and tourism providers who are perceived to have engaged in egregious behaviour. Additionally, religion will remain a crucial premise that is used to influence support for protests generally and boycotts specifically. This study shows that TPB is a good lens through which to explore the perspectives of Muslims in relation to tourism boycotts. The findings generated many considerations from a Muslim perspective and highlight pre-decisional rationalisations Muslims undertake when deciding to boycott tourism destinations. The findings show that respondents considered the outcome of participation in boycotts, observing multiple positive and negative consequences. Participants identified peer pressure as a critical factor to consider in boycott participation along with barriers to take part in destination boycotts. This finding is in line with Hoffmann's (2013) argument that boycott participation is rationally thought through with the aid of many considerations. While religion may influence Muslims to participate in religion-based boycotts, the study shows that the relationship between the two is a complex one. It is also clear that Islam does not represent a homogenous people. Instead,

Muslims hold a diverse array of views regarding themselves, their religion, and the views and actions of others. All of these influence decisions about supporting tourism boycotts.

It is clear from this study that there is a need for further research that explores the tourism experiences of Muslims, including their boycott behaviour. Such work needs to recognise the heterogeneous nature of the global Muslim population, including in terms of which branch of Islam individuals are associated with, how Islam is interpreted and lived in the countries of individuals, and their age and gender. Developing such understandings has the potential not just to ensure the success of boycotts but also the notion of the development of peace and understanding through tourism.

References

Abosag, I., & Farah, M. F. (2014). The influence of religiously motivated consumer boycott on brand image, loyalty and product judgment. *European Journal of Marketing, 48*(11/12), 2262–2283. https://doi.org/10.1108/EJM-12-2013-0737

Aish, E. A., McKechnie, S., Abosag, I., & Hassan, S. (2013). The mystique of macro-boycotting behaviour: A conceptual framework. *International Journal of Consumer Studies, 37*(2), 165–171. https://doi.org/10.1111/j.1470-6431.2012.01108.x

Ajzen, I. (1991). The theory of planned behavior. *Organizational Behavior and Human Decision Processes, 50*(2), 179–211. https://doi.org/10.1016/0749-5978(91)90020-T

Akbarzadeh, S., & Smith, B. (2005). *The representation of Islam and Muslims in the media (The Age and Herald Sun Newspapers).* Monash University Press.

Akram, E. (2007). Muslim Ummah and its link with transnational Muslim politics. *Islamic Studies, 46*(3), 381–415.

Al-Hyari, K., Alnsour, M., Al-Weshah, G., & Haffar, M. (2012). Religious beliefs and consumer behaviour: From loyalty to boycotts. *Journal of Islamic Marketing, 3*(2), 155–174. https://doi.org/10.1108/17590831211232564

Armitage, C. J., & Conner, M. (1999). The theory of planned behaviour: Assessment of predictive validity and 'perceived control'. *British Journal of Social Psychology, 38*(1), 35–54. https://doi.org/10.1348/014466699164022

Bakan, A. B., & Abu-Laban, Y. (2009). Palestinian resistance and international solidarity: The BDS campaign. *Race & Class, 51*(1), 29–54. https://doi.org/10.1177/0306396809106162

Basedau, M., Fox, J., Pierskalla, J. H., Strüver, G., & Vüllers, J. (2017). Does discrimination breed grievances – and do grievances breed violence? New evidence from an analysis of religious minorities in developing countries. *Conflict Management and Peace Science, 34*(3), 217–239. https://doi.org/10.1177/0738894215581329

Blackwood, L. (2015). Policing airport spaces: The Muslim experience of scrutiny. *Policing: A Journal of Policy and Practice, 9*(3), 255–264. https://doi.org/10.1093/police/pav024

Branton, R., Martinez-Ebers, V., Carey Jr, T. E., & Matsubayashi, T. (2015). Social protest and policy attitudes: The case of the 2006 immigrant rallies. *American Journal of Political Science, 59*(2), 390–402. https://doi.org/10.1111/ajps.12159

Carr, N. (2014). *Dogs in the leisure experience.* CABI.

Chaitin, J., Steinberg, S., & Steinberg, S. (2017). 'BDS – it's complicated': Israeli, Jewish, and others' views on the boycott of Israel. *The International Journal of Human Rights, 21*(7), 889–907. https://doi.org/10.1080/13642987.2017.1298093

Chen, M.-F., & Tung, P.-J. (2014). Developing an extended theory of planned behavior model to predict consumers' intention to visit green hotels. *International Journal of Hospitality Management, 36*, 221–230. https://doi.org/10.1016/j.ijhm.2013.09.006

Clark, N. L., & Worger, W. H. (2016). *South Africa: The rise and fall of apartheid* (3rd ed.). Routledge.

Creswell, J. W. (2009). *Research design: Qualitative, quantitative, and mixed methods approaches* (3rd ed.). Sage Publications.

Dunlap, E., Johnson, B., Sanabria, H., & Holliday, E. (1990). Studying crack users and their criminal careers-the scientific and artistic aspects of locating hard-to-reach subjects and interviewing them about sensitive topics. *Contemporary Drug Problems, Spring*, 121–144.

Einashe, I. (2017, July 21). Traveling to America while Muslim. *The New York Times*. www.nytimes.com/2017/07/21/travel/travel-ban-muslim-trump.html

Farook, S. (2007). On corporate social responsibility of Islamic financial institutions. *Islamic Economic Studies, 15*(1). https://ssrn.com/abstract=3159936

Fishbein, M., & Ajzen, I. (1975). *Belief, attitude, intention and behavior: An introduction to theory and research*. Addison-Wesley.

Friedman, M. (1985). Consumer boycotts in the United States, 1970–1980: Contemporary events in historical perspective. *Journal of Consumer Affairs, 19*(1), 96–117. https://doi.org/10.1111/j.1745-6606.1985.tb00346.x

Gardberg, N., & Newburry, W. (2010). Who boycotts whom? A social identity perspective on consumer boycotts. *Business & Society, 52*(2), 318–357.

Higgins-Desbiolles, F. (2006). More than an "industry": The forgotten power of tourism as a social force. *Tourism Management, 27*(6), 1192–1208. https://doi.org/10.1016/j.tourman.2005.05.020

Hoffmann, S. (2013). Are boycott motives rationalizations? *Journal of Consumer Behaviour, 12*(3), 214–222. https://doi.org/10.1002/cb.1418

Holden, A. (2005). *Tourism studies and the social sciences*. Routledge.

Hoyle, B. (2007, June 19). Muslim world inflamed by Rushdie knighthood. *The Times*. www.thetimes.co.uk/article/muslim-world-inflamed-by-rushdie-knighthood-hbgq2r6wmlv

Huefner, J., & Hunt, H. K. (2000). Consumer retaliation as a response to dissatisfaction. *Journal of Consumer Satisfaction, Dissatisfaction and Complaining Behavior, 13*(1), 61–82.

Izberk-Bilgin, E. (2012). Infidel brands: Unveiling alternative meanings of global brands at the nexus of globalization, consumer culture, and Islamism. *Journal of Consumer Research, 39*(4), 663–687. https://doi.org/10.1086/665413

Jevtic, J. (2009). *Global Muslim boycott of MNCs as a method of economic weakening of Israel* [Master's thesis, Central European University].

John, A., & Klein, J. (2003). The boycott puzzle: Consumer motivations for purchase sacrifice. *Management Science, 49*(9), 1196–1209. https://doi.org/10.1287/mnsc.49.9.1196.16569

Maamoun, A., & Aggarwal, P. (2008). Guilty by association: The boycotting of Danish products in the Middle East. *Journal of Business Case Studies, 4*(10), 35–42. https://doi.org/10.19030/jbcs.v4i10.4814

Malykhina, E. (2009, November 13). Updated: Christian group calls for gap boycott. *Adweek*. www.adweek.com/brand-marketing/updated-christian-group-calls-gap-boycott-106676/

Maréchal, B., & Zemni, S. (Eds.). (2013). *The dynamics of Sunni-Shia relationships: Doctrine, transnationalism, intellectuals and the media*. Hurst and Company.

Marshall, A. (2002). *The trouser people: A story of Burma – in the shadow of the empire*. Counterpoint.

Marshall, A. R. C. (2013, June 27). Special report: Myanmar gives official blessing to anti-Muslim monks. *Reuters*. www.reuters.com/article/us-myanmar-969-specialreport/special-report-myanmar-gives-official-blessing-to-anti-muslim-monks-idUSBRE95Q04720130627

Matthews, A. (2018). Ethnographic approaches to tourism research. In W. Hillman & K. Radel (Eds.), *Qualitative methods in tourism research: Theory and practice* (pp. 50–71). Channel View Publications.

McDowell, E. (1993, January 4). Boycotts affect travel industry. *The New York Times*. www.nytimes.com/1993/01/04/business/boycotts-affect-travel-industry.html

Mealer, M., & Jones, J. (2014). Methodological and ethical issues related to qualitative telephone interviews on sensitive topics. *Nurse Researcher, 21*(4), 32–47. https://doi.org/10.7748/nr2014.03.21.4.32.e1229

Minton, E. A., & Kahle, L. R. (2017). Religion and consumer behaviour. In C. V. Jansson-Boyd & M. J. Zawisza (Eds.), *Routledge international handbook of consumer psychology* (pp. 292–311). Routledge.

Morey, P., & Yaqin, A. (2011). *Framing Muslims: Stereotyping and representation after 9/11*. Harvard University Press.

Muhamad, N., Khamarudin, M., & Fauzi, W. I. M. (2019). The role of religious motivation in an international consumer boycott. *British Food Journal, 121*(1), 199–217. https://doi.org/10.1108/BFJ-02-2018-0118

Neusner, J., & Chilton, B. (Eds.). (2008). *Religious tolerance in world religions*. Templeton Foundation Press.

Oliver, P. E., & Marwell, G. (1992). Mobilizing technologies for collective action. In A. D. Morris & C. M. Mueller (Eds.), *Frontiers in social movement theory* (pp. 251–272). University Press.

Parboteeah, K. P., Paik, Y., & Cullen, J. B. (2009). Religious groups and work values: A focus on Buddhism, Christianity, Hinduism, and Islam. *International Journal of Cross Cultural Management, 9*(1), 51–67. https://doi.org/10.1177/1470595808096674

Patton, M. Q. (1990). *Qualitative evaluation and research methods* (2nd ed.). Sage Publications.

Pilger, J. (2000). Inside Burma: Land of fear. *Johnpilger.com: The films and journalism of John Pilger*. http://johnpilger.com/videos/inside-burma-land-of-fear

Pruitt, S. W., & Friedman, M. (1986). Determining the effectiveness of consumer boycotts: A stock price analysis of their impact on corporate targets. *Journal of Consumer Policy, 9*(4), 375–387. https://doi.org/10.1007/BF00380573

Reuters. (2010, November 19). *Immigration law boycott cost Ariz. $140 mln: Study*. www.reuters.com/article/us-arizona-boycott-idUSTRE6AH55W20101118

Scott, J. C. (1985). *Weapons of the weak: Everyday forms of peasant resistance*. Yale University Press.

Sen, S., Gürhan-Canli, Z., & Morwitz, V. (2001). Withholding consumption: A social dilemma perspective on consumer boycotts. *Journal of Consumer Research, 28*(3), 399–417. https://doi.org/10.1086/323729

Seyfi, S., & Hall, C. M. (2020). *Tourism, sanctions and boycotts*. Routledge.

Shaheer, I., Carr, N., & Insch, A. (2019). What are the reasons behind tourism boycotts? *Anatolia, 30*(2), 294–296. https://doi.org/10.1080/13032917.2018.1562948

Shaheer, I., Insch, A., & Carr, N. (2018). Tourism destination boycotts – are they becoming a standard practise? *Tourism Recreation Research, 43*(1), 129–132. https://doi.org/10.1080/02508281.2017.1377385

Smith, N. C. (1990). *Morality and the marketplace: Consumer pressure for corporate accountability*. Routledge.

Thompson Reuters & Dinar Standard. (2018). *State of the global Islamic economy. Report 2018–2019.* https://ded.ae/DED_Files/StudiesAndResearch/SGIE-Report-2018-19_ Eng_1540649428.pdf.

Trentmann, F. (2019). *Consumer boycotts in modern history: States, moral boundaries, and political action.* In D. Feldman (Ed.), *Boycotts past and present: From the American Revolution to the campaign to boycott Israel* (pp. 21–39). Palgrave Macmillan.

Walters, T. (2016). Using thematic analysis in tourism research. *Tourism Analysis, 21*(1), 107–116. https://doi.org/10.3727/108354216X14537459509017

World Population Review (2020). *World population by country.* https://worldpopulationre view.com/

Ysseldyk, R., Matheson, K., & Anisman, H. (2010). Religiosity as identity: Toward an understanding of religion from a social identity perspective. *Personality and Social Psychology Review, 14*(1), 60–71. https://doi.org/10.1177/1088868309349693

15 Questioning Halal tourism motive

In between da'wa, business, and life story

Intan Purwandani

Introduction

Profit-seeking is still considered the main driver of the tourism and hospitality industry (Getz & Petersen, 2005), not only by actors in mainstream tourism but also by those in other, more specialized types of tourism such as cultural tourism; nature tourism; and conservation; Meeting, Incentive, Conference, & Events (MICE); and religious-based tourism. Due to its alleged incompatibility with the contract law applied in the international business system, the Islamic sharia system, along with predominantly Muslim countries applying the system, is often avoided by foreign direct investors (Wilson, 2006).

The growing number of Muslims around the world (Stimage, 2019) is a large market whose demand for specific services needs to be provided not only at home but also on their travels (Akhtar, 2012). Many tourism service providers, not necessarily Muslim themselves, are competing for this large Muslim market (Jeaheng et al., 2020; Ali et al., 2021). This does not mean, however, that all business activities in the Muslim tourism market are profit-oriented.

A study by Purwandani (2018) found that *da'wa* – or a notion of an invitation to Islam – is a driver for some Muslim tourism providers to be in the business particularly in the context of Halal tourism. Da'wa motivated businesses present an alternative view in the conventional tourism industry. This research aims to understand da'wa motivated business in the context of Halal tourism. This study asks the following question: *How do Muslim tourism providers, especially those providing Sharia-compliance facilities perceive and practice da'wa through their business activities?* The urgency of this research is to understand the rationale of Halal tourism providers serving Halal services and facilities. To be specific, the entanglement of da'wa will be spotlighted to the behaviour of Muslim tourism providers who implement the principle of da'wa in their business. Furthermore, the deliberation of 'doing da'wa', which was well-informed attentively throughout the interview process, had been explored, since there is an assumption of a covered relational context between Muslim tourism providers' identities with their life stories, business and da'wa.

DOI: 10.4324/9781003036296-20

Da'wa and tourism

The notion of da'wa itself exists for preaching Islam to all humankind and not exclusively to Muslims (Racius, 2004; Kuiper, 2021). The method/practice of da'wa highly regards the history (the occurrence of Islamic occupancy in a place) and society (the object of da'wa) where da'wa needs to be undertaken appropriately and effectively (Poston, 1992; Toriman, 2012). It also affects local Muslims' understandings and practices toward da'wa. In Islam's classical era, the prophet Muhammad undertook different methods of da'wa in Mecca and Medina (Ansari, 2018). Kuiper (2021) narrated that even though the definition of da'wa denotes the notion of an invitation to Islam, it was done discreetly by the prophet during his life in Mecca. A thriving businessman, the prophet gained the interest of many non-Muslims through his trustworthiness in business. This counts as an act of da'wa. After Hijra (moving) to Medina, the prophet of Muhammad, Peace Be Upon Him (PBUH), shifted to a more public method of da'wa by taking a governmental position and approaching the community until he formed a new government in Medina. At the time of Hijra to Medina, there was no governmental conduct as to what had been administered in Mecca. In the contemporary era, da'wa takes many forms. In Malaysia, a Muslim-majority country that applies Sharia law, da'wa is used to invite and disseminate the teaching of Islam. Some non-Muslims, such as the Chinese, later become *muallaf* (converted-Muslim) (Toriman, 2012). Unlike the da'wa practice in Malaysia, da'wa in North America goes beyond inviting nonbelievers to convert. Da'wa in North America is mainly focused on combating the misconception of Islam, which affects the life of Muslims through threats or discrimination. This practice has started even before the 9/11 attacks. By establishing the institution of Islamic centres to cater for the needs of Muslim practicing their belief, da'wa in North America is also working to deal with misleading publication of information about Islam, not only to invite non-Muslims to embrace Islam but also to create a harmonious society (Poston, 1992; Guzik & Poston, 2020).

Following the previous insights on the manifestation of da'wa in a non-Muslim country, there is a need to explore the practice of da'wa in a non-Muslim country when Muslims are a minority group (Kettani, 2007). The purpose is to create a clear division in the discussion since this research looked into the situation in Spain, a non-Muslim country. In his study, Kettani (2007) examined the challenges and opportunities of da'wa for the Muslim minority in a non-Muslim majority country in Europe. The Muslims have three directions of da'wa:

1. Educate, whether Muslims or non-Muslims, about the Islamic principle from Allah and the prophet Muhammad PBUH with knowledge and understanding;
2. Showcase the principles of Islam by struggling to live and give an example of the right traits of Muslims according to the Islamic teaching;
3. Promote Islam to the society.

In tourism, there is a lack of discussion on the topic of da'wa. Many studies in tourism related to Islamic knowledge mainly focus on the variety of tourism such as Islamic tourism, sharia tourism, and Halal tourism (Al-Hamarmaneh & Steiner, 2004; Zamani-Farahani & Henderson, 2009; Battour et al., 2010; Asih & Asih, 2015; Battour & Ismail, 2016; Henderson, 2016; Rusby et al., 2020). Islamic tourism offers inter-Muslim mobility and its engagement with Islam (Henderson, 2009) while sharia and Halal tourism are used interchangeably to explore sharia-based services and facilities in the tourism industry. Recent studies on tourism and da'wa suggested da'wa as a strategy to balance people's religiosity with tourism activity (Zaenuri, 2018). The notion of 'balance' refers to the act of carrying out actions underpinned by both Islamic tenets and Islamic doctrines. Another research finds that da'wa is embedded in Halal tourism since it facilitates the internalization of Islamic norms (Sarbini et al., 2020). Drawing on the previous studies, it is suggested that da'wa and Halal tourism are interrelated, though further exploration is needed to understand the nature of their relationship. Furthermore, the study about tourism and da'wa was done in the context of a Muslim country, while Halal tourism is now emerging across the globe. By exploring da'wa and tourism in the context of a non-Muslim country, this study may add new perspective, since the notion of da'wa may be perceived differently.

Life story

The 'life story' as a concept simply refers to the life story and experiences of a person (Bluck & Alea, 2008; Bluck & Liao, 2013; McAdams, 1996; McLean et al., 2007). Hence, the narrative and experience are personal. The life story approach is employed in arts, health and medicine, psychology, and migration studies (Titon, 1980; Bertaux & Kohli, 1984; Habermas & Bluck, 2000; Buitelaar, 2006). In addition, life story is about a personal narrative. It becomes a matter of putting it as a material object in the study of tourism as it embodies, embeds, and represents the identity of tourism providers. This story needs to be acknowledged especially as it involves the minority therefore their choices could be heard (Spivak, 2003). In this study, life story become a departure to understand the rationale of Muslim tourism providers to do da'wa by serving Halal tourism facilities. Life story can also be a tool to open up and reveal the minority's personal narratives.

Methods

This research focuses on Muslim tourism providers who understand and use the idea of da'wa in their tourism business. The principle of da'wa in this research's aforementioned aim is to alleviate the elaboration of da'wa, which is also part of a grasped narrative (Wiles et al., 2005; Clarke & Holt, 2010). This study uses an interpretivist approach (Denzin, 1989; DeVault & Gross, 2007) in order to enable a collaborative process of meaning-making between the

Table 15.1 Profile of interviewees

Number	Instution	Muslim and origin identity	Pseudonyms
1.	The owner of Halal restaurant 1	Algerian-born Muslim	P1
2.	The owner of Halal restaurant 2	Algerian-born Muslim	P2
3.	The director of Islamic tour 1	Turkish-born Muslim	P3
4.	The director of Islamic tour 2	Spanish-converted Muslim	P4
5.	Mosque initiator	American-converted Muslim	P5

researcher and participants (Berger & Luckman, 1967). In this case, da'wa is positioned as a reality that has its meaning constructed by both researcher and participants.

Data is presented with pseudonyms for five informants to ensure anonymity, since this study pertains to religion and life story. The profile of the interviewees is shown in Table 15.1. This research departs the argument to respond to the research question on how is the relational context between da'wa in tourism business and Muslim tourism providers' life story? The method of this study, the case study (Mizrahi, 2020) was carried out in Granada, Spain. A case study is employed due to the urgency to obtain in-depth data of an issue (Crowe et al., 2011) as well as detailed investigation of the participants. It also intends to reveal tacit knowledge of the participants' cultures (Rashid et al., 2019).

Findings/discussion

This chapter outlines the entanglement of perspectives and expressions of Muslim tourism providers as they run their Halal tourism business considering their life stories as immigrant Muslims; particularly, why the narration of da'wa is performed by the Muslim tourism providers living in a non-Muslim country in three arguments:

1. Da'wa in Halal tourism businesses because of a responsibility to educate non-Muslims by demonstrating their knowledge about what is needed by Muslims;
2. Da'wa in Halal tourism businesses by doing charity/*sadaqah* to everyone in order to devote a real example of the Islamic ethical system (justice/*adalah*) while opening a discussion to be able to integrate with a non-Muslim society;
3. Da'wa in Halal tourism businesses is required to strengthen the brotherhood between Muslim tourism providers and their business employees as well as Muslim tourists with an aim to revive the Muslim society.

Doing da'wa through Halal tourism: the life stories of Muslim tourism providers

Da'wa, business, and life story – these three elements might have never been disclosed in any research in anthropology particularly on how the life story of someone could potentially alter the way people act and think in every aspect of life, in this particular case, the business of a Muslim enterprise. To bring to light how meaningful is the interrelation between da'wa, business, and life story, an introduction (a terrific conversation) is presented, which involves one of the Muslim tourism entrepreneurs in Granada:

> It is super hard to find Halal food back then. Besides the number of Muslim was still can be counted by the finger, the product of Halal and all the things related to Islam were the susceptible case.
>
> (P1)

Experiencing a hard time in the past is explicitly highlighted in this entrepreneur's answer. The expression of sadness and fear was found during the interview. This section attempted to unveil (his) story with regards to his background as being born Muslim or converted-Muslim and immigrant or Spanish Muslim who live as a minority in Granada, Spain, an untold story of a group in a former Islamic land. The story presented educating non-Muslims; charity/*sadaqah* to demonstrate Islam and the idea of strengthening brotherhood. All of these narratives are explained through societal and historical approaches to diverse life stories.

Educating non-Muslim about Islamic knowledge: against misconception about Islam

In the study, the argumentation on educating non-Muslims either to business partners, neighbours, or mosque visitors about Islam is mostly portrayed by converted Muslims (American-converted Muslim and Spanish-converted Muslim). One narration is told by an immigrant Turkish Muslim, who is the director of an Islamic tour company. This part attempts to conceive the idea of educating non-Muslims in the area of business by analyzing their life stories.

P5, an American-converted Muslim, was the initiator of the establishment of a mosque and has been living there since the early period of Islamic revival around 1970. She had a precarious life, which led her to educate non-Muslims continuously. P5 proposed the idea of da'wa by enabling the mosque as a public space to enlighten non-Muslims with the 'right' knowledge of Islam. She set an aim to rectify the negative public stigma about Islam, which was perceived as a threat previously.

She narrated that in the past, which lasted nearly 900 years, the Al-Andalus region in southern Spain was an area of Islamic civilization until its defeat.

Since then, Islam was seen as an enemy that should never be allowed to return. However, an Islamic revival began from around 1970. She came to the area as a property businessperson who needed to travel across the globe. Following her arrival in Europe, in Luxembourg, the United Kingdom, and finally in Spain, she felt that she found a 'new world' of believing in the existence of God. She converted to Islam in Spain, and built her new life. Following her conversion and moving to Granada, she faced difficulty in performing her prayers.

She understood that the community still found Islam as a threat and expressed their antagonism to Islam. This moment became the turning point to revive Islam in Granada to combat the misunderstanding of the community as well as to unite the community of Granada. She and fellow Muslims, five of them, performed da'wa. This public da'wa was done in the city centre through flyers, direct communication, and public invitation before the establishment of the mosque.

After decades of struggle in building the mosque with severe political and societal rejection and threats, P5 and other first-generation Muslims in Granada are now delighted with the presence of the mosque. From her perspective, this facility is one of the indications of the Islamic society resurrection in Granada. Previously, she and her Muslim colleagues educated non-Muslims publicly in the city centre. Now, she is working to reconstruct the public belief in Islam in the mosque in Granada.

Similar to P5, the director of Islamic tour 2 (P4), a Spanish-converted Muslim, illustrated his life story as one of the factors that led him to educate non-Muslims and respond to the needs of Muslim tourists. He was an influential and successful person before converting to Islam. He was a devout Catholic who used to have a wrong impression of Islam until one day, his curiosity brought him to learn the truth of Islam, and as a result he converted. His family were against him, and he was fired from his job.

> It was my difficult time, but I got the most peaceful soul at that the same time. I could think clearly to teach my closest family and the surroundings through my behavior. Ever since I converted, I started to practice Islam by showing what Muslim needs, while started to familiarize all the things related to it slowly.
>
> (P4)

During the early days of his conversion, he experienced a great challenge in publicizing his new identity as a Muslim. He experienced difficulty in finding Halal foods, in performing prayers on Fridays, in meeting with people after being rejected by his family, and in finding a new career. These challenges guided him to run a business, with a friend, to support the establishment of the mosque as well as become an advocate and educate people of the needs of a Muslim with the use of a travel agency. The education started from educating his family and non-Muslim business partner to recognizing that Halal food is a need of Muslims. It is a cornerstone of the life of the Muslim society in Granada. For this reason, he struggled for a long period to spread his extensive knowledge about Halal food.

At the moment, according to P4, the non-Muslim society in Granada has a misunderstanding on interpreting the term Halal, often linking it to the belief on the way animals are slaughtered for their meat. From his perspective, Halal has a broader definition. In line with this, he, as a travel agency owner, felt the need to become an educator to provide accurate information about the concept of Halal.

The attempt to reconsider the discussion of Halal in a non-Muslim community is not only motivated by the need of adjusting the growing Muslim markets in Granada but also to familiarize the non-Muslim community in Granada with all the notions connected to Islam, so that the next generation will not experience the same difficulty to practice and perform their rituals as a Muslim. This is viewed as a way to ensure that the next generation can comfortably live and reside in their land as a Muslim. Furthermore, he highlighted that this trial is the genuine purpose of da'wa – to present the Muslim society in a good light.

The last decades of the 20th century in Spain and Portugal were marked as the period of resurgence of Islam as a way of life and as a civilization (Vila, 1986; Coope, 2020). During this time, the style of da'wa employed was to educate the non-Muslims of Islam. People from this era of Islamic reawakening, including the director of Islamic tour 2 and the initiator of the mosque, are still managing da'wa in this way. Vila (1986) found that the mosque in Granada deserves a provisional oratory to become a *madrasa* or a place to learn Qur'anic and Arabic studies, not just aiming to learn Islam. This mosque was equipped with adequate tools to teach and discuss Islam with non-Muslims (Rogozen-Soltar, 2017). Meanwhile, to fellow Muslims, the mosque is a place to extensively learn *fiqh* (religious law of Islam), Arabic, and the Qur'an that are essential for the education of next-generation Muslims (Vila, 1986; Rogozen-Soltar, 2017).

Aside from converted Muslims who live in Granada, the director of Islamic tour 2 (P3), a Turkish-born Muslim, understood the idea of da'wa as a way to educate and raise the awareness of his non-Muslim business partners on performing prayer on time. Moving to Granada as a Muslim born in Turkey, the rebirth of Islam in Granada shaped a new way of life for him. Unlike P5 and P4, P3 used to live in a friendly Muslim environment in Turkey, so he was aghast when he first went to Granada, Spain. He struggled to perform the five-time prayers on time. He discovered that the primary factor in performing the prayers on time was the availability of prayer facilities in Granada. Moreover, as a travel agency owner who is always travelling from place to place within and outside Spain, he realized this condition persists due to a lack of attention given to prayer facilities, particularly in tourism businesses.

> I was surprised with the condition of Muslim in Granada when I moved in the first time. Other Muslims and I did not have many options to perform

prayers in the proper place in time. It was an extremely different condition compared to Turkey. I thought it was a region where the golden era of Islam taken place but nothing remained including the flexibility to perform prayer in time at any place?

(P3)

This was expressed with a thoroughly enthusiastic tone when the director of Islamic tour 2 (P3) began to narrate his life story. The difficulty experienced by the director of Islamic tour 2 (P3) in performing the five-time prayers inspired him to accommodate Muslim tourist needs, particularly in performing their prayers. Having a travel agency, he felt he has the power to instruct and teach non-Muslim business partners with his knowledge and understanding of the need to provide a place to pray. When it comes to 'teach', P3 would always perform the five-time prayers on time regardless of the place, such as on the sidewalk, behind the parking bus they rent, or even in other public spaces. He remarked this action was an example of seriously displaying the need to perform the five-time prayers on time. He would teach by explaining the idea behind the five-time prayers, which schedule would regularly change according to the rotation of the sun. The objective was not to force non-Muslim business partners (such as restaurants or hotels) to immediately adjust their services and facilities to incorporate this need but rather to raise their awareness and understanding.

In the case of P3, as he was born a Muslim, da'wa was to educate non-Muslim business partners to arrange a place to perform five-time prayers, a manifestation of the responsibility to help Muslim tourists in a Muslim-friendly environment. In the work of Kettani (2007), the behaviour of P3 could be categorized as a promotion of Islam in the non-Muslim community by giving an example of what regular 'behaviour' is in Islam. One of the examples is the urgency of performing the five-time prayers on time, and so Muslim tourism providers are expected to have an awareness of this need.

In conclusion, P3, P4, and P5 are educating non-Muslims because of their experiences as a converted Muslim and as a born Muslim and encounter their struggles on their practice as a Muslim in public. The fact is mainly the misconception of Islam among the society in general, which results in the lack of awareness and facilities to meet the needs of the Muslims.

Charity/sadaqah: a contribution to everyone and integration to the (non-Muslim) society

In the second aspect of the rationale behind da'wa is found in the life stories of foreign-born Muslims from Algeria who own Halal restaurants in Granada (P1 and P2) and of converted Muslims, such as P4 and P5. It is found that da'wa through charitable donation or *sadaqa* is another way to participate in and showcase the Islamic ethical system by positioning the non-Muslim society as the primary target. This section will investigate the life story of the participants with the objective of da'wa used in their business.

As Algerian-born Muslims seeking financial reward, P1 and P2 experienced difficulty in the early days of their settlement in Granada. They found it hard to find employment as immigrant Muslims from North Africa in the non-Muslim society at the time when the number of Muslims in Granada was few. Both owners of Halal restaurants (P1 and P2) struggled to survive on settling. Their success was not supported by other Muslims since all the Muslims at that time were facing similar obstacles whether internal or external problems. The Muslim community was not yet established.

> I used to experience economic crisis and hardship in integrating to the whole community in my early life here in Granada. I felt that nobody looked at me cause most probably it was the beginning of the Muslim back in Granada. Every Muslim was struggling with it. I was an immigrant as I am today. I got two tests at the same time from Allah. One was the test to persistently practicing Islam. Two was the test to face the difficulty in establishing my life. Ever since, I promised myself that in the future, when-ever I meet Muslim coming to Granada, I would love to help them. They should not be ignored as I experienced. I would make sure, that they are 'safe' here. It is what we are working on today with my sister who owns Halal restaurant 1.
>
> (P2)

> *Bismillah* one coffee for someone, one menu for someone else, one tea for him. I do it all the time whenever I meet Muslim from another country because I know how it feels to be here. A place where is not that 'friendly' to us (Muslim) as a 'visitor'.
>
> (P1)

These quotes are a promise to themselves to do charity especially for fellow Muslims who are coming to Granada, either as a tourist or an immigrant. Their awareness that Granada was not a 'friendly' place to Muslims motivated the owners to release their affection to Muslims. This became the foundation to target giving free food to Muslim clients as da'wa in the tourism business since they experienced an undesirable life when they first arrived. Uniquely, these Algerian-born Muslims discouraged themselves from providing charity in a public fashion. The explicit justification was for the sake of getting *Hasana* (a good reward from Allah).

According to the Qur'an Surah Al-Baqarah verse 271, the essence of pri-vate and unseen giving to those in need is favourable to cleanse our bad deeds. The preference of born-Muslim tourism providers to do a secretive donation is not only because of the hope of gaining reward from Allah but also to experience the feeling of the needy. In contrast, the converted-Mus-lim participants in this study, such as the initiator of the mosque (P5), regu-larly organize the provision of free food in Ramadan or every Friday to the neighbours and mosque visitors in public; they announce this *sadaqah* on purpose. She said they aim to open communication and integrate into society to get 'acceptance' from all people. It did not mean that, after decades, the Muslim society would still be isolated from the heterogeneous community – but rather as a means to maintain the integration process with all societies. At the beginning of the mosque establishment, obstinate refusal was experienced by the Muslim group of mosque initiators. Kettani (2007) signified that this was one of the challenges coming from outsiders that lessen the Islamic identity. Aown (2011) viewed, for non-Muslims, the mosque was one of the informal places to learn about Islam with a possibility of frequent involvement in activities with the general public. So, the Granada societies at that time viewed religious missionary work as a threat. For Muslims, a single mosque serves the entire population, which sometimes means feelings of commonality (Kopp, 2002). From this perspective, the step of opening the mosque to non-Muslim visitors and giving free food regularly seemingly becomes the right path to do da'wa – to initiate social interaction as well as do missionary activities.

The director of Islamic tour 2 (P4), who led the Muslim tourists to buy from a local shop or local restaurants, perceived his action as a way to exhibit the presence of Muslims in the middle of society. This contributes to the local socioeconomics, a component of the Islamic ethical system (Rice, 1999).

> The local association now loves us as the mosque brings business to the area, we help neighbours in need and have now become part of the landscape because everyone wants to visit mosque today.
>
> (P4)

The social effect of doing Islamic charity or giving any gifts according to Islamic teachings is viewed as a tie bind and a bridge to connect people (Hassan et al., 2019) and it can serve as a bridge to embrace not only neighbours but also foreigners, travellers and refugees (Kochyut, 2009). This strategy reflects the life experience of the participants in this study who were once perceived as a threat to Andalusian society. Again, in Kettani's (2007) work, this movement is a part of promoting Islam that reflects being able to integrate and be accepted by contributing real action.

In conclusion, da'wa by giving charity/*sadaqah* considered the background of the Muslim tourism providers. The struggle of the owner of Halal restaurants (P1 and P2), the director of Islamic tour 2 (P4), and the initiator of the mosque (P5) created two different ways of doing charity: in private and in public. The two types of charity have their own objective. For those who experienced economic struggle, the preference of doing charity publicly was discouraged due to the feeling of being needy in the past. Meanwhile, those who experienced explicit rejection from locals at the beginning of the Islamic revival preferred to publicly announce their charity to initiate social integration.

Strengthening Muslim brotherhood: a unity confronts economic and
religious injustice

This section amplifies the story of incoming Muslim people to Granada, either as a tourist or as an immigrant.

> Our struggle began by applying for a job from one shop to another. Until we found an idea to become a hairdresser independently. We did whatever we could to survive at that time. It is extremely not easy even to afford our basic needs.
>
> (P2)

Da'wa is denoted as a way to strengthen brotherhood between the Muslim employee and tourist. It begins with the story of the struggle of the owner of Halal restaurants. Both owners are immigrant Muslims from Algeria, North Africa. Near the end of the 20th century, immigrant Muslims from North Africa arrived in Andalusia to venture into the migrant labour market (Dietz, 2004). Unfortunately, according to the work of Dietz (2004), incoming Muslim immigrants from North Africa (specifically Morocco) were associated with a North African "re-conquest" of southern Spain. At the same time, the migration of Muslims to seek a new life among non-believers poses new and significant problems in economic terms (Hsieh, 2021). This is not only with regards to immigrant Muslims as Muslim tourists also potentially experience injustice in their needs.

Having a lack of economic capital when arriving in Granada narrated the story of experiencing injustice in terms of getting employment. Beyond that, in terms of practicing Islamic rituals, Muslims in Granada have experienced significant challenges. Since that time, Muslims became aware of the importance of encouraging brotherhood with the aim of confronting economic and religious injustices. This strategy is recognized as da'wa by them. For religious justice, the spirit of serving their brothers/sisters led them to satisfy Muslim tourists as they wanted to be satisfied. This action was also seen as a fundamental aspect of the life of their future children. However, looking closely, the narration of da'wa was also influenced by the life story of Muslim tourism providers as a minority in a non-Muslim country willing to educate, integrate, and confront all injustices or horrible experiences in the past by strengthening the Muslim community.

In summary, the rationale behind Muslim tourism providers doing da'wa was because of their struggle to practice Islamic rituals and show their identity as Muslim. Muslim tourism providers also experienced living in difficulty in needs and being viewed as a threat by society. As a result, charity is argued as the right option to create social integration. Finally, Muslim tourism providers in this study experienced difficulty finding a job and practicing Islamic rituals. For this reason, they emphasized the need to create stronger kinship among Muslim community members.

Conclusions

Muslim tourists are a vital market, which makes everyone including non-Muslim tourism providers willing to provide for their needs for profit. In this research, the involvement of Muslim tourism providers to cater to the needs of Muslim tourists provides a new perspective for businesses in the tourism industry. For the Muslim tourism providers who were participants in this research, business was not merely perceived as a sum of money but rather as an expression of spiritual enthusiasm. Business in the point of view of Muslim tourism providers in Granada manifests the concept of da'wa by indirectly implying the Islamic ethical system. Interestingly, da'wa in this research is perceived as spiritual enthusiasm and the result of societal and historical account of business-people. Muslim tourism providers perceive da'wa in business with three primary concepts. First, da'wa is a responsibility to educate non-Muslims. Second, da'wa is doing charity/*sadaqah* to everyone to exhibit an example of the Islamic ethical system (justice/Adalah) while opening a discussion about integration with the non-Muslim society. Third, da'wa is a method of strengthening brotherhood between Muslim tourists and employees.

Basically, as a missionary religion, da'wa in Islam is an invocation to every Muslim in every deed they perform in this world. However, the method and area of doing da'wa are based on the time and place they reside. In other words, da'wa in business also considers societal and historical contexts. The reason for doing da'wa by the Muslim tourism providers in this research was because of their experience in the early years of conversion or living in Granada as a Muslim. They felt the need and felt responsible for educating and helping familiarize people with Islam through establishing public facilities, such as a mosque, which has now become a tourist destination to non-Muslims and Muslims alike. This work's purpose is to combat the misconception on Islam among the society in Granada. Moreover, the act of doing charity to the neighbourhood prompts social integration. Last, the reason of doing da'wa is to toughen brotherhood ties following previous experiences of difficulty in practicing Islamic rituals and finding employment.

References

Akhtar, N. (2012, August 20). The rise of the affluent Muslim traveller. *BBC News*. www.bbc.com/news/magazine-19295861

Al-Hamarmaneh, A., & Steiner, C. (2004). Islamic tourism: Rethinking the strategies of tourism development in the Arab world after September 11, 2001. *Comparative Studies of South Asia, Africa and the Middle East, 24*(1), 173–182.

Ali, F., Mostafa, M. M., Ainin, S., Zalina, Z., & Ahmad, F. (2021). Exploring halal tourism tweets on social media. *Journal of Big Data, 8*(72). https://doi.org/10.1186/s40537-021-00463-5

Ansari, A. (2018). Divine methodology of Dawah. *Islami City*. www.islamicity.org/3143/divine-methodology-of-dawah/

Aown, N. M. (2011). A place for informal learning in teaching about religion: The story of an experienced non-Muslim teacher and her learning about Islam. *Teaching and Teacher Education, 27*(8), 1255–1264. https://doi.org/10.1016/j.tate.2011.07.005

Asih, S. M., & Asih, S. K. (2015). Marketing strategy implementation in developing Sharia tourism in Indonesia. *International Proceedings of Management and Economy, 84*, 133–137. IACSIT Press.

Battour, M., & Ismail, M. N. (2016). Halal tourism: Concepts, practises, challenges and future. *Tourism Management Perspectives, 19*, 150–154. https://doi.org/10.1016/j. tmp.2015.12.008

Battour, M. M., & Ismail, M. N., & Nattor, M. (2010). Toward a Halal tourism market. *Tourism Analysis, 15*(4), 461–470. https://doi.org/10.3727/108354210X12864727453304

Berger, P., & Luckman, T. (1967). *The social construction of reality: A treatise in the sociology of knowledge.* Doubleday and Company.

Bertaux, D., & Kohli, M. (1984). The life story approach: A continental view. *Annual Review of Sociology, 10*(1), 215–237. https://doi.org/10.1146/annurev.so.10.080184.001243

Bluck, S., & Alea, N. (2008). Remembering being me: The self-continuity function of autobiographical memory in younger and older adults. In F. Sani (Ed.), *Self-continuity: Individual and collective perspectives* (pp. 55–70). Psychology Press.

Bluck, S., & Liao, H. (2013). I was therefore I am: Creating self-continuity through remembering our personal past. *The International Journal of Reminiscence and Life Review, 1*, 7–12.

Buitelaar, M. (2006). 'I am the ultimate challenge' accounts of intersectionality in the life-story of a well-known daughter of Moroccan migrant workers in the Netherlands. *European Journal of Women's Studies, 13*(3), 259–276. https://doi.org/10.1177/1350506806 065756

Clarke, J., & Holt, R. (2010). The mature entrepreneur: A narrative approach to entrepreneurial goals. *Journal of Management Inquiry, 19*(1), 69–83. https://doi.org/10.1177/ 1056492609343030

Coope, J. A. (2020). Arabs, Berbers, and local converts. In M. Fierro (Ed.), *Routledge handbook of Muslim Iberia* (pp. 189–207). Routledge.

Crowe, S., Cresswell, K., Robertson, A., Huby, G., Avery, A., & Sheikh, A. (2011). The case study approach. *BMC Medical Research Methodology, 11*, 100. https://doi. org/10.1186/1471-2288-11-100

Denzin, N. K. (1989). *Interpretive biography.* SAGE University Publication.

DeVault, M. L., & Gross, G. (2007). Feminist interviewing: Experience, talk, and knowledge. In S. N. Hesse-Biber (Ed.), *Handbook of feminist research: Theory and praxis* (pp. 173– 198). SAGE Publications.

Dietz, G. (2004). Frontier hybridisation or culture clash? Transnational migrant communities and sub-national identity politics in Andalusia, Spain. *Journal of Ethnic and Migration Studies, 30*(6), 1087–1112. https://doi.org/10.1080/1369183042000286269

Getz, D., & Petersen, T. (2005). Growth and profit-oriented entrepreneurship among family business owners in the tourism and hospitality industry. *International Journal of Hospitality Management, 24*(2), 219–242. https://doi.org/10.1016/j.ijhm.2004.06.007

Guzik, E., & Poston, L. (2020). Daʿwa in North America: The past, the present, and the future. In I. Weismann & J. Malik (Eds.), *Culture of* Da'wa*: Preaching in the modern world* (pp. 160–177). The University of Utah Press.

Habermas, T., & Bluck, S. (2000). Getting a life: The emergence of the life story in adolescence. *Psychological Bulletin, 126*(5), 748–769. https://doi.org/10.1037/0033-2909.126.5.748

Hassan, S. G., Hameed, W. U., Basheer, M. F., & Ali, J. (2019). Zakat compliance intention among self-employed people: Evidence from Punjab, Pakistan. *Al-Adwah', 34*(2), 80–96.

Henderson, J. C. (2009). Islamic tourism reviewed. *Tourism Recreation Research, 34*(2), 207– 211. https://doi.org/10.1080/02508281.2009.11081594

Henderson, J. C. (2016, May 14). Islamic tourism: The next big thing? *The Straits Times.* www.straitstimes.com/opinion/islamic-tourism-the-next-big-thing

Hsieh, Y.-J. T. (2021). Learning language and gaining employment: Problems for refugee migrants in Australia. *Equality, Diversity and Inclusion, 40*(8), 1013–1031. https://doi.org/10.1108/EDI-12-2020-0358

Jeaheng, Y., Al-Ansi, A., & Han, H. (2020). Impacts of Halal-friendly services, facilities, and food and beverages on Muslim travelers' perceptions of service quality attributes, perceived price, satisfaction, trust, and loyalty. *Journal of Hospitality Marketing & Management, 29*(7), 787–811. https://doi.org/10.1080/19368623.2020.1715317

Kettani, M. A. (2007). Muslims in non-Muslim societies: Challenges and opportunities. *Institute of Muslim Minority Affairs Journal, 11*(2), 226–233. https://doi.org/10.1080/02666959008716166

Kochyut, T. (2009). God, gifts and poor people: On charity in Islam. *Social Compass, 56*(1), 98–116. https://doi.org/10.1177/0037768608100345

Kopp, H. (2002). Dress and diversity: Muslim women and Islamic dress in an immigrant/minority context. *The Muslim World, 92*(1/2), 59–79.

Kuiper, M. J. (2021). *Da'wa: A global history of Islamic missionary thought and practice.* Edinburgh University Press.

McAdams, D. P. (1996). Personality, modernity, and the storied self: A contemporary framework for studying persons. *Psychological Inquiry, 7*(4), 295–321. https://doi.org/10.1207/s15327965pli0704_1

McLean, K. C., Pasupathi, M., & Pals, J. L. (2007). Selves creating stories creating selves: A process model of self-development. *Personality and Social Psychology Review, 11*(3), 262–278. https://doi.org/10.1177/1088868307301034

Mizrahi, M. (2020). The case study method in philosophy of science: An empirical study. *Perspectives on Science, 28*(1), 63–88. https://doi.org/10.1162/posc_a_00333

Poston, L. (1992). *Islamic Da'wah in the West: Muslim missionary activity and the dynamic of conversion to Islam.* Oxford University Press.

Purwandani, I. (2018). *Discovering Halal tourism: The preference of devout Muslim tourists and the response of tourism entrepreneurs catering to Sharia-compliance needs: A case study of Granada, Andalucía, Spain* [Master's thesis, Wageningen University and Research]. https://library.wur.nl/WebQuery/titel/2238603

Racius, E. (2004). *The multiple nature of the Islamic Da'wa* [Academic dissertation, University of Helsinki].

Rashid, Y., Rashid, A., Warraich, M. A., Sabir, S. S., & Waseem, A. (2019). Case study method: A step-by-step guide for business researchers. *International Journal of Qualitative Methods, 18.* https://doi.org/10.1177/1609406919862424

Rice, G. (1999). Islamic ethics and the implications for business. *Journal of Business Ethics, 18*(4), 345–358. https://doi.org/10.1023/A:1005711414306

Rogozen-Soltar, M. H. (2017). *Spain unmoored: Migration, conversion, and the politics of Islam.* Indiana University Press.

Rusby, Z., Arif, M., No, J. K. N., & Marpoyan, P. (2020). Development of Sharia tourism in Riau Province Indonesia. *African Journal of Hospitality, Tourism and Leisure, 9*(1).

Sarbini, A., Syamsuddi, Effendi, D. I., & Fakhruroji, M. (2020). Halal tourism as a way of Da'wah in Coastal Muslim communities of Indonesia. *PalArch's Journal of Archaeology of Egypt/Egyptology, 17*(7), 581–590.

Spivak, G. C. (2003). Can the subaltern speak? *Die Philosophin, 14*(27), 42–58. https://doi.org/10.5840/philosophin200314275

Stimage, K. (2019). The fastest growing religions in the world. *WorldAtlas.* www.worldatlas.com/articles/the-fastest-growing-religions-in-the-world.html

Titon, J. T. (1980). The life story. *The Journal of American Folklore, 93*(369), 276–292. https://doi.org/10.2307/540572

Toriman, M. E. (2012). Nature of Islamic Da'wa in Malaysia. *Advances in Natural and Applied Sciences, 6*(4), 572–574.

Vila, J. B. (1986). The Muslims of Portugal and Spain. *Institute of Muslim Minority Affairs. Journal, 7*(1), 69–83. https://doi.org/10.1080/13602008608715965

Wiles, J. L., Rosenberg, M. W., & Kearns, R. A. (2005). Narrative analysis as a strategy for understanding interview talk in geographic research. *Area, 37*(1), 89–99. https://doi.org/10.1111/j.1475-4762.2005.00608.x

Wilson, R. (2006). Islam and business. *Thunderbird International Business Review, 48*(1), 109–123. https://doi.org/10.1002/tie.20088

Zaenuri, L. A. (2018). Dakwah strategies of Sharia tourism: The case of Gili Air, North Lombok. *Journal of Islamic Studies, 22*(2), 237–254. https://doi.org/10.20414/ujis.v22i2.327

Zamani-Farahani, H., & Henderson, J. C. (2009). Islamic tourism and managing tourism development in Islamic societies: The cases of Iran and Saudi Arabia. *International Journal of Tourism Research, 12*(1), 78–89. https://doi.org/10.1002/jtr.741

16 Interactions between Muslim attendees and non-Muslim staff

A study of the Islamic MICE market in Thailand

Songsin Teerakunpisut, Julie Jie Wen, Amie Matthews and Felicity Picken

Introduction

The Meetings, Incentive Travel, Conventions and Exhibitions (MICE) industry includes meetings, seminars, incentive travel, conventions, trade shows, festivals, and exhibitions. Its activities involve many different tourism and hospitality service providers, including transport, pre- and post-conference touring, purpose-built convention centres, exhibition facilities, hotels and catering, and audio-visual services (Rogers, 2008). Irrespective of the term that is employed, MICE "is known for its extensive planning and demanding clientele" (WTO, 2012, p. 46). The common focus for all MICE venues is to attract large groups who usually plan well in advance and have extremely high expectations of the venue. Although demanding clientele are common to a number of tourism and hospitality sectors, in the case of MICE (WTO, 2012) such customers typically spend three to five times more than individual tourists and each conference or event booking may involve between 100 and 1,000 guests. However, with ongoing expansion of MICE infrastructure and increased numbers of stakeholders, the MICE industry has become more complex. Subsequently, the challenges presented by Muslim customer and non-Muslim staff interactions in the industry have also increased.

MICE in Thailand

The development of the MICE industry in Thailand is not well documented (Akkhaphin, 2016; Teerakunpisut, 2018). It was only in 1977 that the International Convention Division (ICD) of the Tourism Authority of Thailand (TAT) was established. This can be regarded as the starting point for recognising the importance of international conventions in Thailand (TCEB, 2014). As MICE is a substantial source of revenue for various members of the tourism and hospitality industries, such as hotel and restaurant sectors, various government bodies have played a key role in attracting more MICE travellers to the country (Akkhaphin, 2016). In 1984, the government and private sectors jointly established the Thailand Incentive and Convention Association (TICA) as a means

DOI: 10.4324/9781003036296-21

of aiding the growth of Thailand as a preferred destination for the MICE sector. With an aim to become the "Tourism Capital of Asia" by 2006, Thailand invested heavily in promoting MICE businesses (TCEB, 2013a, 2013b, 2013c) and turning popular tourist destinations, such as Phuket, into MICE business centres (Campiranon, 2006; TCEB, 2013a). Moreover, several additional improvements in the early 2000s, such as an expanded and improved internal infrastructure, have also contributed to Thailand's importance as a MICE destination. Prior to COVID, MICE was Thailand's second-fastest growing sector (Hua & Batra, 2015) in one of the country's most prominent industries (Sangpikul & Kim, 2009; Kim et al., 2011; TCEB, 2018).

Thai MICE businesses have gained popularity for a number of reasons. These include the fact that Thailand has unique geographical surroundings and a wide array of traditional cultures (TCEB, 2014), is perceived as providing a safe and hospitable environment, and has a very good value for money as well as providing comfortable accessibility (Rogers, 2008). Another of the contributing factors to the substantial growth of the MICE industry in Thailand is the country's location, situated in the heart of Southeast Asia (Campiranon, 2006). Since 2003 Thailand has been listed as one of the top 5 countries for MICE business in ASEAN states (Akkhaphin, 2016); however, it has been ranked as the top destination among MICE visitors from 20 countries (TCEB, 2018).

Since the MICE sector has been recognised by the Thai government as one of the major sources of national revenue and a catalyst to a renewal of the Thai economy, TCEB has invested heavily in the sector. In 2017, as part of Thailand's 12th National Economic and Social Development Plan, TCEB announced government funding of 16 million US dollars for the business tourism sector (TCEB, 2017). This investment appears to have paid off. Along with growth in global and Thai tourism generally, in the 2016 fiscal year the MICE industry fared better than it did in the previous year, with the number of overseas MICE delegates in Thailand recorded at 1,273,465, an increase of 16.19% over the 2015 figure of 1,095,995 (Thammasat University Research and Consultancy Institute (TU- RAC), 2016). Generated revenue was estimated at 3,075.47 million US dollars, approximately 29.78% higher than the 2,933.40 million US dollars recorded in the year 2015. Furthermore, spending per head of MICE travellers to Thailand in the year 2016 rose in all sub-sectors: corporate meetings increased by 34.42%, incentives by 17.84%, conventions by 5.59%, exhibitions by 22.64%, and trade visitors by 7.66% (TU-RAC, 2016; Teerakunpisut, 2018).

Islamic MICE market in Thailand

In addition to the general growth that is witnessed in the Thai MICE industry, there is substantial growth within the Islamic MICE market, supported by more general increases in the number of domestic and international Muslim tourists in Thailand. In addition to the 5.8 million Thais who are Muslim (Sateemae et al., 2015), the country is receiving growing numbers of tourists from Muslim majority countries (TCEB, 2015, 2016, 2018). Given the antici-pated increase in business travellers from the Muslim world and the prospect of increased intra-regional tourism following greater ASEAN economic integra-tion, Muslim MICE travelers represent a huge market to be tapped by Thai businesses and the Thai-Muslim community in particular (TCEB, 2018; Teera-kunpisut, 2018).

The focus of this chapter is on the MICE industry in Southern Thai-land and the extent to which it caters to the Muslim MICE market. It is apparent that MICE is a growing segment in the Thai tourism industry and economy, and Muslim tourists are viewed as one of the most crucial travel markets within the tourism sector. In terms of MICE tourism specifically, in 2016 MICE attracted nearly one million Islamic attendees, which was an increase of 65.43% from 2013 (TCEB, 2016). Indeed, TCEB (2016) indicates that Muslim business travellers are increasingly significant to the MICE industry. However, this large Muslim market is relatively unexplored as a target segment in the MICE industry. Although the MICE industry has expanded internationally over recent decades, the sector has been largely under-researched, especially with respect to Islamic tourism (Altareri, 2016; Teerakunpisut, 2018).

The MICE industry in Thailand, a predominantly Buddhist nation, is cur-rently facing the challenge of diversity because it is expected to provide ameni-ties with options for a variety of customers to observe their religious obligations when attending a meeting or an event. Furthermore, as Muslim-friendly ser-vice has emerged as a new trend in the MICE industry, there is a lack of theo-retical studies in the area of halal hospitality amenities in the MICE context, researching the choices staff make when catering for Muslim customers and the views of this group of clientele during their event. This makes it difficult to understand Muslim requirements and what is needed to improve services to reflect Islamic principles as the MICE industry develops in Thailand. The focus of this study is to recognise the growing number of Muslim clienteles worldwide for the MICE industry in Thailand, and to investigate how focus should be given to improving current services and facilities that comply with Islamic principles.

MICE in Southern Thailand and the growth in the Islamic market

While all of Thailand stands to benefit from growth in the Muslim MICE mar-ket in Thailand, Southern Thailand is well positioned to cater to this demand. About 24.5% of the population in Southern Thailand is Muslim, making Muslims the largest indigenous minority group in the country (Anderson, 2010). The area is known for its "cultural complexity and ethnic diversity" (Horstmann, 2004, p. 76), and since the late 1990s it has experienced sig-nificant tourism and trade growth across national borders (Boonyauva, 2014). This is largely due to its proximity to Malaysia, which, as will be discussed later, serves as a gateway to other Muslim countries, including Indonesia and Brunei.

Thailand – and Southern Thailand in particular – has great potential for Islamic tourism and hospitality because it is close to Indonesia and Malaysia and also offers unique halal cuisines, arts, heritage, and insight into the unique culture of the Malay Muslims. With a diverse population, geography, and easy accessibility, Southern Thailand has been one of the most popular MICE destinations for domestic and international Muslim tourists (TCEB, 2018).

In the south of Thailand, the majority of overseas Muslim tourists are from Malaysia and Indonesia. Geographic proximity, favourable currency exchange rates, ease of passport requirements for Malaysians since July 2010 and Indonesians more recently to enter Thailand all contribute to this tourist growth (TCEB, 2014). According to the TU-RAC (2016) a combined total of more than 230,000 tourists visited Southern Thailand from the predominantly Muslim nations of Malaysia and Indonesia in 2015, more than double the 165,000 tourists who visited Southern Thailand from these countries in 2014. As more than 50% of the Malaysian and Indonesian populations are Muslim (Mastercard CrescentRating, 2016), it can be expected that the number of Muslim tourists will continue to increase, and Muslim tourists will continue to be an important niche market in the southern region of Thailand (Teerakunpisut, 2018).

In addition, three international airports in Southern Thailand offer direct flights to a range of worldwide destinations, including countries with majority Islamic populations, such as Malaysia, Saudi Arabia, Kuwait, Qatar, and the UAE. While the easy accessibility of Southern Thailand makes it one of the world's leading Muslim tourist destinations (Mansouri, 2014) and even though the number of international airports and shopping centres that provide halal food and Muslim-friendly services are increasing in big cities, it is still difficult to find faith-based amenities in most MICE venues in Thailand, including in Southern Thailand. Indeed, the MICE industry faces substantial challenges in catering to Muslim tourists' demands. Therefore, it is urgent to create awareness among the local MICE industry about what halal is and how to prepare facilities, halal food, and delivery services that will meet Muslim visitors' requirements.

Given Islam is a complete way of life and 94.6% of Thai people are Buddhist (Liamputtong, 2014), developing a MICE industry that successfully caters to Muslim clientele is not easy. However, as Samori and Sabtu (2014) point out, one way to attract Muslim customers is by creating special amenities that relate to the principles embedded in the Quran, by which many Islamic consumers abide. While there is a great deal of diversity with respect to religious adherence and practice, as with any religion, Islam involves comprehensive standards, protocols, and guidelines, which inform the lives of its followers (Teng et al., 2013). Services that are consumed by Muslims must meet the general Islamic principles known as "halal", which, as discussed earlier, is a word derived from Arabic that means "allowed, lawful and permitted" (Marzuki et al., 2014, p. 292). It follows therefore that hospitality and customer services for Muslim clientele need to be permissible to be consumed under Islamic law. This means not only that all food should be halal, with no alcoholic beverages served, but it also means the creation of "the right ambiance", architecture and interior and exterior (Hall & Prayag, 2020). Generally, it seems that if the MICE industry is prepared to make Muslim attendees feel at ease in this way, it would attract more Islamic customers (Teerakunpisut, 2018).

Existing hospitality and tourism services catering to Muslim tourists

Some attempts have already been made to tailor tourism and hospitality services in Thailand to the needs of Muslim Thais and Muslim tourists. For example, at both Suvarnabhumi and Don Mueang International Airports in Bangkok, the capital city of Thailand, more prayer rooms have been made available for Muslim travellers in recent years. In addition, an Islamic prayer room is available at a number of large-scale shopping complexes in nearly all tourist-popular provinces throughout Thailand (Mastercard CrescentRating, 2016). With respect to halal food, halal restaurants are growing in big cities of the country such as Bangkok, Chiang Mai, and Phuket, and a number of major restaurants have obtained halal certification. Popular Thai foods such as Pad Thai (noodles stir-fried with tamarind sauce) and Khao Pat (fried rice) have also been certified halal so that Muslim visitors can enjoy popular Thai food (Boonchom, 2016). In addition, advancements in mobile phone technology have contributed to the comfort of Muslim tourists, with various applications providing information on the location of halal food restaurants in the area.

Despite many significant changes in practice across a range of tourism and hospitality service providers, the adoption of halal certification, which is provided by The Central Islamic Committee of Thailand (CICOT), at MICE venue kitchens is slow (Teerakunpisut, 2018). For many MICE venues, the adoption of the standards required by CICOT may involve renovating premises and new facilities, which in turn results in them having to increase venue costs. Hotels in the south of Thailand that incorporate Muslim-friendly services and facilities for Islamic customers are mostly rated two and three stars and most are issued with halal certificates from the Central Islamic Committee Office of Thailand specifically for the hotel kitchen. In contrast, due to their standardised service models, most four- and five-star hotels that are franchised by overseas companies based in the United States of America, Singapore, and the United Kingdom do not have any opportunity to run the business according to halal and Islamic compliance (Teerakunpisut, 2018). Most of the five-star hotels in Southern Thailand are generally not owned by locals but by overseas investors (Mahamud, 2014), making halal certification of luxury hotels very difficult.

Halal tourism involves a new approach for many hospitality venues and poses a number of challenges. However, given the growth in the Muslim market, catering to the needs of Muslim tourists (Mohsin et al., 2016) presents important opportunities for the tourism industry in Thailand given the increased number of Muslims travelling internationally (Puangniyom et al., 2017; Hall & Prayag, 2020). As consuming halal food and amenities are important for Muslims, even when travelling, it is important for the MICE industry to deal with the challenges of making such services available at big and small venues in order to sustain Islamic MICE tourism in Thailand. As such, more needs to be known about the service that MICE venues currently provide, as well as what it is that Muslim MICE customers want.

Identifying the gaps in industry-based and academic knowledge

There are limited studies into Islamic-oriented MICE services and facilities, even though the number of such amenities is growing (Mohsin et al., 2016). Han et al. (2019), who examined halal-friendly destination attributes in South Korea, emphasise that the way in which destinations address Islamic tourists' needs is diverse depending on their perception and understanding of those demands. Further, a study carried out by Mansouri (2014, p. 20) on selected hotels in Bangkok, Thailand, finds that "the investment and adoption of business practices and financial based planning according to the principles of Islam and Shari'a illustrates the potentialities which have been established and are in the process of development". However, no previous study has been carried out to examine the perceptions and experiences of Muslim attendees in the MICE industry in Thailand – that is, whether those potentialities match with the customers' own needs and wants.

While there is substantial general research on Thai Muslims (Putthongchai, 2013), specific research on Muslim MICE customers in Thailand is very limited. Although there are studies on Islamic hospitality services in Malaysia (Hall & Prayag, 2020), which seems to correspond with the Thai context, there are no firm guidelines for MICE operators on how to cater to Islamic customers. This may result from the fact that, as with most religions, there are variations in the levels of religious practice and adherence that different Muslims adopt. There are also regional variations, with Islam in Thailand being identified as having different characteristics to Islam in other parts of the world (Von Feigenblatt, 2010). At the same time, Thailand is, as already mentioned, a predominantly Buddhist country, and Thai identity is often tied to Buddhism (Maud, 2011). It is likely that these factors have an impact on how Muslim-friendly services and facilities are developed in the MICE industry in Thailand.

Methods

In order to address the lack of literature on the provision of MICE Muslim-friendly amenities in the research and explore ways in which Islamic hospitality can be developed in venues, this study took a mixed-methods approach. Identifying that quantitative research was beneficial for the incorporation of a large number of contextual variables but that qualitative research would be useful in providing for richly textured data, we opted to carry out interviews that utilised both close-ended and open-ended questions. In order to capture Muslim and non-Muslim travellers, these were carried out with 18 Buddhist staff, 44 Muslim staff, and 62 Muslim clients in 3 key locations in Southern Thailand. Venues in Songhkla, Krabi, and Phuket were chosen as research areas. The interview data were then analysed to identify key themes and trends, and the demographic data obtained through quantitative questioning was used to compare the results across key variables like nationality and gender. As this study incorporated quantitative and qualitative data, an analysis of the former was performed by the computer program Statistical Product and Service Solutions (SPSS, Version 20.0), whilst for the latter thematic analysis was used.

The research questions began with the notions of "religion" (whether "Islam" or "Buddhism") and "hospitality". When it came to the ideas of 'Muslim-friendly service' in the MICE industry in Southern Thailand, under-examined management issues and also the notion of 'Buddhism', which is regarded as the state religion of Thailand, tended to be contested. Consequently, this study was concerned with highlighting these notions. However, to promote the venue amenity that is seen as halal in the Thai context, understanding of Islamic follower requirements when attending a meeting and an event is essential, and this understanding should be considered as the centre of further MICE halal hospitality and customer service research.

The vast majority of the participants in this study openly shared their religious beliefs and practices and inner thoughts and feelings about the role of religion in their lives. What resulted was a picture of diverse, individualised approaches to religious observance, with behaviour, dress and eating all identified as being influenced by religious principles. In addition to the face-to-face interviews used for accessing the views of MICE staff and Muslim customers, this approach helped the researchers to understand that both Buddhism and Islam are different in many features of prescribing to religious observance for individuals, groups, and societies. This meant that these two groups of participants deliver their meaning and belonging within their culture and link them to concepts of diversity.

Findings

Power of ethnic diversity

As such, the power of ethnic diversity that likely makes catering to Muslim customers more complex has emerged from the interview data. Although this sociocultural phenomenon is not a new power that creates complexity in the current hospitality conditions in Thailand, the growing number of Muslims in the MICE market in demanding amenities that abide by Shari'a rules and a great lack of understanding of Islam can lead to cultural tensions. The MICE sector is currently facing the challenge of diversity because it is expected to provide amenities with options for a variety of customers to observe their religious obligations when attending meetings and events. Further, from an academic perspective little is known about the area of halal hospitality in the MICE context, either from the perspective of staff or clients.

The vast majority (85%) of the Buddhist and Muslim staff who participated in the research indicated that both religious groups had contributed to the development of the rapidly growing hospitality sector in Thailand, including MICE. However, 40% of Muslim staff participants argued that Muslim Thais generally have not received adequate recognition for their role.

Two Buddhist participants, both female and of Chinese-Thai background, expressed their views as follows:

> For MICE Buddhist staff, we practise our religion mentally and do not carry out any religious rituals at work, except on very special occasions. These are rare and involve inviting monks to conduct a holy ceremony and receive food that we have provided. However, I am aware that the five pillars of Islam are significant to all Muslims and I am also mindful of the fact that praying is important to them. Although my boss and I are Buddhist, we allow all Muslim male staff to go to the mosque to pray on Fridays if they do not have work duties. If they do, then they are still allowed to pray at the workplace.
>
> (PKB 1)

> Inevitably I have less in common with my Muslim colleagues than I do with my Buddhist ones. Also, I have found that my Muslim staff are much more likely to interrupt their duties due to their religious obligations than their Buddhist co-workers are. In other words, Muslims, especially males, take more time off work on average than Buddhists, whether it is for their individual prayer routine, or to attend congregational prayers on Friday.
>
> (KBB 2)

Following on from the general stated position of management, two Buddhist male participants of around 45 years old spoke in more detail. Both are senior managers and work in Songkhla but were born and raised in central Thailand. They explained:

> This venue is for people of every faith and no matter whether some (Muslims) cover their hair and neck but not the face, and others (non-Muslim) may dress in western style, they are all treated with the same respect. Although I was born a Buddhist, I am not religious, and do not consider Buddha to be a God I have to worship, asking him to give me a good life.

I put effort and energy into ensuring that people of all religions are treated fairly and with respect at this venue.

(SKB 10)

Even though I respect Buddha as a great man and worship him at the temple, I am aware that for Muslims, worshipping their God plays a vital role in their lives. On this basis, a prayer room has been provided for them in this venue. Furthermore, female Muslim staff are allowed to wear the hijab and male staff are allowed to go to the mosque every Friday afternoon. However, as this venue has no kitchen and all food and beverages are ordered from nearby restaurants for every event, all staff are supposed to have their meals outside the venue.

(SKB 3)

Having looked at the perspectives of Buddhist staff participants, it is pertinent to turn to the views of their Muslim colleagues across the three MICE venues. In regard to being able to follow their religious faith while working at MICE venues, one female Muslim staff participant, wearing a brightly coloured hijab with normal western clothing, said that she was the first in her family, of either gender, to have received a university education. She emphasised that Islam will always come first for her as she is not prepared to compromise her religious faith. She explained she had had the opportunity to work in Chiang Mai, the best-known tourist destination of the northern province of Thailand:

As most Muslim Thais elsewhere, I practice my faith in a peaceful manner and I am proud to call myself a Muslim. I turned down work at a five-star MICE hotel in Chiang Mai around seven years ago because I was not allowed to wear my hijab. My father, an Islamic school headmaster, suggested that I work at a very small Muslim-owned resort in Phuket, my hometown. Here, staff are not allowed to wear revealing garments, and those who wish to wear their hijab may do so.

(PKM 12)

The findings from the previous interview with the Muslim female staff participant show that she exercises her freedom to dress as she wants in Thailand, where there are no laws restricting her from covering herself more than non-Muslim Thai women. It should be noted that, although Thai law allows people of religious faith to wear the clothing of their choice, some workplaces are less tolerant, stipulating that Islamic clothing (such as hijabs) are not allowed. Similarly, men in Thailand who want to wear long beards will not be given employment in the MICE industry, as Thai people have a mistrust of excessive facial hair.

When asked what they knew about their religion, most Muslim staff participants (80%) mentioned that knowing what is considered to be right and what is wrong in regard to Islamic norms and values is of paramount importance to their Muslim way of life. Two participants stated:

> Before I became a mother, I used to think it was not important to pray and wear the hijab, but now I have two small sons, I realise I was wrong and I neglected my Islamic duties in the past. Since this realisation I have devoted more time to reciting the Quran and have discovered that I like it very much. I have also become more aware of Muslim practices, which are allowed or forbidden. However, as I have so many Buddhist friends and feel comfortable with much of the Thai culture, I still participate in some Thai celebrations, which some Muslims do not, but such participation is acceptable only under certain conditions.
>
> (PKM 19)

It is interesting that once the previous participant became a mother, she began to be more mindful of her religious duties. This was echoed by a 40-year-old Muslim male working in marketing:

> My father is a Muslim, but only in name, and my mother was a Buddhist, but converted to Islam when my father asked her to. Both my parents have taught me a little about what is acceptable and not acceptable in Islam. During my teenage years, I felt that my religion limited my freedom, as I liked going to the pub and drinking whiskey, which is clearly forbidden in Islam. However, since I became an adult, my religious point of view has changed and I rely mainly on my religious beliefs for guidance on questions about right and wrong. I am aware of what is prohibited in Islam and I do not have the authority to change it, and anyway I believe that Allah would not teach what it is impossible to practice. The problem usually comes from people around us.
>
> (KBM 10)

The previous interview extracts reflect the responses of the majority of Muslim participants in this study: that they are likely to observe their Islamic practices, such as halal consumption and daily rituals that help them to lead a good Muslim life. However, a small number of Muslim participants (both those who have spent most of their lives studying Islam and those who were born in a Muslim community) state that they are totally 100% committed to all Islamic principles and set themselves the highest standards in carrying out these obligations.

What Islam means to me: diversity in MICE customer beliefs and practices

Most religions are viewed by their followers as a way to provide meaning to life, and Muslims generally believe that only Islam can provide the answer to that question. However, it is evident from the interviews conducted in this study that the participants consider Islam as being more than just a religion but rather a complete way of life that has a direct effect on their wellbeing. The vast majority reported that they felt happier and more satisfied with their lives as a result of embracing Islam. This sentiment is illustrated by the following comments from two participants: a young local female customer in Songkhla, followed by a middle-aged male Malaysian customer in Krabi:

> Islam is crucial for me. I have always felt very happy and proud to have been born a Muslim and mindful of the fact that I can only achieve my goals in life when I strictly follow God's guidance. This means that by following the guidelines of Islam, I am guaranteed a satisfying life while awaiting eternal happiness.
>
> (SK 5)

It is evident from the interviews that participants believe that Islam can not only help meet their spiritual needs but also improve their mental, emotional, and physical health. They reported that their faith, through giving them a good connection with God, allowed them to enjoy life more, while making them better, more relaxed people. One male participant from Krabi around 25 years of age reported:

> Day-to-day issues strongly affect my stress levels and mood. By practicing my religion, I can be thankful for every day and look forward to a better tomorrow since worshipping God changes my outlook on life as a whole.
>
> (KB 2)

Islam is considered by the vast majority of participants as a religion that covers every aspect of life: moral, physical, emotional, economic, and spiritual. It is evident from the interviews conducted in this study that the Muslim customers believe that their relationship with Allah begins in the womb and continues after death. Their belief that Allah has created them brings with it an accompanying sense that they are duty bound to undertake certain responsibilities that need to be done according to Allah's guidance. Most participants reported that, by carrying out these responsibilities with a true sense of commitment, other people will be affected, along with nature and other creatures. This can lead to well-balanced individuals, families and eventually a society in which there will be peace. This is the ultimate purpose of Islam, which is that all participants will worship Allah and thus please him. This is illustrated by a middle-aged female local customer from Phuket, in the following comments:

> In general, my tasks include worshipping and believing in Allah, including making a concerted effort to protect myself from harmful thought and actions, keeping good relationships with other people, showing mercy to

all living creatures, and utilising natural resources and everything around me in a proper manner.

(PK 8)

For many participants, their main objective in wishing to remain within an Islamic environment and by surrounding themselves with Muslim friends seems to be to protect themselves from negative influences and improve their Islamic way of life. Of course, doing this within a MICE venue, which is designed to cater to people of every faith and with diverse beliefs, lifestyles, and behaviours is difficult. To better understand how diversity in Muslim customer beliefs and practices impacts the lives of Muslim customers when visiting MICE venues, more attention needs to be given to the barriers MICE customers feel they face when trying to practice their religion while attending events.

Conclusion

With regards to a discussion of the perspectives of both MICE staff and Muslim customers, this study attempts to explore their awareness of Islamic principles and their perceptions of the halal amenities provided to accommodate Muslims in the MICE industry. The results revealed that, although a number of Muslim customer participants, both locally and internationally, emphasise individualism with respect to practice, which leads to many Muslims observing religious requirements at different levels, they appear not to have faced any difficulties following Islam. However, there were concerns raised by a small number of non-Muslim staff participants emphasising that a number of Muslim customers are still not offered appropriate Muslim-friendly services and facilities, and a few were aware that such services would increase venue costs. In contrast, due to the high cost involved in fully meeting the Muslim requirements and recognition of MICE as a secular business sector, the vast majority of Buddhist participants emphasised that the MICE sector is there to serve the whole community, and not all business travellers want to stay in a venue primarily designed for Muslims. While MICE customer policy generally strives to ensure that individuals of all religious beliefs are welcome, the vast majority of Muslim customer participants felt that the MICE sector in Southern Thailand is not viewed as a progressive Muslim-friendly industry, although it helps them to enlarge their businesses, to share experiences, and to promote their products.

With regard to a discussion of main interview findings from Muslim customer participants, in relation to their assessments of venues and whether they feel that their religious values and principles are respected and/or prioritised, including the impact of Islamic requirements (such as halal food, prayer rooms, and bidet showers) in the MICE industry, the research revealed that as Muslim participants come from a variety of backgrounds, and there are varying degrees of Islamic religiosity that influence their expectations regarding Islamic hospitality services and facilities; as Muslims they have a duty to follow Islamic principles in order to meet the requirements of their faith. As such, many Muslim customers in this study wish to remain within an Islamic environment by surrounding themselves with Muslim friends; however, doing this within a MICE venue that is designed to cater to people of every faith and diverse beliefs, lifestyles, and behaviours is difficult. Although the majority of participants who are repeat Muslim customers, and most are Thai, would hope for a spiritually friendly experience that is in line with Islamic teachings when attending events, they do not necessarily insist on only attending events that are in harmony with Muslim faith. While all Muslim participants reported that most MICE venues have made little effort to provide halal amenities, most overseas Muslims in this study seemed to be more satisfied and less aggressive than local participants, especially in demanding halal food that was prepared by Muslims. Through these findings it appeared that local Muslims were more concerned with creating an environment that is visibly Islamic and expressed a strong wish for better Islamic-focused services, whereas visitors to Thailand appear to be happier to accept a change of environment, culture, and religious traditions. On this basis, it appears that, if such amenities were provided, MICE venues would become more attractive to local Muslims who appear to feel more strongly about the way in which the local MICE sector should address their needs.

References

Akkhaphin, S. (2016). *An evaluation of the potential of Thailand as a MICE (Meeting, Incentives, Conventions, and Exhibitions) industry hub for the international convention industry in Asia* [Doctoral dissertation, Liverpool John Moores University].

Altareri, K. (2016). *Development of multicultural MICE tourism in the Middle East: The case of Saudi Arabia* [Unpublished Doctor of Business Administration thesis, Victoria University].

Anderson, W. W. (2010). *Mapping Thai Muslims community dynamics and change on the Andaman Coast.* Silkworm Books.

Boonchom, O. (2016). *Muslim businesses in Bangkok, Thailand* [Unpublished Doctor of Philosophy thesis, Universiti Utara Malaysia].

Boonyauva, K. (2014). *Corporate social responsibility and Southern Thai culture: A study of multinational corporations in Southern Thailand* [Unpublished Doctor of Philosophy thesis, RMIT University].

Campiranon, K. (2006, September 27–29). *Understanding crisis vulnerability of the MICE sector: A case study of Thailand* [paper presentation]. Global Events Congress, University of Queensland Press, Brisbane.

Hall, C. M., & Prayag, G. (Eds.). (2020). *The Routledge handbook of halal hospitality and Islamic tourism.* Routledge.

Han, H., Al-ansi, A., Olya, H. G. T., & Kim, W. (2019). Exploring halal-friendly destination attributes in South Korea: Perceptions and behaviors of Muslim travelers toward a non-Muslim destination. *Tourism Management, 71*, 151–164. https://doi.org/10.1016/j.tourman.2018.10.010

Horstmann, A. (2004). Ethnohistorical perspectives on Buddhist-Muslim relations and coexistence in Southern Thailand: From shared cosmos to the emergence of hatred? *Sojourn: Journal of Social Issues in Southeast Asia, 19*(1), 76–99. www.muse.jhu.edu/article/400297.

Hua, N., & Batra, A. (2015, June). *Embracing AEC: A brief assessment of MICE sector in Thailand* [paper presentation]. 16th International Joint World Cultural Tourism Conference 2015, 2nd World Tourism Conference.

Kim, S. S., Yoon, S., & Kim, Y. (2011). Competitive positioning among international convention cities in the East Asian region. *Journal of Convention & Event Tourism*, *12*(2), 86–105. https://doi.org/10.1080/15470148.2011.566760

Liamputtong, P. (2014). *Contemporary socio-cultural and political perspectives in Thailand*. Springer.

Mahamud, T. (2014, June 16–17). The potentials of Islamic economic of Muslim minority in Thailand. In *4th International conference on management, 4th ICM 2014 proceedings* (pp. 372–380). Kuta Beach Heritage Hotel, Bali, Indonesia.

Mansouri, S. (2014, January 30–31). *Role of halal tourism ideology in destination competitiveness: A study on selected hotels in Bangkok, Thailand* [paper presentation]. International Conference on Law, Education and Humanities (ICLEH'14), Pattaya, Thailand.

Marzuki, S. Z. S., Hall, C. M., & Ballantine, P. W. (2014). Measurement of restaurant manager expectations toward Halal certification using factor and cluster analysis. *Procedia – Social and Behavioral Sciences*, *121*, 291–303. https://doi.org/10.1016/j.sbspro.2014.01.1130

Mastercard CrescentRating (2016). *Global Muslim travel index*. CrescentRating and Mastercard Asia Pacific.

Maud, J. (2011). Sacred tourism and the state: Paradoxes of cross-border religious patronage in southern Thailand. *MMG Working Paper* 11–04. http://hdl.handle.net/11858/00-001M-0000-000F-49C4-6

Mohsin, A., Ramli, N., & Alkhulayfi, B. A. (2016). Halal tourism: Emerging opportunities. *Tourism Management Perspectives*, *19*, 137–143. https://doi.org/10.1016/j.tmp.2015.12.010

Puangniyom, P., Swangcheng, N., & Mahamud, T. (2017). *Halal tourism strategy to promote sustainable cultural tourism in Thailand* [paper presentation]. CEBU International Conference on Studies in Arts, Social Sciences and Humanities, Cebu, Philippines.

Putthongchai, S. (2013). *What is it like to be Muslim in Thailand? A case study of Thailand through Muslim professionals' perspectives* [Doctoral thesis, University of Exeter]. https://ore.exeter.ac.uk/repository/handle/10871/9321

Rogers, T. (2008). *Conferences and convention: A global industry* (2nd ed.). Butterworth-Heinemann.

Samori, Z., & Sabtu, N. (2014). Developing halal standard for Malaysian hotel industry: An exploratory study. *Procedia – Social and Behavioral Sciences*, *12*, 144–157. https://doi.org/10.1016/j.sbspro.2014.01.1116

Sangpikul, A., & Kim, S. S. (2009). An overview and identification of barriers affecting the meeting and convention industry in Thailand. *Journal of Convention & Event Tourism*, *10*(3), 185–210. https://doi.org/10.1080/15470140903131822

Sateemae, S., Abdel-Monem, T., & Sateemae, M. (2015). Religiosity and social problems among Muslim adolescents in Southern Thailand. *Journal of Muslim Mental Health*, *9*(2). https://doi.org/10.3998/jmmh.10381607.0009.201

Teerakunpisut, S. (2018). *An examination of the influence of Islam on hospitality and customer service standards in the Meetings, Incentives, Conventions and Exhibitions (MICE) industry in southern Thailand* [Doctoral dissertation, Western Sydney University].

Teng, P. K., Jusoh, W. J. W., Siong, H. K., & Mesbahi, M. M. (2013). *Awareness, recognition and intention: Insights from a non-Muslim consumer survey regarding halal labeled food products in Malaysia*. 3rd International Conference on Management (3rd ICM 2013) Proceedings, Vol. 10–11, June, Hydro Hotel, Penang, Malaysia.

Thailand Convention & Exhibition Bureau (TCEB). (2013a). *Introduction to MICE industry (MICE 101)*. TCEB.

Thailand Convention & Exhibition Bureau (TCEB). (2013b). ASEAN Corner Chiang Mai as a world-class MICE destination: News in brief. *MICE Journal, 1*. TCEB.

Thailand Convention & Exhibition Bureau (TCEB). (2013c). Asian century: The age of MICE ASIA. *MICE Journal, 2*. TCEB.

Thailand Convention & Exhibition Bureau (TCEB). (2014). Thailand's rich choices of convention destinations. *MICE Journal, 3*. TCEB.

Thailand Convention & Exhibition Bureau (TCEB). (2015). *Thailand's MICE industry report 2015*. TCEB.

Thailand Convention & Exhibition Bureau (TCEB). (2016). *Thailand's MICE industry report 2016*. TCEB.

Thailand Convention & Exhibition Bureau (TCEB). (2018). *TCEB annual report 2017*. TCEB.

Thammasat University Research Consultancy (TU-RAC). (2016). *MICE Thailand report*. Thammasat University, Bangkok, Thailand.

Von Feigenblatt, O. F. (2010). The Muslim Malay community in southern Thailand: A 'small people' facing existential uncertainty. *Ritsumeikan Journal of Asia Pacific Studies, 27*, 53–63.

World Tourism Organization (WTO). (2012). *MICE industry – an Asia-Pacific perspective*. WTO.

Part VI

Conclusions

17 Conclusion

Emerging trends and future prospects in the muslim travel market

Siamak Seyfi, C. Michael Hall and
S. Mostafa Rasoolimanesh

Introduction

This volume has provided an overview of a number of different dimensions and trends in the contemporary Muslim travel market. As such it highlights the range of different Muslim experiences of travel that exist depending on country of origin and destination, culture, interpretive tradition and position, gender and sexuality, among many other factors. This situation stresses that, while there are clearly commonalities in travel and tourism consumption practices, there are also many differences and reinforces to readers; as Yosry (2021) noted in other contexts, this observation regarding Muslim travel practices provides yet further 'evidence to the rest of the world that Islam should not be defined by the narrow perceptions of the ideologues', wherever they are from.

The religious commonalities that identify followers of Islam should therefore not be seen as providing for undifferentiated tourist behaviours and motivations, even though this is arguably portrayed as such in much of the literature, especially that written by Muslims or those based in Muslim majority countries (Hall & Prayag, 2020a). Instead we are faced with a reality of a rich tapestry of travel practices that deserve a much more informed discussion than that seemingly heavily influenced by often very conservative interpretations from political and religious institutions and leaders (Razzaq et al., 2016; Hall & Prayag, 2020a). These issues will be discussed in the context of the current debates associated with Muslim leisure behaviour while travelling.

Muslim-friendly Tourism

Several studies have suggested that the Muslim-friendly tourism (MFT) market has increasingly become one of the most rapidly growing sectors worldwide and a significant niche market (e.g., El-Gohary, 2016; Mohsin et al., 2016; Arasli et al., 2021; Papastathopoulos, 2022). According to the Mastercard-CrescentRating study (2018), there were 131 million Muslim arrivals worldwide in 2017, which was expected to account for 10% of the global travel market by 2020. Although this increasing number fell to 42 million in 2020 as

DOI: 10.4324/9781003036296-23

a result of the COVID-19 pandemic, a more recent projection from the Global Muslim Travel Index (GMTI) 2021 (Mastercard-CrescentRating, 2021, p. 11) shows that 'the Muslim travel market will recover up to 80% of the 2019 levels in 2023'.

For Jafari and Scott (2014), such growth could be explained by greater hedonic consumption (e.g., recreation, entertainment, and seeing new places) as well as religious motives such as the Hajj and Umrah of Muslim tourists. Indeed, it is important to stress that the vast majority of motives of Muslim leisure travellers are arguably no different to those of secular tourists (Razak et al., 2020). However, while growth in this significant market is undoubtedly occurring, both the nature of the market as well as the notion of growth itself require a more critical analysis than what is often the case, otherwise comments regarding Muslim market growth will start to resemble the oft-stated undergraduate repetition of 'tourism being the world's largest industry'. Repeating something often enough does not make it true. In the case of potential market size growth is representative of population increase, but that does not necessarily translate to increasing travel by Muslims. Instead other factors such as accessibility, income levels, consumption practices and regulation may be far more significant. Similarly, the very notion of what constitutes a Muslim traveller requires more detailed interrogation, with travel by people from some Muslim-majority countries being counted as Muslim travellers on the basis of state definition rather than personal belief systems. While there is insufficient discussion of what might be described as secular or lapsed Muslims or the notion that Islamic religiosity – and therefore the religious dimensions of travel – it may be better understood on a continuum than as a black/white or yes/no concept (Marranci, 2010; Martin, 2010; Anand, 2014; Bayraklı & Hafez, 2019; Vliek, 2020).

With the emergence of the Muslim travel market, various terminology and concepts have been used to refer to either the whole Muslim travel market or its sub-segments, often interchangeably and with little conceptual clarity (Razak et al., 2020). In popular and academic literature, terms like MFT, halal travel, Islamic tourism, sharia tourism, and halal tourism have been regularly used. However, depending on who is using the terms and in what context, the focus of these terminologies has shifted. MFT tends to refer to the tourism segment, which caters to the faith-based needs of Muslim travellers (Razzaq et al., 2016; Hall & Prayag, 2020b). Mohsin et al. (2016) defined MFT as tourism products and services that meet Muslim tourists' needs, such as devotional facilities and dietary restrictions, while adhering to Islamic law. Although the terms halal-friendly and Muslim-friendly are interchangeable, Muslim-friendly service/ facility has been widely suggested by the media and international organisations. For instance, in its report on understanding the demand and supply sides of MFT in Organisation of Islamic Cooperation (OIC) member countries, the Standing Committee for Economic and Commercial Cooperation of the Organization of Islamic Cooperation (COMCEC; 2016) presented a conceptual framework of MFT in terms of three components: core faith-based travel

needs; consumer demands with respect to Muslim travel motivations; and supply side key themes (travel and hospitality services and facilities). According to
COMCEC (2016, p. 19) this framework 'allows destinations and services to
plan a coherent product adaptation/development strategy aimed at the MFT
market'. Battour and Ismail (2016) also suggested four specific attributes for
MFT; Islamic facilities, Islamic morality in general, halalness, and gambling and
alcohol ban. However, such suggestions highlight the way in MFT should best
be understood as a continuum rather than absolute categories (Razzaq et al.,
2016) as well as issues over whether notions such as Islamic morality or halalness, are externally prescribed or determined by the travellers themselves in line
with their own conscience and relationship to God. This is an important issue
given that particular interpretations by governmental and religious authorities
will have implications for the management of product offerings as well as the
external moral framing as to the appropriateness of traveller behaviour and
destination selection.

Issues of definition can also affect marketing strategies. Khan and Callanan
(2017) examined issues of definition in their study of the 'Halalification' of
tourism in the UK. In their content analysis they found no clear difference
between the use of terms (e.g. halal, Muslim friendly, Islamic, Sharia) in popular UK media, UK-based tour operators' websites, and strategies of destinations
popular with Muslim tourists. They also argued that the lack of a clear and
consistent use of terminology along with the lack of halal certification stand-
ardisation may have implications for consumer trust (Khan & Callanan, 2017),
clearly providing an important topic for future research.

While the OIC member states arguably have a competitive advantage for
attracting the major share of the MFT market, the recent growth of this market
as well as emerging non-OIC destinations (e.g., New Zealand. Taiwan, Korea,
Japan) have challenged the leadership of OIC destinations in the MFT segment
as well as potentially requiring a reassessment of Muslim traveller motivations
and tourism consumption practices. Recognising Muslim consumers' needs
is therefore crucial for articulating inclusive service quality and providing a
memorable experience in order to gain a competitive advantage. This is particularly significant as, in light of the COVID-19 pandemic, many countries
and destinations are focusing on the MFT market as part of economic recovery
strategies. For example, Mastercard-CrescentRating (2021) argued that Asia's
travel and hospitality sector should focus more on the halal tourism segment
to help the industry recover, since this section of the market was experiencing
a boom prior to the pandemic in countries such as Japan and Thailand. For
instance, the study of Han et al. (2019) on halal-friendly destination attributes
in South Korea found that almost 60% of international Muslim tourists visiting
South Korea indicated that the availability of halal services and products was
important in selecting this travel destination. Thus, this highlights the need
for hospitality industry stakeholders in non-Muslim countries to address the
specific demands of Muslim tourists and to provide services that are consistent
with their cultural and religious values. Further research is therefore required to

understand what differences exist in comparing between the profile of Muslim travellers between countries.

Millennials and the Muslim Travel Market

Given the relative young age of adherents of Islam compared to other religions, it is unsurprising that millennials have been identified as a significant segment and a key driver of Muslim travel market growth (Salam et al., 2019). The *Muslim millennial travel report 2017* of Mastercard-HalalTrip (2017) indicates that travel among this new generation of Muslims is rising as, with more disposable income, they seek more exotic experiences and far-flung destinations. This is particularly important as the global Muslim population is expected to grow further, with Muslims being the youngest of the major religious groups in the world, with an average age of 23 years – seven years younger than non-Muslims (Lipka, 2016) and with far more purchasing power. Muslims under the age of 30 account for a significant share of millennials in Muslim majority countries, and Muslims are expected to account for 29% of the global young population aged 15–29 (Annuar, 2018). The Mastercard-HalalTrip (2017) report emphasises the increasing importance of the next generation of Muslim travellers to the global tourism industry, as evidenced by shifting global socio-economic trends and potential pent-up demand. According to this study, total expenditure from Muslim millennial travellers (MMT) will exceed US$100 billion by 2025. The study of Abu Bakar et al. (2018b) on characteristics of MMT residing internationally also illustrated the distinct travel needs of this segment of the Muslim travel market. According to their study, MMT seek authentic, affordable, and accessible travel experiences with such travel patterns being observed in pre-trip preparations, during the trip and while sharing digital experiences (Abu Bakar et al., 2018b). Significantly, similar observation were noted by Oktadiana et al. (2020) and Cuesta-Valiño et al. (2020).

Several studies have also highlighted that the global halal tourism sector is driven by millennials (Annuar, 2018; Salam et al., 2019). Salam et al. (2019) argue that MMT place more value on halal certification and conclude that, for MMT, halal and shariah–compliance are the most essential factors in deciding where to eat. Janmohamed (2016) argues that the MMTs are tech-savvy, self-empowered, and enthusiastic consumers who openly embrace both faith and modernity in their identities. This potentially demonstrates how social media may be used in a variety of ways to cater halal products and services to MMTs. Abu Bakar et al. (2018a, p. 8) also noted that

> MMTs make themselves highly accessible and visible online when they travel and the internet serves as a digital bridge for them to easily retrieve information and share their experiences of halal destinations, photos and commentaries on food options online and through sharing applications.

As such, Muslim millennials clearly share many attributes with those of non-religious millennials, although further comparative study would be welcome.

Muslim Female Travellers

Muslim female travellers represent one of the fastest-growing segments within the Muslim travel market (Fajriyati et al., 2020; Oktadiana et al., 2020; Hosseini et al., 2021) and account for one of the top ten halal travel trends (Mastercard-CrescentRating, 2018). According to the Mastercard-CrescentRating (2019) *Muslim women in travel report 2019*, 63 million Muslim women travelled in 2018, spending $80 billion. Muslim women now account for 45% of the Muslim tourism market. For Tilley and Houston (2016), such a growth in the Muslim women travel segment is attributed to more flexibility and a wider variety of destination choices as a result of their increased economic and social independence. Although solo female traveling has been under academic scrutiny, as Hosseini et al. (2021) note, there is a limited available research on Muslim solo female travelers. Nevertheless, as Chapter 2 (this volume) indicates, there is substantial variation in gender related mobility among countries, particularly in terms of the capacity of female tourists to travel alone (Seyfi & Hall, 2019; Dalaman, 2021; Nikjoo et al., 2021; see also Chapters 10–13 this volume). Clearly, the contexts, constraints, and enablers of Muslim female travel require substantially more research, including the relationships that may exist between constraints in a domestic setting with stigmas of solo female traveling and the behaviours that are exhibited when travelling internationally.

Islamic Green Travel Consumption

In light of the existential risks posed by the climate crisis and global environmental change there is widespread interest in the development of more sustainable travel practices, with environmental concerns long regarded as linked to religious beliefs and values (Hope & Young, 1994). Rhama (2021) argues that Islamic teachings support sustainable development. In a similar vein, Sarigöllü (2009, p. 374) notes that the emphasis on fate in Muslim cultures 'would imply a more passive rather than a proactive stance' towards the environment. The empirical study of Rice (2006) on pro-environmental behaviours of citizens in Cairo, Egypt reported that Islamic religious teachings and religiosity were associated with pro-environmental behaviour, thus lending support to the presence of an Islamic environmental ethic.

Research on Muslim-friendly travel and environmentally friendly or sustainable tourism is limited. However, there is some suggestion that green consumption is becoming increasingly important as Muslim consumers seek more than simply halal food and accommodations and start looking for eco-friendly hotels, attractions, transport, and destinations. Thus, Battour et al. (2021) suggest that sustainable halal tourism might be implemented by destinations seeking to accommodate the demands of Muslim tourists. Rhama (2021, p. 3) argues that

> the potential of Muslim tourists to support sustainability could not only satisfy their religious duty but also tremendously support global needs of poverty reduction, empowerment, natural conservation, climate change mitigation and adaptation and any positive impact sustainability could bring.

The Mastercard-CrescentRating (2019) report also underlines that Muslims, like followers of other Abrahamic religions, have intrinsic religious commitments to protect and steward the environment, which might be exploited by destinations. Such aspects of travel culture, though substantially under-researched, may have important implications for tourism consumption and production. For example, Prayag (2020) emphasises that halal certification processes should incorporate more sustainability concerns and asked about whether Muslim travellers practice sustainability and if halal certification takes into account greater environmental issues. Battour et al. (2021, p. 5) argue that 'Muslims are mindful of the positive impact of sustainable tourism as global responsible citizens' and argued that sustainable based new ventures led by halal entrepreneurs will shape the halal tourism services' market in the future. Nevertheless, such perspectives fail to acknowledge the vital role of government regulation in both halal and environmental practices as well the need for more critical assessment of the gaps between attitudes and behaviours with respect to the sustainability of travel and tourism.

Conclusions

This book has outlined a number of significant themes in contemporary Muslim travel practices, many of which require considerably further study. However, further examination also needs to be given to the nature of research and scholarship in this area as well. As Hall and Prayag (2020a) argued in relation to halal certification and hospitality research, many studies in this field appear marked by a lack of critical analysis or a willingness to discuss negative aspects of halal or Islamic tourism, and they surmised that this may be because of not wanting to appear to be critical of either Islam or one's country. In addition, they observe that there is a relative lack of reflexivity in many published works and consideration of how positionality affects both research process and results. Therefore, an important part of future studies in this area is to gain a better contextualisation of the nature of the research process and approach as well as the research subject.

Critical to such research will be further studies on different types of travel in different cultural and national contexts. Ideally, this will include research that highlights the different sharia traditions, the significance of migrant and transnational populations of Muslims, and intergenerational and gender differences in travel behaviours and practices. Such an approach will present a far more realistic and non-idealised assessment of a major travel market segment and of the role of religion, and Islam in particular, on contemporary practices of tourism consumption and production.

References

Abu Bakar, B., Lim, T., Tan, E., & Nair, S. (2018a). An exploratory study of Muslim millennial travellers in the digital age. In *Collaboration and co-creation opportunities in tourism: Proceedings of the International Tourism Studies Association Conference (ITSA 2018)* (pp. 8–14). www. researchgate.net/profile/James-Kennell/publication/339298813_Collaboration_and_Co-Creation_Opportunities_in_Tourism_Proceedings_of_the_International_Tourism_Studies_Association_Conference_ITSA_2018/links/5e4998fc458515072da45279/Collaboration-and-Co-Creation-Opportunities-in-Tourism-Proceedings-of-the-International-Tourism-Studies-Association-Conference-ITSA-2018.pdf#page=17

Abu Bakar, B., Tan, E., Nair, S., & Lim, T. (2018b). 'Halalfying' travel: Reaching for the Muslim millennial travellers. *Proceedings of the Council for Australasian University Tourism and Hospitality Education (CAUTHE) Conference 2018; University of Newcastle.* www. researchgate.net/profile/Eunice-Tan-4/publication/326317708_Halalfying_travel_Reaching_for_the_Muslim_millennial_travelers/links/5b5ee004458515c4b252745c/Halalfying-travel-Reaching-for-the-Muslim-millennial-travelers.pdf

Anand, A. S. (2014). Ethical selfhood and the status of the secular: Muslim identity in Mumbai. *Culture and Religion, 15*(4), 377–398. https://doi.org/10.1080/14755610.2014.982667

Annuar, E. (2018). The rising wave of the Muslim millennial travellers. *Visitor Economy Bulletin, August. Pacific Asia Travel Association (PATA).* http://patachina.cn/ziyuan/?filename=/upload/2019/05/PATA-VE-Bulletin-August-2018.pdf

Arasli, H., Saydam, M. B., Gunay, T., & Jafari, K. (2021). Key attributes of Muslim-friendly hotels' service quality: Voices from booking.com. *Journal of Islamic Marketing.* https://doi.org/10.1108/JIMA-11-2020-0341

Battour, M., & Ismail, M. N. (2016). Halal tourism: Concepts, practises, challenges and future. *Tourism Management Perspectives, 19,* 150–154. https://doi.org/10.1016/j.tmp.2015.12.008

Battour, M., Salaheldeen, M., & Mady, K. (2021). Halal tourism: Exploring innovative marketing opportunities for entrepreneurs. *Journal of Islamic Marketing.* https://doi.org/10.1108/JIMA-06-2020-0191

Bayraklı, E., & Hafez, F. (Eds.). (2019). *Islamophobia in Muslim majority societies.* Routledge.

Cuesta-Valiño, P., Bolifa, F., & Núñez-Barriopedro, E. (2020). Sustainable, smart and Muslim-friendly tourist destinations. *Sustainability, 12*(5), 1778. https://doi.org/10.3390/su12051778

Dalaman, Z. B. (2021). From secular Muslim feminisim to Islamic feminism (s) and new generation Islamic feminists in Egypt, Iran and Turkey. *Border Crossing, 11*(1), 77–91. https://doi.org/10.33182/bc.v11i1.1042

El-Gohary, H. (2016). Halal tourism, is it really Halal? *Tourism Management Perspectives, 19,* 124–130. https://doi.org/10.1016/j.tmp.2015.12.013

Fajriyati, I., Afiff, A. Z., Gayatri, G., & Hati, S. R. H. (2020). Generic and Islamic attributes for non-Muslim majority destinations: Application of the three-factor theory of customer satisfaction. *Heliyon, 6*(6), e04324. https://doi.org/10.1016/j.heliyon.2020.e04324

Hall, C. M., & Prayag, G. (2020a). Emerging and future issues in halal hospitality and Islamic tourism. In C. M. Hall & G. Prayag (Eds.), *The Routledge handbook of halal hospitality and Islamic tourism* (pp. 339–346). Routledge.

Hall, C. M., & Prayag, G. (Eds.). (2020b). *The Routledge handbook of halal hospitality and Islamic tourism.* Routledge.

Han, H., Al-Ansi, A., Olya, H. G., & Kim, W. (2019). Exploring halal-friendly destination attributes in South Korea: Perceptions and behaviors of Muslim travelers toward a non-Muslim destination. *Tourism Management, 71,* 151–164.

Hope, M., & Young, J. (1994). Islam and ecology. *CrossCurrents, 44*(2), 180–192.

Hosseini, S., Macias, R. C., & Garcia, F. A. (2021). The exploration of Iranian solo female travellers' experiences. *International Journal of Tourism Research.* https://doi.org/10.1002/jtr.2498

Jafari, J., & Scott, N. (2014). Muslim world and its tourisms. *Annals of Tourism Research, 44,* 1–19. https://doi.org/10.1016/j.annals.2013.08.011

Janmohamed, S. (2016). *Generation M: Young Muslims changing the world.* Bloomsbury Publishing.

Khan, F., & Callanan, M. (2017). The "halalification" of tourism. *Journal of Islamic Marketing, 8*(4), 558–577. https://doi.org/10.1108/JIMA-01-2016-0001

Lipka, M. (2016). Muslims and Islam: Key findings in the U.S. and around the world. *Pew Research Center.* www.pewresearch.org/fact-tank/2016/07/22/muslims-and-islam-key-findings-in-the-u-s-and-around-the-world/

Marranci, G. (Ed.). (2010). *Muslim societies and the challenge of secularization: An interdisciplinary approach.* Springer.

Martin, R. C. (2010). Hidden bodies in Islam: Secular Muslim identities in modern (and premodern) societies. In G. Marranci (Ed.), *Muslim societies and the challenge of secularization: An interdisciplinary approach* (pp. 131–148). Springer.

Mastercard-CrescentRating. (2018). *Global Muslim travel index 2018.* www.halalmedia.jp/wp-content/uploads/2018/04/GMITI-Report-2018.pdf

Mastercard-CrescentRating. (2019). *Muslim women in travel 2019.* www.crescentrating.com/reports/muslim-women-in-travel-2019.html

Mastercard-CrescentRating. (2021). *Global Muslim travel index 2021.* www.crescentrating.com/reports/global-muslim-travel-index-2021.html

Mastercard-HalalTrip. (2017). *Muslim millennial travel report 2017.* www.halaltrip.com/halal-travel/muslim-millennial-travel-report//

Mohsin, A., Ramli, N., & Alkhulayfi, B. A. (2016). Halal tourism: Emerging opportunities. *Tourism Management Perspectives, 19,* 137–143. https://doi.org/10.1016/j.tmp.2015.12.010

Nikjoo, A., Markwell, K., Nikbin, M., & Hernández-Lara, A. B. (2021). The flag-bearers of change in a patriarchal Muslim society: Narratives of Iranian solo female travelers on Instagram. *Tourism Management Perspectives, 38,* 100817.

Oktadiana, H., Pearce, P. L., & Li, J. (2020). Let's travel: Voices from the millennial female Muslim travellers. *International Journal of Tourism Research, 22*(5), 551–563. https://doi.org/10.1002/jtr.2355

Papastathopoulos, A. (2022). Which hotel services really matter to Muslim travelers? Developing and validating a multidimensional-continuum scale. *International Journal of Hospitality Management.* https://doi.org/10.1016/j.ijhm.2022.103145

Prayag, G. (2020). Halal tourism: Looking into the future through the past. *Tourism Recreation Research, 45*(4), 557–559. https://doi.org/10.1080/02508281.2020.1762044

Razak, N. H. A., Hall, C. M., & Prayag, G. (2020). Understanding halal hospitality. In C. M. Hall & G. Prayag (Eds.), *The Routledge handbook of halal hospitality and Islamic tourism* (pp. 21–52). Routledge.

Razzaq, S., Hall, C. M., & Prayag, G. (2016). The capacity of New Zealand to accommodate the halal tourism market – Or not. *Tourism Management Perspectives, 18*, 92–97. https://doi.org/10.1016/j.tmp.2016.01.008

Rhama, B. (2021). The halal tourism – alternative or mass tourism? Indications of traditional mass tourism on crescent rating guidelines on halal tourism. *Journal of Islamic Marketing.* https://doi.org/10.1108/JIMA-07-2020-0199

Rice, G. (2006). Pro-environmental behavior in Egypt: Is there a role for Islamic environmental ethics? *Journal of Business Ethics, 65*(4), 373–390. https://doi.org/10.1007/s10551-006-0010-9

Salam, T., Muhamad, N., & Abd Ghani, M. (2019). Exploring Muslim millennials' perception and value placed on the concept of 'Halal' in their tourism preferences and behaviours. In C. M. Hall & G. Prayag (Eds.), *The Routledge handbook of Halal hospitality and Islamic tourism* (pp. 130–142). Routledge.

Sarigöllü, E. (2009). A cross-country exploration of environmental attitudes. *Environment and Behavior, 41*(3), 365–386. https://doi.org/10.1177/0013916507313920

Seyfi, S., & Hall, C. M. (2019). Deciphering Islamic theocracy and tourism: Conceptualization, context, and complexities. *International Journal of Tourism Research, 21*(6), 735–746. https://doi.org/10.1002/jtr.2300

Standing Committee for Economic and Commercial Cooperation of the Organization of Islamic Cooperation (COMCEC). (2016). *Muslim friendly tourism: Understanding the demand and supply sides in the OIC member countries.* COMCEC Coordination Office. https://sbb.gov.tr/wp-content/uploads/2018/11/Muslim_Friendly_Tourism_Understanding_the_Demand_and_Supply_Sides_in_the_OIC_Member_Countries%E2%80%8B.pdf

Tilley, S., & Houston, D. (2016). The gender turnaround: Young women now travelling more than young men. *Journal of Transport Geography, 54*, 349–358. https://doi.org/10.1016/j.jtrangeo.2016.06.022

Vliek, M. (2020). (Re) Negotiating embodiment when moving out of Islam: An empirical inquiry into 'a secular body'. In M. den Berg, L. L. Schrijvers, J. O. Wiering, & A.-M. Korte (Eds.), *Transforming bodies and religions* (pp. 159–177). Routledge.

Yosry, H. (2021). From sexual union to the divine – the teachings of Ibn al-'Arabi. *Psyche.* https://psyche.co/ideas/from-sexual-union-to-the-divine-the-teachings-of-ibn-al-arabi

Index